CONTEMPORARY LITERARY CENSORSHIP:

The Case History of Burroughs' Naked Lunch

by
Michael Barry Goodman

The Scarecrow Press, Inc.
Metuchen, N.J., & London
1981

Portions of William S. Burroughs' unpublished material are
quoted with his permission.
Chapter 9 appeared in a somewhat different form under the
title "The Customs' Censorship of William S. Burroughs'
Naked Lunch." Critique, 22, No. 1 (August 1980), 92-
104. Reprinted by permission.
Excerpts from Allen Ginsberg's unpublished notes on the trial
of Naked Lunch are quoted with his permission.
Excerpts from Reality Sandwiches (Copyright 1958, City
Lights) which were read at the Boston trial are quoted
with Allen Ginsberg's permission.
Excerpts from Philip Whalen's "Prose Take 1: VI; 57" are
quoted with his permission.
Excerpts from Naked Lunch (Copyright 1959, Grove Press)
are quoted with permission of the author and publisher.
Portions of a letter from Barney Rosset are quoted with his
permission.
Portions of a letter from William I. Cowin are quoted with
his permission.
Portions of a letter from Norman N. Holland are quoted with
his permission.

Library of Congress Cataloging in Publication Data

Goodman, Michael B
  Contemporary literary censorship.

  Includes bibliographical references and index.
  1. Burroughs, William S., 1914- . Naked lunch.
2. Trials (Obscenity)--Massachusetts--Boston.
3. Trials (Obscenity)--United States. 4. Censorship--
United States. I. Title.
KF224.B873G66   345.73'0274   80-28993
ISBN 0-8108-1398-X

To My Wife, Karen

and

To the Memory of

Joseph T. Bennett

CONTENTS

ACKNOWLEDGMENTS

I am indebted to the criticism, direction, and encouragement of Professor John Thompson of the State University of New York at Stony Brook. Professors Joseph Bennett, Jack Ludwig, and Gerald Nelson of Stony Brook provided ongoing inspiration and faith in this study in addition to critical comment. Professor Kathleen Molz of Columbia University generously and critically read the manuscript. The comments of Lemuel Coley and Tom Gatten have been pointed and welcome. Professor Richard Levine, Chairman of the English Department at Stony Brook, allowed use of department facilities to conduct part of this research and sponsored a grant which was approved by Professor Herbert Weisenger, Dean of the Graduate School at Stony Brook. Miss Mary Bruno, Miss Joanna Kalinowski, and Mrs. Lillian Silkworth performed many favors related to this study. Miss Flora Horowitz typed the final copy of the manuscript.

I am particularly indebted and deeply grateful to Mr. William S. Burroughs. Without his permission to use his letters and inspect other of his documents, this book could not have been accomplished. His work is quoted with his permission. His secretary, Mr. James Grauerholz, provided enthusiastic interest in this study and helped locate many of Mr. Burroughs' unpublished documents.

Mr. Allen Ginsberg allowed me to inspect and quote from the letters Mr. Burroughs wrote to him. These letters are on deposit at Columbia University and are the property of Mr. Ginsberg. I wish to thank him and his secretary, Mr. Richard Elovich. I am indebted to Mr. Maurice Girodias for sharing his recollections of the Paris publication of Naked Lunch with me.

I am grateful to the following individuals who helped me obtain documents, letters, articles, and books: Mr. Jack Lipkind and Mrs. Donna Sammis of the reference department and Mr. Evert Volkersz of special collections at the Ward Melville Memorial Library of the State University of New York at Stony Brook; Mr. Norman Jung, Director of the library at SUNY, College at Old Westbury; Miss Caroline Davis, Curator, and Mr. Edward Lyon of the George Arents Research Library for Special Collections at Syracuse University; Mr. Ken Lohf and Professor Susan Otis Thompson of Columbia School of Library Service; Mr. Robert W. Allison, Assistant Curator of Special Collections at the Joseph Regenstein Library of the University of Chicago; Ms. Nancy Bressler, Associate Curator of Manuscripts at the Seely G. Mudd Manuscript Library at Princeton University; and Professor David Farmer, Director of the Humanities Research Center at the University of Texas at Austin.

Mr. Barney Rosset, publisher and president of Grove Press, opened the files of Naked Lunch at Syracuse University to my research. Miss Sara Uman of Grove Press answered many related questions.

Mrs. Olytha E. Martin, Docket Clerk of the U. S. Postal Service, Office of Administrative Law Judges, provided me with the official record of the Big Table case and with the transcript of the Chicago hearing.

I wish to thank the individuals at the U. S. Customs Service who helped me obtain the records that were still retained on Naked Lunch: Mr. Fred R. Boyett, Regional Director of Customs in New York; Mr. John Atwood, Restricted Materials Branch of the Customs Service in Washington; Mr. Steven L. Pinter, Director of Entry Procedures and Penalties Division in Washington. Mr. Ronald Turbin, attorney for the Customs Service in New York, was especially helpful in guiding my trip through the bureaucratic maze in my efforts to secure records under the Freedom of Information Act. However, the file finally received from Customs was incomplete, though not censored. It began in 1962, or almost two years after the French edition of the book was seized, and did not contain a copy of any of the notices of seizure. A subsequent request for a deeper search yielded nothing, not even a confirmation that the rest of the file had been lost or destroyed. The publication records of Grove Press at Syracuse University, the A. C. L. U. Archives at Princeton University, newspapers, and correspondence were used to supplement the deficiencies of the Customs file on Naked Lunch.

Boston Police Commissioner Robert diGrazia answered my inquiries candidly and promptly, and Retired Sergeant-Detective Edmund Griffin provided valuable information about the arrest. Senator Edward Brooke of Massachusetts and Attorney William L. Cowin took time to share with me their recollections of the Boston trial of Naked Lunch. Joseph A. Laurano, Executive Assistant to the Suffolk County District Attorney, provided the available information on the case, though my request for records on the arrest of the Boston bookdealer for selling Naked Lunch were denied by Massachusetts officials. The commonwealth's Freedom of Information law forbids access to criminal offender records for any study which would result in the publication of the name of the offender. Boston attorney Frank Dardeno, who defended the bookdealer, gave candid information on the matter.

Mr. Joel J. Sprayregen, who defended Big Table in Chicago, was very helpful in securing the records of that litigation and recalling details of the case. Mr. Edward deGrazia, who defended Naked Lunch in Boston, was not available. However, the files of Grove Press at Syracuse contained his correspondence with Barney Rosset pertaining to the case, and provided much information.

Miss Barbara Eichman of the American Civil Liberties Union in New York was instrumental in locating the records on Naked Lunch retained by that organization's national office. She facilitated my access to those records held at the Mudd Manuscript Library at Princeton University. Mr. John W. Roberts, Executive Director of the Massachusetts A. C. L. U., helped locate information on the Boston trial. Mrs. Nancy Graham of the National Obscenity Law Center provided me with information about the anti-obscenity organization Morality in Media. The National Coalition Against Censorship gave me general information on the literary censorship issue.

Professors John Ciardi, Norman Holland, and Gabrielle Bernhard Jackson provided me with their recollections of the Boston trial, and Professor Joel Rosenthal with his of the suppression of the Chicago Review. Professors John Tytell, Pascal Covici, and Thomas Parkinson commented helpfully on my chapter dealing with the Customs censorship of Naked Lunch after it was read at the Burroughs Special Session at the 1977 MLA Convention.

I would also like to thank Mr. Richard Aaron of Am Here Books in Vaduz, Liechtenstein; Mr. Jim Pennington of

Aloes Books in London; Mr. Carl Schinasi of Birmingham, Alabama; Mr. M. J. Wren of The Guardian Weekly, Manchester; Professor Robert Waxler of Southern Massachusetts University; Miss Diana Franklin of the archives at Time, Inc.; Mr. David Goodman of San Francisco; Mr. and Mrs. H. A. Goodman, Mr. and Mrs. Kenneth Goodman, Mr. and Mrs. Fred Kahn of Dallas.

I can only express a small part of my gratitude to my wife, Karen, and to my son, Craig. Throughout this project they remained faithful and devoted. They supported me with sincerity and understanding.

INTRODUCTION

William S. Burroughs' Naked Lunch was the last work
of literature to be proscribed in this nation's struggle between its belief in free expression and its Puritan heritage.
Other books have been the object of more intense censorship
actions. This one is the last complete example of the censorship of literature in the wake of the 1957 Roth Supreme
Court decision because it was censored by academia, the
U. S. Post Office, the U. S. Customs Service, the Commonwealth of Massachusetts, and the city of Los Angeles.

The court trials and other actions against Naked Lunch
provide a moral benchmark. We cannot fail to recognize, in
retrospect, the speed with which we assimilate into the main-
stream of American life that which was once unspeakable.

Frank discussion of sex in print had long been available to men of means and education. The titillating portions
of The Decameron remained in Italian in most translations,
and the descriptions of Roman orgies were appended in Latin
footnotes in Gibbon's The Decline and Fall of the Roman Em-
pire. In the United States the fight against the censorship of
literature is little more than one hundred years old, and coincides roughly with the emergency of mass literacy after the
Civil War. Only with the rise of a literate middle-class did
the discussion of sexual matters in print become a problem.

As debated in the courts, the obscenity issue transformed judges into the public arbiters of literary taste, a
role which had traditionally been the exclusive territory of
the critic and the scholar. As a result many of our most
respected works of literature were banned or castigated for
perpetuating impure morals. Hawthorne's The Scarlet Letter
and Whitman's Leaves of Grass are two noted examples. Fear
of the censor prompted publishers to delete parts of Melville's
Typee and Crane's Maggie: A Girl of the Streets. Anthony
Comstock's anti-obscenity campaign was so successful that

1

toward the end of the 19th century the mere discussion of
sexual themes, or the implication of sex or nakedness, was
enough to have a book altered by a publisher for fear of
censorship. The attitude slowly relaxed until World War I
when sexual intercourse began to be described rather than
implied in novels. Efforts to suppress the discussion of sex
alerted the academic and literary communities to a threat to
the right of free expression.

James Joyce and D. H. Lawrence had broken the sex
taboo by providing their readers with the thoughts of characters engaged in sexual intercourse. When legal battles
were waged over the importation of works by these authors
to the United States, the battle lines for the literary critic
were clear. Once the court allowed the discussion of sex,
its attempts to limit and contain it appear foolish when we
consider the amount of energy expended and the public dollars spent to protect the American reader from himself.
But as a practical matter, opposition to a censorship law or
advocacy of its repeal was a politically dangerous position.

Legal precedent had made a clear distinction between
general censorship and literary censorship, although no law
specified as much. Literature was treated as an exceptional
case, beginning with the lifting of the Customs ban on Ulysses in 1933. The issue was hardly resolved since the legal
definition of "obscenity" remained vague at best. A concerted effort to resolve the obscenity question took place between the Roth case in 1957 and the three landmark decisions
in 1966--Memoirs, Mishkin, Ginzburg. The suppression of
Burroughs' Naked Lunch occurred within the same nine-year
period.

With its descriptions of violent eroticism, Naked
Lunch hit a sensitive cultural nerve more forcefully than other books that dealt with sex through explicit language. It
dealt vividly with the interrelationship of sex and violence,
with sex and cannibalism, with bestiality, with homosexual
exploitation. To a society which wished to view sex as related to affection, the connections Burroughs had made in his
book were intolerable. He challenged an even deeper taboo
and treated sexual motivation in caricature. His book became a controversial topic beyond art in both the popular
press and in scholarly journals. Critics and reviewers took
sides. The alternative publication born out of a New York
newspaper strike, The New York Review of Books, praised
the work of the new author. John Wain, an angry young man

of the 50's, rebuked it. Both sides were extreme in their
praise or excoriation. No one who reviewed the book was
uncommitted. But Burroughs' cartoon treatment of sexual
subjects caught the attention of the censor as well.

When the common enemy of the artist and the critic,
the censor, precipitated legal action, this brought together
literary critics, writers, psychologists, and sociologists to
defend the book whose reputation had preceded its American
publication by almost five years.

The case of the censorship of Naked Lunch illustrates
the struggle to forge a compromise between complete license
in all forms of expression, and the right to discuss sex openly and explicitly in a work of literature. Burroughs' book
tested the critic who found himself defending the legal rights
of a work he considered at the very least tasteless, if not
pornography masquerading as serious literature. In order
to preserve the freedom of expression, some like John Wain
felt literary judgment was being sacrificed.

Most so-called landmark obscenity cases had little or
no affinity to literature. The cases that frame this study--
Roth, Memoirs, Ginzburg, Mishkin--made legal history, but
from a literary point of view, they involve material with little or no interest. Samuel Roth was indicted under the postal
laws for sending books, periodicals, photographs, and advertisements through the mails. The U.S. Supreme Court upheld the lower court conviction of Mr. Roth, reaffirmed the
constitutionality of the obscenity statute, and defined the term
obscene: "whether to the average person, applying contemporary community standards, the dominant theme of the material taken as a whole appeals to the prurient interest." As
far as the court was concerned, contributions by Henry Miller and Aubrey Beardsley to Roth's American Aphrodite did
not alter the dominant theme of the magazine.

The conviction of Edward Mishkin for selling over
fifty books dealing with fetishism, sadism, and masochism
was also upheld by the Supreme Court. The high court upheld the conviction of Ralph Ginzburg, not because of the content of his Eros magazine and The Housewife's Handbook on
Selective Promiscuity, but for the manner in which he advertised his publications. On the other hand, the case of Memoirs of a Woman of Pleasure, also known as Fanny Hill,
ended with a reversal of the Massachusetts ban by the Supreme Court because of the recognized value of the work.

Critics and scholars agreed that it was a classic of 18th-
century erotica.

The recognition of Naked Lunch as a work of art by
the literary community set it apart from the publications involved in the Supreme Court decisions. It was nevertheless
an integral part of the evolving notion of what could or could
not be considered obscene. The trials involving the book
illustrate, in part, the strain that was placed on the literary
community as it defended the right of free artistic expression
against a society which sought to control the content of books
and magazines. Perhaps the obscenity debate had reached
its limits during the nine-year period. The legal system had
either to relent or become a national censor. The literary
community had to reconsider its position on complete freedom
of expression. In general, the discussion of what makes a
work obscene called into question the entire subject of critical
judgment. The Naked Lunch case caught the critic between
a belief in taste and a traditional revulsion for the censor.

This study ends with the reversal of the ban on
Naked Lunch in 1966 directly after the three Supreme Court
rulings. According to Charles Rembar, who argued the
Memoirs case, those decisions signaled an end to the censorship of literature based on obscenity. In the years following
1966, obscenity censorship did not disappear, but the focus
of the debate was no longer on works of literature.

In the following pages, the reactions of the courts and
of critics to Burroughs' book form a major part of the discussion. In narrating the details of the censorship, this
work examines the specific reasons for its proscription in
relation to the issue of literary censorship. However, no
attempt is made here to outline the entire subject of American
literary suppression, since Felice Flanery Lewis has performed just such a survey in her recent Literature, Obscenity,
and Law. Her work proved extremely valuable and influential
as has James Paul and Murry Schwartz's Federal Censorship:
Obscenity in the Mail.

The postal hearing in Chicago and the trial in Boston
are presented in detail from official transcripts. In these
discussions I have followed Charles Rembar's treatment of
the Lady Chatterley's Lover postal hearing in The End of
Obscenity by commenting on the significant points brought out
in trial testimony. The excellent treatment of Tropic of
Cancer's censorship troubles by E. R. Hutchinson (in his

Tropic of Cancer on Trial) has provided a valuable method
for the use of material made available by the Post Office and
the publisher. The discussion of the cases involving Naked
Lunch is based on the transcripts rather than extrapolated
from the summaries and synopses of judges and lawyers in
their rulings and briefs. Literary points are often ignored
by legal professionals in cases of this sort. The drama of
the courtroom also allows us the privilege of witnessing the
adversary relationship which existed between the legal authorities and the literary community on the issue of censorship.

     The Boston trial is recounted from the official tran-
script because it provides the opportunity to place the observations of the witnesses within the context of the proceedings.
Allen Ginsberg, Norman Mailer, John Ciardi, and Norman
Holland were among the witnesses who testified on behalf of
Naked Lunch. Because it involved the entire book, the Boston
case differed from the Big Table hearing which involved
excerpts published in a magazine containing works by other
authors. The two so-called pornographic sections--"A. J.'s
Annual Party" and "Hassan's Rumpus Room"--were not part
of Big Table, but were the focus of the Boston litigation. In
subsequent printings of Naked Lunch, the introductory material
has included numerous excerpts from the Boston trial, suggesting that the trial can be considered as a part of the book.
These excerpts have been placed in the context of the whole
trial including uncomplimentary comments made during cross-
examination by the prosecutor and the judge, omitted in the
editions of Naked Lunch. Since the case against Naked Lunch
was argued by William I. Cowin, who also argued against
Memoirs before the U.S. Supreme Court, the Boston trial
offers a unique opportunity to see the obscenity arguments
which set a national legal precedent applied to a recognized
work of literature.

     The critical opinion of Burroughs' work expressed in
this study has been influenced both directly and indirectly by
the articles and sections of books by the following critics:
John Ciardi, Leslie Fiedler, Ihab Hassan, Alfred Kazin,
Mary McCarthy, Richard Pearce, Theodore Solotaroff, Tony
Tanner, and John Tytell.

Chapter 1

NAKED LUNCH AND OLYMPIA PRESS

On a rainy day in the spring of 1957, Allen Ginsberg brought "a rather bulky, pasted-up manuscript"[1] to Olympia Press publisher Maurice Girodias. In the Paris office he "declared that it was a work of genius"[2] which only turns up once in the life of a publisher. The papers belonged to William S. Burroughs and would appear some years later as Naked Lunch. Girodias recalled his first encounter with the Burroughs book:

> It was such a mess that manuscript: You couldn't physically read the stuff, but whatever caught the eye was extraordinary and dazzling. So I returned it to Allen saying, "Listen, the whole thing has to be reshaped." The ends of the pages were all eaten away by the rats or something.... The prose was transformed into verse, edited by the rats of the Paris sewers. And Allen was very angry with me, but he went back to Bill who was leading a very secret life in Paris....[3]

The chaotic bundle of paper was rejected as almost inaccessible to the average reader not only because of its intentional lack of organization, but also because of its total disregard for the conventions of fiction. It was no wonder the publisher observed that Ginsberg left his office "with an ugly expression on his face."[4]

Maurice Girodias' father, Jack Kahane, owned the English language French Obelisk Press. Among other books he published Henry Miller's Tropic of Cancer, Lawrence Durrell's The Black Book, and James Joyce's Pomes Penyeach. Kahane died on September 3, 1939, as the war approached. Shortly afterwards, Girodias, who had adopted his mother's maiden name for fear of anti-Semitic Nazism, began a publishing firm of his own called "Les Editions du

Chene, which specialized in art books and was quite success-ful"[5] despite his inexperience with technical, financial and commercial matters. He continued to publish art books during the war, and after the war was over he expanded his press to include literature by reviving his father's old publishing house. He began with new printings of Miller's books which sold quite well to American G. I. 's. However, his financial naivete plunged him into debt. He eventually lost the publishing company when a shrewd creditor sold out to a large publishing firm. The loss of the business and a censorship action brought by the French government in 1946 and 1947 against Tropic of Cancer (the first public case since Flaubert's Madame Bovary and Baudelaire's Les Fleurs du Mal were tried) instilled in Girodias "the urge to attack the Universal Establishment."[6]

Broke but undaunted he established Olympia Press in the spring of 1953, using a room at the rear of a run-down bookstore at 13 rue Jacob as an office and a part-time secretary as a staff. The first manuscript he acquired was Miller's Plexus, a carry-over from his father's business connections and a logical place to begin a new operation. At the time, Paris was the base of a new English literary quarterly begun only the year before. It was titled Merlin and its editors and contributors included Dick Seaver (who now heads Richard Seaver Books in New York), poet Alexander Trocchi, and "at a prudent distance George Plimpton."[7] Some of the Merlin contributors wrote for Olympia Press, participating in its unusual production method.

At first the method of operation of Girodias' new press was amusingly simple. When he ran out of money--which was apparently quite often considering his financial discipline--the colorful and innovative publisher would circulate blurbs for imaginary books by writers with odd pen names: Marcus van Heller, Akbar del Piombo,[8] Miles Underwood, Carmencita de las Lunas. He also fabricated eye-catching, fantasy-arousing titles: White Thighs, The Chariot of Flesh, With Open Mouth, The Sexual Life of Robinson Crusoe. As he expected, such titles brought in orders from his readers, enabling him to advance money to an author, often a Merlin contributor, who could then write a manuscript which "more or less fitted the descriptions."[9]

In this way Girodias published his "d. b. 's"[10]--his own shorthand for "dirty books"--in green paperbacks which he called the Traveller's Companion Series. In addition to pro-

viding serious writers with funds in this off-beat manner, he
also published many pieces of literature which American and
British houses would not because of the frank sexual contents
of the books. However, the reputation of the ugly green
paperbacks often spilled over onto the more serious efforts,
making all Olympia Press publications suspect in the minds
of Customs agents.

The staff of Merlin had formed a press called Collection Merlin and eventually joined forces with Olympia. Together the two published an early Beckett novel, Watt, and
English translations of Jean Genet's Our Lady of the Flowers
and The Thief's Journal. In a short time the publishers had
built a strong reputation in both Britain and America for their
willingness "to publish everything that was unconventional and
likely to be outlawed by the archaic censorship rules which
were still being enforced at the time (the early fifties)."[11]
Such a reputation brought Girodias a great many manuscripts
and some pure rubbish. In 1955, though, J. P. Donleavy
sent The Ginger Man and Vladimir Nabokov sent Lolita to the
Paris publisher of English dirty books. However, after the
books received the attention deserved from the literary community, Girodias claimed that he "was repaid in each instance
by the blackest ingratitude."[12] Before publication of American editions, each author went to court over editorial changes
made in the Paris editions. Olympia continued to receive
manuscripts.

Considering the background and reputation of the press,
any serious book which dealt with the subject of sex by shun-
ning euphemism and insinuation in favor of direct factual
discussion would be a natural selection of the press which
assaulted Anglo-American sexual prohibitions. Olympia Press
seemed to be the natural place for Allen Ginsberg to take the
manuscript of Burroughs' book which he claimed would "drive
everybody mad,"[13] and to the author of which he dedicated
his first collection of poems, Howl.

Since Olympia appeared to be the perfect publisher for
Burroughs' book, Ginsberg's disappointment over the rejection of the manuscript was certainly understandable. Nevertheless he suggested that his friend send a chapter of the
unpublished book to Irving Rosenthal, the editor of the Chicago
Review, the prestigious literary quarterly of the University
of Chicago. None of the editors there had ever heard of
Burroughs, but his fiction impressed them as extremely
powerful. What was to become the opening section of the

book was published in the Spring 1958 Chicago Review.[14]
Another section of Burroughs' unpublished manuscript followed in the Autumn 1958 issue.[15]

Chapter 2

NAKED LUNCH AND THE CHICAGO REVIEW

On Saturday, October 25, 1958 The Chicago Daily
News reported a warm front coming up from the southwest.
An escapade of the Crosby brothers was splashed across the
front page, an example of less complicated times or an indication of a very slow news day. Daily News columnist Jack
Mabley, ordinarily a champion of liberal causes, ran his
page-one column next to the weather forecast and the picture
of the Crosbys and their showgirl companions.

The Saturday edition of most newspapers is thin, effort
going into the Sunday issue. Important stories can usually be
delayed a few hours to make the Sunday morning press run.
Mabley's column was not hard news, but opinion. This particular Saturday he expressed his dismay over the declining
literary status of a magazine which he refused to name, but
identified as published by the University of Chicago. By
contrast his position on the worth of the contents of the issue
was quite clear. He characterized it as "one of the foulest
collections of printed filth I've seen publicly circulated. "[1]

Mabley went on to report that the magazine also reflected the social and intellectual feelings of the Beat generation whose members were "young, intellectual, need baths,
and have extreme contempt for the less fortunate than themselves. "[2] He could tolerate that sort of rebellion, but not
the public use of "obscenity. " To him the obscene words
were more than just words, he regarded their appearance in
the literary magazine as a crude gesture flaunted in the face
of respectable society. To underscore the childishness of
that gesture, he compared the publication of the words to
"little kids chalking a four-letter verb on the Oak Street
underpass. "[3] Graffiti had a long way to go before it would
be considered an art form. [4] Only thugs and perverts defaced
property by scrawling obscenities on walls, and Mabley counted
on his readers to make the same association with the magazine writers.

Although his liberal leaning forced him to concede that
he might be a "bluenose" on the issue of public circulation of
obscenity and the increasing legal tolerance of it, he concluded that it was "evidence of the deterioration of our American society" and the use of such words was "dangerous."[5]
His was a curious echo of Ezra Pound's notion that language
and social conditions are inextricable. In Mabley's opinion:

> You can be too priggish, and you can be too
> liberal. We are going overboard in the liberal
> side--in the courts, in literature, in popular
> men's magazines and paper-cover books. [6]

If he had left his opinion as a vague general bombast lament-
ing the death of God, apple pie, and good, clean American
prose, little or nothing would have happened in response to
his column. The sentiment he expressed was not new, nor
terribly well put. He did not leave the matter, however.
In the concluding paragraph of his column he refocused his
attention on the literary magazine which he saw by implication as a single-handed affront to sacred cultural icons. He
did not name the writers of the obscenities. Instead he suggested that the trustees of the University of Chicago "should
take a long hard look at what is being circulated under its
sponsorship."[7]

Above Mabley's column in its masthead, The Chicago
Daily News proudly claimed a circulation of 600,000.

The student editors of the Chicago Review[8] knew the
unnamed publication that Mabley had blasted over the weekend
was theirs. They were amused by "the obvious lack of
knowledge of things literary" and "annoyed that the writers in
the Review had been so completely misunderstood by Mabley
and vicariously by his reading audience."[9] The first public
response to the Mabley column came in an editorial in the
campus newspaper, the Maroon. It charged the columnist
with irresponsibility and called his comments "more an attack on the University than a literary criticism of its publications" which is "of a far more irresponsible nature than the
publication he starts out to criticize." Mabley responded in
his column, "In criticizing half a dozen University of Chicago
students, I reflected on the whole student body, I apologize."[10]

According to the business manager of the Review,
Albert Podell, the editors felt that after the apology the whole
matter would drop. After all, they reasoned, the attack was

directed at the Autumn 1958 issue and specifically singled out
the Beat poets and essayists.   The next issue in winter 1959
had already been blocked out.   It would contain the work of
only three writers--Jack Kerouac, Edward Dahlberg, and
William S. Burroughs.   Of the three, Burroughs was the only
author whose work appeared in the controversial Autumn 1958
issue.   But the editors expressed their optimism prematurely.

Burroughs' contribution to the Autumn issue, "Chapter
2 of Naked Lunch, " had the first position in the magazine.
If Mabley, or anyone else for that matter, began the issue
at the beginning, he would read a great deal of street addict's slang used in the description of a narcotics arrest.
A rather disgusting account of the character Pantapon Rose,
a female narcotics addict, follows as she demonstrates the
pin-and-dropper method of shooting up.   The detailed description of her demonstration appears in a non-authorial narrative, presumably from the point of view of another addict
which helps to explain its exaggerated quality:

> "She seized a safety pin caked with blood and rust,
> gouged a great hole in her leg which seemed to
> hang open like an obscene, festering mouth waiting
> for unspeakable congress with the dropper which
> she now plunged out of sight into the gaping
> wound. "[11]

Although the passage is sexual in its psychological implica-
tions, no four-letter words appear here.   Nor are there any
in the pages which follow this description as they ramble
through a "real scene" of the pin-and-dropper methods and
descriptions of cops, marks, and Chicago.   The random
musings finally focus on the stifling nature of American culture labeled here as "U. S. drag. "   Characteristic of Burroughs' style, the scene shifts abruptly to New Orleans and
to an attempt to buy some heroin.   In this scene is the first
appearance of a word which could conceivably have moved
Mabley to write his blast of the Autumn issue.   Looking for
a local drug pusher in a strange town, the addict attempts to
overcome his paranoia by rationalizing that New Orleans is
"a small place and the fuzz always knows [sic] who is pushing
so he figures what the hell [emphasis mine] does it matter and
sells to anybody. "[12]   Almost twenty years after its publication, the expression "what the hell" is so commonplace as to
be totally innocuous.   Within the context of the story, it
passes almost unnoticed since it is rather tame compared
with the pin-and-dropper description or juxtaposed with this
surreal picture of the oil refineries which surround the city:

> irridescent lakes and orange gas flares, and
> swamp and garbage heaps, alligators crawling
> around in broken bottles and tin cans near
> arabesques of motels, marooned pimps scream
> obscenities at passing cars from islands of
> rubbish. [13]

The region around the city is described as full of "nigger-
killing sheriffs, "[14] and the use of that racial slur may have
upset Mabley as much as the use of "hell. "

But there can be no doubt about the offensiveness of a
word which appears in the dialog of Bradley the Buyer, a
narcotics agent who sucks disgustingly on a Baby Ruth.
Though he never touches drugs himself, he is addicted to
physical contact with addicts.   After Bradley had been
reprimanded by his superior, he pouts alone:

> "I'll just sit in my room, " he says.
> "Fuck [emphasis mine] 'em all.
> Squares on both sides.   I am the only
> complete man in the industry. "[15]

Without a doubt the only word The New York Times still will
not print, "fuck, " caught the columnist's eye.   As if that
were not enough ammunition for Mabley's jeremiad, the
language remains colorful as Bradley, confronted with the
loss of his job, pleads to stay on:

> "Please Boss Man, I'll wipe your ass [emphasis
> mine].   I'll wash out your dirty condums, I'll
> polish your shoes with the oil on my nose.... "[16]

Another word which no doubt offended Mabley appears in a
short description of a Mexican trombone player.   The musi-
cian

> degrades the female sex by forcing his chick to
> swallow all this shit [emphasis mine].   He had
> ideas on every subject: what kind of underwear
> was healthy, when to drink water, and how to
> wipe your ass [emphasis mine]. [17]

In the short space of nine pages of the Autumn 1958 issue
of the Chicago Review the offensive terms "hell, " "nigger, "
"shit, " "ass, " and "fuck" appear.   These then were the
specific words Mabley referred to in his column, and all of

them were found in the excerpt from Burroughs' yet unpublished Naked Lunch.

However, neither the magazine nor Burroughs was
named. But anyone could pick up a copy of the Autumn
Review, just as Mabley had done, and make the connection
himself. He would remember the Burroughs contribution and
the words used, and he would have reason to suspect a recurrence of the same words in a further excerpt from Naked
Lunch. Burroughs was not the only contributor to the issue
in question, not the only author who used questionable words,
questionable in Mabley's terms.

The words "fuck" and "cunt" are used in a poem by
Philip Whalen titled "Prose take 1:   VI:57, "

> I can't eat it, I can't fuck it. It's just beautiful
> ... I think suddenly of a woman's cunt ... I wonder
> what sunrise feels like if one has a cunt? [empha-
> sis mine]18

And "ass" is used in Joel Oppenheimer's poem "More
Nostrum" in the line "an ass [emphasis mine] like a valen-
tine. " "Hell" appears in John Logan's "The House That
Jack Built, " a rambling free-associational recollection of
Mid-Western farm life bordering on the pristine. Logan also
contributed a review titled "Sorrow in the Poet in the Man in
the Animal, " which discusses the theme of sexuality found in
"Sorrows of Priapus" by Edward Dahlberg. Indiana boxer
James Brunot's first publication, "An Opening, " contains the
phrase "Worse than having a god-damned [emphasis mine]
baby"19 embedded almost imperceptibly in recollections of
childhood.

Allen Ginsberg had written two letters to the Review
editors which were published in this issue. In the first
"bullshit"20 appears in almost the first sentence. In the
second, commenting on a poem he had submitted to the
Review, he wrote:

> the copy I sent you last week has [emphasis his]
> form--the fucking [emphasis mine] thing's prac-
> tically iambic pentameter. 21

In the same letter he apologized for the need to rescind his
submission, saying "sorry I fucked [emphasis mine] up on
the deal. "22

With the collection of "hells, " "shits, " "cunts, "
"asses, " and "fucks, " <u>Chicago Review</u> volume 12, number 3,
Autumn 1958 provided enough fuel for moral outrage. Since
the Burroughs article was the only one mentioned on the
cover and since it was the lead contribution in the issue, it
is safe to conclude that the charges of obscenity leveled at
the issue were directed, at least in part, toward William S.
Burroughs' excerpt from <u>Naked Lunch.</u>

Considering Mabley's reaction to the words in the
Autumn issue, and the extensive Burroughs excerpt scheduled
for the Winter issue, Albert Podell asked the editorial staff
their opinion on the possible deletion of similar words in the
future in order to avoid a repetition of the Mabley reaction.
They felt that

> Mabley's remarks made no sense. We would fully
> agree with him that truly obscene matter should
> not be printed, but his standards of obscenity were
> patently ridiculous. To him a few curse words in
> a work were sufficient to warrant the condemnation
> of the entire work as obscene. [23]

No doubt they had in mind the landmark censorship decision
handed down only a year before by the United States Supreme
Court in <u>Roth vs. U. S.</u> [24] Among other tests for obscenity,
Roth stipulated that a work be judged "as a whole, " and not
on isolated passages or individual words. The editors felt
that they were on solid constitutional ground if the matter
ever went to court. At the time, though, the possibility of
legal action seemed quite remote. The material was far
from pornographic.

In response to a debt resulting from a 15, 000-copy
print overrun of the <u>Review,</u> The University of Chicago set
up a five-member Faculty Review Board in 1957 as a watch-
dog over the financial affairs of the magazine to insure that
no such debt recurred. Editorial autonomy remained in the
hands of the student editors. A meeting of the Faculty Review Board had been scheduled for November 3, 1958, only
a week after the appearance of the Mabley article. Editor
Irving Rosenthal and business manager Albert Podell attended
the meeting. Only business matters of the <u>Review</u> were
discussed, and no mention or reference was made to the
<u>Chicago Daily News</u> column. After the meeting, Richard
Stern, Faculty Board Chairman and Faculty Advisor to the
<u>Review</u> asked Rosenthal for a list of contributors scheduled

for the Winter issue because "the Dean wants to know."[25]
Stern's request was indeed extraordinary considering the
staff's tradition of editorial autonomy and the financial nature
of the Board. Even the most casual comparison of contributors to the two issues would reveal William S. Burroughs
and his excerpts from Naked Lunch. The reappearance
raised the possibility of a repetition of the Mabley objection.

Stern's remarks would not have been taken too seriously had Rosenthal not encountered Humanities Dean and
Review sponsor Napier Wilt earlier that afternoon when the
editor went to pick up a requisition form from the secretary.[26] Wilt told him that he had read the Mabley article
and that the Review was in danger of being discontinued, but
he would do everything he could to save the magazine.[27]

After hearing of the conversations Rosenthal had with
Stern and Wilt, the editorial staff discussed the problem again.
It was suggested that the four-letter words which so offended
Mabley and which caused all the unusual behavior in the
University administration could be deleted or replaced by
asterisks. However, they agreed not to expurgate any of
the material, but to publish the articles as the authors wrote
them.

Rosenthal took the manuscripts intended for the Winter
issue of the Chicago Review, except for one which was not
quite ready, over to the University of Chicago Press on
Friday, November 7. He gave press supervisor Robert
Kline the completed requisition form, and took the manuscripts to Tony, composing room foreman, for typesetting.[28]

That afternoon he returned to Wilt's office to discuss
the possibility of inserting asterisks in place of the objectionable words because he was worried about his "duty to
keep the review operating."[29] Wilt told him that alternative
was "puerile," and should only be considered as a last
resort.[30]

Chancellor Lawrence A. Kimpton called a meeting of
the Faculty Advisory Board, the second in a week of that
body which normally met two or three times a year, but this
time without the presence of the student editors. Reuel Den-
ny, Edward W. Rosenheim, Joshua Taylor, and Richard
Stern as Board members were joined by Deans Wilt and
Streeter.[31] Another member, Elder Olson, was on leave of
absence.[32] Kimpton informed the Board that he was under

pressure from people with financial interests in the University and concerned "over the possible consequences of continued adverse publicity. "[33]   He explained that the magazine, while owned by the university, was under autonomous student control.   He asked for advice on what should be done about the forthcoming Winter issue.   Several members expressed concern about the editorial policy because of the San Francisco writers.   Another suggested possible violations of Postal regulations since the journal was mailed.   However, the Post Office had not blocked any copies which were mailed.   In light of subsequent events, though, it is worthwhile to note that this was the first mention of any action against the Review or the material printed in it by a legal or governmental agency. [34]

During the discussion "Dean Wilt and Mr. Stern defended the Review and a majority of those present agreed with them that the Winter issue should be published as planned by Rosenthal. "[35]   Kimpton asserted that the matter was more serious than the others realized and that the financial pressure he was under "was great enough so that if necessary he personally would do something about the Winter issue. "[36]   Although " 'PRESSURE' appeared to be the primary concern of the Chancellor"[37] in calling for action against the Winter issue, he later explained that the Mabley article was "the occasion, but not the cause, for looking into the Review"[38] in the first place.   He decided at the meeting to go along with the others and allow the Winter issue, although he felt it was wrong both legally and artistically. [39]

Rosenthal's term as editor was also brought up at the meeting.   Kimpton observed that some members were "anxious to see a change in editor"[40] but the Autumn issue did not provide sufficient reason.   "Since the Winter issue would have been Rosenthal's last as editor anyway, there would be 'less trouble getting rid of Mr. Rosenthal' then. "[41]

The University's public relations and fund-raising people informed the Chancellor that the Review controversy had made their jobs difficult prior to the meeting. [42]   At the time he was concerned with public relations.   He had undertaken a massive reorganization of the University administration, and the University of Chicago was expanding its physical plant into a ghetto area, encountering another "public relations" problem.   Though he would later deny it, pressure influenced his actions toward suppressing the Winter issue. [43]

As far as anyone present at the meeting could determine, no effort was then being pushed to force the suppression
of the Winter issue. However, something was going on in the
administration over the Mabley article. Dean Wilt urged
Rosenthal to wait and see before expurgating the issue. [44]

On Monday at 9:30 a.m. Rosenthal took the remaining
manuscript to the University Press office. He asked Tony
for the others, wanting to insert the one he had just brought
into its proper position. Tony told him that he didn't have
them and to see Mr. Kline instead. "Kline didn't have them
either but said 'the administration has them.' "[45] He assured Rosenthal that he'd call as soon as the manuscripts
came back.

The action by the press was at least unorthodox and
unethical, since the manuscripts were the property of the
author and the Review, and not available publically before
publication. The printer was obliged to protect the manuscript for the owner.

Kline called Rosenthal at 10:30 a.m. and told him that
both the manuscripts and the requisition form had been in the
comptroller's office, but they had just been returned to the
press. Rosenthal went to the office to find the papers in
disarray as if they had been dropped and put back together
in no particular sequence. After straightening them up and
inserting the manuscripts he had brought in earlier that
morning, "he turned them back to Tony, with Kline's permission. "[46]

On Tuesday Chancellor Kimpton called a noon meeting
of the nine-member Committee of the Council of the University Senate in order to discuss the Chicago Review. Although
he had already received advice from other faculty and administrators on the magazine, he sought the comments and
opinions of this committee. He began the meeting with the
assertion that the history of the publication had brought on
"the circumstances by which it achieved an unwanted notoriety. "[47]

Kimpton explained that the Review was owned by the
University which was legally and financially responsible for
it, but the student editorial staff was not answerable to the
University. It was unlike other student publications which
were "under the purview of the Dean of Students, "[48] or the
other University journals whose "editors are appointed by and

responsible to the University. "[49] He told the members of the committee that he and the trustees felt the controversy was an administrative problem. However, he recommended that "some remedial action should be taken without any undue delay [because the editorial staff had not changed], and there is some reason to believe that the tone of the new issue will be gamier than that of the number presently under criticism, "[50] bringing with it further attacks from the local press.

As the Review's faculty advisor, Richard Stern was also present at the meeting. Although he too objected to the low quality and bad taste of the Autumn issue resulting from the editors' fascination with Beat writers, Stern nevertheless defended the magazine as a valuable publication "unique as a serious literary medium run entirely by students. "[51] In his opinion as a literary critic, it compared well with similar journals published by adult scholars and artists. The success and international recognition of the magazine, he maintained, was largely attributable to the student editorial autonomy traditional with the Chicago Review.

The committee members agreed with Kimpton that "the University could not continue to allow its name to be used on a periodical whose staff owed no responsibility to the institution. "[52] They could not agree on a course of action, though. If they simply dropped the magazine, they may not only lose a valuable publication, but also appear to have censored the Review indirectly through a cut-off of money. For the University to do nothing, on the other hand, would also bring unfavorable comments from the press. The meeting ended with the committee unresolved on the appropriate response, but allied with Kimpton in the belief that something should be done.

Rosenthal went to the press on Monday, November 17, to check on the galley proofs. Tony told him they were not in the print shop and to check with Kline who had previously picked up the manuscripts. Rosenthal asked Kline for the papers. The supervisor of the shop went to his safe, gave them to the editor, [53] and said:

> Sorry, but things have been very busy around here lately. Just haven't had a chance to set them up.

> [Rosenthal:] But that never happened before. The composing room seems clear.

[Kline:] Well, we're really very busy.

[R:] When will they be typeset?

[K:] I don't know right now.

[R:] Can you give me a date?

[K:] Not right now.

[R:] Well, can you give me a date when you can give me a date?

[K:] I have to speak with my supervisor. I'll call you at the end of the week. [54]

Rosenthal went to Dean Wilt to find out what had happened to precipitate Kline's strange evasiveness in answering questions about the manuscripts.

Wilt told the editor that "Burroughs, Kerouac, and the San Francisco poets generally could not appear in the Winter issue." [55] However, they might be permitted to appear individually in subsequent issues since the stories and poems had already been accepted for publication. He suggested that Rosenthal seek permission to have a note printed in a revised Winter issue explaining that situation. [56]

After the refusal to set the material in type, Wilt saw only three alternatives open to the editor. Rosenthal could: 1) attempt to publish the issue as it stood at the risk of the loss of University funds; 2) change the contents of the issue to conform with the administration demand that it be "completely innocuous;" [57] or 3) resign as editor. The first possibility was ridiculous because without typesetting, publishing was impossible. The second had been ruled out from the beginning as puerile. The last, Rosenthal's resignation, would not solve the basic question of publication and editorial autonomy. If he resigned, the decision would have to be made by his successor. Under the circumstances, he chose to present the alternatives to the editorial staff at a meeting he had called for the next day.

After outlining the alternatives, Rosenthal asked if anyone on the staff could accept the editorship under those conditions. Hyung Woong Pak said that he could; and since he was the only one present who could do so in good conscience,

Pak was elected editor-in-chief on the spot. A sense of duty
and commitment to the existence of the magazine as a viable,
autonomous literary periodical forced Rosenthal and six members of the staff to resign in protest.

As far as the staff was concerned, the problem was
solved. They had voted not to break up the Winter issue as
Wilt had suggested. Only Pak considered that alternative
viable. [58] Ironically the administration had slated a meeting
that afternoon to debate its course of action.

At 3:40 p. m. the Council of the University Senate met
to discuss the question of the Chicago Review. Richard
Stern was present as Mr. Cate, who has been characterized
as Kimpton's enforcer in the Faculty Senate, [59] reported the
substance of the November 11 meeting to the full Council.
After his statement, he asked Stern if he wished to add anything he may have left out. The magazine's advisor replied
"that Mr. Cate's was as complete a report as he had ever
listened to, and he had nothing to add unless there were
questions." [60] Stern was later chastised by students for his
failure to stand up for the magazine, but the resigned sarcasm
of his response to Cate's question indicates his awareness of
the editorial resignations and the hollowness of the meeting he
was attending. He had done what he could to save the Winter
issue, but at this point he must have been prudently acquies-
cent.

A discussion followed in which Kimpton was asked to
comment on the future of the magazine. He said that he
hoped "a new editor could be found and the board reconsti-
tuted ... to reflect the literary taste and judgment of the
Humanities faculty." [61] Considering the resignations, his
suggestion was ironic.

A Mr. Weinberg observed that the current issue was
not in the fine tradition of the early Chicago Review when it
boasted the world's best young writers as contributors. In
his opinion the punitive actions taken in response to Mabley's
article were partially the result of the loss of prestige.
Stern hastily contradicted Weinberg by observing that of all
the "little magazines," the Review had enjoyed exceptional
circulation figures. He informed the Council that the Summer
1958 issue devoted to Zen Buddhism printed and sold 5, 700
copies.

As comic relief a Mr. Allison admitted to those discussing the problem that he had "never heard of the magazine

and did not know what the reporter was referring to when he
read the critical column in the Daily News. "[62] His confession of ignorance confirmed the student editors' initial reaction that the controversy would pass quickly because few
people would recognize the reference to the Chicago Review.

Chancellor Kimpton, however, was less indifferent,
and obviously more powerful. The issue offended him, and
"he was resolved to do something about it."[63] He stated
flatly that the University would assume the financial liability
of repaying subscribers if the magazine were dismantled.
The general sentiment of the Council favored some alternative
to stopping the magazine. Kimpton suggested that Dean Wilt
be urged to resolve the dilemma. The members agreed.
Kimpton had succeeded in convincing the faculty to recommend
the action which had already taken place.

Cate then moved that the discussion not be made a
part of the record because it was not advisable. However,
several members felt that a public airing of the facts was
healthy, and passed a substitute motion authorizing the
secretary to report the statements made during the discussion. [64] Despite this attempt to keep the content of the
meeting secret, the suppression of the Winter issue had been
achieved with the backing and support of the Faculty Senate.
The University had stopped the Winter issue without a direct
confrontation, or the appearance of repressiveness. It had
censored the material by Burroughs and the others nevertheless.

The Student Government began an investigation of the
suppression of the Winter issue on December 2, 1958, and
issued a report of their findings on January 28, 1959. Although the report found the University of Chicago administration culpable, [65] that was pale solace for the editors who
needed money to have the issue printed outside the University. In order to gather the funds, a benefit poetry reading
by Allen Ginsberg and Gregory Corso took place on January
29. The reading and donations from patrons of The Shaw
Society of Chicago which sponsored the event brought in
enough money to print the suppressed issue and to begin "a
literary magazine in Chicago which would not be subject to
the review of a Chancellor loyal to the philistines."[66] The
reading also caught the attention of Nelson Algren.

The author of The Man with the Golden Arm and A
Walk on the Wild Side sneered at the Beats who had staged

the poetry reading in defense of the Chicago Review. Though
much more articulate, he voiced much the same sentiment as
Mabley had done a few months before:

> Never before us, someone has noted, has any
> people enjoyed such a plentitude of physical
> luxuries while suffering such a dearth of emotional
> necessities. Never before has any people set itself
> a moral code so rigid while applying it so flexibly.
> Now, in gaining affluence so great that we can af-
> ford to support infantilism as a trade followed by
> professional infants, we score another first. [67]

Perceiving the Beat writers as children or as a symptom of
deteriorating American morality was not new. Algren objected to the content of their message, but not to their right
to express it openly. His was a critical, not a legal judgment. As the controversy over the Burroughs and Kerouac
contributions moved beyond the academy, the distinction between free expression and critical assessment would become
muddled and lead to more controversy.

Chapter 3

BIG TABLE, BURROUGHS, AND THE POST OFFICE

Following the repressive censorship action taken by
the University of Chicago administration which forced him to
resign as editor, Irving Rosenthal remained firm in his commitment to publish the material. He found a new little
magazine to be titled Big Table, begun by former Chicago
Review poetry editor Paul Carroll. A poet himself, Carroll
had taken the position of permanent editor. Because of the
acrimonious events at the Review, however, he sympathetically
and enthusiastically turned over the editorship of the first
issue of Big Table to Rosenthal, who intended to serve as
editor only for the first issue in order to publish the entire
contents of the suppressed Winter 1959 Chicago Review.
Carroll would resume his position for subsequent issues.

The publication of the suppressed material in Big
Table #1 signaled a victory for the student editors who had
resigned in protest. Buoyed by the publication, Rosenthal,
in introducing the issue, pointed an accusing finger at the
University administration whose actions forced the resignations of all but one student editor. [1] He then took the opportunity to dare the administration to tell the whole story
publicly. If they did not, he would publish the full report
of the student committee investigating the incident in a later
issue of Big Table. The need for that never arose since the
report was subsequently published by the University of Chicago unexpurgated. [2]

The euphoria over the victory gained in publishing
the material was short-lived, though. A new danger which
would not surface until late April of 1959 promised to be
more formidable than the extra-legal suppression by academia.
The second round of trouble would not originate from a University administrator, but from another journalist. The
danger would not appear in the Chicago newspapers; it was
set in motion, in part at least, when literary editor of The

Capitol Times of Madison, Wisconsin, August Derleth, received a review copy of Big Table #1.

As author himself, Derleth was prolific, boasting as
early as 1942:

> I write because I must, because I have plots and
> material to keep me writing for more years than
> I can possibly live, and I want to put it all down
> as quickly as I can. [3]

He wrote poems, novels, children's books, science fiction,
biographies. He wrote local Wisconsin stories collectively
called the Sac Prairie Saga. He wrote for and was co-founder
of a periodical collection of horror-detective stories titled
Weird Tales. But it was as a journalist, a literary editor,
that the "burley-chested blond"[4] would have a chance to comment on the new Bohemian literature so alien to his own
taste.

Though the philosophical differences between Burroughs and Derleth appear obvious, several interesting
similarities exist. Both have a tendency to "get the stuff
out, leaving to subsequent novels the revision and refine-
ment."[5] Both published what may be considered science
fiction. Burroughs was hailed as a new writer for the future
in the science fiction journal S. F. Horizons,[6] on the publication of Nova Express. His fiction was at least as weird as
Derleth's horror stories. Derleth was closely associated
with the works of H. P. Lovecraft.

Though Burroughs and Derleth exhibit eccentricities
and some thematic similarities, each writer's perception of
his audience is quite different. Derleth explained his attitude
this way:

> In the overwhelming majority of my books I am
> primarily an entertainer [emphasis mine]. Little
> more than the primitive storyteller who had a
> place at his tribal fire. I believe in communicating
> as simply and directly as possible, as freshly as
> I can, and am not interested in various literary
> 'isms--though I keep up with everything from the
> avant garde to the academicians--and I am not
> troubled at being out of the main stream of con-
> temporary American writing. [7]

Burroughs also cares little for literary "isms" and the main-
stream of writing, but his relationship to his audience is
strikingly different. For him

> there is only one thing a writer can write about;
> what is in front of his senses at the moment of
> writing.... I am not a recording instrument....
> I do not presume to impose "story" "plot" "con-
> tinuity." ... I am not an entertainer [emphasis
> mine]. [8]

Though they shared a tendency to revise slightly or not at
all, Burroughs totally rejected the idea of the writer as
entertainer, while Derleth embraced it.

No avant-gardist, Derleth requested a review copy of
Big Table # 1 because it contained the suppressed contents of
the Winter 1959 Chicago Review, and by virtue of that enjoyed
advance notoriety and reputation. He expected, therefore,
examples of a valid literary movement unfairly censored; he
found offensive rubbish instead.

He could have let the matter drop, choosing not to call
further attention to the magazine, or he could have printed a
damaging review in his literary column the way Jack Mabley
had done. Like their Chicago counterparts, Madison readers
would have noted the new magazine as unworthy of a second
glance. Derleth was no dilettante, however, and decided that
the material was foul enough to warrant direct action. He
contacted the postmaster in Chicago.

Derleth did not file a formal complaint with the Post
Office because the magazine was already suspected of violating
the laws designed to keep obscene matter from the mail.
Joseph F. Kozielec, a Chicago postal clerk in charge of
second-class mail, had previously questioned the "mailability"
of Big Table # 1. [9] He felt the issue conformed to the law
which excluded from the mail:

> Every obscene, lewd, lascivious, indecent, filthy
> or vile article, matter, thing, device, or substance
> ... [which] is declared to be nonmailable matter
> and shall not be conveyed in the mails or delivered
> from any post office or by any letter carrier.... [10]

The law, commonly called "The Comstock Act" after its avid
19th-century lobbyist Anthony Comstock, had been originally

written to prevent the mailing of any literature, device, or
drug dealing with abortion. It was expanded in 1873 and
1876 to include material which was considered obscene.
Other additions to The Comstock Act provided for the seizure
and detention by the Post Office of suspected magazines and
other material under "mail block" provisions. [11] The laws
set the Post Office up as the official national censor, as
well as seller of stamps.

At the time Big Table # 1 was mailed, then U. S.
Postmaster Arthur Summerfield enjoyed the reputation as a
well-known hardliner on pornography and obscenity. He
wanted tougher postal laws prohibiting obscene material, and
in a lobbying effort he set up a permanent display of confiscated books, abortion devices, and other contraband in the
Post Office Department. The display was intended to graphically demonstrate for congressmen and members of visiting
women's groups the extent of moral depravity and degradation
which was turning the mails into an open sewer. Summerfield's display room was dubbed the "chamber of horrors. "
With the coming of Camelot in 1961, the new Postmaster
General did away with the dramatic display of his predeces-
sor. In 1959, however, the number of arrests for obscenity
violations under the Comstock Act was increasing. Big Table
1 was one of "315 arrests after about '4, 000 separate in-
vestigations' of alleged violations of the Comstock Act"[12]
made by the Post Office in the fiscal year which ended June
30, 1959.

Although August Derleth did not file a complaint, he
had "evidenced a desire"[13] to testify against the magazine in
a hearing to determine its mailability. Considering the
nearly unanimous nature of the adversary relationship which
existed between the Post Office and literary critics on the
issue of obscenity censorship, Derleth's desire to testify cannot be taken as an idle whim.

On March 18, 1959, Albert Podell, the business
manager, took several hundred copies of Big Table # 1 to
the Chicago Post Office for mailing. [14] He obtained an application form for second-class mailing privileges from Joseph
Kozielec, filled it out, and returned it. [15] The space on the
form which called for the number of magazine subscribers
was left blank, [16] and for this reason "the application was
held in the Chicago Office pending the receipt of the required
information. "[17]

"In the meantime the postmaster at Chicago enter-
tained doubt as to the mailability of the publication and on
April 3, 1959, a copy was transmitted to the director of the
Division of Postal Services for a ruling. "[18] The director in
turn sent the copy he had received to the Post Office's
General Council for a legal opinion concerning Big Table #1.

Reports from subscribers and advertisers that they had
not yet received copies of the first Big Table concerned the
magazine's editors.   Other than the mention of unreceived
copies, nothing had been communicated to them that the issue
was in any trouble.   However, the past experiences with the
Chicago Press and with the University of Chicago was enough
to arouse their paranoia and draw them to the conclusion that
the Post Office had seized the copies deposited for mailing.
Since they had no official word, they subsequently sent a
telegraph message to the General Council of the Post Office
in Washington, D. C. asking for information about the
missing copies.   The Chicago authorities had evidently referred them to the Washington attorney who replied:

> Mailability of "Big Table" magazine under considera-
> tion.   Expect decision Monday, [April 20]. [19]

Monday, April 20, passed without the promised ruling,
and another telegram was sent on Thursday requesting an
immediate decision on the magazine's mailability.   A request
was also made for a late May or early June hearing in the
event of a negative answer. [20]

On Friday, April 24, Post Office General Council
Herbert Warburton, convinced that there was enough doubt
about the magazine under the Federal law, wired the editors:
"Big Table Magazine of questionable mailability.   Hearing
will be set and formal notice furnished you early part of
next week. "[21]

Richard S.   Farr, Acting Assistant General Council
of the Post Office Fraud and Mailability Division, sent Albert
Podell a letter informing him that a hearing had been scheduled for June 2 at 10:00 a. m. in room 5241 of the Post Office
Department Building in Washington.   Since the rules governing
such mailability actions were being revised, Farr added that
he would send a formal notice confirming the hearing date as
soon as the new rules were adopted.   He estimated that the
notice would be sent in two weeks and that it would contain
the Post Office's position

that there is probably cause to believe that the
Spring issue of "Big Table" is nonmailable under
18 U. S. Code 1461 because of its obscene and
filthy contents with particular reference to the
articles entitled "Old Angel Midnight" and "Ten
Episodes from Naked Lunch."[22]

Farr sent the informal notice and a copy to the Chicago postmaster, directing him to serve the notice in person and to
file the copy. He also stipulated that the copies of the
magazine should continue to be held, and additional mailings
detained and reported to Washington.[23] The action effectively
banned Big Table #1 from the mail.

Albert Podell did not receive the April 30 notice addressed to him, but was told of its contents by newspaper
reporters.[24] He called the Post Office to confirm the information, and after several hours delay, they blamed the failure
to deliver the notice on some errors in Farr's letter. They
assured him, however, that he would get his copy eventually.
Not totally reassured, Podell asked that the letter be read to
him over the phone. It was.

Without attempting a formal answer to the charges,
Podell wrote General Council Warburton posing several
questions and requests.[25] He asked for the locations of the
magazines held and a list of the addresses. He asked for
the release of the twenty-one advertisers' copies in order to
prove that ads were inserted before Big Table could be paid.
And if that were denied, he asked for permission to open the
envelopes and remove the correspondence and invoices which
were then two months late.

Podell did not stop there, however. He asked Warburton for permission to mail several hundred copies to
critics, editors, publishers, professors, scholars, and lawyers
in order to solicit testimonials for use in the defense at the
mailability hearing. He further specified that the mailing be
air-mail, special-delivery and paid for by the Post Office because their actions had caused the financial losses already suffered by the magazine.

He asked if the term "obscenity" could be defined more
clearly, and if it were necessary for him to be present at the
hearing in Washington. Such a trip represented an unaffordable
expense.

Podell's letter was an arrogant challenge of the postal bureaucracy.

Podell sent the letter by registered mail and a copy to his friend Irving Rosenthal who had moved to New York City. He confided to Rosenthal that he was forced to release the story when reporters found out about the action against Big Table. He directed him to look at the requests he had made, and with the glowing pride of protest predicted, "Those poor bastards in Washington will go crazy."[26]

Sobered by the inevitable court battle and the anticipated refusal of his mailing request, he asked Rosenthal to secure a few testimonials for the magazine. He also provided a breakdown of the seized copies: 122 for Ferlinghetti's City Lights Book Store, 122 for the Folklore Center, 122 for the Paperback Gallery, and 21 for advertisers.[27] Copies had been secured by Ferlinghetti and the Paperback Gallery. The list, however, explains why Podell left the space on the second-class mailing application unfilled and unaccompanied by a list of subscribers. The list and the subscribers simply did not exist. To be fair, they could not exist since the magazine was begun under less than the ideal circumstances which would have provided a few subscriptions.

Joel J. Sprayregen, the Chicago attorney from the American Civil Liberties Union who had been assigned to the case, wrote to Rowland Watts in the New York Office to explain the Big Table situation on May 8. He insisted that he would try to get a change of venue on a possible violation of due process unless a local hearing were provided.[28]

May 11, Rosenthal went to the A. C. L. U. office in New York to deliver the copy of the letters he had received from Podell. He thanked them for taking on the Big Table case, adding that he had no other place to turn.[29]

On the 14th, Albert Podell finally received the official letter from the Post Office sent on April 30 which contained the informal notification of the hearing in Washington in early June.[30] Podell signed for the letter at the Post Office, and the receipt was sent to Washington.[31]

Melvin Wulf of the A. C. L. U. directed Joel Sprayregen to begin his preparations openly since it was no secret that the organization was interested in Big Table. New York Post

reporters had approached them first for information, and
when they ran a story the association would be clear. [32]   On
the 24th the Post ran the story of the Post Office objections
to the Burroughs and Kerouac contributions to Big Table,
mentioning the Chicago Review and the A. C. L. U. [33]

Assistant General Council Richard Farr answered
Podell's letter to Warburton on the 22nd. He informed him
that a formal complaint was being filed against the magazine
and would be served according to the new regulations which
were published on May 19. He enclosed a copy and then addressed the points Podell raised previously by first assuring
him that the list of addresses would be provided by the postmaster.

He directed Podell to consult a lawyer on the hearing
requests and he rejected the request for an additional mailing,
completely ignoring the demand that the Post Office pay for it.
However, he had no objection to the withdrawal of the copies
addressed to advertisers, and assured him that on written request they would be turned over to him by the Chicago agent.
Finally Farr defined "obscenity" by quoting Roth:

> whether to the average person, applying contem-
> porary community standards, the dominant theme
> of the material taken as a whole appeals to pruri-
> ent interest ... [and] a thing is obscene if, con-
> sidered as a whole, its predominant appeal is to
> prurient interest in nudity, sex, or excretion, and
> if it goes substantially beyond customary limits of
> candor in discription or representation of such
> matters. ... [35]

Complying with the new regulations, the docket clerk
directed the Chicago postmaster to deliver the formal complaint against the magazine and the notice of hearing in person. [36] The hearing was set for June 4th at 10:00 a. m. in
room 5241 of the New Post Office Department Building. [37] As expected, the formal complaint suggested that
there was probably cause to believe Big Table violated U. S.
Code 18, Section 1461 because " 'Old Angel Midnight' and
'Ten Episodes from Naked Lunch' were 'obscene, lewd,
lascivious, indecent, and filthy.' "[38] Edward Carlick was
assigned to serve as hearing examiner, [39] but he became ill
and was subsequently replaced by William A. Duvall. [40]

Paul Carroll, founder and editor of the magazine, re-

quested that the hearing be moved to Chicago. He reasoned
that the magazine was published, edited and impounded there,
the witnesses were there, and he could not afford to go to
Washington. He asked that the hearing be postponed to the
week of June 21-27 even if the move were denied. [41]

Carroll received the Post Office letter containing the
complaint and the notice of hearing. [42] Chicago Postmaster
Carl A. Schroeder forwarded the receipt Carroll signed to
Washington. [43]

Joel Sprayregen, acting as the magazine's attorney,
formally asked for a continuance and change of venue, adding
to Carroll's reasons his own need for time to prepare the
case. [44] He confessed to Melvin Wulf in New York that an
effective presentation could not be made unless there were
more time, [45] because he wanted to use Allen Ginsberg, Jack
Kerouac, and William Burroughs as witnesses. [46]

Wulf told Irving Rosenthal of Sprayregen's choice of
witnesses. [47] He wrote to the Chicago lawyer that as far as
he knew, Burroughs was in Europe, but planned a trip to
New York in late June or July. Though he knew him only
through letters and the stories of Allen Ginsberg and Gregory
Corso, Rosenthal felt strongly that Burroughs would be unwilling to testify because of his desire to remain as anonymous as possible. He added, in strict confidence, that there
were things in Burroughs' past which would prove damaging
in the eyes of the hearing examiner, if the Post Office
lawyer were sharp enough to uncover them. Rosenthal no
doubt had in mind Burroughs' drug addiction and the accidental
shooting of his wife in Mexico City some years before.

In his opinion, Jack Kerouac could not be persuaded to
testify. Not only was he painfully shy, but he refused to participate in the Big Table benefit reading with Ginsberg and
Corso. In addition, his drinking posed the problem of his
effectiveness as a witness in court. [48]

Allen Ginsberg was in San Francisco and informed
Rosenthal that instead of testifying, he would rather write a
comment for submission as evidence. The poet explained
that he would be too flip to be of much help. [49] All the
reasons aside, Rosenthal concluded that as a practical matter,
no one could pay for the trip even if they all could testify.

After reading Rosenthal's explanation, Sprayregen did

not pursue the idea of using the three to serve in the defense of Big Table at the hearing.

In Washington on June 1st William A. Duvall asked for advice from the Post Office's general council on the request to move the hearing to Chicago. [50] The lawyer had no objection and agreed with Big Table that it would indeed be a financial hardship for them to go to Washington. Although the other reasons were dismissed as irrelevant, [51] the changes in time and location were approved. [52]

Acting on the advice of the Post Office lawyer, Duvall set the hearing for June 23rd at 10:00 a. m. in Chicago. [53] He advised Sprayregen of the changes and informed him that the hearing would be held in room 616 of the Main Post Office Building on VanBuren and Canal. [54]

New York attorney Herbert Levy advised the A. C. L. U. that the Big Table case could be won, if not at the Post Office level, certainly at some Federal Court level. But to do this, he considered it essential that a full-dress presentation be made, complete with expert testimony and statements from the authors. It was clear that a solid record be established "to overcome the obviously psychologically bad effect upon the Post Office officials of the use of four-letter words." [55] Joel Sprayregen was already committed to such a presentation, but without the testimony of Burroughs and Kerouac.

Sprayregen anticipated the forthcoming battle. He quipped to Melvin Wulf, "I wanted to have it set to co-incide with the Playboy Jazz Festival in early August, but you know how impersonal bureaucracy is. [56]

Under the postal regulations governing obscenity in the mail, which were being debated in Congress at the time, the Post Office had a mandate to act both as prosecutor and judge in matters of postal law violations. Some reformers and most civil libertarians feared the possible abuse of the Constitutional guarantees of free speech and press if the Post Office were to act as autonomous censor. Considering the tough stand taken by Postmaster General Summerfield, the editors and lawyers for Big Table had something to fear from a postal hearing.

The press in addition to the A. C. L. U. took up the cause. In an article in late May, The Nation described the Post Office's delays in a distinctly belligerent and sarcastic

tone. [57] The unsigned story called Kerouac and Burroughs'
contributions "steamy prose about a seamy world . . ."[58] and
concluded that the subject matter would

> attract the noses of Post Office snoopers. Reading
> with their noses, these civil servants found in the
> pages of Messrs. Kerouac and Burroughs the words
> they expected to find, and they decided that the
> issue should not be delivered. [59]

Though the stand taken by The Nation was quite clearly opposed to censorship for any reason, the case at hand involved not the emotional issue of literary values versus public
morality, but the authority of the Post Office to impound
several hundred copies of Big Table #1 without proper notification. The problem was more frustrating than complex, and
The Nation perceived it correctly by mentioning that Constitutional precedent was clearly on the side of the magazine,
not the Post Office. However they saw that realistically
"the weight of bureaucratic arrogance is on the Post Office's
side, and it is a formidable weapon when used against private
citizens of limited resources."[60]

Postmaster Summerfield "personally became an active
combatant in the anti-obscenity effort,"[61] and if the past
actions of the Post Office were any indication, Big Table had
reason to fear any impoundment. Gershon Legman's Love
and Death was impounded. It was

> a serious, vehement condemnation of the emphasis
> on sex and sadism in postwar American literature
> and movies. On one or two occasions Legman's
> polemic uses four-letter words; beyond that it can
> hardly be reproached, and presumably no court
> would ever find it obscene. But the Postal lawyers
> did, and Legman was driven out of business by
> their 'temporary' mail block. [62]

Had the A. C. L. U. not chosen to take on the Big Table case,
the magazine could have been slowly censored by inaction,
and might have died for lack of funds to mount the case in
the proper Federal court.

In arguing for a longer interim impounding period
before the House Committee on Obscene Matter Sent Through
the Mail, the Big Table case was used as a typical example
of the slowness of the procedures and as an illustration of

the need for more time. The report of that committee explained that material could be barred from the mail

> only after a quite lengthy administrative proceeding. An amendment to this statute in 1956 authorizes the Postmaster General to issue an interim impounding order, detaining the purveyor's mail for a period of up to twenty days to give the Department an opportunity to complete the administrative procedure required to issue an "unlawful" order. Experience has shown that this is not a sufficient period of time to complete such a proceeding. [63]

This Post Office explanation demonstrates its arrogance by its failure to consider the rights of speech and press. Its plea for a longer period seemed reasonable within the workings of a bureaucracy, but the Constitution was intended to protect the rights of individual citizens, not the convenience of agencies. The practice of impounding material such as Legman's book and the delays experienced by Big Table appear to be harassment and abuse of public office. Only as a last resort could the Post Office be accused in these matters of benign incompetence.

Joel Sprayregen prepared a formal answer to the charges brought against the magazine. [64] In his statement he denied the allegation that Big Table was obscene by calling it the work of serious writers expressing ideas of "social importance protected by the First Amendment to the U.S. Constitution." [65] With the obscenity definitions set down in Roth in mind, he said the magazine was not conceived to arouse the sexual desire of its readers or of the community as a whole. He stressed its literary nature and asserted that it was neither hard-core pornography nor prurient in appeal. [66]

He then attacked the postal law itself, calling it "vague and ambiguous in law and in fact." [67] He argued that by failing to spell out exactly what was prohibited, the law severely limited the expression protected by the Constitution. The law was also questionable because it provided for a block of an item before a proper hearing, and was then an illegal prior restraint. The regulations also granted judicial power to the Post Office hearing examiner, and violated the Constitution which granted that power only to the courts.

In proper legalese, masking no doubt a sense of

sarcasm, Sprayregen pointed out that the rules governing the proceedings were published five days after the notice of hearing was officially sent. [68] Finally Sprayregen asked for the charges to be dropped because he considered the issues to be constitutional and not within the power of the hearing examiner or the Postmaster General to resolve.

The answer to the charges was intended to make a solid record for future court actions and appeals since Sprayregen had no realistic hope that the charges would be dismissed before the hearing. He anticipated the hearing on June 23rd with hopeful resignation that the fight to free Big Table would take a great deal of time and effort.

The suppression of the Burroughs material by the University of Chicago, and the subsequent actions taken against Big Table inspired Olympia Press publisher Maurice Girodias to reconsider his previous rejection of the manuscript of Burroughs' Naked Lunch. [69] By the end of July, an English language, French edition of The Naked Lunch was available outside the United States.

Chapter 4

BIG TABLE OBSCENITY HEARING

Part I

Postmaster General Summerfield ruled that Lady
Chatterley's Lover by D. H. Lawrence was obscene under
18 U. S. Code 1461, and barred it from the mail on June 11,
1959. On Tuesday, June 23, 1959, William A. Duvall, Post
Office Department Hearing Examiner, began the proceeding
to determine the obscenity of Big Table #1, and thus its
mailability under 18 U. S. Code 1461. He immediately denied
a motion by Joel Sprayregen that the charges leveled against
the publication be dismissed. The presentation of evidence
began.

Post Office attorney J. Carroll Schueler, in his
opening statement, asserted the worthlessness of Big Table
#1. The lawyer got directly to the point.

> It is our position that this magazine is obscene
> and filthy. And it has no redeeming value; that
> it is conceivable that there are literary critics
> who would state that certain essays or poems
> contained in this magazine have some literary
> merits. These people are not able to speak for
> the average member of the community. It is
> conceivable that the average member of the
> community would find in this book anything but
> filth, and it is the effect of this magazine on the
> average member of the community that we must
> concern ourselves with. [1]

He made it clear that the opinions of literary critics in this
matter would hold little or no weight, interpreting the
"average person" concept outlined in the Roth test for obscene material in an embarrassingly literal sense.

The attorney went on to explain that the contents of
the work offended the community standards because it ex-
ceeded "the present critical point and compromise between
candor and shame (p. 26)." It was also the position of the
Post Office that the magazine used filthy and obscene words
sordidly, and described sexual acts and parts of the human
anatomy graphically.

After Schueler completed his opening statement, Sprayregen asserted that the rules of evidence applied in this
hearing, and therefore moved that the opening descriptions
and conclusions be stricken from the record. Reminding the
Big Table lawyer that Schueler's was an opening statement
and not intended to be based on established evidence, Hearing
Examiner Duvall overruled the motion.

Sprayregen waived his right to make an opening statement, choosing instead to "rely on the witnesses and evidence
which I will introduce (p. 27)."

Schueler began the presentation of his case by calling
to the stand his first and only witness, postal clerk Joseph F.
Kozielec. The clerk had received the copies of the magazine
for mailing and the petition from Podell for second-class
mailing privileges on March 18. He had also served on
Podell and Sprayregen the first notice of hearing on May 14.
He explained that his "duties consist of answering inquiries
over the phone and through correspondence, matters pertaining
to second class and to help patrons process second class
authorizations or applications (p. 29)." He informed the court
that he became curious about the contents of the magazine only
after he was unable to verify the number of subscribers to
the publication. That information was not supplied on the
application form submitted by Podell. If the clerk had seen
Podell's letter to Irving Rosenthal on May 8, 1959, [2] he would
have determined that there were no subscribers. Neither the
clerk nor the postal court, however, were aware of the literal
absence of subscribers, only of Podell's failure to fill in the
proper blank on the application form calling for a number.
According to Kozielec, when Podell was unable to verify the
subscriptions with individual order receipts, he wrote the
Postal Service Director in Washington on April 3 for an
opinion on the mailability of the magazine (pp. 30-32).

Schueler asked the clerk to identify a copy of the
magazine which was then submitted and accepted as evidence.

On cross-examination Sprayregen established that there was a delay of fourteen days, from April 30 to May 14, in the receipt and the subsequent delivery of the original notice of hearing to the editors of Big Table. Duvall interrupted to ask Kozielec to explain, as best he could, the reason for such a delay. The clerk said that Podell had two addresses listed on the application, each served by a different branch Post Office. When the letter could not be delivered at one, it had to "come back through channels again through the Post Office before it could be remitted (p. 37)" to the other address. At the risk of being facetious, the Post Office is the only organization which would, or could, plausibly use such an answer to explain a two-week delay in the delivery of a letter within the boundaries of a city.

Schueler, Sprayregen, and Duval had no further questions of Kozielec and he was excused.

Schueler offered into evidence a "notarized statement furnished the complainant by an individual by the name of August Derleth who is the Director of Arkham House Publishers, Sauk City, Wisconsin in the nature of a critique of the magazine, Big Table (p. 37)." Sprayregen asked to see the material which also contained a biographical booklet on Derleth, and a note referring to an article in Who's Who in America on the man. In other obscenity cases such evidence offered by defenders of publications on trial was routinely disallowed as hearsay, or accepted only as evidence of recognition, not for purposes of substance. Anticipating the trouble he would have with his own evidence in the forms of written criticisms, Sprayregen returned the papers and declared:

> I will make no objection to this type of evidence being introduced on the condition, which I assume when I attempt to introduce similar evidence it will be received without objection (p. 38).

Before making a ruling on whether or not to allow the exhibit as evidence, Duvall asked why Derleth was himself not in court to deliver his opinion. Schueler explained "Mr. Derleth evidenced a desire to come here but he could not. He is teaching school and could not get away (p. 39)." Though Duvall realized the written evidence was strictly hearsay, he was going to allow the statement to be received as evidence because neither lawyer raised an objection. He added that he would only accept the opinions of qualified critics.

In his statement, Derleth wrote that his experience
as the literary editor of The Capitol Times of Madison,
Wisconsin, as book publisher, and as author of numerous
books gave him "at least a minor claim to some knowledge
of what constitutes a work of literary merit."[3] He explained that he had become interested in the magazine because of the suppression of its contents by the University
of Chicago, and because it promised to be an example of
avant-garde literature which he thought should be heard
without the University's censorship. Before he received his
copy for review, he considered the contents of Big
Table #1 to have been the unfortunate target of a tendency
toward censorship in the country as a whole. The articles
proved to be a disappointment to Derleth's stimulated ex-
pectations. Ordinarily a man of many words, he got
directly to the point, heaping corrosive criticism onto the
object of his disappointment.

> I am sorry to have to say that in my considered
> opinion the overwhelming majority of the material
> in BIG TABLE 1 has no literary merit whatso-
> ever. I have here specific reference to material
> titled "Old Angel Midnight," by Jack Kerouac;
> "Ten Episodes from Naked Lunch," by William S.
> Burroughs; and "Three Poems," by Gregory
> Corso, which are for the most part undisciplined
> prose, far more akin to the early work of experi-
> mental adolescents than to anything of literary
> merit. Though two contributions by Edward Dahl-
> berg, "Further Sorrows of Priapus," and "The
> Garment of RA," are works of some merit, they
> occupy so few pages in the magazine as to be
> negligible in the issue, and do not represent an
> important contribution to literature.[4]

The literary worthlessness of the material found in Big Table
#1, as expressed by Derleth, would be the point which
Schueler would bring out over and over during the course of
the hearing. With the completion of the testimony of Joseph
Kozielec, the submission of a copy of the magazine, and the
acceptance of Derleth's written statement, Post Office Department attorney Schueler rested his case.

Since the Post Office had nothing further, Sprayregen
again moved that the case against Big Table be dismissed.
Duvall denied the motion, and the hearing continued with the
presentation of the case for the magazine.

The Post Office case was similar to others involving questions of obscenity in which the book or magazine itself is perceived by the court to be the best evidence of its nature. Schueler went further than other government attorneys by submitting a critique of the publication, though the prevailing opinion expressed by Duvall considered such information as hearsay. Sprayregen intended to establish as strong a record as possible, loading the transcript with information and packing the record with statements with an eye towards the appeal which he felt would follow.

Since the Post Office was intentionally unspecific in its accusations, a short description of the magazine and its controversial contents may help clarify the legal issues before the defense of Big Table is reviewed.

The cover of the magazine, with its broad red, white, and blue stripes on the front and white stars on a blue field on the back, could not have been perceived in a sexual way, though it may have been interpreted as a political caricature of the American flag. Any disrespectful similarity to the flag was not mentioned either before or during the hearing. The first white stripe at the top of the front cover contains the title "Big Table #1" and the price "$1." On the red stripe, directly below, in white letters reads: "Jack Kerouac Old Angel Midnight," and "The Complete Contents of the Suppressed Winter 1959 Chicago Review" in blue.

Under the red stripe another white band contains "Edward Dahlberg" in blue, and "The Garment of Ra," "Further Sorrows of Priapus" in red. The blue band at the bottom of the cover reads in white "William S. Burroughs Naked Lunch"; and in red "And Power, Army, and Police by Gregory Corso."

The inside front cover and the flyleaf are covered with advertisements for New Directions, Faulkner's books published by Modern Library, Noon day magazine, and Beacon paperbacks. A few brief notes on the contributors is followed by the table of contents. The biographical note on Jack Kerouac declares interestingly, "The title 'Big Table' was his suggestion."[5]

If one were confused by the reference to the suppression made on the cover, Irving Rosenthal's "Editorial" provided a summary of the events and the subsequent publication of Big Table.

The first story, Kerouac's "Old Angel Midnight, "[6]
assaults and stuns the equilibrium of the reader with its utter
formlessness and chaos.   It is in the same moment complete
gibberish and a privileged peek into brief flashes of sub-
conscious insight, interwoven with Zen philosophy and lapsed
Catholic imagery.   A liberal gloss would struggle to call the
story the impressions of the fallen angel, Old Angel Midnight,
as he experiences earth and decrys god in the earthiest
terms:

> Ya damn hogfuckin lick lip twillerin fishmonger!
> Kiss my purple royal ass baboon! Poota! Whore!
> You and yr retinues of chariots & fucks! Devadatta!
> Angel of Mercy! Prick! Lover! Mush! Run on
> ya dog eared kiss willying nilly Dexter Michigan
> ass-warlerin ratpole!... [7]

The colorful bombast appears quite early in the story, and
the most myopic illiterate searching for obscene words would
be very successful with this excerpt and with the rest of the
story as well. [8]   In either its diction or in its overall message, though, the character of the Kerouac narrative could
hardly be considered erotic.   Because of the excess of
Joycean experimentation, which in this case leads more often
to confusion than epiphany, the charge of boredom may more
easily be leveled against Kerouac's contribution to Big Table
#1 than one of obscenity.   Boredom, however we may wish
the contrary, is not illegal.

Edward Dahlberg's "Further Sorrows of Priapus"[9]
appears in four sections--essay-like, historical fictionaliza-
tions.   The heading of each identifies its contents: "On the
Persian Tyrants, " "On Discovery and Sorrow, " "On War and
Alexander of Macedon, " "On Wisdom and Old Age. "   Although similar to Pound's Cantos, the history presented here
in prose form is even more obscure.   Yet some interesting
and fresh treatments of Alexander and Magellen save the contribution from complete lifelessness, in spite of its Who's
Who quality.   For the postal censor the Dahlberg story had
no interest at all.   Not a single word was questionable, as
far as obscenity.   August Derleth's statement freely admitted
the limited literary value of "Further Sorrows of Priapus, "
but did not have enough weight to save the entire magazine.
Derleth had of course pitted the use of obscenities against
literary value, a questionable endeavor in court at best,
though essentially the point upon which the debate over
obscenity censorship raged at that time.

Dahlberg's other contribution to the magazine titled
"The Garment of Ra"[10] rambles through fifteen sections of
rather heavy-footed blank verse. Like the other story, it
too is heavily dependent on historical themes and on Egyptian
and biblical characters. One would have to stretch his definition of obscenity to apply it to this poem.

"Ten Episodes from Naked Lunch"[11] by William S.
Burroughs presented a less complicated problem for the
postal authorities. Within the fifty-seven pages of its text,
no less than forty questionable words, obscenities, "four-
letter words," and "Anglo-Saxon words" pepper the candid
narrative. [12] Far from any association with prurience, the
words appear in a context of violence and disgust associated
with drug addiction. They are also part of the imitated
language of individuals drawn in exaggerated fictional caricature of con-men, narcotics agents, addicts, cripples,
Arabs, homosexuals, bureaucrats, sheriffs, judges, doctors,
vaudevillians, perverts--all of whom act out their stereotyped,
flat personalities as if passively projected on a movie screen.
In the full version of Naked Lunch published later, Burroughs
would comment on this trademark of his fictional style that
he considered himself a "recording instrument. " Such a
claim to passive reportage in fiction writing reflects Burroughs' training as an anthropologist at Harvard, but it also
allows him to analyze often deviant behavior, free of pre-
determined judgments. It is generally within the fictional
recreation of the speech of street people that the obsceni-
ties--"turd, " "shit, " "fuck, " "asshole, " "cunt, " "bull shit, "
"ass, " "bastard, " "crap"--are used to achieve verisimilitude.
If anything the speech of the characters and the street scenes
created by Burroughs in the excerpts from Naked Lunch, like
an Eisenstein montage of static frames, flash across the
page, projecting the illusion of rapid movement and precipita-
ting a feeling of disgust or nausea in an audience. The
postal law forbids the lewd and lascivious, but not the disgusting. Disgust is hardly a major factor in the sexual
arousal of the average reader.

The final contribution to Big Table #1 consists of
three poems dedicated to Allen Ginsberg by Gregory Corso
titled "Power, " "Army, " and "Police. " The first explored
external political power as an undesirable alternative to the
internal power of an individual. "Army" delivers an im-
passioned anti-war statement. And "Police" recalls several
encounters with lawmen--as a youth, through the newspapers,
at a poetry reading, in a patrol car, and in a stationhouse.

None of the three Corso poems in Big Table contain an
obscenity of any kind. In retrospect, the poems should not
be considered more than average free verse, valued more
for where they appeared, than the sentiments they express.
Held up to other "Beat" poems, they appear stiff and often
dull.

Its questionable use of obscenities aside, Big Table
#1 certainly did not qualify as everyone's type of literature.
It could hardly be termed obscene when compared to the
hard-core pornography then being circulated. Nevertheless,
the Post Office's belief in the magazine's obscenity neces-
sitated a Postal hearing, not such a far-fetched notion when
one considers that Mr. Summerfield's "anti-obscenity publicity
had even included a stamp cancellation reminding the public
at large, constantly, to 'Report Obscene Mail to Your Postmaster.' "13

Confident that legal precedent was on his side, but
enough of a realist to be pessimistic concerning the final
outcome of the postal hearing, Joel J. Sprayregen began the
presentation of his case in defense of Big Table #1. He
wanted to build a strong record for what he anticipated as a
long series of appeals before a final reversal in a higher
Federal court.

Paul Carroll, Big Table's president, editor, and publisher, was the first witness to offer testimony (pp. 40-77).
He noted that he had received his M. A. in English literature
in 1952 from the University of Chicago. He had taught at
Notre Dame, Loyola, and the University of Chicago. He also
mentioned that several of his poems were published in
periodicals, he had held numerous poetry readings, and he
had published a translation of St. Jerome's letters.

In his opinion Big Table #1 represented an important
attempt to publish a new movement in contemporary American
fiction. Because the material was serious, it called for un-
hampered availability to readers. According to Carroll, the
seizure of several hundred copies of the publication by the
Chicago Post Office fettered the public availability of the
magazine.

Sprayregen asked Carroll to explain why material by
each of the four authors was included in the issue. The
editor commented on them individually. The story by Jack
Kerouac, "Old Angel Midnight," was included for two reasons.

In its fictional technique, it represented "a serious attempt
to continue and develop the very prose style and stylist
technique (sic) devices invented and articulated by James
Joyce (pp. 45-46)." In terms of American Literature, Carroll continued, that style had its roots in the writing of
"Cooper, Thoreau, Walt Whitman, and in many ways Mark
Twain ... [and] extends to the Twentieth Century to such
writers as Hemingway, [and] Sherwood Anderson (p. 47)."
He considered Kerouac the heir of this tradition which, among
other things, placed supreme importance on the consciousness of the individual. His reasons for including the Kerouac
contribution in the first issue of Big Table suggested no low-
minded appeal, prurience, or tawdriness.

He suggested to the court that the selections by Edward
Dahlberg were chosen because of the writer's twenty-year
critical reputation as a distinguished prose stylist. Burroughs, on the other hand, was represented in the issue not
because of his established reputation, but because he had, in
the opinion of the editor, the potential of becoming a major
influence on American fiction. He explained, "In the writing
of William Burroughs we had come upon an American prose
stylist of considerable power who is articulating an area of
the contemporary scene in a lucid, honest manner (p. 48)."
In his estimation Burroughs was writing in, and was heir to,
the tradition of authors which included Poe, Baudelaire,
Rimbaud, Verlaine, and Jarry. Carroll defined that tradition
as "an attempt to find a meaning for one's existence outside
of the accepted mores, sociological, philosophical and religious
of the existing societies. It is an attempt, actually, at
religous experience which the writer feels is either inaccessible or perverted in the society in which he is living (p.
49).

Another factor in the selection of the Burroughs
material lay in "the quality of his satire of the contemporary
American scene (p. 50)." Carroll compared Burroughs to
Swift, and pronounced the author of the excerpts from Naked
Lunch to be the first powerful American satirist since
Nathanael West. Carroll illustrated the point by reading
from the "Clem and Jody" section, beginning on page 110 of
the magazine. Duvall asked the witness if he could look at
the section, did so, then declared, "We have the book in
evidence. I would prefer you proceed with your oral testimony, (p. 51)" indicating the hearing examiner's reluctance
to have the questionable words and descriptions read aloud
in the hearing room.

The final contribution to the magazine, the three
poems by Gregory Corso, were included as the work of a
serious and responsible contemporary poet, though Carroll
conceded his stature was the subject of critical debate.
Before Carroll could describe Big Table's intended audience
Post Office lawyer Schueler objected that the "book has to
be judged by the reactions of the people in whomever's hands
it may fall (p. 57). " A small debate followed between the
two lawyers over the precedents governing the interpretation
of an intended audience in an obscenity case. Duvall directed
them to return to the case at hand. One can presume,
though, from Schueler's objection that he interpreted the
audience to legally include, along with the educated, the so-
called "most vulnerable mind" in the community, i. e. children. The most vulnerable mind concept in censorship cases
was set forth in the 19th-century British case Queen vs.
Hicklin, and formed the model for the anti-obscenity laws in
the United States. The Roth decision in 1957 all but castrated
the most vulnerable notion with the assertion that its ultimate
effect would reduce all reading material to the level of a
child. [14]

The Roth decision to the contrary, Duvall sustained
Schueler's objection and refused to allow Carroll to describe
the intended readership of the magazine. Sprayregen's effort to have the editor state for the record "whether in
publishing Big Table #1 he had a calculated intent to arouse
sexual desires in average people"[15] also met with a challenge.
Duvall sustained the objection, explaining that the Post Office
was not interested in the intent of the publisher or the
magazine.

Sprayregen rephrased the question and asked Carroll
for a description of the average reader of Big Table. He
informed the hearing that his magazine was typically read by
a college graduate "who reads serious works of literature
with the intention of not merely entertainment, but of finding
deeper insights into his own condition and the life around
him ... to learn some of the truths of life from that literature. "[16] Sprayregen had established an important distinction
for the record. Big Table was no hardcore smut rag intended for secret bathroom reading, but a literary quarterly,
written by serious authors for serious readers.

Once he had established the seriousness of the magazine, he turned to the objectionable diction of the contributions. Sprayregen asked Carroll his opinion of what the

hearing examiner termed the "repeated usage of certain terms that were referred to at the hearing as four-letter words or Anglo-Saxon words."[17] Carroll acknowledged his awareness of the presence of the questionable words at the time the material was submitted, and then selected for publication. They were allowed to remain because they "were germane to the serious artistic purpose of these writers (p. 17)." He added that the words used in Big Table could also be found in existing and widely accepted works of literature. The explanation was calculated to establish a contemporary community standard of acceptability of the questionable words in print, and constituted an effort to convince Duvall that Big Table should be considered as literature. If the hearing examiner conceded that the magazine was literature, it would then fall under the protective umbrella of the previous court decision involving the release of Joyce's Ulysses from a Customs ban. The release of Ulysses in December 1933 allowed the use of explicit language for artistic and scientific purposes. The establishment of Big Table as literature was an important factor in Sprayregen's case.

In an effort to underscore Big Table as an example of serious literature for a select, educated audience, Sprayregen asked Carroll how the publication was distributed. He replied that it was handled by two firms which carried literary quarterlies and quality paperback books. To his knowledge the magazine was sold in the Chicago area in the better book stores like Brentano's. In establishing its routine distribution, over Schueler's strenuous objections, Sprayregen joined with the leading constitutional experts on obscenity Lockhart and McClure who strongly believed that literature and pornography were circulated and sold differently.[18] Though its above-board marketing does not prove its position as literature, considered with critical opinion of its serious intent, the charge of obscenity would be weakened. Sprayregen submitted advertisements for Big Table as further evidence of the manner in which sales were solicited. The ads appeared in the Village Voice, The London Magazine, and Evergreen Review.[19] Copies were entered in the record.

Having established for the record the serious intent of the publisher in selecting the material directed toward a college-educated audience interested in literature, Sprayregen completed his direct examination of Paul Carroll.

After a lunch recess, Post Office attorney J. Carroll Schueler began to cross-examine Paul Carroll. He questioned the publisher rather intensely on six major points: 1) Carroll's opinion of limits imposed on an artist's use of certain words; 2) Carroll's connection with the Chicago Review and the subsequent suppression of the Winter 1959 issue by the University of Chicago; 3) William S. Burroughs' reputation as a writer and Allen Ginsberg's description of the material as "too raw" for American censors; 4) Kerouac's contribution to the magazine; 5) Burroughs as a social satirist; and, 6) Carroll's background as a literary critic. Under the attorney's questioning, Carroll was often impatient, belligerent, and arrogant.

In questioning the publisher on the artist's use of words, Schueler asked if he believed in "absolute liberty for an author to use any words known to him (p. 78)." Carroll replied that "a serious writer ... is warranted to use any word that would articulate and throw light on what he is trying to write and present to the reader (p. 78)." The qualification implicit in the response signaled the lawyer to attempt to eliminate the distinction made.

> Schueler: I am simply asking your opinion, whether you believe a hack can use any words in writing a story....
>
> Carroll: May I focus your question for my own benefit, please. I've tried to describe earlier how I think the responsible and serious artist trying to articulate a subject has complete freedom in the selection of words, to bring out the full dimension of his subject. Regarding other kinds of writing, I'm afraid I feel you are trying to get me to say that I think complete license is permitted. The answer is no (pp. 79-80).

In the spirit of egalitarianism, Schueler had tried to erase any distinctions between writers and their use of language. Carroll clung steadfastly to the notion that there were writers called artists who enjoyed privileges, by virtue of their seriousness, not granted to others. [20]

Frustrated in his effort to have Carroll describe an example of a non-serious artist, Schueler urged him to be more specific about James Joyce, the writer used as a general illustration of a serious artist. He replied that a serious artist generally is, like Joyce: "The man who tells the truth about the human condition as he knows it. If he necessarily has to use certain words to bring out that truth, he has carte blanche in my opinion. This is a responsible artist without whom we are blind (p. 82)." Carroll was only willing to grant unbridled use of the language to serious artists, not to anyone who owned a typewriter or a pen.

Schueler then turned to the relationship of the Big Table editor with the Chicago Review. Sprayregen objected to that line of questioning as irrelevant to the case. Duvall let it continue because the matter, and Mabley's article as well, had been mentioned by Irving Rosenthal at the beginning of the magazine. After some confusion concerning the date of the Chicago Review issue which was suppressed by the University of Chicago, Schueler was finally instructed that the Winter 1959 issue, which came out in 1958, was not to be called the Winter 1958 issue. The date and its explanation exasperated the Post Office lawyer to the point of anger, as he asked Carroll why the issue was barred. The Big Table publisher explained:

> The reason why the Chicago 1959 Review was suppressed was that [the] Chancellor did not want a further scandal at that time. It was not on literary grounds. It was based on the grounds of the potentiality of further scandal, which in my opinion, they didn't want to go through because of certain financial interests made to the university. They didn't want to jeopardize their reputation. It was not literary grounds (p. 85).

Carroll may have been moved to deny any literary basis for the suppression twice by Schueler's implication that the material had previously been considered obscene by the University of Chicago. That would bolster the Post Office contention that the same material had no literary value and was indeed obscene. Though he did not coax Carroll to call the suppression literarily inspired, he did succeed in placing on the record the prior supression of the material by the University. The motive for the action would be less important than the action itself.

Satisfied with a minor victory on that point, Schueler asked the witness a series of questions about Burroughs' background as a writer and about Carroll's knowledge of his work, leading up to this revealing exchange:

> Schueler: Would you characterize any of Burroughs' writings as raw?

Carroll: Raw?

Schueler: Raw.

Carroll: Would you please explain that word.

Schueler: I think we are well aware of the word
itself, raw.

Carroll: Raw, like a fellow murdering his wife is
raw.   I mean--

Duvall: Mr. Carroll, you take your meaning of
the word raw and see whether it would apply to
any of the writings of Burroughs.

Sprayregen: Your Honor, I object on the ground
that--on the point that I don't see what the characterization of writing as raw has to do with the legal
issues at stake in this hearing.   I assume that if
writing is raw it may nevertheless not be obscene.

Duvall: Well, I would assume that this is a preliminary question, and he is asking his opinion as a
man who's qualified to give such an opinion.

Carroll: My--in my understanding of the word
"raw" I would say emphatically yes.   If I could
describe briefly what my understanding of that
word is, it is an articulation of the more brutal
aspect of the human condition--I have particular
references to the Shakespeare [of] Othello,
Macbeth, Hamlet, reference to some aspects of
Anderson, Ernest Hemingway, in particular The
Sun Also Rises, I would describe them as raw
works of literature.   In this way, I would say
his work is raw.   Sections of his work, the overall effect of Mr. Burroughs is raw.   In that understanding of the word (pp. 88-89).

Eventually Schueler revealed the reason behind the seemingly
pointless questions over the word "raw. "   The term had been
used in a letter from Allen Ginsberg to Paul Carroll which
was subsequently printed in the Chicago Review, Autumn 1958.
Burroughs' work is referred to in this way:

Most of his work [is] too raw but I asked for him

to send something palpably printable by U. S.
censors standards. [21]

As soon as Schueler read the reference into the record, both
Carroll and Sprayregen explained that the opinion expressed
in the letter was Ginsberg's, not Carroll's. The publisher
went on to explain that he felt that if certain passages of
Shakespeare were translated from the Elizabethan to the contemporary vernacular, they would also be too raw for the
censor. He informed the hearing that the letter in question
had been received before he had read any of Burroughs'
work, admitting that his initial thought at that time was,
"either he [Burroughs] was a psychotic or that this kind of
writing was very powerful, indeed (p. 94). "

In an effort to badger Carroll into an admission that
"raw" had a sexual or obscene interpretation, Schueler repeated questions several times. The publisher was steadfast,
Sprayregen finally objected, and before the Post Office lawyer
could rule, Schueler changed his line of questioning to
Kerouac's writing style. He quickly returned to the Burroughs contribution, asking, "Do you believe this social
criticism, as you have called it, would be valueless or in-
articulate if it were not for so-called four-letter words
being used?" Carroll replied, "Yes, I quite honestly do
(p. 99). "

Before he completed his questioning of the witness,
the lawyer asked Carroll, in an apparent effort to discredit
him as a qualified literary critic, to list his book reviews
and critical articles. When Carroll did so, the effort was
thwarted. The Post Office attorney ended his cross-examination of the Big Table publisher.

On redirect Sprayregen attempted to reemphasize
Carroll's ability to make critical literary judgments, and to
clarify his belief that Burroughs' social satire was not only
perceptible to the average reader of the magazine, but
certainly not intended to be erotic or prurient in any way.

On recross Schueler asked Carroll what kind of person the magazine was intended to serve. He replied:

Carroll: A serious reader of literature, I would
say. Not necessarily a college graduate in the
statistical sense of the word, but one who reads
serious literature with the intents of the--to learn
some of the truths of life from that literature.

Schueler: Would you agree with me that that is
not the true average reader in the United States?

Sprayregen: I think we could use some further
definition.

Schueler: I think we are all aware of what I am
asking. I am sure Mr. Carroll is.

Carroll: Well, of course, I would say that's not
the true average--I would--I wish that it were. I
may also add this, please, that our use of the
United States mails is too--

Schueler: We have testimony that--

Carroll: You are trying to establish for whom the
magazine is intended. You're trying to get me to
say it's not for the average reader (pp. 105-106).

He had clearly confused the exasperated Carroll, causing
him to appear contradictory and inconsistent in describing
the intended audience. Had he agreed with the lawyer that
the audience was specialized, the concession would not have
been damaging to the case. Schueler's obvious purpose was
to show that the magazine was not fit for certain segments of
the population, children for instance. However, Schueler
would have been more in line with the interpretation of the
law had he tried to establish the nature of the adult audience
which picked up Big Table, instead of pushing tenaciously for
an ambiguous interpretation of the average.

Neither Sprayregen nor Schueler had any further
questions of Carroll, but the hearing examiner wanted several
points clarified. Duvall wanted Carroll to explain how Kerouac
"writes and reduces to writing the workings of the uninhibited
mind (p. 106)." The publisher felt that the writer tried to
record the actual experience of his mind while meditating on
a particular subject. The technique, he continued, was
similar to the free association of psychoanalysis or the im-
provisation of jazz. It was "uninhibited not in a moral or
religious sense, but uninhibited in a literary sense (p. 107)."

Duvall asked if Carroll could expand on a statement
made previously that part of Burroughs' work was a record
of his attempts to find outside society the reasons for its
existence. He instructed the hearing examiner that an author

often searches for meaning in ways prohibited or censored by
an existing society, because to him that society is corrupt
and incapable of encompassing the full dimension of the human
experience. Duvall wanted to know if a writer uses language
to explore such dimensions. Carroll agreed that language was
used that way, adding: "Merely because he doesn't use
language that would be used in church on Sunday or at the
Kiwanis Club, doesn't necessarily mean that he should not
be read by that society (p. 110)." Duvall brought the discussion back to the specific use of words in Big Table:

> Duvall: I am referring in part to his language,
> and in part to the scenes and situations described,
> such as lesbianism, homosexuality, various matters
> of that type. I think you will agree that they are
> purely outside the mores of the community.
>
> Carroll: May I add this? The more recognized
> piece of great literature is Socrates--I mean,
> Oedipus Rex by Socrates (sic). The experience
> of that play is incest, which is surely outside the
> mores of any society. Should that play be put on,
> shouldn't it? Shouldn't it be read--should it be
> read? The experience actually of the man who
> sleeps with his mother and kills his father. The
> experience of a fellow who is terrible, violent
> psychotic, jealous. The experience of Hamlet,
> the murder of his brother (sic), should these plays
> not be read by the accepted society. That's the
> question. I think Burroughs takes his place in this
> tradition, of one who writes about areas of this
> experience that are not accessible to the average
> person. But by writing about them as a social
> satirist, and presenting them in such a way, the
> average person can gain a deeper insight as to
> what is happening in our very day, in front of our
> noses. This is my literary feeling on this....
> I'm sorry if I was giving a lecture (pp. 110-111).

Duvall dryly informed the publisher that the issue at hand was
not whether an author should, or should not write on a particular subject, but whether the language he chose was acceptable by the standards of the community. To Carroll,
Burroughs was entitled to write about his experience truth-
fully and vividly because he was "one of the damned (p. 112)"
who could make us understand our own identity better.

No one had further questions of Paul Carroll, and he was excused.

As the publisher of Big Table Carroll could hardly be negative in his testimony. At worst his responses would be perceived as understandably biased. The next witness, on the other hand, had no association with either Big Table, the Chicago Review, or the University of Chicago. He was Hoke Norris, a book reviewer for the Chicago Sun-Times. After he was sworn in, he identified himself before the hearing as a former Neiman Fellow at Harvard University, a novelist and short story writer, and literary critic. Norris' Harvard background and his position on a big city daily made him the literary superior of August Derleth.

Sprayregen began his examination of Norris by asking him to evaluate Big Table # 1. He replied that the contents of the magazine represented a "serious, valid, international literary movement (p. 116)" which voiced a socially signifi- cant "protest against a world which can produce a bomb that can blow up a city with one blast (p. 118). " Though Norris respected Kerouac's attempt to trace the "wanderings of a mind back through the caverns of experience (p. 122)" in a manner similar to James Joyce and Gertrude Stein, his literary judgement was that "Old Angel Midnight" didn't quite come off (p. 122).

The Burroughs excerpts, however, enjoyed more suc- cess in using free association techniques to communicate the inner workings of the mind. Norris explained that "wild figures, disjointed associations between objects and words, sentences, and paragraphs, places (p. 122)" found in the text all contributed to the overall effect on an audience as a peek inside the mind of a narcotics addict.

Norris considered Corso's three poems to exhibit a good grasp of the language, a feeling for the precisely drawn image, and a great deal of wit. He felt that they were the best contributions in the magazine. His praise, though ex- tremely positive, stresses subtly the potential of the poet rather than the accomplishment.

Surprisingly the most recognized of the contributors and the one least controversial in terms of the obscenity laws drew the most pointed criticism from Norris. Concerning Edward Dahlberg's contributions, he admitted that he "couldn't quite figure out what he was about (p. 124). " They did represent something of literary value, though, as a "rather pallid rewrite of Plutarch with some nice turns of phrase ... [and] pleasant description. "[22]

In an effort to establish the normality of the maga-zine, Sprayregen asked the reviewer if he found any signifi-cance or meaning in the kinds of advertisement in Big Table # 1. Even the most cursory comparison of the ads in a literary magazine and a so-called "girlie" magazine would yield obvious differences. Before Norris could comment, Schueler objected that the witness was not called to testify about ads. Sprayregen explained that a reviewer would re-view the whole work including the ads. Those ads may in-fluence his judgement by indicating to him the type of maga-zine it is, its purpose, and its intended audience.

> Duvall: I don't see how the advertisements that are contained in here give any indication as to the type of audience that the publisher is appealing to. I would assume that the publisher would take an ad from any business concern. After all, a pub-lisher would like for his publication to be financially successful, presumably.

> Sprayregen: If we found an advertisement in this magazine for a stag movie, I think we might be permitted to draw certain inferences from that.

> Duvall: But there are none.

> Sprayregen: That is precisely the point on which I have testimony.

> Duvall: All right, sir, you have testimony on that point from the book itself. That is the very best evidence as to what is in the book--the book itself.

> Sprayregen: The objection is sustained then?

> Duvall: Yes (p. 125).

The hearing examiner's stand on the point of the magazine as the best evidence of its own character exemplified the depth of his obdurate position on the issues involved in the hearing. The more Sprayregen and the witnesses called to testify explained and interpreted the text, the more tenaciously Duvall clove to the dictum that the book spoke for itself. It

may have been sound as a legal principle, but the absurdity
of its blind application was not without its demonstration immediately after Sprayregen posed another question to Norris.

> Sprayregen: In reading and evaluating Big Table
> One, as a literary critic, were you aware of any
> intimate detailed descriptions of sexual activities
> in that volume?

> Schueler: Objection. The magazine speaks for
> itself.

> Sprayregen: If the magazine spoke for itself, your
> honor, we wouldn't have to be here today. Writing
> does not exist and did--and is not produced in a
> vacuum (p. 126).

As reasonable men outside a courtroom, neither Duvall nor
Schueler would assert that every book is fully apprehensible
in all its supposed complexity by anyone who reads it. But
they were in a courtroom and a short argument followed on
the point. Duvall resolved the dispute by concluding "that
in view of the fact that this is opinion testimony, and opinion
testimony is not binding on me when I go to make my decision,
I am going to let the witness answer (p. 128)." Duvall had
taken a rather safe detour around the issue by calling the
testimony nonbinding. When Norris was allowed to answer
the question, he said that he did not consider the descriptions
in Big Table #1 to be sexual.

Sprayregen then questioned the witness on the use of
certain words in the text. Norris felt that the four-letter
words used by Kerouac and Burroughs were germane to the
serious purposes of their contributions. Any substitution of
euphemistic synonyms for the words would be ridiculous in
the context of the stories. Though he gave no specific examples, one can imagine the silliness of substituting "copulate
off" for "fuck off" in Kerouac's "Old Angel Midnight." Norris
did say that the words which appeared in the magazine "refer
to the natural functions, or the organs with which those natural
functions are performed (p. 128)."

Sprayregen then asked the critic's professional opinion
on three items: 1) whether he had noticed any changes over
the last thirty years regarding the use of four-letter words
and of sexual descriptions in serious literature; 2) whether
the objectionable words found in Big Table #1 could be found

in widely accepted books; and, 3) whether the works found in
the magazine were designed to arouse the reader sexually.
Schueler objected to all three lines of questioning. The first
two were called irrelevant; the third called for Norris to
offer testimony which he was not qualified to deliver. Schueler
contended that the point required training as a psychologist.
Duvall sustained the objections.

The Big Table lawyer turned to the question of the
intended audience. He asked Norris to describe the average
reader of the magazine, instead of the intended audience.
The critic replied that any sophisticated reader interested in
serious, avant-garde literature would appreciate the issue.
He added quickly, however, that large segments of the population would not be interested in the magazine because "it's
just the nature of the avant-garde publications to appeal to a
small group (p. 138). " Rather than draw further attention
to the reference to a limited audience, Sprayregen completed
his examination on that weak legal note.

Schueler then grilled the witness on his qualifications
as a literary critic, making the point strongly that Norris
had only been "a literary critic for less than one year (p.
138). " Confident that the point had placed the witness on the
defensive, the lawyer attempted to follow up on the comparison
made in direct examination between Kerouac's use of Anglo-
Saxon terms with a similar use by Whitman and Stein. Sprayregen of course objected, and Duvall sustained it.

Thwarted only for a moment, the Post Office council
asked Norris if as a critic he felt that it was his duty to inform his readers that a piece of writing was "the meanderings
of a narcotic's mind (pp. 139-140), " no doubt a reference to
Burroughs' contribution and to his reputation as a drug addict.
The newspaper critic replied that since narcotics addiction
was of public concern, he would certainly mention that a work
illuminated the social problem. In effect his answer had
turned the pejorative implication of the question around to
show the subject of addiction in a socially valuable way.
Schueler followed with a series of questions concerning the
process of critical judgement, Norris' perceptions of his own
critical opinion as superior to that of the average person, and
the diverse range of critical opinion. After establishing that
critical opinion was never predictable, nor absolute, even
among critics, Schueler grilled Norris on the relative merits
of Big Table # 1.   The Sun-Times literary critic admitted that
his opinion was consistent with the majority of other profes-

sionals. He considered the publication of the magazine as an
important literary and cultural phenomenon, while simultaneously holding back praise of its contents.

Schueler then turned to the use of the so-called dirty
words in the text. The lawyer wanted to know if Norris felt
that the meaning of the stories would suffer if those words
were removed and replaced with equivalents. Norris replied

> I would know in reading this that the characters
> about which this is written would not use synonyms,
> that is the accepted synonyms. They would use the
> synonyms that are unacceptable. That is what I
> meant [by] it would be ridiculous to replace these
> with other words (p. 145).

True to the demands of literary realism which formed the
essence of almost all writing in the 20th Century after
Dreiser, Joyce, and Hemingway, the critic had placed himself squarely on the side of the free use of any words for
the sake of realism. Norris had no real choice. The only
alternative was Philistinism, difficult to defend and more
difficult to believe. The writer's use of words, then, formed
a privilege critics were ready to grant. The legal system
was less progressive in its attitude toward the use of certain
words.

Before Schueler had finished his questions, Norris
mentioned that he had reviewed the magazine unfavorably in
the Sun-Times (p. 147). He was quick to point out that the
magazine still had literary merit, though it was not great
literature. The beats, after all, had fomented a heated
critical debate which neither negated nor diminished the
magazine's seriousness according to Norris. As far as the
Post Office lawyer was concerned, the question boiled down
to a less complicated distinction, indicated by his last question of the witness:

> Schueler: Do you believe all writings that are
> published have literary value?
>
> Norris: Oh, no (p. 147).

After Sprayregen had Norris reemphasize the seriousness of the magazine, Duvall asked a few clarifying questions.
The hearing examiner wanted to know why the critic had reviewed the magazine in the first place. Norris mentioned

some of the same reasons August Derleth had given for his
interest in Big Table. The contents were the topic of local
controversy, the beats were a topic of national interest, and
two beat poets had recently read in Chicago in support of the
magazine.

Duvall: Your criticism of the book was adverse.

Norris: Adverse in general, yes sir.

Duvall: And I think you stated that your--in your
estimate of the book you are in the majority of the
critics with whom you are acquainted whose criticism you read?

Norris: Yes, sir. That is an impression.

Duvall: Yes all right, sir. That is your best
opinion?

Norris: Yes, sir (p. 150).

Duvall had nothing further.

Sprayregen could not leave such an impression and
hastened to have Norris say that if the magazine were not
a serious representation of an important literary movement,
he would not have considered it for a review at all. Norris
stated flatly, "I avoid shabby, cheap publications for review
(p. 150)," implying that Big Table was no such document.
He had made a critical, rather than a legal distinction in
writing an unfavorable review. The subtlety of that action
never penetrated the awareness of the hearing examiner. [23]
With his astute answers and candid, honest opinions now in
the record, Norris left the stand. It appeared as if the
effect of his testimony had little influence on Duvall who would
make a ruling on the magazine.

The third and final witness for the defense was Hans
W. Mattick, a sociologist, psychologist, and criminologist.
He had received an M. A. in Sociology from the University of
Chicago. During World War II he served as an administrator
in P. O. W. camps. He was the former assistant warden of
the Cook County Jail, Sociological Actuary and Research Sociologist for the Illinois State Parole Board, and President of
the Illinois Academy of Criminology. His entire testimony
was confined to the Burroughs excerpts. Through Mattick's

responses, Sprayregen strove to establish the social and
scientific importance of those descriptions found in the episodes from Naked Lunch.

Based on his experience as a prison warden and
criminologist, Mattick considered drug addiction to be a
serious social problem. Since it was defined as a criminal
activity, he felt addiction forced "persons to resort to various
other kinds of crime in order to support their habits (p. 153). "
To underscore the seriousness of the problem, he reminded
the hearing that an entire Federal bureau was organized to
deal with it.

Asked what use the Burroughs article might serve,
he replied that in teaching a course in criminology he:

> would certainly refer my students to the article by
> Mr. Burroughs as being an excellent example of
> the fantasy life of an addict and as such makes a
> rather significant contribution of [sic, to?] our
> understanding some portion of the drug addict's
> problem (p. 154).

He also considered the experience articulated in the excerpts
from Naked Lunch to constitute a serious delineation of the
addict's thoughts as well as an objective description of drug
use. The facts in the story rang true from Mattick's own
knowledge of the scientific literature on drug addiction and
from his experience with addicts in prison. "But its main
value, " he went on, "is its first-hand account from the stand-
point of one acquainted with the problem and apparently
speaking uninhibitedly about both the joys and sorrows of the
addict (p. 156). " Other first hand accounts were taken from
addicts in artificial situations, usually in official custody or
under confinement.

Duvall interrupted the questioning to ask if it were
necessary for Sprayregen to establish Burroughs as a drug
addict since it had not been done so either in direct testimony
or in the magazine itself. Chilled by the remark, the lawyer
suggested that the issue of the hearing involved the quality of
the work, not the conduct of the author. Duvall pointed out,
though, that Mattick's comments assumed that the narrative
could only be the product of an addict. The witness conceded
that

> if he indeed has never used drugs, this is a very
> remarkable sympathetic and vicarious experience

which he is delineating and is a true image as far
as I know. . . .

[However] I am in no position to make an accusation because that is a legal matter, which I can
not comment on (p. 158).

He considered the text to be fictionalized autobiography, since
the facts and impressions could only have been written by
someone with first hand knowledge.

As a sociologist Mattick was asked his professional
opinion concerning the use of four-letter words in the Burroughs excerpt. It appeared to him that the expletives in
question were used to express hostility, and not to refer to
or describe sexual activity. The words appeared to lend
emphasis to the forms of expression "used verbally among
drug addicts and prisoners in general, as I have seen them,
as well as others in the army (p. 160). "

A short comment from the witness on the realism of
the text would have been appropriate at this point, but Mattick had not listed himself as a literary critic, and he was
not allowed to discuss the literary merit of the publication.
Duvall did not allow him to testify on the allegedly sexual
arousal of the stories by Burroughs and Kerouac. The
hearing examiner called such information irrelevant to the
case. The ruling was no doubt influenced by Mattick offering
a letter "on the relationship between criminal figures in
literature and the criminal in the open (p. 166)" published in
the American Scholar as his credentials as a literary critic.

On that point Schueler ended his questioning. As with
the other witnesses, Duvall had some questions of his own
for the criminologist.

Duvall: Mr. Mattick, based on your testimony, it
is my impression that you feel that this article by
Burroughs is good primarily for people who are
drug addicts or for people who are treating drug
addiction, as a therapeutic bit of reading?

Mattick: Yes, I think in terms of understanding
the nature of the drug addict, and his emotional
and psychological organization (p. 167).

Unwilling to have the testimony of his witness end on the

limiting implication that the Burroughs article would only be
of use to addicts and to those who treat them, Sprayregen
asked if any serious intelligent reader, not necessarily trained
as a sociologist or a criminologist, or an addict himself,
would find the excerpts from Naked Lunch to illuminate the
problems and sufferings of drug addiction. Mattick, of course,
agreed that it would contribute to the serious reader's understanding of the problem.

As Mattick stepped from the witness chair, the case
looked less promising for Big Table. The tenaciously conservative rulings on the part of the hearing examiner on the
testimony indicated that his reception of the case for the
magazine was at the very least cool. Yet Sprayregen, it
should be recalled, had a more long-range purpose in mind.
The testimony of the witnesses had created a strong record
on which the issues could be argued on appeal. Sprayregen
had introduced a number of constitutional questions which
could only be decided in a Federal court, not at an administrative hearing.

But Sprayregen had not finished the presentation of
his entire case. After the witnesses, he introduced as
evidence "twenty-four letters from writers, critics, educators,
clergymen, publishers, and a psychiatrist."[24] The hearing
examiner accepted the letters as evidence that, in the opinion
of the writers, Big Table #1 had both literary and social
value. He qualified his acceptance of the letter, however,
informing Sprayregen that only the views of competent critics
on the literary value would be allowed to remain in the
record. Duvall would reject the written statements containing opinions on the alleged tendency of the material to
arouse the prurient interest of the average reader as not
germane to the case. He told Sprayregen that he would rule
on each statement individually as he read them. As Sprayregen had done previously on other rulings which he considered ill-advised, he took formal exception to the hearing
examiner's decision to choose which letters and which parts
of letters would be allowed in evidence.

He then submitted a collection of nine articles on the
philosophy and literary importance of the Beat Generation.
Again, Duvall reserved a ruling on the evidence until after
he had an opportunity to read and inspect the material.
Sprayregen also submitted a statement on the new acceptable
use of Anglo-Saxon words which was part of Malcolm Cowley's
testimony at the Lady Chatterley's Lover hearing. Duvall
said he would rule on it after he read it.

With the submission of three exhibits, Joel Sprayregen concluded the presentation of his evidence. Still curious over the financial matters of the magazine, Duvall recalled Paul Carroll for further questioning. The publisher said that the potential of a larger, nation-wide audience for Big Table would not be out of the question and that he would welcome the sale of his journal at newsstands where "people might buy a magazine of serious literature."[25] But at the moment he hoped for no more financial success than to pay himself a salary, after establishing a permanent pay scale for Big Table contributors. He told Duvall that he had made a verbal contract with the contributors of the first issue to pay them "fifty dollars apiece, but we haven't been able, financially, to pay them yet, but we will be (p. 181)." Carroll was allowed to step down after revealing the thinness of the journal's shoestring budget.

Schueler began his final argument with the declaration that he did not intend to make a closing statement. He said, rather, that he was "willing to rest on the record that had been made in this case (182)." The record established: 1) Big Table #1 was mailed, 2) it was obscene, and 3) the evidence revealed "an extreme difference in critical opinion of the literary value of the magazine (p. 183)." The Post Office lawyer interpreted the lack of critical consensus to mean that the literary value the material possessed "would not render an obscene or filthy article not obscene (p. 183)." In other words, he took the "social value" test laid out in the Roth case to require that the value and the obscenity be weighed against each other, the dominant quality prevailing. Others interpreted the "social value" test for obscenity to mean that a work with any value could not be banned as obscene. At the time of the Big Table hearing, this point from Roth was very much at issue and would remain so until the 1966 clarification of the point by the U.S. Supreme Court. Duvall would nevertheless base his decision on the weighing of value against obscenity. Schueler ended by directing the hearing examiner to find "as a consideration of law that the magazine in question is obscene, lewd, lascivious, indecent or filthy, and is non-mailable matter under 18 U.S. Code 1461 (p. 183)."

Sprayregen closed with a discussion of recent U.S. Supreme Court decisions on the obscenity question. He concluded that:

> only so-called hard-core pornography, dirt for
> dirt's sake, as used in some of the opinions, may

be banned by the government, and that works which
have redeeming social importance and value which
are produced with a serious literary purpose such
as Big Table, cannot be considered obscene (p.
187).

The two interpretations of the Roth "social value" test could
not have been more at odds. Each reflected the complexity
of the issue as interpreted by the legal and literary communities. The quality of the confusion can be seen in a
comparison Sprayregen made in defense of Big Table. He
cited a ruling handed down the week before the Big Table
hearing in which Postmaster Summerfield pronounced
Lawrence's Lady Chatterley's Lover obscene because the book
was filled with minute sexual descriptions. [26] Sprayregen
reasoned that even though the language in the magazine went
beyond the customary limits of candor in description, none
of those descriptions were of intimate sexual relations, nor
did they appeal to sexual interest. Big Table, then could
not, like Lady Chatterley be banned under the postal law.

Turning to the facts involved in the case, Sprayregen
observed "that obscenity is a mixed question of law, fact,
and also partially a constitutional question (p. 191)." He
reminded the hearing examiner that the Post Office's case
consisted only of the magazine itself and a statement of
August Derleth that it was obscene. He stated that each of
his three witnesses and twenty-four critics said the publication was serious. He then launched an attack on the methods
of cross-examination employed during the hearing by Schueler,
concluding that his questions reflected:

a view point on the part of the Governmental
administrators with the--which I submit is
directly in violation of the principles of the
first amendment to the constitution which
guaranteed free expression, guarantees the
right of every American to decide for himself
what is good and what is valid and what is not
so good in the arts (p. 193).

Sprayregen asked that the hearing examiner find as a matter
of fact that Big Table #1 was not obscene, contained literature
produced with a serious purpose, and was expression protected by the First Amendment. On the question of law, the
lawyer asserted that if the questions of fact were granted, the
legal and constitutional points need not be reached.

His statement concluded, Sprayregen moved for the hearing examiner to render an immediate oral decision. Duvall explained that he had not read the magazine in its entirety nor had he had the opportunity to read the exhibits. Under those circumstances a fair judgement was physically impossible at that time. He denied the motion, and instead availed himself of the option to deliver a written decision within five days of the date of the hearing. Both lawyers waived their right to submit additional written briefs on the matters of law and fact in the case. Duvall closed the hearing at 5:22 p.m.

Part II

The hearing had been a long, tiring one for Joel Sprayregen. His frustration surfaced in a comment he made after the proceedings to a reporter covering the case for the New York Post:

> The Post Office would do well to remember that its job is to deliver the mail, and that Americans are free to decide what they will read. [27]

His comment ran the next day, June 24, in the New York paper, marking the first large circulation periodical outside Chicago to give the incident involving the Burroughs and Kerouac stories any coverage.

In his June 27 magazine column poet and critic for the Saturday Review, John Ciardi, summarized and evaluated the actions taken against Big Table by the Post Office. The intellectually snobbish tone adopted in his comments were no different than any other intellectual writing in favor of free literary expression. Flippantly he referred to the postal officials who screened printed matter for possible violations of the obscenity laws as "scholar-inspectors." [28]

He of course anchored his invective on literary and legal precedent by mentioning the landmark Ulysses case. However, in illustrating the social value concept as part of the legal definition of obscenity, he chose the then recent and obscure case of "Howl" heard in a San Francisco court. Since lawyers and critics recognized the U.S. Supreme Court's Roth decision as the contemporary source of a legal definition of obscenity, Ciardi's mention of "Howl" is curious. His reference indicates not so much an ignorance of the law, as it suggests that Ciardi's information was supplied by someone, like Allen Ginsberg or Irving Rosenthal, who was clearly sympathetic to Big Table and to Beat writing. If this were not the case, Roth would certainly have been used as the logical illustration of social value because of its recognized authority by both lawyers and laymen.

Ciardi's defense of Big Table before the Post Office's allegations should not, though, be interpreted as his aesthetic approval of the works in question. Like most critics in matters related to obscenity, he drew a clear line between artistic disagreement and legal culpability. William A. Duvall, like other hearing examiners before him, muddled the issue by never separating the two very different reactions to obscenity.

Ciardi, nevertheless, found himself defending "Old Angel Midnight" even though he was "no admirer of Kerouac's assaults on near-prose. "[29] The critic did consider the writer to possess "a substantial gift, however much the gift may be smothered by indiscipline. "[30] As far as the attempts to ban the material on the grounds that it was obscene, he observed, "it is impossible to conceive how any average man can go on reading the stuff, let alone be corrupted by it. "[31] Advising the Post Office what course of action they should adopt, he could not resist sarcasm:

> I would suggest to our guardians in the Post Office Department, as a ponderable principle of law, that dullness precludes excitation of the centers, and that by the test of dullness, Kerouac's writing is as unimpeachable as Federal prose. [32]

Not all of the material in Big Table was quite as disappointing to the Saturday Review critic. The literary value of Burroughs' "Ten Episodes from Naked Lunch" impressed him. He mentioned the frequency of four-letter words, concluding that " ... such obscenities--if obscenities they are--are inseparable from the total fabric and effect of the moral message. "[33] Contrary to the Post Office allegation, Burroughs' work represented that of "a writer of great power and artistic integrity engaged in a profoundly meaningful search for true values. "[34] In his opinion, neither of the works could intelligently be labeled obscene by a reasonable court, implying that the administrative proceedings by the Post Office against this magazine and other publications were unreasonable.

In spite of the intransigence of the Post Office, Ciardi had faith that if the case were fought to a high enough court, Big Table would be released. The question, though, involved more than the ultimate outcome. He expressed his concern over the procedures which gave to the Post Office the power to act as both Judge and prosecutor by asking:

> And when the editors have won the release of Big Table #1, what assurance have they that it will not begin all over again with Big Table #2? Is this the true intent of the Post Office Department: to force a safe and sane sixteen-year-old sweetheart conformity upon all writing, by making it financially disastrous to venture beyond the literary standards of a postal inspector, who yet seems to enjoy peeking into other people's more promising mail?[35]

Because the extra-legal harrassment outlined circumvented normal due process of law through the courts and also invited the possibility of official abuse, it cried out for change. For Ciardi and others, the Big Table case resurrected the spectre of government censorship of literature, believed to have been settled with the release of Ulysses. The possibility fueled the writer's rhetoric as he defined his opposition to the censorship of literature rather eloquently: "All censorship is a disaster that begins in ignorance and seeks to culminate in demagoguery. "[36]

More than rhetoric or publicity, John Ciardi's article placed the approval of the literary establishment on the Big Table cause. The glowing reception of the publication by the Village Voice[37] and the Wagner Literary Magazine[38]--representatives of more specialized, iconoclastic audiences--was now joined by the more prestigious, conservative Saturday Review. His article solidified the issues. Like Hoke Norris, most critics opposed censorship as a general principle, demanding the freedom to make an aesthetic judgement apart from a legal one.

A work which used obscenities could often be considered simultaneously as serious literature and not achieve literary greatness, an obvious truism to any student of literature. But the distinction, reasonable enough in its capacity to embrace conflicting appearances, made little legal difference. Ciardi expressed as much in his article which Sprayregen tried to submit as evidence after the hearing. Duvall refused

it as after the fact. [39]   In fact the literary judgement of
Kerouac's prose may have provided additional support for the
prosecution's contention that the story had no redeeming social
value.

On the contents page of the Saturday Review issue
following the Ciardi article, a three-quarter page ad in the
form of an open letter from Grove Press publisher Barney
Rosset detailed the Post Office ban handed down a few weeks
earlier on Grove's edition of Lady Chatterley's Lover. [40]
The publisher, interested at the time in publishing Burroughs'
Naked Lunch in America, had run solidly into Summerfield's
army of postal inspectors over the obscenity issue.

Considering the volatility of the censorship issue,
Ciardi's editorial on the Big Table matter brought an expected response.   Praising his efforts on behalf of the
magazine, novelist John Clellen Holme wrote:

> Fortunately, prurient post-office officials, and
> university chancellors with weak stomachs, will
> continue to resemble so many intellectual Keystone
> Cops as long as people like Ciardi have their eyes
> open. [41]

Supporters of what was quickly becoming a cause celebre were
not strictly confined to writers or individuals associated with
the staff of the magazine.   An alumnus of the University of
Chicago, G. Scott Wright, Jr. of Weston, Connecticut, expressed his disapproval of the actions taken by Chancellor
Kimpton in suppressing the material when it first appeared
in Chicago Review.   He taunted the administrator whose
"adolescent concerns with football and public morals [were]
not in the tradition of the once-respected institution of higher
education. "[42]   Ridiculing the actions of the Post Office he
asked rhetorically, "What kind of mind must a man have to see
dirty pictures where others see masterpieces?"[43]   No doubt
the alumnus from conservative Connecticut had articulated
the central question which makes obscenity so difficult to
define, much less to regulate.   But all of the responses to
the actions against Big Table and Chicago Review generated
by Ciardi were not positive.

A detractor from Minturn, Maine, Helen W. Beurstorff,
was moved to verse:

> Both good and bad T. V. I've seen,
> And read new novels.   But

> There must be something in between
> Clean Western yarns and smut.
> (I agree with Summerfield.)[44]

To agree with the Postmaster General meant approval of his
definition of smut. As practiced by his office, anything which
described sex explicitly for any reason or contained pro-
fanities of any kind regardless of context was barred from the
mail as obscene material. His past arbitrariness in the application of the regulations and his bureaucratic userpation of
legislative and judicial power precipitated a great deal of
concern in the academic community. To any writer or critic
or publisher, it seemed certain that if the Post Office could
have such power with the use of individual words regardless
of context, the next logical step then would seek to regulate
ideas, whether or not they had any prurient interest.

Ciardi's article drew an inevitable response from the
University of Chicago. Acting as spokesman, Richard G.
Stern, the Chairman of the Faculty Advisory Board of the
Chicago Review, [45] impeached the facts laid out from his
point of view. He informed the Saturday Review audience
that the three issues of the magazine had been used by then
editor Irving Rosenthal "as a showcase for one group of
writers."[46] According to Stern's letter, when Rosenthal
planned a fourth issue, the University intervened because the
"purpose of the magazine was to display a spectrum of the
finest imaginative and intellectual work available, and that he
could not print the same group of writers in the next issue."[47]
Informed of the underlying motives behind the suppression,
Stern took them at their word as he noted that the "restric-
tion" allowed for the publication of each article individually in
the future. But that explanation had by the summer of 1959
been disproved by the report issued by the students who investigated the matter, as well as by the absence of the
articles in question in subsequent issues.

Stern continued to defend the University's action calling
it intellectually motivated. He countered the charge that the
decision had been precipitated by the preponderance of four-
letter words, asserting that no one in the administration
"ever objected to reading any word qua word or description
qua description."[48] Because Stern had initially worked with
the editors to get the articles published, his present statements against the material were particularly annoying to
them. Since he repeated the reasons given for the suppression by the University and distanced himself from the decision

making process, he could not have been accused of complicity
had he ended his response to Ciardi at this point.

But possibly tempted by the need to justify his new
position and to put the editors on the defensive, Stern made
some startling charges and disclosures. He denied that the
magazine was even read by a faculty member and certainly
not censored. If this were true, the suppression was even
more reprehensible. The denial was followed by this thinly
veiled accusation:

> But the faculty board will pass on the intellectual
> responsibility of student editors: those who print
> the work of cousins; those who print comic strips;
> and those who rob the till will be asked either re-
> form or resign. [49]

The assertion left the impression, and wrongly so, that
Rosenthal was related to the Beat writers and that he was
guilty of stealing funds from the magazine. [50] Ciardi challenged Stern to substantiate these "hidden charges and offered
reasonable magazine space for that purpose, "[51] but he never
took the opportunity to do so.

A rumor had persisted ever since Big Table was banned
that the Post Office was somehow connected with the University of Chicago. Stern also addressed himself to this issue.
But in an attempt to refute the rumor, he instead gave it
greater substance by disclosing:

> Recently a number of us saw a Postal Inspector
> about the proposed banning of Big Table. All of
> us objected to the proposed banning, and all of us
> would be willing to testify to the serious intent of
> the contents. [52]

The revelation created a disturbing contradiction. It made
little sense for any university official to testify in court on
the serious intent of the work which had been suppressed by
his institution for lacking such seriousness. One can only
speculate, and then read Stern's comments on this point with
deep sympathy for a faculty advisor obviously caught between
university politics and his intellectual scruples. Silence may
have proved the more prudent action than responding to
Ciardi's article. [53]

Another response to the Ciardi article clarified whether
or not the four-letter words which Jack Mabley found so of-

fensive back on October 25, 1958 had any influence on the
University's decision to stop the Winter 1959 issues of the
Review. The journalist described the terms he found in the
Autumn issue as similar to the "dirty words on railroad under-
passes."[54] Fairfax M. Cone, a Trustee of the University of
Chicago, must have been acquainted with the Mabley article.
It is more than mere coincidence which influenced Cone to
use an image related to the railroad to describe what he found
offensive in the suppressed issue of the Chicago Review. In
his opinion "there were ... a number of pages that were
shocking in precisely the way certain short, nasty words are
when these are chalked on the side of a boxcar or building."[55]

Cone brought into focus any confusion over the motive
of the university administration concerning their actions:

> ... Rosenthal and his witless friends were required
> to stop publishing obscenities that no university
> could condone in a student publication. Intellectual
> freedom was not at stake. The objection was to
> some specific printed lines that Mr. Ciardi failed
> to quote in his impassioned discussion. [56]

There could be no doubt that the material was suppressed
because of the use of questionable words. The questions of
literary merit and diversity had been invoked to mask the
censorship of the material because it contained obscenities.

Cone's startling candor was followed by a response
from August Derleth, the only literary expert to submit a
written statement supporting the Post Office in its case
against Big Table #1. He restated his general opposition to
censorship, and his reasons for supporting the censorship of
the magazine. But in contrast to his official statement, no
doubt feeling the less restrictive atmosphere of a literary
journal, he embellished his position with this immaculate
periodic sentence:

> It does not even have the literary merit of an
> average pulp-magazine story, or that kind of
> weary entertainment afforded by the tru-confessions
> periodicals, and the average newspaper story, with
> its occasional misuse of language, is vastly superior
> to it. [57]

Consistent in his statements both for the court and for the
Saturday Review, Derleth clung tenaciously to his defense of

the literary status quo, a valid critical position. Legally,
however, the ground was as solid as Mississippi bottom land
in Spring.

H. W. Pak, who had taken over as editor of the Review when Rosenthal resigned, responded with pleasure to
Ciardi's defense of Big Table. He compromised his praise,
though, by suggesting that the success of Big Table was
dependent on its former association with the Review. Pak
obviously felt the need to dispel the rumor that he had accepted the editorship under limiting editorial conditions. He
stated emphatically that he had accepted the position only
under the guarantee of full editoral autonomy.

The controversy over Big Table, as argued in the
Saturday Review, ended with an apology from Ciardi for mis-
quoting Chancellor Kimpton and, a confession of his personal
confusion over the facts. Nevertheless he concluded that
the magazine was indeed censored despite all the contrary
statements by officials of the University. Feeling a bit uneasy about the absolute nature of his conclusion, Ciardi
softened by extending an offer:

> Should the University of Chicago through one of
> its official spokesmen, care to make a clear state-
> ment, Saturday Review will print it subject to space
> limitations. We hope the University of Chicago will
> join us in viewing the matter seriously, and that
> it will accept this invitation to clarify the record. [58]

In subsequent issues of the magazine no clarifying statement
was published on the matter from the University. [59] In retrospect their silence signified prudence rather than an admission of impropriety. Despite Cone's suggestion that even the
Saturday Review would not publish the words in question, past
decisions of the high court suggested that work could not be
suppressed only on the appearance of certain words.

In rendering his decision on the obscenity of the
material in Big Table #1, William A. Duvall would be conservative in his interpretation of the concept of obscenity.

Chapter 5

THE DECISIONS OF THE POST OFFICE

William A. Duvall filed his decision with the Post
Office Department on July 9, over two weeks after the
hearing. The delay was caused by the late receipt of the
transcript and the late submission of an exhibit by Sprayregen, the Ciardi article "Bookburners and Sweet Sixteen. "[1]
As promised, he ruled on whether or not the three exhibits
submitted by Sprayregen would be allowed to serve as
evidence.

Sprayregen submitted a copy of Malcolm Cowley's
testimony on the use of "Anglo-Saxon" words in modern
literature in an "attempt to establish the contemporary community standards as to the acceptability of certain language. "[2]
Duvall rejected it as "not appropriate in a hearing of this
character. "[3]

Nine groups of articles and parts of books were submitted as evidence of Jack Kerouac's stature as an artist,
and as discussions of the philosophy and literature of the
Beat Generation. The exhibit attempted to establish the
seriousness of the authors, distancing their work from
pornography. Duvall refused to allow the material into
evidence. He did, however, permit the articles to accompany
the record as rejected exhibits, though they did "not relate
to the specific issues involved in this proceeding. "[5]

The rejection of these two exhibits did not damage the
case for their purpose was to beef up the record. On the
other hand, the third amounted to a substantial entry, con-
sisting of twenty-four letters from such distinguished critics
as Jacques Barzun, Kenneth Burke, Hugh Kenner, Lionel
Trilling, and Thomas Parkinson. Norman Mailer, Allen
Ginsberg, Le Roi Jones, James Laughlin, Robert Creeley,
and John Ciardi were also among those who wrote in defense
of the magazine. [6] As he promised at the hearing, Duvall

read the letters, excised what he considered the portions irrelevant to the case, and appended the acceptable parts to
his decision in fourteen singlespaced pages. [7]

Duvall concluded:

> I have read all these comments and the perusal of
> them substantiates the testimony of Mr. Norris
> that, while critical appraisal of this publication
> varies, the majority of such critical opinion is
> averse. [8]

He pointed out that in the majority of the written statements,
the contributors were considered serious writers.   Most of
the critics did not express an opinion on the literary merit
of the book, and he confessed that he discounted some of the
letters because they had been submitted by "members of the
cult or adherents to the so-called literary movement of the
beat generation."[9] He identified Ginsberg, Ferlinghetti, Jones,
and Mailer as members of the cult of Beat writers.   Even
though it is clear from his White Negro[10] that Mailer shared,
or wanted to be associated with the beliefs of the Beats, he
nevertheless was not a member.   It was an understandable
mistake on Duvall's part, but an error which was, according
to Sprayregen, "an example of government's incompetence"[11]
in literary criticism.   So Mailer's profound critical evaluation:

> Burroughs may prove to be one of the most
> important American writers to be printed since
> the War, [12]

was slighted by Duvall as the enraptured declaration of a
devotee.

The comments allowed to remain affect a critical tone
appropriate to the discussion of a literary work which com-
mands attention.   Hugh Kenner commented on the impact of
the Burroughs excerpts:

> One arises from its perusal impressed by the
> author's virtuosity, and I believe enlightened by
> what has been set before me, but certainly un-
> tempted to try for one self the experience de-
> scribed. [13]

Although Hans Mattick had testified to the value of Burroughs'
contribution as a deterent to the use of heroin, Kenner's men-

tion of the same value clearly negates the charge of the utter valuelessness of the material. His comments also praise the writer's stylistic ability. Other critics made similar statements on Burroughs' style.

Kenneth Burke, for example, described the value of the literary technique:

> In my opinion, many passages in this collection are stylistically interesting and valuable. They possess a certain turbulance or saliency that, being attained at times by inventiveness and imaginativeness, are good for literature. [14]

A critical evaluation of this sort could hardly be made of worthless pornography, or worthless stories regardless of content. Burke's compliments, it appears, had little influence on Duvall.

He was more persuaded by the literary judgements of Thomas Parkinson whose assessment of the material in Big Table, while not complimentary, reflected a general feeling about Beat writing.

> Please let me add, not to hedge on the matter, but to declare my own literary judgement, that I find much of Burroughs' work tedious, repetitive, and dull. [15]

However, if his evaluation were taken as criteria for proscription, then the legal and literary perception of obscene material would become twisted indeed. Very little printed matter could be mailed under those restrictions. Duvall confused critical assessment with legal judgement. When he totaled the positive and negative reactions to Big Table, Parkinson's honest criticism carried the same negative weight as if he had described the journal as the foulest smut, rather than just dull reading.

The absurdity of Duvall's interpretations is demonstrated in his efforts to explain his conclusion. For example, John Ciardi declared his critical reservations about the works this way:

> I may confess to some personal disagreements of aesthetic principle here and there in the writing, but in general it must certainly be recorded as work of substantial artistic accomplishment. [16]

Ciardi's qualification recognized that the material had literary
worth.   But his statement undergoes a substantial change in
Duvall's paraphrase of the sentence quoted above:

> Mr. Ciardi regards the work as being of substan-
> tial artistic accomplishment, but he says that he
> must confess to some personal disagreement of
> aesthetic principle here and there in the writing. [17]

By reversing the order of the clauses, Duvall had shifted the
emphasis from the praise of the artistic accomplishment of
the writing to the rejection of the aesthetic principles of the
Beats.   At the very least the hearing examiner could be
guilty of being unqualified to determine the literary value of
a piece of writing because he had no formal training as a
literary critic.   But the issues in this case called for him to
perform just such an evaluation.   His I-know-dirt-when-I-see-
it attitude hardly provided a healthy criteria for literary
judgement.

In determining which of the twenty-four letters would
be allowed as evidence, Duvall excluded a statement made by
Lionel Trilling.   He considered it a general declaration of
the critic's opposition to all literary censorship.   Similarly
a statement by Jacques Barzun was disallowed as not germane to the case because he compared Big Table's diction to
current literary standards, an area of discussion Duvall considered inadmissible.   The letters were allowed for the
limited purpose of establishing the merit of the magazine,
and Barzun commented on its intent:

> In this respect (intention and power to raise lustful
> thoughts), the contents of Big Table 1 are totally
> ineffective when compared with such classics as
> The Decameron or the Tales of La Fontaine, or
> with current paperback fiction at 25 cents such as
> is sold in every drugstore and on every newsstand
> in this country. [18]

Peyton Place, Lady Chatterley's Lover, Sanctuary, The Sun
Also Rises, and Butterfield 8 were some of the titles he had
in mind, but his conclusion concerning the alleged prurient
appeal of Big Table was, of course, deleted from the record
because Duvall considered it a general comment on the standards of obscenity.   The exclusion of the Trilling and Barzun
statements illustrates the arbitrariness of the hearing examiner's ruling on the twenty-four letters.   Duvall in effect

judged the statements of literary professionals, making himself the ultimate literary standard in this case. Perhaps Duvall may not have been guilty of putting his thumb on the scales of justice when he weighed the lone written opinion of August Derleth against those of Burke, Trilling, Kenner, Barzun, Ciardi, and Mailer; but his rulings on the letters provided negative statements on the magazine--the opposite purpose of their submission.

After ruling on the evidence, Duvall addressed the case as a whole. In his opinion it called for a determination of whether or not the magazine was "obscene" or "filthy" or both. In order to make such a decision, he outlined the legal definition of obscenity. Just as Sprayregen had done, the hearing examiner quoted the Roth definition.

> Whether to the average person, applying contemporary community standards, the dominant theme of the material taken as a whole appeals to the prurient interest. [19]

But Duvall noted that the Big Table lawyer had quoted only part of it. An important qualification had been eliminated. Duvall explained that the following clause had been overlooked: "unless excludable because they encroach upon the limited area of more important interests. "[20] However, the "more important interests" upon which the Burroughs and Kerouac material encroached was never made clear. Noting that Sprayregen had built his case on the right of free expression, Duvall quoted from Bread vs. Alexandria 341 U.S. 622:

> The First and Fourteenth Amendments have never been treated as absolutes. Freedom of speech or press does not mean that one can talk or distribute when, where, and how one chooses. Rights other than those of the advocates are involved. By adjustment of rights we can live with full liberty of expression and an orderly life. [21]

The case upheld a municipal law forbidding the solicitation of sales at a private residence without the prior consent of the owners or occupants, and it had been cited in Roth in reference to the "more important interests" clause. In other words, he interpreted the clause to mean that the rights of the individual should be respected.

Big Table never solicited readers or subscribers

door-to-door or by mass-mailing. It was in fact the inability
of Albert Podell to produce a list of subscribers which initiated the Post Office action. But the act of subscribing is in
itself a consent given by the reader to allow the publication
into his home. The Post Office never produced evidence that
the publishers included anyone on a mailing list or sent a
copy to anyone without his consent.

One can also speculate that the evocation of the "more
important interests" clause amounted to an effort to protect
the moral fabric of society as applied in obscenity cases. A
written expression of that notion might cast the hearing
examiner as an evangelist rather than as a judge. But it is
not unreasonable to assume that an educated man, not a
literary professional but a college graduate, would consider
that all literature should necessarily have a high moral purpose. Where the literary community would see art in the
avant-garde themes and in the amoral stance of so much of
20th Century realism, hearing examiners might interpret the
absence of moral judgement in the discussion of sex as
obscenity. Much to his credit, Duvall refrained from de-
livering a sermon as he evaluated the contents of Big Table
#1 under the legal definition of obscenity.

To him "Old Angel Midnight" amounted to little more
than printed characters on the page. The story was "a series
of letters or groups of letters interspersed with words that
mention the private parts of the anatomy, bodily functions and
various types of sexual perversions and aberrations expressed
in terms of the lowest vehicle that can be used to convey their
meanings. "[22] Duvall pulled no punches; the four-letter words
alone were sufficient to classify the whole magazine as obscene.

Although Burroughs posed a more complicated problem
for the hearing examiner, he was able to describe the excerpts from Naked Lunch in a similar fashion:

> While there is more of a narrative, better de-
> scription, and intelligible satire in the article
> by Burroughs, it is also plain to the reader
> that the vile, vulgar, and filthy language used
> far outweighs whatever literary merit there may
> be to the article. [23]

Both articles, according to Duvall, established the tone which
dominated the entire issue. Because the two stories were
obscene, his argument continued, the "dominant interest" of

the magazine taken "as a whole" was obscene. The logic of
the argument was classically unrelenting. But his initial
premise that the material was obscene reveals a fault in the
substance, as well as the process, of his argument. The
material in question was never demonstrated, only asserted
to be obscene. The cyclic nature of the argument calls
Duvall's conclusion into question.

Duvall did concede, however, that the magazine was
not obscene because of its appeal:

> Concerning the obscenity of this publication, if that
> term is confined to its connotations of sex and a
> prurient interest there in, it is my view that this
> publication would not arouse the interest of the
> average reader in sex, and I so find. [24]

But he hastened to add that the definition of obscenity in Roth
included a reference to the American Law Institute's Model
Penal Code which branded as obscene anything which goes
"substantially beyond customary limits of candor" in descriptions or representations of sex, nudity, or excretion. In applying this expanded interpretation to Big Table, Duvall concluded: "This publication most assuredly is obscene and I
so find. "[25]

In addition to the term "obscene, " the statute also
barred "filthy" material from the mail. Duvall felt that he
must also rule whether or not Big Table was filthy. He
referred to Justice Louis D. Brandeis who had called "the
filthy" a distinct branch of literature and defined it with the
"popular meaning of the term. "[26] "Having in mind this
definition of filthy, " Duvall concluded, "I think that the publication Big Table #1 is filthy. "[27] He conceded the serious
intent of the authors, but he added, on the basis of the written
testimony introduced by Big Table, that "the writings were
not meritorious. "[28]

Duvall repeated his findings in his closing remarks:

> Upon the basis of the foregoing findings of fact, I
> conclude that as a matter of law Big Table #1 is
> nonmailable under the provisions of Section 1461,
> Title 18, United States Code. [29]

Sprayregen received the adverse decision, and informed Rowland Watts and Melvin Wulf of the American Civil

Liberties Union in New York that he planned to go through
the motions of an appeal within the Post Office Department.
As far as he was concerned he had made "a damn good
record"[30] and needed to persuade the A. C. L. U. Board
to let him pursue the case into the Federal court to gain the
release of the magazine.

Sprayregen filed a formal statement with the Post
Office Docket Clerk on July 17 which bore the title "Appeal,
Memorandum, and Exceptions."[31] In it he repeated the
arguments he had presented at the hearing. However, he
added several comments and registered several disagreements
with the Initial Decision. Sprayregen mentioned that Duvall
ignored the issue of due process by failing to consider the
one and one-half month delay by the Post Office in notifying
Big Table of the confiscation. The Big Table lawyer also
felt that the hearing examiner misunderstood the testimony of
Hans Mattick, because he had commented during the hearing
that the witness believed Burroughs' work appealed only to
drug addicts. Sprayregen noted that Duvall's impression was
wrong, and that Mattick had explained that any intelligent
reader could expand his understanding of the drug problem
by reading the Burroughs piece.

Sprayregen considered Duvall's failure to consider the
serious intent of the authors as a misinterpretation of legal
precedent. He cited Sunshine Book Co. vs. Summerfield 335
U. S. 372 (1958) which allowed the author's intent in the determination of the obscenity of a publication.

Duvall's exclusion of the articles on the Beat movement was interpreted as bias. It was apparent to Sprayregen
that the hearing examiner had given greater weight to the
testimony which opposed or qualified the type of writing
represented in the magazine. He indicated that the classification of Norman Mailer as a member of the cult of Beat
writers demonstrated Duvall's unsuitability to dictate to the
American people what they should and should not read. In
other words, Sprayregen felt that the postal hearing examiner
was not qualified as a literary critic, nor able to serve as
the arbiter of public literary taste.

Sprayregen took issue with Duvall's use of the "more
important interests" clause from Roth. As far as he was
concerned, the clause which restricted free expression in
certain instances "clearly referred to uninvited soliciting,
lobbying, child labor, and espionage."[32] In addition to the

misapplied clause, Sprayregen felt that Duvall had also distorted the Roth definition of obscenity by ignoring the require-
ment that obscene material exhibit a predominant appeal to
the prurient interest. After all, he reasoned, Duvall admitted
that Big Table #1 did not have such an appeal to sex. [33] But
in spite of the admission that the material could not arouse
anyone sexually, and also in the absence of testimony which
demonstrated the ability of the magazine to sexually excite,
Duvall nevertheless affirmed that the material could "arouse
the salacity of the reader to whom it is sent."[34] Of course
Sprayregen pointed out the obvious contradiction in the hearing
examiner's assessment, and registered his strong opposition
to the consideration of that judgement in any further determination of the obscenity of the material.

In addition to Duvall's misapplication of precedent and
his misinterpretation of testimony, Sprayregen also objected
to the manner in which the hearing examiner ruled on the
admissibility of the statements of critics as evidence for Big
Table. He expressed his opposition to the procedure as extremely arbitrary:

> The idea that government may censor writings
> deemed unmeritorious is rather unique in this
> country. Roth seems to say that only writings
> so unmeritorious as to be socially worthless can
> be banned. But the examiner chooses to disregard
> the opinions of the twenty-six qualified witnesses
> and affiants for Big Table; all of whom say, at the
> very least, that the magazine is not so unmeritorious
> as to justify government suppression. [35]

The lawyer for the magazine could have expressed his outrage
in stronger terms, but he was writing a formal appeal. He
concluded with a request that the action against Big Table #1
be overturned, and that the magazine be dispatched through the
mail immediately.

But in a statement released to the press, Sprayregen
was less formal in articulating his feelings:

> Since the Post Office has proclaimed eagerness to
> chloroform the nation's bookshelves, the decision to
> ban Big Table comes as no great shock. Big Table
> has now entered the distinguished company of authors
> banned by the Post Office, among whom are Ben-
> jamin Franklin, Dr. Freud, Ovid, Aristophanes,

James Joyce, and D. H. Lawrence. Since the Post
Office persists in labelling Big Table 'obscene' despite the contrary opinions of 26 distinguished critics,
educators, writers and psychiatrists, one might suspect that there is more obscenity in our government
censors' minds than on the printed page. But Postmaster General Summerfield has said he doesn't
care what the critics say; so we have known all
along that Big Table's position--which is essentially
that postal officials have no authority or competency
to tell the rest of us what serious literature we can
read--can only be vindicated in the Federal courts. 36

The Post Office Department received a petition from
the lawyer handling the Big Table case for the government, no
longer Schueler, that the date for filing a reply to the appeal
be extended. 37

The Post Office Department Judicial Officer assigned
to the Big Table case, Charles D. Ablard, granted the extension. 38 He had presided over the case of Lawrence's Lady
Chatterley's Lover, decided only the month before. Charles
Rembar, who argued for the release of the Lawrence book at
the previous postal hearing, commented on Ablard:

> Though he was an employee of the department,
> there was no question about his fairness. He
> reached a strange result--or rather strangely
> failed to reach a result--but this was not due to
> any lack of integrity. Nor was there any question
> about his ability; he knew his subject, and ran the
> trial well. 39

J. Carroll Schueler was replaced by Saul J. Mindel,
who was selected to handle the Big Table appeal. Mindel had
successfully argued the case against Lady Chatterley before
presiding Judicial Officer Charles D. Ablard. On August 3
Mindel filed his "Complainant's Reply Brief on Appeal. "40
After summarizing the findings of the hearing examiner,
Mindel stressed that language considered lewd or obscene was
not a form of expression protected by the First Amendment
guarantees of free speech. He then quoted part of the definition of obscenity:

> A thing is obscene if, considered as a whole its
> predominant appeal is to prurient interest, i. e. ,
> a shameful or morbid interest in nudity, sex, or

excretion, and if it goes substantially beyond customary limits of candor in description or representation of such matters.[41]

Applying these guidelines to the magazine, Mindel concluded
that: "Taking Big Table as a whole, there is insufficient
countervailing 'art' to reduce its obvious obscenity and filth
to a subordinate level."[42] As Duvall had done, he cited the
testimony of Hoke Norris as representative of the unfavorable
critical opinion. Mindel berated Sprayregen's argument for
the literary merit of the contents of the magazine, and declared that such a position "tempts us to quote Pope's qua-
train (sic) about the Monster Vice which, when too prevalent,
is embraced."[43] He should have quoted Pope, not para-
phrased him.

Mindel urged, finally, that the decision of the Hearing
Examiner be adopted and that the Chicago Postmaster be instructed to dispose of the magazines held there.

Also on August 3 Joel Sprayregen sent a notice to the
Post Office Department officially complaining about the July
31 extension granted to the postal lawyer in filing his appeal.
He was irritated more that he was not notified of the change,
than that the deadline was lengthened from five to ten days.[44]

He informed the Judicial Officer that the delays had
placed a severe financial hardship on the magazine because
it depended on the mails for distribution. In objecting to the
extension request, he was "not seeking to harass understandably
busy postal attorneys," but the magazine had "been deprived of
its mailing privileges since March 18,"[45] almost six months.

This complaint was for the record since it was filed
the same day Mindel submitted his reply brief to the docket
clerk. However, it emphasized that Big Table considered
the delays by the Post Office a form of harassment.

On August 12, 1959, supplied with William Duvall's
"Initial Decision," the official record of the case, a corrected
transcript of the June 23rd hearing, and briefs from both
Sprayregen and Mindel, Judicial Officer Charles D. Ablard
reviewed Docket No. 1/150, the Big Table case, on appeal.
He handed down a "Departmental Decision" as the ranking
authority with final jurisdiction to resolve the contested decisions of hearing examiners.[46]

Ablard mentioned the dispute over the change in regulations governing mailability, the delay in delivery of formal
charges, the continuance of the hearing from June 4 in Washington to June 23 in Chicago, and Duvall's initial decision
barring Big Table from the mails.   He also mentioned the
occurences at the University of Chicago, Chancellor Kimpton's role in the suppression of the Chicago Review issue,
and the birth of Big Table.   He noted that the Post Office
allegations were directed toward Kerouac's "Old Angel Midnight" and Burroughs' "Ten Episodes from Naked Lunch," and
not toward the two stories by Edward Dahlberg and the three
poems by Gregory Corso.   He also referred to the agreement
among the witnesses concerning the serious intent of the
writers, and the confusion over the literary merits of their
contributions.   Ablard then observed:

> Both of the alleged obscene and filthy articles
> are esoteric writings which are difficult to read
> since they are written in unintelligible language
> with very little connection in thought. [47]

Indirectly, this suggests that he believed the articles had a
tenuous claim to literary merit at best.

He turned to the question of obscenity and repeated
the criteria outlined in Roth.   He also relied on Roth's
use of the American Law Institute's Model Penal Code to
define "prurient": "The prurient interest is an exacerbated,
morbid, or perverted interest growing out of the conflict between the universal sexual drive of the individual and the
equally universal controls of sexual activity." [48]   Duvall ruled
that the material in Big Table was obscene because it ex-
ceeded the limits of candor in description, not because it appealed to the reader's prurient interest.   Though Ablard
agreed with Duvall's final conclusion that the publication was
obscene, his reasons were altogether different:

> The matter is obscene but only because of the
> definition provided by the Institute of the word
> "prurient. "   The articles portray sexual matters
> and subjects in a most exacerbated, morbid, and
> perverted manner.   The language used exceeds
> any four letter Anglo-Saxon words which may be
> found in current contemporary novels.   They dis-
> cuss defecation, the genitals, sexual relations,
> perversions, and aberrations in the lowest type
> of language.   I believe the publication appeals to
> prurient interest. [49]

Ablard recognized that Duvall had applied an erroneous definition of obscenity in his findings against Big Table, but was
nevertheless convinced by the material itself that it was
obscene and appealed to the prurient interest.

On the assessment of the literary value of a work,
Ablard was aware, as Duvall apparently was not, that

> policemen, district attorneys, law judges and
> jurors are poorly qualified as art critics; prose-
> cution and conviction should depend as little as
> possible on their appreciation of poems, painting,
> sculpture or dance. [But] we know that even profes-
> sional critics differ widely in evaluating works of
> art and entertainment, and that tastes are constantly
> changing so that art criteria introduces an unde-
> sirable element of uncertainty into criminal law. [50]

In comparing the critical abilities of the lawmen with the
professional, Ablard had arrived at the conclusion that literary
value was subject to fad and whim beyond the toleration of
legal judgement. He would therefore treat the "expert" testimony as opinion, not fact. Considering this stand on critical
opinion, he made no attempt to ascertain the literary merit
of the contents, but chose to interpret the obscenity law as
a mandate for the determination of dominant appeal. Without
the benefit of supporting testimony from either the government
or evidence presented at the hearing, he concluded that Big
Table #1 "has the characteristic of appealing to prurient interest more than any other. "[51]

Ablard also objected to the use of individual words in
the issue:

> Although much of the language in the articles is
> unintelligible to the average reader, it is noted
> that the words dealing with excretion and sex are
> most intelligible and explicit in their vulgarity. [52]

The words appeared in the Burroughs and Kerouac
articles and constituted the dominant theme of the magazine
in spite of the Dahlberg and Corso contributions. According
to Ablard, the Kerouac story was a contributing factor in the
dominant theme not only because it was first in the issue,
but also because Kerouac was recognized as the dean of Beat
writers.

Despite his conclusions and in striking contrast to the workman-like quality of Duvall's written statement, Ablard ventured a short, sensitive, and informal philosophical comparison of the rights of the artist--writers in this instance--to free expression and the community's toleration of the compromise between, in the words of Judge Learned Hand, "candor and shame." Taking the position of enlightened judge bound by law and duty to protect the entire community, Ablard asked rhetorically:

> How far may we go when explaining or advocating nudism? adultery? homosexuality? lesbianism? If indeed these are ideas which are protected by the First Amendment, there must surely be some limitation on the manner of expressing them to the viewer or the reader.
>
> Kerouac has every right to criticize society and Burroughs every right to explain dope addiction but it is my opinion that the right to express those ideas does not carry with it the constitutional right to express them in the manner which has been done in this publication. [53]

Ablard had penetrated to the central conflict at issue in this case, the right of individual expression versus the right of the community. Overlooking the strictly personal nature of reading a book, he took the side of the community in ruling Big Table #1 obscene, filthy, and non-mailable. He adopted the facts established at the hearing and accepted Duvall's decision, disallowing the list of exceptions Sprayregen had made.

Complying with Rule 14 of the Rules of Practice in Proceedings Relating to Mailability, Ablard directed the Post Office in Chicago to continue to hold the impounded issues of Big Table pending further instructions. Before he could order the issues destroyed, all legal recourse had to be exhausted, and Big Table still retained the option of action against the Post Office in Federal District court.

Chapter 6

APPEAL AND DECISION IN FEDERAL COURT

U. S. Postmaster General Summerfield accelerated what he called a crusade against smut by urging postal workers to be alert for it, by imploring citizens to return any obscene material they received to their local post office, and by lobbying for stronger anti-obscenity legislation in Congress. On August 12 Summerfield delivered a speech titled "Our Responsibilities and America's Future" before the Annual Convention of the National Rural Letter Carriers Association in which he described the mail-order smut business as "the most insidious racket of our time."[1] This particular speech was included as part of the Congressional Record by Kansas Senator Andrew Schoeppel. It was similar in content to many of the speeches the postmaster had given before women's organizations as part of his crusade.

Summerfield was not alone in his concern over obscene material in the mail. In the New York Daily News a four-part series by Richard McGowan investigated the pornography business. His headlines reflected the commonly accepted notion that printed pornography was part of the cause of juvenile delinquency: "Billion $ Cesspool: Sadism and Sex Ladled Out to Kids."[2] Another four-part series on the corrupting influences of the smut trade ran in The Chicago Sun-Times and was written by Alfred C. Roller. His articles described the efforts of Chicago Postmaster Carl Schroeder, U. S. Postmaster Summerfield, and the Cincinnati-based Citizens for Decent Literature. He also perpetuated the belief that pornography was a cause of juvenile delinquency. One of his headlines declared boldly: "How Smut Seduces Youths to Violence."[3]

Congresswoman Kathryn Granahan's House Post Office Committee held hearings during the summer of 1959 on the problem of obscene material sent through the mail. Witnesses from church groups, women's organizations, and the

government came before the Committee and testified to the
truth of the causal relationship between printed filth and the
corruption of youth.   The Report issued by the committee
echoed the popular feeling of both the witnesses and the
general public when it observed:

> the character of juvenile delinquency has changed as
> a consequence of the stimulation of these publica-
> tions, being no longer the thoughtless, mischievious
> acts of children, but are reflected in acts of vio-
> lence, armed robbery, rape, torture, and even
> homicide, [with] which the vicious and vile publica-
> tions conditioned the minds of our children. [4]

Its conclusions were also based in part on the belief that
good ideas produce honest citizens while lewd and distorted
ideas result in evil consequences and "a pollution of our
thought supply. "[5]   The offensive material included "comics,
horror magazines, and other publications" which contained
"anti-social and vicious pictures and reading material. "[6]

Not only did the Report outline the effects of the
obscene matter, it also described the Post Office procedure
for dealing with it, and emphasized the difficulty the department encountered in keeping the mails free of it.   A 1958
change in the 1865 anti-obscenity statute provided for prosecution of offenders in the jurisdiction of delivery, as well as
deposit.   Even though the changes provided for a twenty day
interim impoundment period, the Post Office said in the Report that it needed at least forty-five days to complete the
administrative procedure required to issue an order against
suspected material. [7]

To illustrate its procedure in dealing with obscene
material, the Report reproduced in its entirety Charles D.
Ablard's "Departmental Decision" in the Big Table case.
The administrative handling of the magazine was "typical of
those conducted by the P. O. Department under the authority
of 18 U. S. C. 1461, the criminal obscenity statute, which
also gives the Postmaster General authority to withhold from
dispatch matter which is obscene. "[8]   Although it was mentioned that the case could still be tried in Federal District
Court, the impression given by the Report was that no appeal would be filed.

Considering the manner in which the case was presented, a reader of the report unfamiliar with the magazine

could easily conclude that Big Table was the same type of obscene comic book or horror magazine which was turning young boys into juvenile rapists and murderers. Even if they knew that the book contained four-letter words, most juveniles would not have been able to read beyond page one. The citation of Big Table by the committee as a typical Post Office obscenity case indicates the government's failure to recognize the not so subtle difference between the subject matter and the audience the literary quarterly strove to achieve, and that of so-called pornography. It was not, as implied, sent indiscriminately through the mail, running the risk of falling into the hands of children. [9] As was emphasized at the hearing, Big Table was directed toward a college-educated audience and solicited no subscriptions by mass mailings.

Contrary to the use of the case in the Report on Obscene Matter Sent through the Mail, Big Table was not typical of the 315 arrests made after 4,000 obscenity related postal investigations that year. [10]

On August 26, 1959, [11] Joel J. Sprayregen and Bernard Weisberg filed a complaint in Federal District Court against Carl A. Schroeder, the Chicago Postmaster, on behalf of Big Table. [12] In it the lawyers called for "declaratory relief," i.e. that the judicial officer's decision be declared invalid and that a preliminary injunction be issued which would bar the Post Office from seizing, impounding, and refusing to deliver the first issue of Big Table.

They asserted that the magazine was protected by the first amendment, and charged that the detention of the magazine was illegal because it was executed without a warrant. Because no judicial hearing took place, Sprayregen claimed that the administrative procedure of the Post Office violated the Constitution by denying Big Table due process of law. They said that the decision of the judicial officer was "arbitrary and capricious," [13] and that as a result the magazine had suffered "incalculable and irreparable damage." [14]

The court considered the pleas and arguments on September 18, then denied the motion for a preliminary injunction and declaratory relief. The denial was formally recorded on October 15, 1959. [15]

Both the Post Office and Big Table filed motions with the court calling for a "summary judgement" in the case.

That is, both parties conceded that the facts of the case were
not in dispute, but rather the rulings handed down based on
those facts were in question.

　　　　Joel J. Sprayregen filed a brief with the Illinois
Federal District Court on February 1, 1960.[16] In it he
argued what he perceived as the three central issues in the
matter: 1) that Big Table was not obscene and thus non-
mailable because it was an expression of social importance
protected by the First Amendment; 2) that section 1461 of the
U.S. Code did not give the Post Office the authority to act
as it did in this instance; and 3) that the Post Office censorship system violated the First and Fifth Amendments.

　　　　In his brief he argued the social importance of the
magazine. His efforts to discuss the contemporary community standards were disallowed at the hearing. He noted
that a difference existed between "hard-core pornography"
and works of "erotic realism, " and using the Ulysses precedent, he explained that "erotic realism" was associated with
works of literature which were afforded the full protection of
the First Amendment by virtue of their artistic values. Both
Duvall and Ablard conceded that Big Table was not hardcore.[17]

　　　　Sprayregen also discussed the community standard concerning the use of particular words in other works which dealt
uneuphemistically with sex and defecation. "Like Lady Chatterley's Lover and Ulysses, " he observed, "Big Table 1 contains a number of 'four-letter' words. But unlike these books,
Big Table #1 is wholly devoid of intimate description of sexual
and excretory activity. "[18] Compared with the explicitness of
the two books previously cleared by Federal Courts of obscenity charges, the magazine on trial, according to Sprayregen's
argument, could hardly exceed those limits of what the community would tolerate in expression. He reminded the court
that since Duvall excluded all evidence designed to establish
the community standard, the statement Ablard made, that
Big Table's language went beyond any use of "four-letter
Anglo-Saxon words which may be found in current contemporary novels, "[19] was clearly unsupported by the evidence submitted. Sprayregen concluded that by looking at the four
letter words and seeing only " 'dirt for dirt's sake, ' the Post
Office had again ignored the uncontroverted evidence and the
law. "[20]

　　　　In order to correct the absence of a standard of acceptability in literary expression, he offered the views of

several critics, and provided a list of thirty "widely accepted
and honored contemporary works which frankly and explicitly
portray both normal and deviant sexual themes."[21]   He
emphasized that books like Faulkner's Sanctuary and Mailer's
The Naked and the Dead served as a standard, but by no
means stood as the outer limit of what could be expressed
in print.

Taking a hypothetical position, Sprayregen said that
even if Big Table could not be compared with reputable and
serious publications, a comparison with "distasteful 'men's,'
'girlie,' and 'adventure' magazines widely if lamentably read
and circulated in our society"[22] would demonstrate Big Table's
dissimilarity with them.   He noted for the court that "the
Post Office has accepted 'men's' magazines for mailing ...
[and] could safely tolerate the passage of Big Table #1 through
the mails to its subscribers. Any contrary finding is pre-
mised on a wholly arbitrary and capricious determination of
contemporary community standards."[23]   He concluded his
discussion of standards with a specific example.   According
to his brief, Big Table #1 was sold at a Chicago art festival
the previous summer and was accepted by the community
present which included several plainclothes policemen who did
not choose to act against the open and public sale of the
magazine.

Having established that Big Table was well within the
limits of expression, Sprayregen turned to the intent of the
authors.   He quoted from John Ciardi's article on the Big
Table controversy, cited the testimony affirming the serious
intent of both Burroughs and Kerouac, and contrasted it with
the absence of evidence submitted to the contrary.   The Lady
Chatterley's Lover decision[24] provided a method for the determination of literary merit based on "the sincerity and
honesty of purpose of an author as expressed" by the unity
of the book and the development of the theme.[25]   In the
lawyer's opinion, both Duvall and Ablard in their decisions
had ignored the uncontradicted evidence which demonstrated
those qualities in the writers.

Other cases involving obscenity noted that the manner
in which a work was distributed aided in the assessment of
the material as obscene or not.   Sprayregen pointed out that
Big Table was published and distributed in a reputable fashion,
reminding the court that its open sale and distribution by a
handler of literary quarterlies and quality paperbacks had been
established at the hearing.   His irritation over the disregard

the postal examiners showed toward the evidence presented
on the method of distribution and his awareness of the Post
Office's anti-pornography campaign resulted in an extremely
passionate rhetorical explosion in Sprayregen's brief:

> But Big Table #1 is not thrust from under the
> counter by leering merchants of smut for sale
> to those seeking a shabby thrill. It is not cir-
> culated by furtive peddlers in schoolyards and
> locker rooms. It is not trespasser in the mail-
> boxes of those who do not wish to receive it or
> whom might be repelled by it. It is not adver-
> tised on the homegrounds of the prurient minded,
> nor do its cover and promotional material snicker
> suggestively. Its advertisers are as reputable and
> their advertisements at least as dignified as those
> appearing in newspapers. No shady enterpriser
> has imagined that he could solicit any interest in
> degrading wares by advertising in Big Table #1.
> The price is more than one need pay for a cheap
> vicarious thrill. [26]

Sprayregen then explained another Post Office misinterpretation of the evidence. The decision returned by Duvall and
supported by Ablard interpreted Paul Carroll's desire for the
financial success of the magazine as pandering to dirty minds
for profit. The desire for profit had been equated with proof
of obscenity. Sprayregen labeled that part of the postal
decision absurd.

In an effort to place on the record the material which
was intended to show the serious intent of the authors but
disallowed at the hearing, Sprayregen submitted several
articles and clippings along with his brief. One clipping
which had not accompanied the official record was a page
from the December 28, 1959 Time magazine. It contained
the names of eleven people nominated by Time readers for
"Man of the Year." Jack Kerouac was listed along with
Pope John, President Eisenhower, and Vice-president Nixon.
The nomination showed the national recognition Kerouac enjoyed as a writer. But the letter printed in the magazine
nominating Kerouac may have been a subtle prank played on
Time. The letter read:

> Jack Kerouac and a Beat Generation that howls all
> over the world as a protest against dehumanization.
> Migual Grinberg, Buenos Aires. [27]

Taking the verb "howls" as a suggestion, "Grinberg" could
be a pseudonym for Allen Ginsberg, author of Howl and close
friend of Kerouac and Burroughs. This, however, does not
undercut the appearance of Kerouac as a nominee, since he
was well-known enough to be included among the other nomi-
nees no matter who submitted his name.

Another article which appeared after the postal hearing
was also submitted as evidence of the importance of Kerouac
and Burroughs as writers. Life magazine ran Paul O'Neil's
caustic article on the Beat generation titled "The Only Rebellion Around."[28] The Life photo spread showed what it considered a typical Beatnik's room, each item in the picture
numbered and identified in an accompanying legend. The
picture provided a perjorative image of Beats for the American public. However, Sprayregen was quick to use the unfavorable article advantageously in his arguments for Big
Table. Although Beats were treated unsympathetically, he
pointed out that Burroughs and Kerouac were listed as
exceptions:

> A few Beat writers demonstrate that gift of phrase
> and those flashes of insight which bespeak genuine
> talent ... Jack Kerouac has been unable (although
> he comes close) to disguise a real feeling for life
> as it is lived along the truck roads and tenderloins
> of America. William Burroughs has a terrible and
> sardonic eye and a vengeful sense of drama.[29]

As a final bit of new evidence of the serious intent of
the writers, Sprayregen included a two-page letter from
Harold Rosenberg, Longview Foundation Program Director, to
Paul Carroll. The letter announced the foundation's literature
awards which were intended to stimulate the progress of American literature with "awards of $300 ... made annually for
outstanding work in poetry, fiction, and essays appearing in
publications which cannot pay for contributions or which pay
inadequately."[30]

The awards were determined by a panel of writers who
selected the recipients from contributors to little magazines.
The winners were chosen "on the basis of their contribu-
tions."[31] The panel was no conglomeration of literary pre-
tenders, but included such authors as Saul Bellow and Alfred
Kazin.[32] Edward Dahlberg received the essay award for
"Because I Was Flesh," in Big Table #2, and for "A Literary
Correspondence," in the Spring and Summer 1959 issues of

Sewanee Review. Gregory Corso was awarded the prize for
poetry for his contributions to Big Table and to Evergreen
Review. But the award for fiction was extremely important
to the Big Table obscenity case. It went to William S. Burroughs for his "Ten Episodes from Naked Lunch" in Big
Table # 1. The award certainly provided very strong evidence
of the literary merit of the Burroughs contribution to the
magazine.

        Sprayregen explained that in rejecting evidence on the
literary merit of Big Table, Duvall had cited the Lady Chatterley's Lover decision. 33 Based on that decision Duvall felt
that a publication must receive massive critical acclaim to
qualify for consideration as literature. Sprayregen, on the
other hand, felt that it allowed for a fair evaluation in cases
not involving great literature and in the absence of wide critical comment. In other words he believed the intention of the
court was designed to accommodate literary experimentation
which often gets little attention because of the limited audience
it may reach through literary journals and little magazines.
The position taken against Big Table, he argued, would sti-
fle artistic experimentation. His argument echoed Professors
Lockhart and McClure's touchstone legal article in which they
warned against arbitrary applications of obscenity definitions
as injurious to the free exchange of ideas in print. 34

        Sprayregen concluded his argument for the literary
merit of the magazine:

                to establish its right to be free from postal cen-
                sorship, then, Big Table # 1 need not prove that
                it is great literature. It is enough to show, as the
                record here does abundantly, that the work is
                recognized as literature. 35

On the basis of his statements the magazine could not be
considered obscene because it was recognized as literature
by critics, marketed as literature by its publisher, and did
not exceed the contemporary community standards for decency
in print. It therefore had social value, and because it has
such value, he argued, it was fully protected by the First
Amendment.

        The Big Table attorney then turned to a discussion of
the validity of the laws under which the magazine was charged.
According to Sprayregen, the original intent of Congress in
passing 18 U.S. Code Section 1461 gave the Post Office the

power to impound material only after a violation had been
determined in Federal court. The original Big Table hearing,
he argued, should have been heard first in Federal court.
Sprayregen noted that a 1956 amendment to the postal regulations allowed the Post Office an interim period of twenty days,
before a hearing, to impound material in extreme situations.
He explained that the Congressional intent of this amendment
was directed toward fly-by-night operations which used the
mails to defraud or to peddle pornographic material. [36] Under
Section 1461, he maintained, the Post Office did not have the
right in this case to impound material and then declare it
obscene in its own administrative court.

Only under Section 1463 could the Post Office act as
it had done in this case, because that part of the law governed
the use of questionable words and pictures only on the covers
and wrappers of magazines. Big Table's cover was quite innocuous. [37] In his opinion the Post Office believed that it had
the power to impound material without a hearing under Section
1461. In practice that interpretation would grant the power
to financially destroy publications "by impounding without
notice or hearing several successive issues. "[38] As far as
the Big Table lawyer was concerned the statutes severely
limited the Post Office in what actions it could properly
take, [39] and if it did seize material, it could only be held for
twenty days without hearing, not the fifty-seven day period
Big Table experienced. [40] He urged the court that the law
be confined

> to its originally intended design, i. e. , punishment
> of offenders and resultant exclusion of obscenity
> from the mails through the process of the criminal
> law, and not through unauthorized administrative
> censorship. The difference between these two
> methods cuts to the core of the First Amendment.
> One method sanctions interference with freedom of
> communication only after obscenity has been proved,
> before a court or jury, beyond a reasonable doubt.
> The other permits infringement of First Amendment
> freedoms by administrative fiat. [41]

Not only did a seizure without a hearing violate the First
Amendment, Sprayregen contended that it also denied the 14th
Amendment guarantee of due process of law. He explained
that seizure by the Post Office "leaves the bookseller or
publisher with but one real alternative to lift prior restraint:
he must initiate an independent civil action in the district

court to 'prove' that he has not violated a criminal statute.
A more pervasive prior restraint in published material can
hardly be imagined. "[42]

Having completed his statements on the facts and on
the laws, Sprayregen appealed to the better judgement of the
court:

By forecasting the probable Supreme Court decision
that postal censorship under Section 1461 is un-
constitutional, this court will be doing no more than
condemn a censorship system which has already
condemned itself during years of absurd and irresponsible decisions. Books 'banned' by the Post
Office under Section 1461 at one time or another
included Ulysses, For Whom the Bell Tolls, Elmer
Gantry, Candide, Lysistrata, and From Here to
Eternity. [43]

Sprayregen counted on the unwillingness of the judge to be
classified as a boor by censoring a work similar to the
modern classics he named. He also felt that censorship
practiced by a government agency would appear as distasteful to the tradition of democracy in the eyes of the judge as
it appeared in his own.

He reminded the court that Big Table was a serious
artistic experiment, and that the Post Office's decision was
"arbitrary, capricious, not in accordance with law, contrary
to constitutional right, in excess of statutory authority or
short of statutory right and unsupportable by evidence. "[44]
He requested that the court rule in favor of Big Table #1 and
remove the restraints imposed upon it.

On March 25, 1960, Robert Teiken and Charles Purcell
on behalf of the Post Office moved for a summary judgement
in favor of the ban on Big Table previously imposed by Duvall
and upheld by Ablard. [45] The lawyers asserted that 18 U. S.
Code Section 1463, which gives the Postmaster General the
authority to issue regulations for administrative enforcement,
and 18 U. S. Code Section 1461, which calls for Federal
judicial determination of fact, were one and the same.

They also argued that obscenity was not a form of
expression protected by the First Amendment. Since Big
Table #1 might be obscene, they contended, the constitutional
issues raised by Sprayregen did not apply in this case. They

felt obscenity, not expression, was at issue, and they considered the delay of 57 days before the hearing a minor issue. They called the figure inaccurate, but admitted that it could not have been less that 43 days. They blamed the delay on the two addresses Big Table provided, which complicated the delivery of the notices. Teiken and Purcell called for a re-affirmation of the ban against Big Table #1.

Sprayregen filed a reply brief opposing Teiken's motion.[46] He took issue with their assertion that obscenity, not expression was at issue in this case. A similar case, Smith vs California[47] in which a Post Office seizure without a hearing was deemed an inhibition of constitutionally protected publications, was cited.

He ridiculed the excuse offered by the Post Office attorneys in explaining the 57-day delay, saying that two addresses should have made delivery of the notice of hearing easier, not harder. Of the case presented by the Post Office based on the magazine itself, and the decisions of Duvall and Ablard, Sprayregen observed:

> If this is substantial evidence and if such evidence is enough, the Post Office is a censor beyond control.[48]

Finally he again called for the cancellation of the ban against Big Table #1.

The decision was now in the hands of Federal Judge Julius J. Hoffman.

On June 30, 1960, in the United States District Court, Northern District, Illinois,[49] Judge Julius J. Hoffman reviewed the official record and the briefs submitted by the opposing lawyers. The case posed five broad questions to him: the appropriateness of his court for the issues, the propriety of the call for summary judgement, the application of the "substantial evidence" rule, the legality of the Post Office rulings, and most importantly the obscenity of Big Table #1.

Since the first two questions were not disputed by either side, it was routine for him to affirm that the issues were being argued in their proper forum, and in the proper manner. However, he noted that the constitutional rights which Sprayregen claimed were violated by the original seizure did not need to be resolved in order to reach a satisfactory

conclusion in the case. Though he did not consider them irrelevant, he was not compelled by the facts to rule on the
constitutional questions.

No new facts were introduced, so summary judgement
was appropriate. If there had been, a new trial would have
been called. Hoffman noted that the magazine had not been
disputed as evidence by either side, and he felt that the
record contained enough testimony on its literary merit for
him to render a new judgement on its obscenity.

It was Sprayregen's contention that the Post Office had
violated the publisher's right of free expression by ruling
Big Table obscene without "substantial evidence. " He asked
that the Post Office decisions be ignored because the case
should have been heard in a Federal court in the first place.
Hoffman conceded that though the arguments were "persua-
sive, " he was forced to reject the position because "the
result would be not only to deny well-established precedent,
but to exceed the bounds of judicial review ... needlessly. "50

Having ruled on the procedures and the statutes, Hoffman then addressed the obscenity of Big Table #1. Neither
of the Post Office's administrative rulings was binding on the
judge's review of the facts. The appeal called for a re-
examination of the evidence, and a new trial if it were claimed
that the Constitution had been violated. He noted that a new
trial was not an absolute necessity because the appeal provided the required review of the facts. He cited two cases
which he felt allowed for a broader review of the facts than
is usual. 51

At this point Hoffman addressed the constitutionality of
the statute authorizing the Post Office to determine "obscene"
matter and bar it from the mails. Although he considered
that the point was one which demanded a legal decision, the
claim was not appropriate in this instance. He felt that if
the magazine had been found obscene on proper grounds, then
it would have been a suitable test case for the regulations
governing obscenity, and appropriate for a judicial reexamina-
tion of the Postal law as well. The opportunity to use Big
Table as a challenge to the constitutionality of the law was
missed.

Before Hoffman could make a new ruling on the evidence, he had to consider the Post Office's decisions. Based
on the record and the evidence, he felt that "the conclusion

reached by the Post Office that <u>Big Table #1</u> was obscene was
not supported by substantial evidence ... and therefore must
be set aside. "[55] He then began his review of the evidence
by mentioning the legal definition of obscenity and pointing
out Ablard's definition of "prurient. " By calling the magazine
obscene, Hoffman felt Ablard had judged the manner of expression. Because Ablard limited the words used to the single
inference that they only appealed to the prurient interest,
Hoffman reasoned that he voided the possibility that they could
be used without that effect.

In noting Duvall's decision, Hoffman pointed out that
the hearing examiner admitted that even though the contents
of the magazine went beyond the limits of candor in sexual
discussion, it did not appeal to prurience. Duvall's original
declaration was important to Hoffman and still carried significance, not because a hearing examiner in obscenity cases
has technical expertise, but because he sees and inspects all
kinds of erotic literature in the course of his duty. Such
exposure implied a more sophisticated basis for judgement
than the average person's. He had seen fit to declare the
magazine's lack of prurience, and Hoffman would consider that
opinion on the central point of the appeal of the contents. By
declaring the absence of prurience, Duvall provided a loop-
hole large enough to overturn his original ban.

Hoffman then turned to the magazine itself. As he
saw it, a close look at the whole work was necessary to
determine its theme. Even if it contained "an overwhelming
galaxy of four-letter, Anglo-Saxon words or other expressions usually consigned to the category of obscene parlance, "[53]
it need not appeal to a salacious interest in sex. The use
of obscenities in a work was insufficient to classify it as
obscene. In this instance the use of "shit" and "fuck" violated
a cultural and social taboo to be sure, but not the law.

The test of obscenity required the court to recognize
the literary setting of the disputed expression. It could then
consider the author's intent, the literary merit, and the demands of literary technique. Hoffman noted, however, that
an unbalanced reliance on abstract or academic literary
judgement should be avoided, and observed that, "the legal
standard of obscenity is not intended to serve as a protection
for <u>semantic</u> liberalism under the guise of free speech. "[54]
The First Amendment, he explained, encompassed the free
expression of an idea, not the license to use any language.

The law also stipulated that the contemporary community standards of obscenity be applied. In Hoffman's
opinion this added the "living concept of social freedom, or
ordered liberty"[55] to the law. He struggled to describe the
Kerouac story, but nevertheless called it a stream-of-
consciousness dialogue between God and Man as a critique
of the world. He conceded that the story was full of words
which were not overtly used by the average person, but concluded that "any libidinous effect those words might commonly
have could not possibly occur from their present position
among other printed characters which sometimes rise to the
dignity of a word and sometimes do not. "[56] Although he felt
the article rarely departed from gibberish and was peppered
with obscenities, it did not deal with sex more than it dealt
with anything else. No doubt he considered it the barest
excuse for literature, but it was protected by the right of
free expression.

Burroughs' "Ten Episodes from Naked Lunch" presented a recognizable story concerning the life of a narcotics
addict to Hoffman. Though some of the situations dealt with
sex, he considered them representational. They dealt with
morbid and perverted sex--the eating of genitals and sex
while hanging. In spite of those scenes, Hoffman concluded:

> The dominant theme or effect is that of shocking
> the contemporary society, in order perhaps to
> better point out its flaws and weaknesses, but that
> clinical appeal is not akin to lustful thoughts. [57]

The Federal judge had identified, as both postal officers had
not, the essential satiric nature of the Burroughs episodes.
He also noted the opinions of the writers and critics that the
material was intended to be serious literature. In spite of
the adverse critical opinion, the magazine was entitled to
experiment with new techniques. Hoffman concluded "that
Big Table #1 could not be found obscene as a matter of
law. "[58]

After finding that the evidence presented at the hearing
and the arguments on appeal did not support the obscenity
charge, Hoffman addressed the second charge, that the magazine was considered non-mailable because it was "filthy. "
The judge considered the test for filthy material as essentially the same as the Roth obscenity test, and since the
material could not be found obscene, it could also not be found
"filthy" under the same evidence. He concluded:

> The motion of the plaintiff for summary judgement
> is allowed and the order of the Post Office Depart-
> ment declaring Big Table #1 non-mailable will be
> set aside. [59]

Judge Julius J. Hoffman, who later presided over the trial
of the Chicago Seven, [60] had ruled in favor of the Kerouac
and Burroughs articles in Big Table #1.   Almost fifteen
months after it was first banned as obscene, and almost two
years after it was suppressed by the University of Chicago,
its right of free expression was regained.

However, the Post Office could still appeal Hoffman's
decision, and did so shortly after the ruling.

But on August 11, 1960, attorneys for the Post Office
"appeared before Chief Judge William Cambell ... to announce
that the appeal would be dropped. "[61]

Joel Sprayregen reacted to the victory:

> Big Table #1 can now take its place alongside
> Ulysses and Lady Chatterley's Lover as monu-
> ments to the ability of our democratic legal insti-
> tutions to resist the onslaught of government cen-
> sors who seek to impose their own literary taste
> on all Americans. [62]

His assessment following a lengthy legal process, though
understandably exuberant, contains a common perception of
the motives of a government censor.   The assumption that
Americans are too dim-witted to choose what they should and
should not read, and therefore the government should choose
for them, is not only alien to the tradition of the free exchange of ideas, but it is a dangerous policy.   It implies that
the government should choose, as arbiter of public taste, what
an individual should think as well as read.

Chapter 7

THE CUSTOMS CENSORSHIP OF NAKED LUNCH[1]

Grove Press was interested in publishing Burroughs' Naked Lunch ever since parts of it began to appear in Chicago Review. After Maurice Girodias' Olympia Press issued the book in France in 1959, Grove requested a copy of the edition and expressed its desire to publish it in the United States. Informed that copies of the book never arrived in New York, Miss Fran Muller of Olympia Press wrote on September 21, 1959, "I am surprised to hear that you did not receive the copies of 'The Naked Lunch' we have sent to you."[2] Mildly alarmed on receipt of this information, Judith Schmidt of Grove replied to Miriam Worms of Olympia on October 14, 1959 with the suspicion that the book might have been seized by Customs inspectors.[3] At that time the obscenity of the Burroughs excerpt in Big Table #1 was being appealed before Judge Hoffman. The contents of the magazine were still considered obscene because the rulings of the Post Office Department had not then been overturned.[4] In addition to the past litigation, the Customs' tenacious enforcement of obscenity laws made the possibility of a seizure at the border quite real for Judith Schmidt. Alarm then was not a groundless response when a copy of the book did not arrive from Paris.

Since no word from Customs came to her, Schmidt explained her suspicions to Worms and requested that she send copies of the Olympia Naked Lunch "in a plain wrapper; by air mail, " adding that "at least we'll know by its arrival or non-arrival, if it's the French or American authorities who are stopping it."[5] Presumably Schmidt believed that the U. S. Customs would suspect an unmarked package from Paris sent to Grove Press of containing contraband books. The seizure of certain French books was not uncommon, but the publishers were confused about which government initiated the action against Naked Lunch. Previous actions by Customs may have added to their confusion.[6]

Also on October 14, 1959 Joel J. Sprayregen, the
attorney handling the Big Table ban, wrote to Grove's lawyer
Charles Rembar filling him in on the actions against the
magazine. [7] Because of the publisher's plans for Burroughs'
work, the information was at once welcome and ominous.
The censorship action guaranteed interest in the book, while
simultaneously indicating a costly court battle.   If Big Table
#1 were vindicated in court, nothing prevented individual
municipalities and states from further censorship action
against the whole of Naked Lunch.   Just such legal cat and
mouse entangled Miller's Tropic of Cancer when Grove published it in America.   Fifty suits greeted Tropic, [8] making
the publisher quite cautious with the Burroughs book.   Grove
was also embroiled in a fight to reverse the Post Office ban
against Lady Chatterley's Lover.   In spite of its caution,
Grove was in the vanguard of the fight against literary censorship in the late 1950's and early 1960's.

Judith Schmidt continued her requests for copies from
Paris, hoping to secure one upon which to base the American
edition and comply with Burroughs' desire to have the French
edition serve as the authority.   Since all copies sent to the
office address, as well as ones sent to her home address and
that of Rosset, failed to arrive, she was forced to conclude
that their mail was being monitored by the Customs Service.
Even though Grove had received a typescript of the book by
April 1, 1960, Schmidt continued to request copies from
France because Grove was now obtaining them for the several
American individuals who wanted the book.   In order to
eliminate itself as the middleman, Schmidt sent the addresses
of those people directly to Olympia Press.   She sent a form
letter to those requesting a copy which explained that Grove
was securing Naked Lunch by having Olympia mail it directly. [9]
In this way Schmidt hoped to circumvent the need to send the
book to the Grove Press address, which she believed was
monitored by the Customs.

The first official indication that Naked Lunch had been
classified as obscene and confiscated came on August 29,
1960, almost ten months after the seizure of the book was
first suspected.   On that date three notices were sent from
Customs Deputy Collector Irving Fishman to Barney Rosset
informing him that a total of five copies had been seized. [10]
At the time of the seizures, obscenity cases were almost
exclusively handled by Irving Fishman in New York and Reuben
Klaben in Washington.   Fishman was tough on obscene material
and boasted at the time, "In the past 15 years ... we have had

only a few tentative protests [of obscene material seized by customs.] But in not one case has the complaint gotten as far as the courtroom. "[11]

Under Title 19, Section 1305 of the United States Code, commonly referred to as the Tariff Act of 1930, the service is required to prevent specified items from entering the United States. The law bars

> any obscene book, pamphlet, paper, writing, advertisement, circular, print, picture, drawing ... or other article which is obscene or immoral.[12]

In 1960 that meant sexually explicit or "dirty" books of the type often smuggled into the U.S. by adventurous individuals in handbags or under coats or dresses. For quite some time smuggling was the only way an American in his own country could read D. H. Lawrence, James Joyce, or Henry Miller. Recently other contraband has replaced the printed word in its power to evoke fear, shame, disgust, and outrage. But in 1960 the printed word, especially its illegal or improper use, set massive agencies into motion.

The official procedure of the Customs in executing the mandate of Section 1305 calls for a random examination of three percent of all packages arriving at the port.[13] If any item is considered "obscene," the U.S. Attorney is notified. He files an action in Federal District Court and a judicial rather than an administrative determination is made whether the material is obscene by contemporary standards or not. The Customs also considered the seal on first-class mail from overseas inviolate. Suspected mail was only opened and inspected after receiving authorization from the addressee. If no consent were given to open and inspect the contents of the package, Customs returned it to its sender. In the case of the seizure of Naked Lunch it appears plausible that the book was detected by some method other than random chance.

Unconvinced by the probability of a random inspection to uncover a specific title, one might speculate that the involvement of the Customs in the Naked Lunch case was a result of the routine monitoring of the international correspondence of publishers reputed to handle so-called "dirty books." In an effort to verify this notion, John Atwood of the Restricted Materials Branch of the Customs Service,[14] was asked how Customs could single out a package with a

book in it for inspection. He replied that cases such as the
Naked Lunch seizure were usually the result of an individual
Customs Officer using, according to Atwood, "alert methods
and techniques." He was then asked to comment on an example involving Grove Press and Olympia Press in an effort
to obtain a more satisfying explanation of the bureaucratic
description of the Customs' detection methods. He was told
that at the time of the seizure Maurice Girodias and his
Olympia Press enjoyed a world-wide reputation as a publisher
of avant-garde and sexually explicit books--books that some
considered obscene. Barney Rosset's Grove Press daringly
published innovative and sometimes explicitly frank books like
Lady Chatterley's Lover in the United States when other
houses refused. Considering the reputations of these two
publishers, Atwood was asked if this were enough to alert the
officers of the U.S. Customs and warrant monitoring of the
overseas correspondence between Grove Press and Olympia
Press for suspected contraband books. To this specific
characterization of the Customs' methods, Atwood replied
calmly, "I'd rather not comment on that." It seemed quite
clear that specific details of the "alert methods and techniques"
remained closely kept information.

However, once a book was suspected of being obscene,
the procedure was relatively simple. The work under suspicion was sent to Huntington Cairns, [15] who acted as a literary
consultant to the Customs Service. He in turn notified Reuben
Klaben and Irving Fishman whether, in his opinion, the book
in question was liable under the Tariff Act. But how was a
particular book selected and obtained for Cairns' evaluation
in the first place? The illusive "alert methods and techniques"
mentioned by Atwood seem to provide the answer.

The method outlined above suggests that the mail of
suspected recipients of obscene material was routinely monitored. Atwood would not comment on this notion, either to
confirm or deny its possibility. In the Customs file on
Naked Lunch no documents appear which would disprove the
monitoring of packages. [16] Since direct supporting evidence
is irretrievable, a conjecture based on the facts and circumstances which remain is not improper. Considering the experience of Judith Schmidt and Miriam Worms in attempting
to mail Naked Lunch from Paris to New York, the unavoidable
conclusion persists that the Customs Service routinely monitored the packages sent between the two publishers. It is
ludicrous to believe that the routine, random inspection of
three percent of all packages would net identical contraband

books sent to the home and business addresses of both Barney
Rosset and Judith Schmidt over a period of months.   But
evidence which would indicate the manner in which the book
was detected does not exist in the file.   However, an incident
which occurred around that time involving the seizure of an
Olympia Press book helps to clarify the Customs' attitude
toward the French publications.

Former Fortune magazine editor, member of the
A. C. L. U. Board of Directors, and resident at Stanford University's Center for Advanced Studies in the Behavioral
Sciences, Daniel Bell returned from a trip to Europe in the
fall of 1958.   At the port of New York, a Customs inspector
confiscated his copy of Jean Genet's Our Lady of the Flowers
purchased in France.   The book was published by Olympia
Press.   According to Bell, when he opened his bag, the inspector saw the distinctive green color of the unhidden book
and immediately said, "Oh, you have there some of those
Parisian books. "[17] The inspector told him that "all Olympia
Press books are confiscated on the presumptive basis that
they are obscene. "[18] When Bell pressed the inspector to affirm the existence of a list of contraband books, he said yes
and escorted him into an office where another officer showed
it to him.   The inspectors did not inform him of his right to
contest the decision that the book was obscene, but asked him
to sign a form authorizing its destruction.

Bell wrote the A. C. L. U. of his experience.   They in
turn contacted Irving Fishman of the Customs in New York
for an explanation.   The A. C. L. U. had heard of instances of
the Post Office confiscating all the titles of a publisher, but
not the Customs.   Questioned by Mel Wulf, Fishman stated
that there "is no list of books to be seized and there is no
instruction requiring all Olympia Press publications to be
seized. "[19] However, Fishman did offer an explanation for the
action: "over the course of time [inspectors] have found so
many books printed by Olympia to be excludable that they
might seize them all on the hunch that it is probably obscene. "[20] Informed of Fishman's reply, Bell insisted on the
list and the Olympia Press policy based on his experience.

Executive Director Patrick Murphy Malin of the
A. C. L. U. then wrote to Secretary of the Treasury Robert B.
Anderson on December 30, 1958[21] informing him of Bell's
experience.   Malin objected to the apparent policy of seizing
all works published by Olympia Press on the presumption of
obscenity as contrary to the American tradition that each per-

son and publication be judged individually. He objected to the existence of a list of contraband books, because it implied their obscenity by administrative fiat and not judicial decree. He also complained of the Customs' negligence in informing an individual of his right to protest a seizure.

The A. C. L. U. received an acknowledgement of their letter and the promise of a full reply. On January 20, 1959 after no reply, the A. C. L. U. politely urged an answer. When none came Malin wrote again on March 10, 1959, explaining that if no reply was forthcoming the A. C. L. U. would be forced to release the story to the press. On March 16, 1959 (about the same time Big Table was deposited in the Chicago Post Office for mailing) Assistant Secretary of the Treasury A. Gilmore Flues replied to Patrick Malin that although the book in question was obscene under Section 1305, the Commissioner of Customs was releasing the book to Bell for purposes of research. Flues denied the charge of a blanket ban of Olympia Press books,

> While this firm also publishes books found to be obscene within the meaning of section 305 of the Tariff Act, it is not our practice either to list or to bar all books published by it. [22]

Malin then thanked Flues in a March 30 letter, and asked him to issue guidelines to inspectors to avoid recurrence of the Bell incident. The Treasury Department replied that the incident was the exception rather than the rule and informed the A. C. L. U. that the New York Customs had been advised of the inadvertence of the inspector to inform Bell of his rights. [23]

Bell got his book back, even though the Customs denied any central list of banned books, a blanket ban on Olympia Press, or improprieties in confiscation procedures. Aside from obvious illustration of the workings of the Customs, the Bell incident is linked to the seizure of Naked Lunch in a most surprising way. Government agencies place a number and letter code on communications for filing and reference. On both letters sent from the Treasury Department to the A. C. L. U. concerning the Bell matter (March 16 and May 20, 1959) the code "PEN 633. 11" appears. On the papers in the Customs file on Naked Lunch appears the code "PEN 633. 11K". Since the Bell seizure preceded the Naked Lunch seizure by more than a year, the similar code numbers indicate that the Customs perceived a relationship between the two books, most

likely that both were publications of Olympia Press. The
circumstances of the seizures of Naked Lunch published after
the Bell incident indicate that the Customs Service was indeed
on the alert for any book published by the Paris house. Contrary to the denial by the Treasury Department, Irving Fishman's suggestion that his agents from long experience suspected the ugly green books as obscene constituted an unofficial operating procedure for both mail and passenger packages. Some years later after consulting with Fishman, J. A.
Sigler wrote in his article "Customs Censorship":

> There does exist, for internal use, a file of titles
> and a list of the disposition made in specific cases.
> From time to time instructions are issued from the
> Washington headquarters to collectors of customs
> which serve as guidelines, but for the most part
> these are by way of comment on current interpreta-
> tions by the Federal Courts. [24]

The keeping of an unofficial list by Customs on court actions
suggests yet another method used to detect obscene material.
In the case of Naked Lunch, use of this method might have
alerted collectors to the possible obscene nature of Naked
Lunch independently of any association with Olympia Press.

A reference to the Big Table case and its relationship
to Burroughs' book in an October 2, 1962 Customs Service
memo from Eleanor Suske to Irving Fishman[25] shows that
close attention was paid to Federal cases involving obscenity
charges. Customs checked for the possibility of the books
appearing as contraband. The same memo also referred to
the publication of the book in the U. S. by Grove Press. That
information was mentioned in the correspondence to Customs
of a recipient of contraband material, and demonstrates that
all correspondence was painstakingly combed for leads to
contraband. It also indicates a concerted effort by the agency
to stop the flow of contraband books.

When Big Table was detained by the Post Office Department for a hearing to determine its "mailability," the
official notice of the hearing was sent on April 30, 1959 to
Albert Podell by Richard Farr, Acting Assistant General
Council for Fraud and Mailability. An unexpectedly revealing
name appears at the bottom of the notice as one recipient of
a carbon copy. This name as a recipient indicates a strong
and vigorous working relationship between the Post Office and
the Customs Service on obscenity related matters. A copy of

the notice of hearing was sent to "Mr. R. Klaben, Bur. Cus.,
Treas. Dept. ". [26] Reuben Klaben, of course, handled matters
of obscenity for the Customs, along with Irving Fishman. The
routine notification alerted the Customs of the possibility that
the book could qualify as contraband. The April 30 notice
alerted the Customs of the possible obscenity of Naked Lunch
even before Maurice Girodias decided to publish it, because
it was not until June 1959 that Girodias contacted Burroughs
seeking another look at the manuscript, [27] almost a month
and a half after a copy of the notice was sent to Klaban.
The facts clearly indicate that the Customs Service knew of
Burroughs' work, and had cause to consider it obscene even
before it was published by Olympia Press in Paris. If the
matter had received a hearing, these facts indicate evidence
of prior restraint.

The action begun by the Post Office against the material in Big Table #1 ended with Judge Hoffman's decision on
June 30, 1960 to overturn the ban. Because this decision
came in Illinois Federal District Court, the Customs Service
reexamined its earlier ruling that Naked Lunch was obscene, [28]
but continued to adhere to it nevertheless. The Customs
later reiterated its position in a February 21, 1961 letter:

> The Bureau [of Customs] is still of the opinion
> that the book The Naked Lunch, is obscene under
> section 305 of the Tariff Act of 1930. [29]

The independent decision of the Customs to continue to consider Naked Lunch as contraband in spite of the removal of
the postal ban on the excerpt in Big Table should not ob-
fuscate the strong co-operation between the two government
agencies in identifying and apprehending obscene books.

The publication on November 30, 1962 of an American
edition of Naked Lunch generated a great deal of interest in
both the literary and legal communities. Shortly before U.S.
publication Huntington Cairns requested that Reuben Klaben
give him the Paris edition so that he could once more review the book and make a new recommendation on its obscenity. [30] Klaben in turn asked Fishman to forward a copy.
Along with the book Fishman sent a memo reminding Klaben
of the February 21, 1961 opinion that "the book was obscene
under section 305"[31] in spite of the lifting of the Post Office ban against the excerpt in Big Table. Two months later
Fishman requested notification of any change in the ruling on
the book, adding that it had been published in the U.S. by
Grove Press. [32]

In February 1963, about a month after Theodore
Mavrikos was arrested in Boston for selling a copy of Naked
Lunch to undercover vice-squad officers, [33] Harold F. Shapiro
of the U.S. Attorney General's office sent the following statement to the Commissioner of Customs:

> It is the opinion of this division that it would not
> be appropriate or desirable to institute forfeiture
> proceedings under section 305 of the Tariff Act
> against copies of the above-named book [The Naked
> Lunch by William S. Burroughs] which have been
> seized and detained by Collectors. [34]

The book was then ordered released to the persons from whom
it was seized, effectively cancelling the ban and bringing to an
informal end the Federal censorship of Naked Lunch--almost
simultaneously with the beginning of censorship action in
Boston.

Before this discussion turns to the Grove Press publication and the censorship case which followed in Massachusetts, a look at the writing of Naked Lunch is called for.

Chapter 8

BURROUGHS AND THE WRITING OF NAKED LUNCH

William S. Burroughs, Jr. offers this picture of his father working on Naked Lunch in Tangier:

> There was an orgone box in the upstairs hall in which my father would sit for hours at a time smoking kif and then rush out and attack his typewriter without fair warning. If typewriters could think, Bill's would instantly sympathize with the story of Pearl Harbor. [1]

And Paul Bowles described the living and working conditions of the writer:

> He lived in a damp little room whose single door opened onto the garden of the Hotel Villa Muniriya. One wall of the room, his shooting gallery, was pock-marked with bullet holes. Another wall was completely covered with snapshots, most of which he had taken on a recent trip to the headwaters of the Amazon....
>
> During the two years when I saw Bill regularly in Tangier, he took only kif, majoun and alcohol. But he managed to take vast amounts of all three. The litter on his desk and under it, on the floor, was chaotic, but it consisted only of pages of Naked Lunch, at which he was constantly working. When he read aloud from it, at random (any sheet of paper he happened to grab would do) he laughed a good deal, as well he might, since it is very funny, but from reading he would suddenly (paper still in hand) go into a bitter conversational attack upon whatever aspect of life had prompted the passage he had just read.... [2]

However, the composition of the manuscript began before

Bowles and Burroughs' son witnessed him madly typing in
Tangier.

Burroughs' first book, Junkie, had been published in
1953 by A. A. Wyn and Company. It appeared as an Ace
paperback along with a reissue of Maurice Helbrant's Narcotic
Agent published in 1941. He confessed to his friend Jack
Kerouac a year later that work on a second novel progressed
haltingly:

> I am having serious difficulties with my new novel.
> I tell you the novel form is completely inadequate
> to express what I have to say. I don't know if I
> can find a form. I am very gloomy as to the
> prospects of publication and I'm not like you Jack,
> I need an audience. Of course a small audience. [3]

The reason he was discouraged over the progress of his
present work followed in another letter to Kerouac. This
time he enclosed an example of the kind of writing which
evoked the hopelessness he had previously articulated. Ever
since the publication of his first novel, he had expressed his
need to write to make money. The prospect of receiving a
great deal of money for a piece of popular fiction from a
magazine appealed to his immediate needs. The result of
his efforts, though, was less than he had hoped.

> I sat down seriously to write a best seller Book of
> the Month Club job on Tangier. So here is what
> comes out first sentence:
> "The only native of Interzone who is neither
> queer nor available is Andrew Keif's chauffeur,
> which is not an affectation on Keif's part but a
> useful pretext to ["get" crossed out] break off
> relations with anyone he doesn't want to see.
> 'You made a pass at Arachnid last night. I
> can't have you to the house again.' People are
> always blacking out in the Zone whether they
> drink or not. No one knows for sure what he
> did last night.
> Arachnid is the worst driver in the Zone. On
> one occasion he ran down a pregnant woman in
> from the mountains with a load of charcoal on
> her back, and she miscarried a bloody, dead
> baby on the street, and Keif got out and sat on
> the curb stirring the blood with a stick while
> the police questioned Arachnid and ["ended up

an" crossed out] finally arrested the woman. "
I can just see that serialized in Cosmopolitan or
Good Housekeeping.   I mean it's hopeless, Jack.
I can't write in a popular vein. [4]

His attempt to hide his frustration with a joking reference to
the magazines is halfhearted at best. His desire to write
popular fiction and his frustration over his inability to do so
was a bitter realization in light of his need for money. [5]

In his personal letters Burroughs often included short
sketches which were the written counterpart of the routines
and skits he had performed for his friends.   Later some of
these sketches were included almost word-for-word in Naked
Lunch. The passage he had included in his letter to Kerouac
late in 1954 appears in Naked Lunch, [6] and as accurately as
can be determined, is the first fragment of Naked Lunch.

The letter which satirized Tangier also included a note
revealing the identity of Andrew Keif.   He wrote: "P. S.
Andrew Keif is Paul Bowles: of course. "[7] It is surprising
that Bowles is treated in such a macabre fashion, considering
the professional and social friendship of the two writers.   But
at this time Burroughs was not yet part of the artist colony
of Tangier, and he felt alienated from the writers and artists
there.   Bowles became a convenient symbol of that community.

Another section of Naked Lunch was enclosed in a letter
to Allen Ginsberg. [8] It contains a scene in which the character, Dr. Benway, tells an anecdote of a man who taught his
anus to talk.   Its tone suggests political satire rather than
an off-color, high-school joke.   In the letter the story is not
framed as a tale told by Benway, but describes the carnival
character who has achieved such anal control as a "novelty
ventriloquist act. "   However, the man's anus begins to
develop on its own, finally taking over the man by sending
out a transparent jelly that covers his entire body, except
for his eyes.   The story appears in Naked Lunch[9] directly
from the letter to Ginsberg.   Burroughs bluntly points out
that the story represents the fate of bureaucracy:

a virus takes root ... and grows, always repro-
ducing more of its own kind, until it chokes the
host if not controlled or excised.   Bureaus cannot
live without a host, being true parasitic organisms. [10]

In the same letter to Ginsberg, Burroughs once again
confessed his desire to write a narrative which could be sold.

He mentioned to his friend how he got ready to write. Before he began to compose the anecdote of the talking asshole,
he said that he had avoided the work of writing by

> reading magazines, making fudge, cleaning my
> shot-gun, washing the dishes, going to bed with
> Kiki, tying up the garbage in neat parcels and
> putting it out for the collector--(if you put it out
> in a waste basket or any container they will steal
> the container every time ...)--buying food for
> dinner, picking up a junk script. So finally I say
> "Now you must work," and smoke some tea and
> sit down and out it comes all in one piece like a
> glob of spit: the incredibly obscene thinly disguised
> references and situations that slip by in Grade B
> movies, the double entendres, perversions, sadism
> of popular songs, poltergeist knockings and mutter-
> ings of America's putrefying unconscious, boils
> that swell until they burst with a fart noise as if
> the body had put out an auxiliary ass hole with a
> stupid, belligerent Bronx cheer. [11]

The narrative of the talking asshole was not exactly what
Burroughs had set out to write, a piece he could sell to a
magazine. Instead of novelistic prose, the more he forced
himself to impose a plot on his material, the more he was
thrust into a form of madness in which only extreme ideas
came to mind. His use of marijuana while writing might
have released suppressed ideas, and it explains Burroughs'
report to Ginsberg that the sensations he experienced while
writing the piece were similar to automatic writing. He felt
as if a hostile independent force produced the story.
Evidently marijuana eased the inhibitions he had at the
time he put his pen on the paper, but the result
was not the marketable story he sought. His desire to write
something he could sell and his dismay over the result are
understandable since he had run out of money the month before, was without food or heroin, and was forced to sell
his typewriter. The loss of his typewriter meant that he had
to work in long hand, a situation he considered a disaster. [12]

   When Burroughs sent the letter which contained the
"talking asshole" episode to Ginsberg, he provided a glimpse
into his working habits, the nature of his writings, the intent of the prose, and his frustration over his inability to
write for a popular market. He had set out to write a best
seller, and wrote political, social satire instead--extreme in

its explicit and vivid anal imagery. The material was hardly
suitable for any glossy magazine in the early 1950's or possibly in the 1970's for that matter. He would later consider
that "it was a very dim period. "[13]

        Disappointed, he nevertheless took the effort in his
stride and began to work on a straight action story in the
Raymond Chandler style. [14] It was, according to Burroughs,
about a super heroin so addictive that only one shot was
needed to start a habit. The narrative begins with two
detectives who are sent to arrest a character referred to as
"me. " They take the character in for experiments with the
drug, and he kills them both. When Burroughs wrote to
Ginsberg, he had reached this point in the story with the
main character on the lam.

        He later moved to the native quarter of Tangier close
to the house of Paul Bowles, who was said to be in Ceylon
at the time. A friend of Burroughs' was renting the Bowles'
house so he had access to the writer's books. He wrote to
Kerouac that he was trying to adopt his technique by writing
down immediate feelings and sensations in an effort to trans-
mit the facts directly, and included this sample:

        Sitting in front of the Cafe Central in the Spring
        like, rainy sunshine. Sick. Waiting for my
        Eukodol. A boy walks by and I turn my head,
        following his loins like a lizard turns its head to
        follow the course of an ant. [15]

Aside from its obvious concern with drugs and homosexuality,
it indicates clearly the method Burroughs used in writing
fragments of Naked Lunch. As he explained later, "I am a
recording instrument. "[16]

        In addition to the writing experiment using Kerouac's
method, he also included another sketch about his character
Andrew Keif. The scene concerns Keif, the homosexual, and
his desire to "live a normal life. [He] sees a female Reichian
analyst who attaches electrodes to his penis and inserts an
orgone sprayer in his anus and tells him to relax and let the
orgasm reflex take over. "[17] The social satire is rather thinly
disguised. It was also part of the same manuscript he had
described to Ginsberg a few days previously.

        He explained to Kerouac that the book was shaping up
as a fight between scientists who have discovered an "anti-

dream drug that will excise the intuitive, empathizing, sym-
bolizing, myth and art creating faculties [and] a few counter-
conspiritors ... trying to obtain and destroy the formula."[18]
He admitted to his friend that it would certainly contain a
lot of violence and shooting, and he described the opening
scene. Two cops have come to arrest him because he is
slated as the guinea pig in one of the anti-dream drug experiments. The cops expect a routine bust, unaware of the
full details of their assignment. The outline of the story
was changed in only one detail from the description he had
given to Ginsberg. The super heroin of the earlier version
was changed to an anti-dream drug, resulting in greater
allegorical tone. But this time Burroughs included a section
of the text in his letter to Kerouac. It was indeed in the
Chandler style.

> I snapped two quick shots into Hawser's [sic] belly
> where his vest had pulled up showing an inch of
> white shirt ... O'Brien was clawing at his shoulder
> holster, his hand stiff with panic. I shot him in
> his huge, red forehead about an inch below the
> white hair line.[19]

This excerpt, like others which were included as part of
letters, appears as part of a scene in Naked Lunch.[20] His
letters to Kerouac and Ginsberg provide his thoughts on the
Hauser and O'Brien section at the time of its composition.
However, the version which appears in the book has the
detectives looking not for a super heroin or an anti-dream
drug, but "books, letters, manuscripts. Anything printed,
typed or written."[21] The shift from drugs to printed
material suggests another shift in the symbolic meaning,
and it indicates that Burroughs wanted the episode involving
the two cops to extend beyond fictionalization. The earlier
draft versions point toward a more realistic than fantastic
episode.

An incident involving Burroughs, which occurred later
that year in Tangier, closely parallels the Hauser and O'Brien
plot. Describing the episode in third person, he wrote that
during the

> late afternoon of December 13, 1955 ... author
> Bill Burroughs was writing a letter in his pent-
> house quarters. Suddenly a stream of men, some
> carrying guns, opened Burroughs' door and looked
> in. The explanation is that [the building] is for

> sale and these were the guides for the 'Black
> Bernouse,' none other than the ex-Sultan of
> Morocco Mohammed ben Arafa. [22]

The episode, however, occurred after Burroughs had written
the Hauser and O'Brien section. The coincidence was an
example of what he called writing the future.

Written as a hard-boiled detective narrative, the
Hauser and O'Brien episode is stylistically similar to the
beginning of Naked Lunch, the "I can feel the heat closing
in" section. When placed together, the two sections provide
a coherent plot and were probably written at the same time
in early 1955 in Tangier, then separated for the novel. In
fact they were restored to their original order for the
beginning of Dead Finger's Talk, a British edition of material
taken from the Naked Lunch manuscript. [23]

The letters to Kerouac and Ginsberg in late 1954 and
early 1955 from Tangier provide a unique revelation of the
author's intent at the time of composition, his attitude toward
his fiction, and his general state of mind. These letters also
demonstrate the autobiographical nature of the fiction, the
surreal quality and spontaneous composition of some of the
episodes, in addition to Burroughs' conscious perception of
the non-linear, non-novelistic quality of his work.

He continued to send excerpts in letters to his friends.
Another section of Naked Lunch was included in a letter
written to Kerouac on May 24, 1955. [24] It involves a routine
in which purple-assed baboons are hunted from motorcycles.
The homosexual overtones of the scene are obvious. [25] The
purple-assed baboon recurs in Burroughs' writing, most
notably in an article he wrote on the 1968 Democratic National
Convention in Chicago in Esquire. [26] In that article the baboon
became the personification of politician "Homer Mandril"
through a process of fictional metamorphosis, a characteristic
of his work after Naked Lunch.

But what kind of circumstances surrounded the writing
of Naked Lunch? Did it spring full-blown from the head of
the Harvard graduate, or are there events in the author's
life which contributed to the poignancy of his fiction?

A letter Burroughs wrote Ginsberg in April 1952
provides an early indication of his preference for the surreal
and the grotesque in social comment. He had just finished

the manuscript of his first novel Junkie, and had designated
Ginsberg as his agent in New York. It was Ginsberg who
handled the contract negotiations with Wyn and Company.
Like most publishers, they wanted some information for the
introduction and requested a short capsule biography from the
author. Irritated by the vagueness of their request, Burroughs exploded with the following satire of dust-jacket
biography:

> Now as to this biographical thing, I can't write it.
> It is too general and I have no idea what they want.
> Do they have in mind the "I have worked--but not
> in the order named--as a towel boy in a Kalamazoo
> whore house, lavatory attendant, male whore, and
> part time stool pigeon. Currently living in a re-
> modeled pissoir with a hermaphrodite and a suc-
> cession of cats. I would rather write than fuck--
> what a shameless lie. My favorite hobby is tor-
> turing cats. We have quite a turnover especially
> in the Siameses. That long silky hair cries for
> kerosene and a match. I favor kerosene over
> gasoline. It burns slower. You'd be surprised at
> the noises a cat can make when the chips are
> down" routine like you see on the back flap?[27]

Since he felt he could not write it, he then asked Ginsberg to
do it for him. However, he wanted him to tell Carl Solomon,
who was handling the biographical material for Junkie, that
he did not mind a reference to his homosexuality as long as
he was not presented as a limp-wristed stereotype. In his
instructions to Ginsberg, he parodied that stereotype, and
this may have been an outgrowth of his work on a sequel to
Junkie which carried the tentative title Queer.[28] Burroughs'
letter to Ginsberg exhibits his ability to duplicate the voice
and tone of a character type, as well as his disdain for the
common image of the homosexual. The preference for
satiric written expression evident in this and other letters
demonstrates that his caustic social criticism was not limited
to his published work, but was part of the author's letter-
writing style before it became part of his novels. Naked
Lunch was his first published exhibition of the fragmented
satires, and an obvious contrast to the matter-of-fact prose
of Junkie. One can safely conclude that much of Burroughs'
fiction was first worked out in letters to his friends Jack
Kerouac and Allen Ginsberg.

The informality of a personal letter provided Burroughs with great freedom. It is no wonder that Naked Lunch

contained many of the fragments, routines, parodies, and
black jokes he had written in letters.   The epistolary style
fashioned the novel as an art form, and it was that style
in which Burroughs was able to first liberate his imagination
and capture on paper his bizarre social visions.   His inability to write conventional narrative provided the cause for
the stylistic innovations of Naked Lunch.   Sex, drugs, politics,
addiction had been the subjects of earlier novels by other
writers.   But Burroughs treated these social problems as
black jokes, turning the taboo into a demonic laugh. [29]

Wyn asked Burroughs for additional material for
Junkie.   They were especially interested in material which
would clear up an obvious hole in the plot.   In the book the
junkie is married, and his wife who is mentioned in several
scenes which occur in Mexico, merely disappears after those
sequences.   The editors wanted that cleared up.

Clarification proved difficult for Burroughs.   Personal
and emotional reasons prevented him from dealing with the
subject.   A tragic incident reported in the New York Times
offers an explanation:

Stunt Shooting of Wife Denied

MEXICO CITY, Sept. 7 (AP)--A wealthy Texas
cotton grower denied today that the fatal shooting
of his wife last night resulted from his firing at
a glass of gin on her head in William Tell fashion.
William Seward Burroughs, 37, a descendant of the
adding machine family, declared he dropped his
gun, it fired, and his wife dropped fatally wounded. [30]

This report subsequently became the basis of many rumors
about the incident.   It was, however, a very serious matter
which was quickly taken before the Mexican officials:

MEXICO CITY, Sept. 10--William S. Burroughs of
a prominent St. Louis family was held today for
trial on a charge of fatally shooting his wife.
Judge Eduardo Urazia Jimenez ordered "formal
prison" on a homicide charge for the 37-year-old
grandson of the Burroughs adding machine inventor.
That is the Mexican Court preliminary to a trial.
Court officials declined to say when the next
hearing would be held.   Mexican law requires a
decision in a criminal case within a year.   Bur-

> roughs counsel has not asked for his release in
> [sic] bond. The judge's order followed the hearing
> of two witnesses, whose testimony backed Bur-
> roughs' own story that a pistol had gone off acci-
> dentally while he was looking to see whether it was
> loaded. [31]

It is not altogether clear exactly how Burroughs' lawyer was
able to obtain a ruling of accidental death, but suffice it to
say that Burroughs was allowed to leave Mexico on bond, and
return to the U. S.   He left his son William Jr. with his
parents Laura Lee and Mortimer Burroughs in Palm Beach,
Florida, where they owned and ran a gift shop called Cobble
Stone Gardens.

The shooting had an intense emotional effect on Burroughs and remains one of the personal events in his life
which is not treated in his fiction straight-forwardly as are
drug addiction and homosexuality. It may be that because
homosexuality and drug addiction are defined as deviant social
behavior with varying degrees of intensity from one historical
period to another, and from one nation to another, that Burroughs could deal objectively with his own experiences with
drugs and sex. But homicide is universally unacceptable.
Accidental homicide carries with it the internal guilt of
violating the strongest taboo without the catharsis of external
social punishment.

The editors at Wyn wanted Burroughs to write about
a most devastating event only months after it occurred for
inclusion in Junkie. He replied to his friend Ginsberg:

> About the death of Joan.   I do not see how that
> could be worked in.   I wish you could talk them
> out of that idea.   I will take care of her dis-
> appearance. [32]

But Wyn persisted in its desire to have the plot filled in.
Burroughs offered an alternative that Ginsberg could take
to the publisher:

> I wonder if Wyn would agree to leave the wife out
> altogether. Since she only appears once it seems
> simpler to cut out that single reference instead of
> trying to sandwich her into the narrative. This is
> just a suggestion. If Wyn wants her in there she
> will be in there. I myself would be glad to drop

the subject of the wife altogether.   Please let me
know on this point. [33]

Frustrated over the haggling concerning the subject of the
wife in the novel, and painfully aware that the year allowed
to decide all cases in Mexico was drawing rapidly to an end,
Burroughs offered this final solution to the problem:

> I have inserted references to my wife here and
> there.   She does not disappear.   She has no
> bearing on the story and therefore she is only
> mentioned casually and occasionally.   The last
> reference is "My wife and I were separated at
> this time."   Now if they insist I can insert a
> drunken car accident and some jail scenes.   I
> know that it would be an artistic error and that
> it does not belong in this book.   If they want it
> I will write it.   Alternatively they could simply
> cross out all references to her.   Like I say she
> has no bearing on the story whatever. [34]

But in spite of his suggestions to the publisher, the wife was
allowed to remain in the manuscript without inserting any
explanation of her disappearance.   Yet the incident was the
type of occurrence which would not lie still.   When Junkie
was reissued by itself it carried an introduction which repeated the episode:

> One of the more lurid incidents in his past was
> the accidental shooting of his wife in a "William
> Tell" experiment ... demonstrating his markman-
> ship by attempting to shoot a champagne glass off
> her head and killing her in the process.   For this,
> in Mexico City in about 1950, he was acquitted. [35]

Obviously relishing the sensationalism of the accident, the
editor plunged into the heart of the rumor spawned by the
New York Times reference to William Tell in reporting the
story in September 1951, not 1950.   The gin glass of the
newspaper report is transformed into a champagne glass,
adding what the editor thought to be a touch of decadence to
the sordid event.

The rumors surrounding the shooting were to pro-
liferate rather than diminish.   Burroughs' son William Jr.
wrote about the episode in an article about his life with his
father for Esquire, some years later,

Ginsberg ... told me one cold New York China-
town night that ... she was driven by a death wish,
as of course anyone is who makes a habit of speed.
He said he had the morgue photograph if I wanted
to see it, but I chuckled uneasily and said something to the effect of "maybe later." It was a cold
night after all and the picture was overtone.
   So mama was tempestuous to say the least.
One night at a party in our house when everyone
was drinking or stoned, she placed an apple or an
apricot or a grape or myself on her head and challenged my father to shoot. Bill, usually a good
marksman, missed. "Accidental Homicide: Cause
of Death: Cerebral Hemorrhage" (at least). So I
can remember no details of the apartment or my
mother. Is there a psychiatrist in the house?
"The past is fiction," my father says, which may
or may not be true. But I tend to agree that what
is essential is true. 36

Burroughs, Jr. narrates a version similar to the others with
a few embellishments. He suggests that the incident was
not an accident, but instigated by his mother in order to
fulfill her death wish. He also implies that the shooting may
not have been an accident by referring to his father's reputation as a good marksman. Burroughs always carried a
gun reflecting a life-long fascination. He later explained the
shooting in an interview after the publication of Naked Lunch.

   I had a terrible accident with Joan Vollmer, my
   wife. I had a revolver that I was planning to sell
   to a friend. I was checking it over and it went
   off--killed her. A rumor started that I was trying
   to shoot a glass of champagne from her head William Tell style. Absurd and false. 37

He considered the unfortunate event an accident, and so did
the Mexican authorities. More importantly, though, his account demonstrates the depth to which he was affected by the
shooting. Because of it, among other things, Mexico takes
on a sinister character for Burroughs in his fiction. His
new attitude toward the country is in stark contrast to many
glowing letters he had written to Kerouac extolling the virtues
of life in that country for an American with limited funds. 38

   In Naked Lunch, for example, the narrator recalls an
incident which occurred in "Cuernavaca or ... Taxco."39

He observes a woman named Jane, the name Burroughs used in Junkie for his wife Joan, talking over a drink with a

> pimp trombone player ... [who] is one of those
> vibration and dietary artists--which means he
> degrades the female sex by forcing his chicks
> to swallow all this shit....
> So he is putting down junk and coming on with
> tea. I take three drags, Jane looked at him and
> her flesh crystallized. I leaped up screaming "I
> got the fear!" and ran out of the house. Drank
> a beer in a little restaurant--mosaic bar and soccer
> scores and bullfight posters--and waited for the
> bus to town.
> A year later in Tangier I heard she was dead. [40]

Unable to confront the shooting of his wife, accident or not, Burroughs treats the incident in fiction as a bizarre psychic episode, maintaining places, people and possible the way in which it is remembered. In Naked Lunch the accidental shooting of his wife rendered fictionally as "her flesh crystallized" remains a vivid image of death, an image the sad product of experience.

Allowed to leave Mexico on bond, Burroughs stayed for a while with his parents in Florida. He then traveled most of 1953 in South America. [41] From South America Burroughs set out in 1954 to join the artists' colony in Tangier.

From there he wrote letters to his friends filled with observations of the people he met. He had settled into a rooming house which he referred to as a whore house, and which others called a male brothel. The owner of the place was a Dutchman named Tony. In a letter to Jack Kerouac, Burroughs mimicked the thick Germanic accent of the owner who constantly complained about the rumors which linked him with narcotics.

> Tony ... keeps casting me reproachful glances in
> the hall and saying: "Ach thirteen years and never
> before I hoff such a thing in my house. And since
> two weeks are here in Tangiers two good English
> gentlemens I knew since long time with them I
> could make gud business except my house is so
> watched at. "[42]

Letters such as this demonstrate the relative ease with
which he was able to duplicate a voice on paper. Not readily
shown in his first published book, his ability to capture
voices convincingly appears fully developed in Naked Lunch,
especially in the County Clerk and Benway sections. Without
the caricatures, the black humor of Naked Lunch would merely
be sour, disconnected ravings.

In addition to his observations, he also expressed in
his letters his frustration at being snubbed by the Tangier
expatriot literary society--Paul Bowles, Truman Capote,
Tennessee Williams. He told Kerouac that he was trying to
kick his drug habit and that his Arab boy Kiki was a great
emotional help. [43] Since the shooting death of his wife, Burroughs had begun to express in letters his emotional attach-
ment to Allen Ginsberg. His vulnerability and the sincerity
of his affection for his friend is touching in its expression
and its desperation. [44] His affection for Ginsberg would
mature into lasting friendship, but the passion and rejection
he expressed were painful then.

In September 1956 Burroughs "began writing full time
and the material from which Naked Lunch was later ab-
stracted ... was produced at that time."[45] A year later, on
September 20, 1957, he advised Allen Ginsberg, who was
again acting as his agent, that the material in the manuscript
should not be arranged chronologically, and that material
written for his unpublished Queer should not be included with
the new pages. It was his feeling that the material he was in
the process of writing did not present a cohesive unit like a
novel. Rather, "it is a number of connected--by theme--but
separate short pieces."[46]

Burroughs also mentioned work on a theory which he
felt would explain morphine addiction. After reading a book
on the operative action of antibodies and antibiotics, Burroughs,
who attended medical school briefly in Europe in the thirties
after graduating from Harvard, concluded

> that morphine must in some way, dissolve or
> blanket the cell receptors thus taking over the
> vital function of protection and nutrition becoming
> literally the skin of the cells, so that the cells
> undergo a recessive simplification and become para-
> sitic in the morphine medium ... Incidently this
> theory resulted from the necessities of the novel
> ... that is scientific theories and novel are in-

separable. What I am evolving is a general theory
of addiction which expands into a world picture with
concepts of good and evil. [47]

Only a week before he explained this theory to Ginsberg,
Burroughs' Arab boy Kiki was murdered in Madrid by a
homosexual Cuban singer who became enraged when he saw
the boy with a girl. The Cuban stabbed Kiki in the heart
with a kitchen knife and then attacked the girl. Neighbors
came in, the Cuban ran, but he was later caught by the
police. Burroughs felt remorse over the incident, referring
to it, however, in a controlled tone, "Poor Kiki."[48] The
incident, as far as fiction is concerned, demonstrates the
close proximity Burroughs lived to violence and death.

During the writing of Naked Lunch, a great deal of
chaos and violence surrounded him, even if his letters to
Allen Ginsberg, Paul Bowles, and Jack Kerouac record only
the most striking episodes in the author's life. At the time
Kiki was murdered, Alan Ansen's ex-boy went to France,
murdered a cab driver, and shot himself when police arrived
to arrest him. [49] Ansen was a friend of Burroughs who
shared a room with him in Tangier and later helped him
organize the manuscript of Naked Lunch.

Not only did Burroughs struggle to understand and
kick the drug habit, but he also fought to understand his own
homosexuality. He wrote to Allen Ginsberg[50] that he felt he
was closer to a resolution of this condition which he referred
to as an illness. His awareness came to him in a dream
he had in London in which the homosexual and heterosexual
aspects of his personality met. The heterosexual personality
appeared as an adolescent who after twenty-five years of
imprisonment in the body of a homosexual expressed his
hatred for the homosexual personality. The conflict between
the two was influenced by another entity which Burroughs
could not identify completely. This third presence made it
impossible for the heterosexual to reclaim the body. The
articulation of this dream ended with an expression of the
need for a consolidation of all the personality traits which
appeared in the dream.

Any Freudian would begin to take notes feverishly at
the mention of parts of one's personality as separate beings.
Though a simplistic explanation would be schizophrenia, the
narrative of the struggle between the two segments of his
personality for dominance is more likely Burroughs' metaphoric

explanation of his own dream. In his work characters are constantly changing from within, being taken over by protoplasmic forces, mutating into insects; which is, no doubt, Burroughs' way of explaining just this kind of personality conflict in fiction. The hanging scenes of "A. J. 's Annual Party" employ the changing of characters into one another during the sexual acrobatics of the blue movie. Burroughs had been studying the relationship between morphine and schizophrenia on a clinical level. That is, he began to question the metabolic significance involved, if any, in the low incidence of cancer found in both heroin addicts and in schizophrenics. But the personality struggle, though it is described schizophrenicly, is an attempt to resolve intense homosexual guilt. The guilt and repression is vividly described in the image of a heterosexual boy imprisoned in a straightjacket of homosexual flesh.

By this time Burroughs was working feverishly on the book. Writing had become for him as addictive as his heroin habit. [51] He explained that the book which had become an obsession, superimposed several narratives in which characters wander back and forth from the U. S. A. , South America, Tangier, and Scandinavia. Like his own personality, which he had described earlier as a composite of many characters, he considered the book as having only one main character called variously Benway, Carl, and Lee. All three were manifestations of the same personality which was extrapolated from his own experience. Like Twain, another native of Missouri, Burroughs used places from his own experience for the settings of the episodes which occur in Naked Lunch. [52]

In the fall of 1957, Burroughs perceived the book he was writing as a saga of lost innocence, the Fall. [53] It was not without redemption obtained through an understanding of the life process. The theme seems almost scientific in its emphasis on the redemptive quality of knowledge. Psychologically the perception of knowledge as curative is Freudian in its faith in the intellect. And redemption was on Burroughs' mind.

> The only way I can write narrative is to get right
> outside my body and experience it. This can be
> exhausting and at times dangerous. One cannot be
> sure of redemption. [54]

The reference to the method of writing suggests a schizophrenic state achieved in order to obtain a narrative. The

method is of course dangerous psychologically.   Taking such
a risk, as Burroughs pointed out, did not always guarantee
that the result would be redemptive.   In the case of some
of the more lurid parts of the narrative, the social reaction
was censorship rather than praise, leaving redemption outside the limits of society.

Not only did the project underway run the risk of not
obtaining redemption, but the feverishness with which Burroughs wrote during this period was not without its small
emotional hazards.   One consumed with a project often per-
ceives the world's events as directly related to that project.
While not manifesting clinical paranoid behavior, Burroughs
was disturbed enough by the crash of the Tangier to Madrid
plane, and the possibility that a letter of his containing a
section of his manuscript was destroyed with the plane, that
he wrote to Ginsberg:

> all hands dead and all mail lost.   The letter [with
> the manuscript] may have been on that plane.   So
> let me know when you receive this.   I will send
> the rest along as fast as I can get it down and in
> condition. [55]

At the time he had no takers for the Naked Lunch manuscript.
Still concerned over the fate of the manuscript, he again
wrote to Allen Ginsberg. [56] The substance was the same, did
Ginsberg get the manuscript, or were his worst fears that
the material was destroyed in the plane crash true.

Ginsberg, however, had plans for the fragments he
received.   Scrawled at the bottom of the last letter from
Burroughs was a Paris address and phone number.   The
name "Girodias" and "first floor" are there also.   The hand-
writing, though similar to Burroughs' is that of Ginsberg.
He of course was planning to show the Naked Lunch material
to the French publisher.   When Ginsberg arrived with the
amorphous pasted-up manuscript, the publisher rejected it
as too inaccessible for the average reader.   The encounter
between the two must have taken place in Paris between
November 10, the date of the letter with the address scrawled
at the bottom, and November 25, 1957.

On that date Burroughs mentions the rejection of the
manuscript by Olympia Press. [57] He took Girodias' refusal
in his stride, considering it a rejection of the form of the
manuscript and not of the totality of its substance.   The ac-

ceptance for publication of a fragment by <u>Black Mountain Re-</u>
<u>view</u> also helped soften the bad news. In addition the pub-
lishers at the <u>Chicago Review</u> showed an interest in Beat
writers, which held out a strong hope for publication. Burroughs promised Ginsberg that he would send them a section
of his work.

During this period Burroughs confided with Ginsberg
that he had confronted his original trauma over homosexuality.
He called the horror of the confrontation enough to make him
fear that his heart would stop. In fact he reported severe
pain in the sciatic nerve along the buttock as well as throughout the body. He used the medical terms "sciatica" and
"intercostol neuralgia [sic]" to describe the sensations he
felt. He said he was fed up with homosexuality, and expressed his desire to have a woman because he no longer
desired boys. He felt too that he was never intended to be
a homosexual in the first place.

He was also fed up with Tangier and its homosexuals.
He expressed his disgust for a fellow named Barney Bliss
who had a preference for sex with eight-year-old Arab boys.
Burroughs mockingly told Ginsberg that the fellow could only
make the sheepish excuse that he felt "inadequate with older
people. " Burroughs' disapproval of the man's practice was
strong and he branded the practice of sexually using eight-
year-old boys as belonging to a particularly undesirable part
of hell.

The judgment he made on the lecherous actions of
Bliss is appropriate because he had again changed his mind
concerning the meaning of the book he was writing. Before
he considered it a saga of lost innocence; now he viewed it
as a modern inferno. [58] It is no wonder he expressed doubts
about his own homosexuality to Ginsberg with the accompanying
revulsion of the acts of Barney Bliss. He had placed the
events of his novel in the context of redemption. And since
the novel was largely based on personal experience, the concept spilled over, calling for a judgment of his own actions
upon which the fictions were based.

On December 4, 1957[59] Burroughs mentioned to Kerouac
the manuscript he had been working on, at times up to ten
hours per day. He explained that the narrative was an attempt
to incorporate the sections that deal with Interzone--Bur-
roughs' fictional name for Tangier, but he did not enclose
examples.

Instead he sent two sections to Allen Ginsberg to give to Paul Carroll of Chicago Review. [60] He confessed that his writing habit had turned into a full-fledged compulsion, "I literally don't find ten minutes from the time I get up glued to this fucking typewriter."[61]

By December 8, 1957, Alan Ansen had arrived in Tangier to live with Burroughs, who by that time had written one hundred pages of new material.

He finally received a copy of the excerpts of his work which had been published in Black Mountain Review in February 1958. [62] He confessed to Ginsberg at the time that he was still addicted to opiates, paregoric.

Burroughs then decided to move to Paris and take up Allen Ginsberg's old room at a hotel at 9 rue Git Le Couer. The address was the residence of Beat writers called the "Beat Hotel."

Early 1958 brought a minor confrontation with Kerouac's mother. Evidently she had intercepted one of the letters Ginsberg had written to her son Jack, and became enraged at what she read. She wrote insulting letters to both Ginsberg and Burroughs, telling them that they could not see Jack anymore because they were sexual degenerates and drug addicts. Burroughs quoted part of the letter he had received to Ginsberg. "You are unfit to be talked to as human beings you and your dirty books and dirty mind and dirty dope."[63]

She barred Jack from seeing Ginsberg because he was Jewish. This racism upset Burroughs whose liberal tolerance did not extend to the sentiments expressed in the letters written by Kerouac's mother. But more upsetting to him was Kerouac's attempt to support his mother's slurs and simultaneously befriend them both. The relationship between Burroughs and Kerouac cooled considerably after that. [64]

Burroughs had relapsed and he wanted to go to London and take Dr. Yerbury Dent's apomorphine cure. Apomorphine is a strong emetic used to treat cattle, and was used by the British physician to cure alcoholism. Dent also tried the treatment with success on heroin addicts, but he only treated two patients at a time because he employed a great deal of personal guidance along with the apomorphine. Though Burroughs had visited the London doctor once before, his relapse called for an additional treatment. He was also ready

to leave Paris for a while because he was constantly interrupted by Ginsberg's friends and others staying at the hotel.
He found the place at once stimulating and distracting. However, he was not to go to London for the cure until late that
year.

Before he left Paris he received word that the Chicago
Review had accepted some excerpts from Naked Lunch for
publication. He expressed his excitement to Paul Bowles,
who by this time had become a frequent correspondent. He
told him that "Chicago Review is completely sold on my work,
publishing it in sections."[65]

August of 1958, the traditional month for vacations,
found Burroughs again in Tangier. He found a situation there
not totally to his liking. The police had begun a crack-down
on the homosexuals. He considered the situation extremely
repressive--beatings of Arab boys by police to get names of
homosexuals, and jail for those arrested. [66] In spite of the
crack-down, Burroughs' two-week stay in Tangier was rest-
ful, and since he worked on his novel while there he also
found the time productive. Nevertheless he advised Bowles
against returning to Tangier if he could. [67]

Upon his return to Paris, Burroughs found himself
living next door to Brion Gysin, a painter who would become
a life-long friend of the writer. Gysin had experienced in
painting a conversion similar to Burroughs' in writing. For
Burroughs his experience was so strong that he said he would
quit unless he could "reach a point where my writing has the
danger and immediacy of bull fighting."[68]

In October 1958, Burroughs went to London to undergo
the cure for drug addiction from Dr. Dent. This time he
would be there with a Harvard friend Jack Stern. A second
section of his work had been scheduled for publication in
Chicago Review. Only the lack of money for the stories
dampened his euphoria. He told Bowles that

> Rosenthal, the editor of Chicago Review is the only
> editor who really understands what I am doing ... I
> don't know if Jay Laughlin has seen the Ms. or
> not. [69]

Bowles had asked if the manuscript of Naked Lunch had been
considered for publication by the New Directions publisher.
His question indicates that he felt the work to be of the right

literary quality for New Directions. He also felt the publishing house daring enough to publish the text.

By Christmas 1958, Burroughs had spent a few weeks in London taking Dent's apomorphine treatment. He was off heroin and the Chicago Review intended to publish more excerpts from Naked Lunch. Feeling the spirit of the season he sent identical Christmas/New Years cards to both Paul Bowles[70] and Allen Ginsberg.[71] He told Bowles that he would like to meet him in England. To Ginsberg he excitedly asserted that he had broken through to another level of being, achieved ability to affect a physical change in what had once been only a subjective one. He explained that once when he was high on hashish, he looked at his hands in a mirror and saw them thick and pink with white tendrils extending out like vines or roots. A friend in the room who was not high looked over and asked what was wrong with his hands, remarking that they were thick and pink.[72] The discovery and the publication of his work signaled a positive turn for Burroughs.

His elation, however, was jolted by the decision of the Board of Trustees at the University of Chicago to suppress the Winter 1959 edition of Chicago Review. Although the decision by the Trustees was made early in November 1958, word of their action did not reach Burroughs until January 1959.

Considering the depression that normally is associated with drug withdrawal, the news of the Chicago Review must have been particularly hard to bear when we recall that Burroughs felt that Irving Rosenthal was the only one around who understood his work. He expressed his disappointment to Paul Bowles,

> The Chicago Review folded out from under me.
> Also I was announced in The Nation as an international homo and all around sex fiend.[73]

He concluded that:

> looks like Naked Lunch is finished. As to whether it will ever be published in a complete form I have no idea at this point. Complications and the manuscript scattered all over Europe.[74]

In early January 1959 Big Table prepared to publish

the excerpts from <u>Naked Lunch</u> censored by the University of
Chicago. In the United States and Britain no book publisher
would dare touch all of the Burroughs book for fear of
further censorship.   The prospects for an unexpurgated edition
of the book looked bleak indeed.   But after a benefit reading
for the <u>Chicago Review</u> was given by Allen Ginsberg and
Gregory Corso, a few publishers offered to bring it out in
an expurgated edition. [75]   The caution displayed by the publishers colored Burroughs' perception of his work, forcing
him to consider the deletion of certain parts which may have
been pornographic.

     Later that spring Burroughs returned to Tangier for
another visit.   On this trip he became involved in an opium
scandal. [76] A yacht captain on the skids named Stevens whose
ship was impounded in Gibraltar was arrested in Tangier for
trying to sell one-half of a kilo of opium which he had obtained from a supplier called Old Black Joe.   After the police
interrogated them both, one of them implicated a friend of
Burroughs' named Paul Lund, the British gangster after whom
Burroughs modeled some of the characters in <u>Naked Lunch</u>,
and another "American with glasses."   Burroughs was that
other American.   It seems that he had thought of selling a
little marijuana in Paris and wrote to Lund asking if he could
deliver some "Moroccan Leather goods" to him in Paris.
He eventually dropped the project before it got off the ground,
but the letter he wrote to Lund was on Captain Stevens at
the time of Stevens' arrest in Tangier.   The police concluded
that Burroughs was the Paris connection for the opium, and
obtained his name and Paris address from the letter found on
the ship's captain.

     Like the opening line of <u>Naked Lunch</u>, Burroughs
"could feel the heat closing in. "[77] He felt that he was on
the top of the suspect list of the French customs agents.
By April 21, 1959, though, he was back in Paris at the Beat
Hotel, after spending an anxious period in Tangier, in fear
the police would rush into his apartment and place him in
custody.   However, the Moroccan police never caught on that
Burroughs was in Tangier at the time of Captain Stevens' arrest.   Even more ironic, Burroughs was with Paul Lund when
the police searched Lund's apartment.   From the safety of
Paris Burroughs wrote Ginsberg about the search:

          Miraculously--no passport check of my person, not
          to mention the five grams of O[pium] in my pocket
          at the time. [78]

If the police had discovered that it was Burroughs in the
apartment with Lund, his presence there and the opium in
his possession would have provided very strong evidence to
support their theory that the American with glasses was the
Paris connection they sought. The five grams of opium would
have sealed the case. Burroughs was indeed lucky, but he
was not out of trouble. He was still wanted by the police
for an explanation of his involvement. The Lund/Stevens
incident coincidentally resembles the beginning of the Hauser
and O'Brien section of Naked Lunch written almost five years
previously. [79]

A copy of Big Table #1 had arrived from the United
States on Burroughs' return to Paris from Tangier. The
magazine impressed him as a first-rate job. He was not
aware, however, of the actions taken against the publication
by the Post Office, nor of the hearing scheduled for June to
determine whether or not the magazine was obscene under
the provisions of the U.S. Postal laws.

Unaware that the censorship of his work now extended
beyond Chicago Review to include Big Table, Burroughs began
to make plans to travel to New York in late June or early
July for a meeting with Grove Press on the possible publication of Naked Lunch. Allen Ginsberg had set up the meeting
between Rosset and Burroughs. Burroughs told Ginsberg that
he wanted to work with Irving Rosenthal on the preparation of
the manuscript and that he was prepared to guarantee Rosset
the delivery of a publishable manuscript by the end of the
summer. [80]

The arrival of word late in May of 1959 that Big
Table had been censored by the Post Office altered Burroughs' plans for publication considerably. On May 18, 1959,
he was more convinced than ever by the recent action that
the book could not be published in its entirety by any publisher. The Big Table controversy did not go unnoticed by
the sharp eyes of French publisher Maurice Girodias. The
actions by the University of Chicago and by the U.S. Post
Office created an interest in the material and generated
curiosity which no ad campaign could have achieved. The
suppression of Burroughs' work caused Girodias to reconsider
his rejection of the amorphous collection of typewritten pages
which Allen Ginsberg had presented to him in Paris almost
two years before.

According to many accounts, [81] Girodias sent Sinclair

Beiles to Burroughs' apartment at 9 rue Git Le Couer.   Burroughs recounted the whirwind of events which dissolved his
depression to his friend Paul Bowles:

> I have sold <u>Naked Lunch</u> to Olympia Press ... He
> --Girodias the editor--read the manuscript one day,
> waiting with a contract the next morning.   Not bad
> terms either.   In the past month I have edited the
> entire manuscript, corrected all the proofs and it
> rolls off the presses today.   Looks like a good
> deal so far as concerns loot. [82]

His excitement ran unabated, and for good reason; the impossible had happened to him.   The book he had all but given
up hope of having published was being issued in record time.   He
wrote to Allen Ginsberg with the news of his good fortune,
adding a few details on a possible U.S. edition:

> I am sure the deal I made with Olympia was the
> best deal I could have made.   I saw Jack fucking
> around five years with American publishers.   And
> no book is ever out less than a year from date of
> acceptance.   Of course the two pornographic sections
> --Hassan's Rumpus Room and A. J.'s Annual Party
> are in a very important part of the structure.   I
> had exactly ten days to prepare the MS for the
> printers.   Pressure welded the whole book together
> into a real organic continuity which it never had
> before.   The book will be out this week ... I don't
> make mistakes.   Not any more I don't.   This was a
> unique opportunity.   Selling to a U.S. publisher is
> now going to be easier--all I have to do is jerk out
> 2 chapters which are right together.   In short I can
> prepare the Ms for American or English markets in
> five minutes.   I will send you a copy which I should
> have like I say in a few more days. [83]

Burroughs' suggestion that "A. J.'s Annual Party" and "Hassan's Rumpus Room" could easily be deleted for American
and English editions indicates not only the author's awareness
of the tight sex censorship situations in both countries, but
also his willingness to have even an expurgated edition of the
book in print.   Evidently he felt that the book could be published without the two chapters even though he realized that
the two chapters were central to the structure of the novel.
It was his opinion that an expurgated edition would have the
best chance of publication outside of France.   For that reason

he chose to publish the book in Paris with Girodias' Olympia Press and have at least one edition in an unexpurgated form.

He explained the logic of his decision to Ginsberg:

> Please understand that Girodias is in a unique
> position to publish original and valuable work that
> more orthodox and committed publishers would not
> touch.   Who else would have published Naked Lunch
> FIRST??[84]

His rhetorical question brings the desperation he felt prior to the acceptance of the book by Olympia back into painfully sharp focus.   Who indeed would have published the whole Naked Lunch in the United States when the Post Office was actively fighting to maintain the legality of its ban on the excerpts found in Big Table.   However the decision to publish in Paris was not without complications.

Many of his friends who had worked to find a publisher for the book were caught flatfooted by his decision to publish with Olympia Press.   Irving Rosenthal had made some preliminary contacts, and Ginsberg had of course set up a New York meeting with Rosset.   Burroughs apologized to Ginsberg:

> I appreciate, God knows, your efforts and those of
> Irving [Rosenthal].   The present confused situation
> --I received telegrams and letters from publishers
> I never heard of in regard to arrangements of which
> I know nothing, acrimonious complaints that the
> book has been promised them by Rosenthal and
> taken out of their hands by Girodias--the present
> situation is entirely my fault.   I think Girodias will
> make a deal with Barney Rosset on the American
> edition.   As he put it to me straight (over a black-
> bird pastry) in his new restaurant (and he does come
> on straight) "This is a complicated business full of
> angles.   I know them--you don't, let me handle it.
> You will have to trust me. "[85]

Girodias had impressed Burroughs as not only smart beneath his timid and confused manner, but lucky as well.   The publisher had convinced him that he could save the writer money by subtle manipulations.   For example he could reduce taxes from 90 percent to 10 percent by transferring money to a Swiss branch office.   Burroughs let Girodias handle the contract negotiations for an American edition with Barney Rosset.

However, the contract he signed required that one
third of the money received from the sale of the English
language rights would go to Olympia Press. [86] The clause
was not standard since most contracts give the publisher no
share of the sale of rights. The situation can be explained
by Burroughs' naivete and by the remote possibility that an
unexpurgated edition of the book would be issued by another
publisher. He was, after all, in desperate need of money,
and publication under any circumstances was welcome. In
retrospect his oversight was costly, but understandable given
the rapidity of publication.

At the time he was finishing the manuscript of the
book in Paris, Burroughs had an anxious encounter with the
French police. They had an order for his arrest, but did
not get around to serving it until late July. He spent twelve
hours in jail and a day in what he described as the Kafkaesque
French bureaucracy. They were looking for marijuana, not
heroin. The police found some hashish, and Burroughs was
fined for possession. [87]

The arrest concerned Burroughs because he was named
in the still unresolved opium case in Tangier involving Paul
Lund and Captain Stevens. He thought that the police knock
at his door at eight in the morning was related to that case.
Only an oversight by the authorities kept him out of jail on
the charges pending in Tangier, but his presence in Paris
had been confirmed by the arrest and fine on charges of
possession.

Shortly after his arrest he received a telegram from
Interpol concerning the Lund/Stevens case. He confessed his
despair over the prospects of the situation to Ginsberg, admitting that the matter looked bad. He blamed himself for
associating with someone with a reputation like Lund's in the
first place, and told his friend:

> I am writing a short deposition with regard to
> Naked Lunch. This is essential for my own safety
> at this point. Naked Lunch is written to reveal
> the junk virus, the manner in which it operates and
> the manner in which it can be brought under control.
> This is no act. I mean it all the way. Get off
> that junk wagon boys its going down a three mile
> grade for the junk heap. I am off junk in sickness
> or in health so long as we both shall live....
>   The two chapters of Naked Lunch that have been

described as pornographic are intended as a tract
against Capital Punishment in the manner of Swift's
Modest Proposal. If you want to drink blood and
eat hangings go to it boys. But leave us make it
a Naked Lunch.

I hear the boys in the back room say "Burroughs pulla the switch." Well maybe. Wouldnt
you? I am not playing to lose. In fact I'm not
playing at all. I mean it.

If you can get the beatnicks off the junk route,
then maybe other routes wont be so difficult as they
are now. [88]

The reference to the hanging scenes as a tract against
capital punishment, then, seem related to Burroughs' need to
present a convincing interpretation of those passages which
would simultaneously appease the censor, on the one hand,
and the judge in Tangier on the other. It was indeed Burroughs who first compared the scenes with Swift, allowing
the issue of capital punishment to overshadow the more psy-
chosexual explication of the hangings. [89]

Burroughs' deposition against heroin, partially the
product of the possibility of jail in Tangier as a conspirator
in an international drug smuggling operation, was published
in Evergreen Review and later in the American edition of
Naked Lunch. It carried the same title in both instances:
"Deposition: Testimony Concerning a Sickness." It provided a suitable explanation for passages in the book and
occurrences in his life which could be easily misinterpreted.
Just because he was under the gun in Tangier should not
suggest that his disclaimer was dishonest. Junk was a dead
end for him.

The charges in Tangier hung heavily over him. Burroughs had a great deal to lose now. His career as a writer
had taken a dramatic turn. From the utter despair at the
beginning of the summer of 1959, he was now scheduled for
a Life interview in Paris in early October. He sought advice
from Brion Gysin.

Following Gysin's suggestion, he admitted before the
judge hearing the Lund/Stevens case that he had indeed written
the letter to Lund found on Stevens at the time of his arrest.
The judge, who turned out to be an understanding man, said
that he did not want to make a big deal out of Burroughs'
connection with the other two. However, he did not want to

be treated as a fool either.   Burroughs insisted that he was
not engaged in any trafficking, nor did he intend to be.   He
also told the judge that he did not want to see or talk to any
underworld figures since he had his own work, his writing,
to attend to.   The judge freed him on his own recognizance.
Burroughs was fined and given a suspended sentence.   The
minimum fine of $500 seemed a small price compared with
jail and the unwelcome publicity which would have accompanied it. [90]

        With the affair in Tangier cleared up, Burroughs
could return to writing.   It was at this time that he began
to mention L. Ron Hubbard, the founder of the Church of
Scientology. [91]   His interest in the philosophy cum religion
lay principally in its "auditing" techniques designed to ex-
ternalize personality.   Burroughs had just discovered a writing
technique which externalized the process of writing.   He later
termed his discovery the "cut-up" method.   Cut-ups were
just that.   A page of typescript or any written matter was
divided into four sections and then literally cut into quarters
with a scissors.   The parts were rearranged, and the result
was read.   Often cut-ups yielded only gibberish, but Burroughs was able to select the more imaginative lines from
the chaff.   Although the text of Naked Lunch was not written
by this method, Burroughs admits that much of it appears as
if it were.   He felt that cut-ups introduced the spontaneous
random factor into writing, liberating it from static linguistic
combinations and associations.   He saw in the technique of
Scientology the promise of liberating the personality.   In
short, both were methods which worked.   He was to renounce
both cut-ups and Scientology years later, however.   He formally lashed out at Hubbard's techniques in a review of a
book on Scientology. [92]   At the urging of Brion Gysin he
quietly dropped the cut-up method.   While Burroughs was able
to create some interesting effects with cut-ups, imitators
using the same technique produced only laughable jumbles
of words. [93]   The writer who makes the selections, then, was
more important than the technique.

        After the publication of Naked Lunch by Olympia Press,
Burroughs was faced for the first time with the notion that he
was a professional writer.   His name began to circulate in
literary circles, and his benign encounter with the court over
the trafficking allegations proved a good omen.   In early
October 1959 two Life reporters named Snell and Loomis
visited Burroughs at 9 rue Git Le Couer.   He considered
them both "amusing and knowledgeable characters."[94]   They

spent over fourteen hours with Burroughs and he felt that
they would write an interesting article with "brilliant" pictures. He praised them to Ginsberg:

> The Life interviewers here are two far out cats
> with real appreciation for my work that cant be
> faked. Of course they have nothing to do with
> the final form of the story. [95]

Ironically the article which did appear in later November 1959
was not sympathetic in its treatment of the Beats. Its author
Paul O'Neil portrayed them as absurdly as he could. But
his treatment of Burroughs appeared less irreverent. The
work of Snell and Loomis resulted in this faint praise.

> For sheer horror no member of the Beat Genera-
> tion has achieved effects to compare with William
> S. Burroughs ... The Naked Lunch could be de-
> scribed as an effort to communicate the degrada-
> tions of addiction in epic tones ... [96]

Lawrence Ferlinghetti, founder of the City Lights Bookstore
and press in San Francisco, was also spared caustic criticism. But most were not. To the Life writer, and by extension the vast readership influenced by the magazine, the
movement was to be soundly dismissed:

> The bulk of Beat writers are undisciplined and
> slovenly amateurs who have deluded themselves
> into believing their lugubrious absurdities are art
> simply because they have rejected the form, style
> and attitudes of previous generations and have
> seized upon obscenity as an expression of "total
> personality. "[97]

The Beat movement did not represent to Life a serious
artistic alternative, only a rejection of the past with no
workable replacement.

     The photo of Burroughs within the article shows him,
paper in hand, sitting on the edge of a bed. It is certainly
not one of the "brilliant" shots he thought was taken during
the interview.   The Life article, in words and pictures, defined Burroughs for many millions of Americans as a com-
paratively serious member of an otherwise uninteresting and
adolescent literary movement.   The notoriety received from
the article was bittersweet.

In the fall of 1959 Barney Rosset attended the Frankfurt book fair. According to Burroughs the Grove Press publisher was negotiating the details of a contract for an American edition of <u>Naked Lunch</u> with Maurice Girodias. [98] To his discovery of a new writing method and the techniques of Scientology, he could add the prospects of American publication of his book.

Burroughs continued to discuss his new writing discovery in a letter to Ginsberg in later October:

> I have a new method of writing and do not want to publish anything which has not been inspected and processed. I cannot explain this method to you untill you have necessary training. So once again and most urgently believe me there is not much time. [99]

He was working on a book titled <u>Minutes to Go</u>[100] with Brion Gysin, Sinclair Beiles, and Gregory Corso. It was a collection of writing experiments using the enigmatic technique, the cut-up method. The cut-up method excited Burroughs, but a sudden delay occurred in the plans for American publication of <u>Naked Lunch</u>. He was disappointed over the reversal and told Ginsberg:

> Oh uh I don't know what is going on between Rosset and Girodias he told me it was "premature" to sign a contract. [101]

Grove Press was certainly concerned over the real possibility of a censorship action against <u>Naked Lunch</u> if it published an unexpurgated edition. Its desire to have the option to leave out the so-called pornographic sections prompted Girodias to go slow on the contract.

Other prospects for publication appeared as winter approached. Under rather bizarre arrangements, Girodias secured a contract for a German edition of <u>Naked Lunch</u>.

> Limes is publishing L. N. [sic] contract signed processing through Switzerland where it is registered in the name of a Turkish widow resident of Hong Kong branch office in Amsterdam. Girodias is such a devious who you never know to whom you are a speak. [102]

And in spite of the court battle still being fought over issue number one with the U.S. Post Office, Burroughs sent another manuscript to Paul Carroll at Big Table.

During the last months of 1959 events and discoveries had a profound influence on Burroughs' perception of himself. He signed a letter to Ginsberg, "Not even I know exactly who."[103] Previously he signed letters with playful aliases such as "that Junky writin' boy," but the expression of doubt over his own identity here seems less innocent. Whatever else was happening, Burroughs felt that the change was a good sign which manifested itself in new methods of seeing, thinking, and writing.

As the year ended Burroughs' career was, at the age of forty-five, finally set. For better or worse he was a professional writer, defined as such by his own admission before the judge of the Lund/Stevens case and to the Life reporters. He had written, but he had not totally convinced himself that he was a writer even as late as the Spring of that year. With the publication of Naked Lunch he could no longer avoid the demands of the profession which would now direct his life.

Burroughs went on to explore the cut-up method. It appealed to him as a method which could reproduce the spontaneity of Naked Lunch. The method promised new intellectual connections by simply cutting and rearranging the pieces of prose. It was also a technique similar to many experiments with film, music, and dance. Although that period of Burroughs' writing career is interesting, there is not room to explore it here.[104]

The book published in Paris now began to create subtle tremors in the legal and literary communities in the United States. The following chapters record its publication, reception, censorship and trial in the U.S.

Chapter 9

THE GROVE PRESS PUBLICATION

Grove Press was a maverick publishing house known for its unorthodox approach to the book business. [1] It was receptive to the literary avant-garde, and was interested in Burroughs' work for possible publication after excerpts appeared in Chicago Review and Big Table. Reflecting the depth of its interest in publishing Naked Lunch, Joel Sprayregen wrote to Grove's lawyer Charles Rembar with details of the censorship actions taken by the Post Office against Big Table. [2] The lawyer would not have written had the publisher not planned to publish the book, and considering those plans, information about the censorship of even a part of the book would be of great interest to Grove Press.

However, as soon as Maurice Girodias published an unexpurgated edition of Naked Lunch in Paris, Barney Rosset began to negotiate a contract for an American edition. On November 11, 1959, he sent a proposal to Girodias, who was acting as the author's agent in landing a U.S. contract. [3] Specifically, Rosset suggested a $2,500 advance against royalties of 10 percent of the first 5,000 hardbound texts sold, $12\frac{1}{2}$ percent to 10,000, and 15 percent over that figure. He also wanted to have the paperback rights.

The financial terms, however, standard, were not the element of the contract which most concerned Rosset. The record of Naked Lunch's legal encounter with the Post Office and Grove's suspicion of a U.S. Customs seizure of the Paris edition prompted the publisher to request that the warranty clause be left out of the contract. Such a clause is usually regarded as the author's guarantee of the legality of the work, i.e. the work does not contain any libelous, scandalous, or obscene material. Customarily the author agrees to pay the costs if the book is legally challenged, the charges made against royalty payments by the publisher. Any excess cost would be owed by the author. Because Grove Press felt that

the nature of the contents of the Burroughs book would make
its challenge in court inevitable, Rosset's suggestion to leave
out the warranty in this case provided a strong incentive to
the author to grant Grove the U.S. rights to the book.

Girodias responded rather quickly and excitedly to Rosset's proposal. [4] He expected some favorable publicity on
Burroughs to appear shortly in Life magazine. And in a subtle gesture to increase the demand for his product, he informed Rosset that he had already sold the rights to Naked
Lunch to French and German publishers. Saying that he
needed a very good American contract, he refused the gradu-
ated royalty scale which Rosset offered, in favor of a $17\frac{1}{2}$
percent royalty and an advance of $3,000. He explained that
the request was made because he felt that the appearance of
a U.S. edition would ruin the sale of his own English-language
French edition.

But again the money was not the essential issue; the
content of the American edition was. Girodias asked Rosset
if it was his intention to publish Burroughs' book with or without the sections that the author himself was prepared to drop
--"Hassan's Rumpus Room" and "A. J.'s Annual Party."
Considering the censorship situation in America, it was not a
simple decision for Rosset to make. Mindful of that, Girodias
nevertheless pushed for early publication. He suggested that
the book be out in the U.S. by Spring 1960, only a few months
away, and not the fall as Rosset mentioned. He finally informed Rosset that after they agreed, the actual contract
would be drawn up by Swiss literary agent Odette Hummel. [5]

Rosset sent his reply to Girodias' amended terms, explaining that it was his feeling that the only stumbling block
to Spring publication of Naked Lunch was Girodias himself. [6]
It was his understanding that before the present negotiations,
Olympia was in no hurry to have another English language
edition of the book because it had a rather large printing itself to sell, around 2,500 copies. [7] However, Rosset now
felt that the details could be worked out for a contract with
Grove Press, since Girodias had obviously changed his mind.

Rosset agreed to the $3,000 advance and the $17\frac{1}{2}$ per-
cent royalty, but only on those copies over 25,000. He offered instead 10 percent on the first 15,000; $12\frac{1}{2}$ percent after
that on softcover sales. The substantive item though, was not
money, but whether or not Rosset intended to publish an edition which contained the two so-called pornographic sections.

He told Girodias that he planned to delete the two, and challenged the Olympia publisher not to publicize his own edition
as the only complete or unexpurgated edition. [8]   Voicing his
own worst fear, he reminded Girodias that word of that sort
of textual difference travels fast and should be limited, if
possible, to allow the U. S. edition a chance to sell.   Rosset
assured Girodias that the time it would take him to come out
with a text would provide ample opportunity for Olympia to
sell many of their copies.

Like a well-seasoned angler, Girodias did not answer
immediately, but waited until he received another letter before he addressed the new terms.   He suggested to Rosset
that the book sell for $5.00 and that Burroughs receive a
15 percent royalty on the first 15,000 copies; $17\frac{1}{2}$ percent
above that.   On Rosset's suggestion for an unexpurgated
American edition, Girodias commented coyly:

> Well, I can't promise that the fact that my edition
> is complete and yours is expurgated can remain a
> secret, even if I refrain from advertising the fact
> ... But people discover those things, and journalists
> always like to appear well-informed, whether their
> information is relevant or not. [9]

He added optimistically that the decision to drop the questionable sections would eliminate the possibility of any legal trouble.   Nevertheless the offer to exclude the warranty clause
was valuable as well as welcome, and he reminded Rosset
that Odette Hummel in Geneva would handle the contract.

After the Christmas of 1959 Rosset agreed to most of
the terms and sent a draft contract to Girodias, asking that
he have it translated into French for Mme. Hummel. [10]   She
in turn drew up a contract in English and French, with slight
royalty modifications, and sent it to the U. S. for Rosset's
approval. [11]

Instead of a signed contract, he replied with nine suggested changes.   Most of his alterations dealt with the royalty
scales, payment dates, reduced royalty for "remaindered"
copies, and the payment of the advance in three installments.
However, two suggestions reflect Grove's need for some lee-
way with the book.   Hummel had asked that the book be issued within twelve months of the signing; Rosset wanted eighteen.   He also wanted the option of choosing whether or not to
include the two questionable sections.   This no doubt reflected

a slight change of heart after receiving the limp assurances on the matter from Girodias. [12]

In response Hummel suggested that the advance be paid half on signing, half two months later, instead of in three installments. She explained that this was according to Burroughs' direction, suggesting to Rosset that the author needed the money. [13] She agreed with the royalty, payment, and remaindering changes. She also extended the time limit to eighteen months as requested. Most important was her agreement to allow Grove the option of including the two sections.

Rosset agreed to the new terms, [14] and Hummel sent the final contract signed by Burroughs and herself for Rosset's signature on February 20, 1960. [15] However, on receipt of the contract Rosset noticed that Hummel had added a clause calling for the publisher to guarantee to fight and pay for any legal case the book might incur. Grove was willing to relieve the author from such an obligation, but it was not willing to go that far itself. Grove crossed out the qualification saying that it must be allowed the freedom to decide whether or not to take appropriate legal action in defense of Naked Lunch. They also amended the publication rights provisions to assure Grove's retention of those rights should the book be legally proscribed. [17]

In spite of those qualifications, Burroughs was himself excited by the prospect of an American edition of the book--a development he assumed would not take place for many years, if at all. Although he was convinced at that time that Grove Press would only publish an expurgated version in the U.S., and he was not even remotely aware of the publication date, the signing of the contract was the kind of good news he rushed to share with Paul Bowles. [18]

Rosset and his staff began their preparations for publication, though they suspected that Naked Lunch had been seized by the U.S. Customs Service. The book had of course gained an audience following the publication of excerpts in both Chicago Review and Big Table. Nevertheless, Rosset felt the controversial subject matter of the text and Burroughs' idiosyncratic, often impenetrable style required an explanatory introduction for the more general reader. The publisher wrote to John Ciardi, asking him to write an introduction for Grove's forthcoming edition. [19] Considering the role the poet played in the Big Table struggle, the choice

was wise and logical. However, Ciardi regretted that he must
refuse the offer because of previous publishing commitments. [20]
The idea of using another writer to introduce the book was
soon dropped because Burroughs himself wanted the opportunity
to do the job himself. He was fed up with the misconceptions
beginning to surface about his book. Along with a prefatory
note of his own he explained to Grove, "I mean I get tired of
people telling me they lost their lunch reading my Lunch."[21]

Aside from obtaining introductory material, the most
immediate problem facing the publisher was editing and
proofreading the text. Considering Burroughs' unique
spelling, syntax, and style, this was no routine task. The
proofreaders of the Olympia Press edition had "corrected"
some dialect spellings and constructions which also had to be
restored. The former editor of the Chicago Review, Irving
Rosenthal, was chosen for the job. Allen Ginsberg also
helped. By July 18, 1960, Rosenthal had been paid for sixty
hours of editing and proofreading work. [22] Late that month
Burroughs wrote to Rosenthal to clarify some questions concerning spellings, foreign words, and textual additions. [23]
Regarding the format of the U. S. edition, Burroughs told him
that the form of the Olympia edition was the way the text took
shape and that it should remain that way. He did not want
the text altered, nor did he want additional spacial interrup-
tions or chapter headings which Rosenthal had suggested.
However, he did like the suggestion that the article "Deposition: Testimony Concerning a Sickness" be included in an
appendix. In addition Burroughs wanted to include some of
his own illustrations, inspired by the calligraphy of Brion
Gysin, and placed between the main text and the appendix. [24]

Ginsberg, who had been working with Rosenthal, read
the author's letter, and on July 29, 1960, he wrote to him
with some comments, advice, and suggestions. [25] He urged
that the material Rosenthal wanted to add be allowed to be
set in type so that Burroughs could look at them and approve
their inclusion. After all, Ginsberg reasoned, the additions
could always be eliminated from the galley proofs at no cost.
Only additions to the galleys cost money. Including the additions cost nothing.

Ginsberg also urged Burroughs to allow the spacial
breaks and chapter headings to be added. But he did not like
the idea of including the "deposition" essay. He argued that
not only would it detrimentally alter the dramatic impact of
the end of the book, but it was also available elsewhere in the

Evergreen Review and in a forthcoming collection of essays
by and on Beat writers. [26] To bring about a quick resolution
to this and other issues regarding the American edition of
Naked Lunch, Ginsberg included a questionnaire for Burroughs
to check either yes or no on the unresolved points.

Burroughs answered Ginsberg's questions right away by
filling in the appropriate blanks and writing a letter of explanation. [27] He agreed with all but one of his friend's suggestions, the deletion of the essay. Not only did he want the
essay included, but he wanted to include a cut-up of it, the
way he had intended the essay to appear in Evergreen Review. [28]

In early August Burroughs sent a copy of the completed
questionnaire to Grove Press editor Richard Seaver, directing
him to contact Allen Ginsberg for further details. He wanted,
too, some clarification on their decision to publish the book
in expurgated or unexpurgated form. [29] That decision, however, was complicated by the formal seizure of the French
edition by the U.S. Customs late that month. [30]

The speed with which the American publication of
Burroughs' book progressed was unexpectedly affected by
another development. Henry Miller, whose books had been
banned since the thirties, suddenly decided to sign a contract
with Grove Press for an American edition of Tropic of Cancer.
Though his decision was not formally announced until April
1961, it had been made months before. [31] Miller's choice
startled the literary community which had assumed that if
Tropic of Cancer were ever published in the U.S. it would be
done with Laughlin's New Directions. A factor turning Miller
to Rosset may have been Maurice Girodias, whose father Jack
Kahane published the book in Paris in 1934.

In spite of the complications caused by Miller's decision,
Burroughs was anxious to receive the galley proofs of his own
so that he could see the changes and additions both Rosenthal
and Ginsberg had made. [32] The proofs were sent to him in
early 1961. [33]

Miller was to enter the promotion of Naked Lunch as
well. In gathering testimonials for the book, Rosset received
one from Girodias which did not appear on the dust jacket or
in advertising flyers. On December 8, 1960, Miller had
written Girodias that he found Naked Lunch boring, adding
that the Marquis de Sade bored him too. Nevertheless Miller

did acknowledge Burroughs' unquestionable talent as a writer. 34

It was not Miller's lack of enthusiasm for the book,
but the imminent publication of his own which forced Rosset
to postpone the publication of Naked Lunch in the U.S. until
after Tropic of Cancer was in print. 35 Throughout the spring
and into the summer of 1961, Girodias pressured Rosset,
urging him to issue Burroughs' book quickly. 36 Finally in
September Rosset cabled the French publisher that plans to
publish Naked Lunch that fall were going forward.

A five-page publicity flyer was drawn up announcing
the October 31, 1961, publication of Burroughs' book at the
relatively high list price of $6.00. The text of the flyer con-
tained praise from Norman Mailer, Jack Kerouac, Robert
Lowell, John Ciardi; Burroughs' autobiographical introduction
from Junkie; and parts of Alan Ansen's anecdotal sketch published in A Casebook on the Beat. 37

But the shadow of Henry Miller would again affect the
publication of Naked Lunch. For the first few months of the
summer of 1961 shortly after it was published, Tropic of
Cancer sold so briskly that it was listed sixth for the entire
year on the Best Seller list. 38 By the end of the summer,
however, ominous events dampened any euphoria over the
book's future. Brentano's and Doubleday refused to carry it
in their shops, and the Chicago Tribune refused to print its
title in its list of best sellers. 39 Then legal actions against
Tropic of Cancer were initiated in Boston and Dallas. Out
of fear that pirate editions would soon appear to fill the
vacuum created by the book bans, Rosset rushed a paperback
edition into print by October 10, 1961. 40

Another event occurred during the fall of 1961 to delay
the publication of Naked Lunch in addition to the censorship
of Miller's novel. As a student at Harvard in the 1930's,
Burroughs wrote a scatological satire of F. D. R. 's administrative appointments, complete with officials with names like
"Transvestite Lizzie--Congressional Librarian" and "Lonny
the Pimp--Ambassador at Large. " In October 1961 it was
published under the title "Routine: Roosevelt After Inaugura-
tion" in Floating Bear #9 edited by LeRoi Jones and Diane
diPrima. Two Postal Inspectors and an FBI agent arrested
Jones for sending obscene material through the mail on October
18, 1961. 41 He was brought before a grand jury where he
testified for two days, reading for hours everything from

Ulysses to Catullus and other works which had been labeled
"obscene" at one time or another.   Since the grand jury refused to return an indictment, the case never went to court
and was dropped.

By the end of October, partially because of the action
against the Burroughs story in Floating Bear #9, Grove had
once more postponed the publication of Naked Lunch.   The
legal actions against Miller's book also made publication of
Naked Lunch an extremely risky venture.   In a very short
time Grove Press was beseiged with court actions against
Miller's book.   Over fifty cases were initiated across the
United States, making it impossible for Grove's attorney,
Charles Rembar to exercise his role as trial lawyer in each
instance. 42   Out of necessity he prepared a general legal
packet for use in defending the book.   Because the obscenity
action against Tropic of Cancer was so widespread, Publisher's Weekly concluded:

> The year 1961 saw a reversal--perhaps only
> temporary--of the trend toward freedom from
> censorship for serious works of literature ...
> despite favorable anti-censorship precedents at
> the federal level, a book can be banned effectively
> in large portions of the United States. 43

In the eyes of Grove Press, the actions against Floating Bear
#9 and Tropic of Cancer provided enough evidence of the trend
toward increased censorship and prompted their delay in the
publication of Burroughs' book.   In accepting Miller's book,
Grove had decided to go to court with any bookdealer arrested
for selling it.   It proved to be a terribly expensive policy,
bringing the publishing firm to the brink of financial collapse. 44
The legal fees they had incurred made them quite cautious in
their handling of any new book which promised to add to their
financial and legal burden like Naked Lunch.

Girodias did not understand Rosset's reasons for in-
vesting so much money and effort in the defense of the Miller
book.   Personally he wanted him to publish Naked Lunch as
soon as possible. 45   Rosset tried to explain to him that he
had to indemnify the booksellers against criminal arrests for
selling copies of the book.   If he did not provide such assurances, he believed, no one would handle the book at all for
fear of going to jail. 46   The recent refusal by Doubleday and
Brentanos to stock the Miller book was fresh on his mind.
He reasoned that the investment was necessary, and that the

legal problem had to be addressed because if it were not, then the same resistance by retail book stores would surely happen to Burroughs' Naked Lunch.

Burroughs, on the other hand, was more understanding of the need for a publication delay than was Girodias, who was squeezed for operating funds by his new restaurant venture in Paris. Burroughs wrote to Rosset in December:

> I am sorry to see the differences between you and Girodias take such an acrimonious turn--My own position remains clear and unchanged: I agree with you that it is not practical to publish Naked Lunch at this time in America. I feel it is most important to put the Novia [sic] Express first as preparation [sic]. I feel that you are the only logical publisher for Naked Lunch in America. Of course, Girodias's impatience is understandable. [47]

Grove Press placed Naked Lunch on a back burner, and Burroughs went ahead with preparations for the publication of Nova Express.

Rosset again wrote to Girodias on January 31, 1962 to try to convince him that the delay was necessary. [48]

By the summer of 1962 Burroughs was back in Paris and thirty or forty pages into a new book which he said contained "scenes and concepts more 'obscene' than anything in Naked Lunch."[49] He wrote to Rosset concerning the progress of the publication of his books.

He replied that he intended to publish Nova Express early in 1963. He added that he had scheduled Naked Lunch for late 1962 or January 1963 because of the recent favorable decisions in court on Tropic of Cancer which relieved some of the censorship pressure on sexually candid works. [50]

In August 1962 Burroughs was invited to participate in the Edinburgh Writer's Conference. He saw the conference as an opportunity to provide some valuable publicity. [51] However, he was not moved to go to Scotland by the promise of publicity alone, rather he was "principally motivated by all expenses paid and [the] prospect of seeing twenty-five Cuban writers who are scheduled to appear."[52] The publicity generated there would accelerate Rosset's plans to publish Naked Lunch.

Chapter 10

WRITERS' CONFERENCE, CONTROVERSY, AN EDITION IN PRINT

In Edinburgh, Scotland on August 20, 1962, a five-day conference devoted to literature, organized by British publisher John Calder, began in McEwan Hall on the University campus.[1] It was part of the Edinburgh Arts Festival, and attracted an audience of around two thousand.

The standing of the novel was the topic of discussion at the opening session. Mary McCarthy, in her efforts to assess the American novel, asserted that the national novel was dying. She qualified her statement by saying that she did not wish to suggest that there was nothing going on in the American novel. On the contrary, in her opinion a great deal was happening in narrative fiction. She explained that Bellow, Malamud, and Updike were examples of the American tendency toward autobiography, self-examination, and childhood regression.

She then began to discuss the books she had read recently in which she found excitement, curiosity, and even displeasure. Such novels indicated to her that something was happening. Among the books she cited were Nabokov's Lolita and William Burroughs' Naked Lunch. McCarthy admitted that even though they were radically different books, both were examples of the novel at some international level, reflecting what she described as conditions of exile and statelessness. To her these conditions not only provided a new subject for the novel, but also characterized the future of humanity. She predicted that the subject might appear as grotesque mass tourism, or be fictionally rendered as an aimless roaming across the face of the earth.

Her mention of Burroughs signaled the first attention paid his work by the world literary community. Most members of the audience were unaware of his book. Such high

praise from McCarthy of an unknown work by an unknown writer created a stir in the audience and among the conference
participants, [2] and promised to erase Burroughs' anonymity as
a writer.

In a not too subtle criticism of McCarthy's praise of
Naked Lunch, David Daiches lectured:

> Now this is the only communion possible you see,
> [a] cocktail party turned into the ritual of communion,
> if you can get a swollen up cocktail party. I think
> that most modern novels in America have been con-
> cerned not with lunches, but with the smallest cock-
> tail party. [3]

Colin McInnes observed that "Henry Miller crossed perhaps
with Algernon Charles Swinburne was the daddy of William
Burroughs. "[4]

The state of Scottish writing was the topic of discussion on the second day of the conference, Tuesday, August
21.   The rather bland discussion erupted into a shouting match
between Alexander Trocchi and Hugh MacDiarmid. [5] According
to one press account of the session, the rowdiness was caused
in part at least by a carafe of whiskey on the dais.[6]

The next session on Wednesday was led by Norman
Mailer.   The topic was the writer and commitment.   The
shouting match of the day before acted as a catalyst, pro-
ducing loose alliances of spirit at the conference--the younger,
less established writers challenging the conservative, established ones.

Mary McCarthy presided over the Thursday, August
23rd discussion.   The topic, censorship, promised to be one
on which every writer could agree, since censorship represents
the antithesis of written expression.

After a Dutch and a German publisher spoke on the
topic, Williams S. Burroughs was introduced so that he could
add his thoughts on censorship. [7] In his opinion the nature
of censorship depended heavily on who exercised the control.
He explained that in the middle ages it was the Church against
heresy; in communist countries, the government against politics.   But the worst form, according to Burroughs, occurred
"in English speaking countries [where] the weight of censorship
falls on sexual word and image. "[8]

The writer then called into question the right of any government to decide what people should think, even under the often invoked excuse that such actions were taken to protect impressionable children. He considered that excuse false because they were already exposed to a daily barrage of images calculated to arouse desires through radio, T. V., movies, and comic strips. Asking rhetorically what the removal of all censorship would do, he asserted, "not very much."[9] But he went on to qualify his statement by saying that the removal of censorship could result in the creation of an atmosphere in which serious, scientific investigation of human sexuality could exist. He noted that Wilhelm Reich had tried to study the subject scientifically, but was rewarded with the indignity of dying in a Federal prison while serving a sentence as a quack.

After the comments of several other writers including Norman Mailer, Mary McCarthy asked Burroughs to elaborate on his idea of the vested interest of the censor. She wanted him to clarify for her exactly why he felt the capitalistic world chose to suppress books dealing with sex over other topics. She suggested that the monogamous marriage represented to the modern mind the force which held the world together, as religion held the medieval world together. Burroughs agreed with her observations, and he added that sexual censorship was indeed complicated, and involved the channeling of the sex drive into the making and buying of consumer goods. Advertising, he said, had just these goals at its core.

Mailer added:

> I think if there is any cause I would fight for to the very end, it is precisely to fight censorship, and a book would have to be meritricious in the extreme before I would feel it was at all honorable not to fight for it.[10]

In his stand against censorship, Mailer had pulled a punch.

Several other writers commented. Then Maurice Girodias spoke on the topic. He was there by virtue of his reputation as the publisher of many censored books. He said that censorship was like the tip of an iceberg. Its presence was an indication of a vast amount of repression beneath. According to the Paris publisher of Naked Lunch, the real danger of censorship was the intolerance of diversity manifested in the social conformity in the West, as well as in the communist East.

The future of the novel was the discussion topic for the last day of the conference, Friday, August 24, 1962. The session was chaired by several writers including Mailer and McCarthy. And the first speaker asserted that James Hogg's Confessions of a Justified Sinner was as much a part of the new novel as the "junkie sex novel which is very much the American novel of the present ... Certainly when one is talking about future of the novel, one is not looking forward to an eternity of novels about drug addiction."[11] He did not consider the drug addiction theme as the determining factor for future novels because it explored new states of consciousness rather than new forms of consciousness. His comments were a clear rejection of the praise which had been given at the conference to Burroughs' Naked Lunch.

After several other speakers, Mary McCarthy vehemently defended the American novel against the charge leveled by the first speaker that it was strictly a junkie-sex novel. She listed Faulkner, Bellow, Mailer, Updike, Malamud, Capote, and Salinger as exceptions, and defended the attack on Burroughs by praising Naked Lunch as "some kind of study of free totalitarianism."[12]

David Daiches spoke after Alexander Trocci, Stephen Spender, and Norman Mailer. The novel, in his opinion, had a future because it had the power to illuminate human experience. He predicted that the novel would absorb more of the techniques of poetry and drama. As far as the subject matter was concerned, he felt that "much more interesting things [were] going on than junkies and sex."[13] The novel born out of the middle class, he asserted, would focus on "problems which are much more concerned with the anguish of the individual in society than with the comforts provided by society to the individual."[14]

After Daiches sat down, Mailer, in introducing the next speaker, quipped that drugs and sex were indeed fit subjects for the novel. The next speaker was William S. Burroughs, and he began by telling the writers gathered in McEwan Hall that in his writing he was acting as a mapmaker, an explorer of psychic areas. Mentioning man's steps into space, he said,

> If writers are to travel in space/time and explore areas opened by the space age, I think they must develop techniques quite as new and definite as the techniques of physical space travel.[15]

He explained that he was doing just that in his own writing. His technique was an extension of the cut-up method developed by Brion Gysin, a close friend of Burroughs' and a contemporary painter. He called the technique the fold-in method, and said it was designed to extend the limits of choice open to the writer. He then explained how the fold-in method worked for the audience,

> a page of text, my own or someone else's is folded down the middle and placed on another page. The composite text is then read across, half one text and half the other. [16]

The result is then edited as any other page of text. The best results were obtained, Burroughs added, when he used pages dealing with similar subjects. Anticipating misunderstandings, he added that the technique might be useful to some writers in some instances, and not for others.

An Indian writer startled by the content of Burroughs' remarks demanded, "Are you being serious?"[17] Burroughs replied, "Of course."[18]

Mailer, who had taken over as moderator, took advantage of the interruption to say:

> Out of respect for what I consider your vast talent and because you have not taken much trouble to speak before, we are going to break the rule in your case ... and we are going to give you an extra five minutes. [19]

In his concluding comments Burroughs said that his current work was concerned with the survival of the human race and with exposing social criminals. Colin McInnes followed with his feeling that the novel was strong because of the great diversity of forms. He urged the audience to make an effort to inform themselves of the art, or nonrealistic, or experimental novel; and to consider it an obligation to obtain some of the works of Henry Miller, Norman Mailer, and William Burroughs.

During a discussion session which followed, Stephen Spender asked if Burroughs' technique was similar to something a rocket maker might be doing. In his opinion the fold-in method sounded more like medieval magic than modern science. Burroughs explained that his method was similar to

the flash-backs in a film, and nothing "so vague as any analogy between rocket makers."[20] He reiterated that the same
method had been used in music and film for years.

Mailer and others asked about the technique. It appeared to Burroughs that they had overestimated the degree
of arbitrariness in his method. He assured them that it was
not as arbitrary as it sounded, but he could not demonstrate
it for them because it was after all "a technique and like all
techniques, something to experiment with, something to do,
rather than something to talk about."[21]

A member of the audience informed Burroughs that an
experiment had been performed in which the sonnets of Shakespeare were recorded on tape, the tape cut up, the pieces
spliced together at random, and the result, recorded by a
stenographer, was simply printed. He then asked if Burroughs considered the experiment serious, because to him it
was nothing more than a mix-up. Burroughs replied cautiously, "I would consider it an interesting experiment. It would
depend entirely on the results."[22] The session ended after
some comments by McCarthy, and Mailer closed the 1962 International Writers' Conference in Edinburgh with the hope
that the writers would all get together the next year.

The New York Times Book Review columnist Raymond
Walters, Jr. discussed Burroughs since he had become the
topic of debate at the conference. Walters made the following
remarks about the author whose Naked Lunch was yet to be
published in the United States:

> At Edinburgh, when Norman Mailer joined Mary Mc-
> Carthy in proclaiming William Burroughs the writer
> of this century who'd most deeply affected the literari
> cognoscenti, the hall was drenched in puzzled silence.
> No one present, it seemed, had ever heard of Bur-
> roughs.
>   It would have been almost--though not quite--the
> same in this country ... He's long been living in
> such places as Paris and Mexico and now occupies
> a position roughly comparable to that of Henry Mil-
> ler before the war. His fellow countrymen know
> him only as the author of "the Naked Lunch" and
> other Paris-published works whose spicy content
> raises the gorge of the customs officials and other
> keepers of American morals.[23]

Walters' comments reflected approval of the book by the literary community, not merely of the book itself, but of its
stand against restricted expression. Any work praised by
respected writers would find its champions if it were banned.

In addition to the recognition Burroughs received, the
conference also resolved Barney Rosset's problem of publishing the United States edition of Naked Lunch either expurgated, or unexpurgated; or at all. Now that Burroughs
had won the support of Mailer and McCarthy, he would risk
the almost certain censorship of an unexpurgated edition.
The writers gave credibility to both the subject matter and
the style of Naked Lunch, something Allen Ginsberg's years
of promotion had not been totally successful in obtaining.
Burroughs emerged from the Edinburgh conference as a writer
able to chronicle the chaos and flux perceived to be the human
condition following the concentration camps and atomic bombs
of World War II. He was seen by his supporters as a serious, well-informed, and unhysterical novelist who having returned from hell, was back to tell us all.

In an effort to capitalize on the favorable publicity,
Rosset pushed for early publication. On September 19, 1962,
while attending the book fair in Frankfurt, Rosset cabled
Milton Perlman at the New York office, asking for a publication date for Naked Lunch. The next day Perlman replied
that Burroughs' book would be out on November 15, 1962. [24]

The date of publication confirmed, Grove Press turned
to the physical preparation of the text. The New England
printer who had produced the American edition of Lady Chatterley's Lover, Halliday Lithograph Corporation, promised to
be a logical choice for printing the text. An order was sent
out, [25] but much to Grove's astonishment, the firm's owner,
Russel Halliday wrote on October 11, 1962:

> We are in receipt of your print order for Naked
> Lunch by Bunngus [sic]. This order I am returning
> as I will not allow my name to be associated with
> this type of literature for reproduction in my
> plant. [26]

Undaunted by Halliday's refusal, Rosset contracted with the
Book Press in Brattleboro, Vermont to print Naked Lunch.
This company had done work for Grove before--Tropic of
Cancer. Reflecting Rosset's caution, the agreement with this
printer included a clause which indemnified the company in
the event of legal action. [27]

Grove Press also made efforts to convince a book club to include the Burroughs book as a selection, and drew a response from Lionel Trilling, who was with Mid-Century Book Club at the time. Trilling described the text as one that he did not personally admire, or one that he thought his subscribers should admire. However, it was a book they might want to read, he felt, because several people thought it to be a work of genius, and because it was sure to be widely discussed. [28]

The publication date had been moved up, and Rosset circulated a flyer on October 30, 1962, announcing to booksellers that Naked Lunch would be published on November 20, 1962. This flyer contained the praise of other writers found in previous publicity material, but this one also included part of Julius J. Hoffman's opinion which reversed the postal ban on the excerpts in Big Table. In addition, a sixteen-page pamphlet containing reviews and excerpts from the book accompanied the flyer. A post script on the flyer from Rosset reflected his anticipation of a series of court battles similar to the ones which greeted Tropic of Cancer the previous fall:

> One more word about censorship. You know best what the situation is in your area and we would advise you to exercise your own discretion. Should you nevertheless run into any censorship problems, we may be able to lend information and advice, although we will not be able to bear legal expenses. Naturally, we reserve the right to use our discretion in distribution of Naked Lunch. [29]

The book was published on November 20, 1962, in the United States. It had been anticipated for more than three years. It sold briskly; through March 14, 1963, 14,236 copies were purchased. [46] Critical reception in newspapers and literary magazines was extensive and diverse.

Chapter 11

CRITICAL RECEPTION

The publication of Naked Lunch in the United States had
been anticipated by some critics as either the death knell of
civilized man, or the next step in the progress of the English
novel beyond Joyce. Burroughs' book was perceived as excellent or deplorable. Its coming had been anticipated since Allen Ginsberg dedicated Howl to Burroughs with the dramatic
warning that Naked Lunch was "an endless novel which would
drive everyone mad. "[1]

It was also seen as literature brutally manhandled by
repressive forces at The University of Chicago and by the
U.S. Post Office because it discussed sex candidly. Grove
Press publisher Barney Rosset had fought heroicly to erase
the social and criminal associations of such discussions in
print. It took a great commitment for Rosset to buck a legal
and literary establishment whose knee-jerk response was a
prudish rejection of printed sexual discussion.

The reception of the book in this country, however,
began shortly after it was published in Paris, and undoubtedly
helped create a great deal of anticipation for its American
edition. The laudatory extreme appeared in early 1961 in a
literary magazine published by a small liberal arts college
located on Staten Island, New York. In spite of its unembar-
rassed shower of praise, the article demonstrates the excitement Burroughs' work generated:

> To date there have been less than one hundred pages
> of William Burroughs' writings published in this
> country ... and yet his reputation as an artist is
> unparalleled among those who know his work. And
> this high opinion is held over a wide segment of the
> literary spectrum--from Allen Ginsberg to John
> Ciardi to Alfred Kazin and higher frequencies. Now
> the publication of The Naked Lunch definitely estab-

lishes Burroughs as America's greatest prose writer
to appear since the War.... In fact, to be fair to
Burroughs, The Naked Lunch is somewhere up there
with Huckleberry Finn and the other stars of our
galaxy.[2]

If one were not aware of the limits of Burroughs' style, the
undisguised hyperbole might fall into the same category as
Whitman's own reviews of his 1855 edition of Leaves of Grass.
However, the exaggeration aside, the article indicates the
anticipation of a major book.

After the Chicago hearing of Big Table John Ciardi had
said as much in his Saturday Review column; and in Advertisements for Myself Norman Mailer expressed his anticipation of the finished book after seeing the same excerpts:

> the excerpts in Big Table were more interesting I
> thought, than anything I've read by an American in
> years. If the rest of William Burroughs' book is
> equal to what was shown and if the novel proves to
> be a novel and not a collage of extraordinary frag-
> ments, then Burroughs will deserve rank as one of
> the most important novelists in America and may
> prove comparable in his impact to Jean Genet.[3]

Mailer's support did not diminish, though the book in its final
form did have the collage effect he had feared. Not only did
he praise Naked Lunch at Edinburgh, but also responded favorably to a Grove Press request for a statement on the book.
His now well-known assessment that Burroughs was "the only
American novelist living today who may conceivably be possessed by genius" appeared in a sixteen-page publicity booklet,
along with other testimonials from Terry Southern, E. S.
Seldon, Robert Lowell, Jack Kerouac, and John Ciardi.

Seldon announced that the publication of Naked Lunch
in the United States signaled "one of the most impressive
literary debuts of the past century."[4] Southern concluded,
"It is safe to add that for the new generation of American
writers the work of William Burroughs is by far the most
seriously influential being done today."[5] Ciardi said Burroughs "is a writer of great power and artistic integrity engaged in a profoundly meaningful search for true values."[6]
And Jack Kerouac called him "the greatest satirical writer
since Jonathan Swift."[7] Robert Lowell called Naked Lunch
"one of the most alive books written by any American for
years."[8]

The publicity, the censorship, and the subject matter of the book excited the anticipation of its American publication. The repressive atmosphere toward sexual candor in print had cleared significantly in the year and one-half of Kennedy's Camelot. For better or worse, the literary community found itself obliged to defend any book against the charge of censorship if it possessed the slightest literary value. William S. Burroughs' Naked Lunch would test that commitment. The book would test it more profoundly than did Miller's books or the Fanny Hill reissue for the simple reason that sections of Naked Lunch made sex a grotesque example of desire, often turning into scenes of cannibalism. The lunch was indeed naked.

After Grove published the book in late November 1962, it was reviewed in major newspapers and magazines. On November 20 the reviewer at The New York Times noted its prior publication in Paris and observed caustically, "it is somewhat barnacled with notoriety."[9] He mentioned the stir Burroughs caused at the Writer's Conference, and conceded that the praise it was given made it important. However, he was disturbed by the literary trend which he thought it signaled:

> The book's general format is banal, as it should be I suppose, to provide a meeting ground for the insufferable sinner and the insufferable prig. To avoid both, I advise avoiding the book.[10]

This first critical evaluation of Naked Lunch by a nonsympathizer was a cautious rejection of the highly praised volume. It was symptomatic of the underlying split in the literary community's attitude toward the book. Hints of it had appeared during the postal hearing, for example, when Lionel Trilling agreed to support the legal rights of the material in Big Table without conceding its literary importance. The Times review that Tuesday suggested the importance of the book as a literary event, not as literature. The Sunday reviews were to follow, however.

Herbert Gold, who reviewed the book for the Sunday New York Times Book Review, was not as dismayed by the appearance of the book as the daily reviewer. While not quite the bold praise found in the publicity material circulated by the publisher, Gold's review admired Burroughs' ability to handle the "black humor of addiction" which was alien "to that evolution of characters and actions within society which is traditional to the novel."[11]

The same Sunday Richard Kluger, general editor of
books at the now defunct New York Herald Tribune, also noted
the absence of the traditional elements of plot, character,
time, and place in Burroughs' book. He suggested that such
concerns did not matter in Naked Lunch, observing, "What
matters as in all abstract art are the effects created, and
Burroughs' effects are stunning. He is a writer of rare
power. "[12]

On the West Coast, Curt Gentry noted that the long
build-up before publication worked against Naked Lunch as
far as he was concerned. He acknowledged that the publicity
could have distorted his sense of balance and that the praise
could inevitably result in disappointment. He had also read
the excerpts in Big Table and found them "disgusting. "[13]
Against such formidable odds, Naked Lunch would have to be
quite a book. He admitted, "It is. "[14] Responding to the
charge that the book was hardcore pornography, he asserted
that the contrast was striking because "Naked Lunch portrays
a world where the epitome of pleasure is relief. "[15]

Criticism in the national news magazines was mixed.
Newsweek mentioned the notoriety of the book, the controversy
generated at Edinburgh, the charge of pornography, and the
defense of parts as Swiftian satire. Its praise was qualified:

> It is indeed a masterpiece, but a totally insane and
> anarchic one, and it can only be diminished by at-
> tempts to give it any social purpose or value what-
> ever. [16]

But without a demonstration of the book's social value, it
would most certainly be banned in the face of obscenity law
violations.

By contrast the praise was not qualified in Newsweek's
chief competitor, Time; it was non-existent. The reviewer
linked Burroughs to the Beat movement which was described
as a failed, almost ludicrous experiment. He discounted the
praise given at the Writer's Conference and its record of
censorship as elements unrelated to the worth of the book itself. He did admit grudgingly that the book commanded attention for the simple reason that Burroughs knew what he was
talking about. The review then included the following, rather
sensational synopsis of Burroughs' life gleaned from fact and
from rumor:

> Chairbound souls, however, we'd put up with a lot
> from an author who had been there and back, wheth-
> er 'there' is the top of Everest or the depths of the
> soul. Burroughs has been there, all right; he is
> not only an ex-junkie but an ex-con and by accident
> a killer. In Mexico, having acquired a wife, he
> shot her between the eyes playing William Tell with
> a revolver. (The Mexican authorities decided it was
> imprudentia criminale and dropped the whole matter.)
> He has even been in the army but not for long; he
> reacted to being drafted by cutting off a finger joint,
> and was discharged with the notation 'not to be re-
> called or reclassified.'[17]

The personal attack, calling him an "ex-con" and a "killer,"
prompted a quick response from Burroughs. At the time he
was living in England, and he obtained council in order to
sue Time for libel. In March of 1963 a suit was filed with
the Queen's Bench Division of the High Court of Justice in
London. The court eventually ruled in Burroughs' favor, but
it was a pale victory for him. Time deposited the "con-
temptuous sum of five pounds five shillings (about $30.00 at
the time) with the court for damages to Burroughs."[18] He
took the sum from the court in January 1964 which terminated
the law suit. At the time he tried to read a statement in
open court, but the judge refused permission. Burroughs had
beaten the magazine, but at the cost of an insulting judgment,
reflecting what the court deemed the value of the damage to
the writer's reputation.

The Queen's Bench decision was not the only bad news
to come from England. One of the angry young men of the
1950s, novelist John Wain, reviewed Naked Lunch for New Republic in an extensive article. He compared the book to Os-
sian and Peyton Place, books "whose interest lies not in their
own qualities but in the reception given to them in their own
time."[19] He dismissed it as the "merest trash, not worth
a second glance," not because it was an obscene book, but
because it was "unreservedly on the side of death," while
even a pornographic novel was on "the side of something
describable as life."[20]

Wain's blanket rejection brought a quick reaction from
Richard Kostelanetz, critic of contemporary American literature and one of the few who consistently defended the writer
in the critical debate. He blasted Wain as an important avant-
garde figure for affirming the British literary establishment

which he had challenged only ten years before. In his opinion
the belief in and the rigorous defense of the need for an af-
firmative art, the superiority of the clean experience, and
everyday notions of the Good Life in criticizing Naked Lunch
disqualified Wain "from saying anything significant about the
new in modern literature."[21] On the other hand Kostelanetz
found the book to be Kafkaesque in its capacity to communicate the simultaneity of terror and comedy. Naked Lunch,
he felt, was truly exciting and original.

George Siegel called Wain's position "the most errant
philistinism."[22] He noted that he had rejected the book because other critics overestimated it, and concluded, "such
overestimation is a fact of our time and Mr. Wain's reputation as a novelist is surely an instance of it."[23] Kay Boyle,
however, sided with Wain in rejecting Naked Lunch. She
asked rhetorically:

> By what odd combination of circumstances and de-
> fenses had Naked Lunch become the yardstick for
> measuring critical acumen? Who in the world is
> afraid of Naked Lunch? Kafka, despite Mr. Koste-
> lanetz's insistence would never have got beyond
> the first page.[24]

Florence Howe, on the other hand, considered the book favorably not just as a statement against drugs, but also as an
"anti-Utopian anti-novel."[25] For her the ultimate horror of
Burroughs' vision of homosexual sex was in its relation to
death and the omission of birth through reproduction. In
short the book was a vivid depiction of moral, political, sexual,
and intellectual annihilation.

The Wain article exposed a raw nerve in the literary
community. Although the battle lines were not clearly defined,
they were nevertheless present. For its supporters who found
it to be serious literature; it was a funny, dirty book. For
others, it was just a dirty book. Drug addiction, death, and
homosexuality were not new themes, but no other book had
combined the three in a coalescence of black humor as did
Naked Lunch.

In a review for Commentary, Alfred Chester articulated
the quandary Naked Lunch presented to the intellectual community. Personally he felt that the course of the contemporary
novel had previously abandoned any attempt "to decide what is
good in a universe in which all things are equal and equal to

nothing. "[26] He cited the French novelists as examples of
that theory and compared Burroughs to them by saying, "Burroughs is actually Robbe-Grillet without tears. "[27] Far from
continued praise, however, the rest of his review is filled
with biting criticism, and contrary to Mailer's opinion, Chester did not consider the book to be a work of genius. Rather,
the first half was readable without skipping, and the last half
was skippable without reading.

The reviewer for New Statesmen confessed his confusion over the notoriety and praise given to Burroughs by
Mailer and McCarthy. He admitted he was unable to understand it because no one had provided a key to the work. It
was a work that was in his opinion "largely devoid of either
positive merits or interesting faults. "[28] He felt the book was
not innovative, but insipid, and nothing more than a "hunk of
raw, bleeding verbiage, " adding, "I find it hard to fathom
what quirk led Mary McCarthy to praise The Naked Lunch. "[29]

David Malcolm, in The New Yorker, dismissed the
claim that Naked Lunch was commendable because of its innovative structure. He scoffed, "The work ... has so little
structure, being a mere hectic accumulation of anecdotes and
fantasies, that it might as fittingly been issued in a paper
bag as between hard covers. "[30] The interest and importance
of the book lay in it as a raw document of personal history.
Malcolm was perplexed by the claim that the so-called pornographic sections were intended as a tract against capital punishment. He admitted difficulty in determining the exact sections meant to be Swiftian satire, settling on the hanging sequences in "A. J. 's Annual Party. " As satire in the "A
Modest Proposal" tradition, they missed the target. Con-
trasting Swift and Burroughs, the reviewer felt the latter "so
emphatically bent on making horror stark upon the page that
he accomplished little else. "[31] Finally he ridiculed the prose
style by holding up a sentence from Naked Lunch and one from
Edgar Rice Burroughs for unflattering comparison.

At this time a newspaper strike in New York City
helped to split the literary community. A new publication
emerged to fill the vacuum left by the struck dailies. The
New York Review of Books appeared in the absence of The
New York Times Book Review, and would soon compete with,
and eventually replace it as the standard literary periodical in
the United States. In its premier issue, Burroughs' Naked
Lunch was reviewed by Mary McCarthy. Her admiration for
the book had not flagged in the months following the Writer's
Conference, and in her review she praised the book,

> The best comparison for the book with its aerial
> sex acts performed on a high trapeze, its con men
> and barkers, its arena like form, is in fact a cir-
> cus. A circus travels but it is always the same, and
> this is Burroughs' sardonic image of modern life. [32]

She also compared Burroughs and Swift, saying that both were
obsessed with excrement, horrified by female genitalia, and
disgusted with politics. Aside from a satiric style, both
shared an anthropologic regard for man as well as a soured
utopianism. However, McCarthy found Burroughs' factualness
and his unsentimentality his most courageous qualities.

Lionel Abel in the Partisan Review treated Naked Lunch
as an ominous indicator of the future. Asking if it were indeed literature and what human need the book satisfied, he
suggested:

> Very probably there is a metaphysical need in many
> people which cannot nowadays be satisfied by the
> "high" experience of ethical decision, speculative
> wonder, communion with nature or with others. [33]

He felt that whatever the need was, it should cleave literature
to life, not split it from humanity--a quality he found lacking
in the book. In spite of the novel's lack of literary merit, Abel
concluded that it would be considered, judged, and even admired as literature.

In November 1963, almost a year after U. S. publication, the Times Literary Supplement reviewed Naked Lunch
along with three other books by William S. Burroughs--The
Soft Machine and The Ticket that Exploded both from Olympia
Press and Dead Fingers Talk from Calder. The anonymous
British reviewer was not kind in his judgments of Naked
Lunch because he had the totality of Burroughs' work for
comparison. He agreed with John Wain, and blasted the book
as pornography masquerading as literature.

> Glug, Glug. It tastes disgusting even without the
> detailed but always callous homosexual scenes and
> the unspeakable homosexual fantasies--pure verbal
> masturbation--that figure so largely in the Olympia
> Press volumes. [34]

The review brought an instant response from readers which
was sustained for the next ten weeks.

British publisher John Calder was the first to respond. He resented the insinuation that the reputation of other writers he published--Beckett, Robbe-Grillet, Ionesco, Piaget--would suffer because they appeared in the same catalogue with Burroughs. He defended the unpleasant subject matter of his book by explaining that Burroughs' intention was to expose the corners of the mind which had resulted in Auschwitz and threatened a nuclear holocaust.

The reviewer responded with the charge that Burroughs' books were mindless, repetitious, and unorganized. He said flatly, "The case against William Burroughs is that he is a second-rate writer who would have attracted little critical attention if it were not for his shock effects and his forced inaccessibility."[36]

Edith Sitwell and Victor Gollancz praised the reviewer for rejecting the book. Eric Mottram of King's College, University of London attacked the review as unscholarly.[37] The reviewer noted that because others took him seriously did not make Burroughs a serious writer.[38] A week later R. C. Kenedy, whose books were published by Calder, denounced the reviewer's suggestion that all Calder's authors would suffer by association with Burroughs.[39]

John Calder wrote again and expressed his disappointment that writers like Sitwell and Gollancz would dismiss the book without reading its contents. He believed their emotional response was part of their generation.[40] Gollancz denied having never read the book, and charged that Calder's remarks were of no consequence since in his opinion the publisher could not tell the difference between poetry, tragedy, or fiction.[41]

Another correspondent, Margaret Kennedy, defended the negative review of Naked Lunch as an example of a badly needed return to critical assessment in the press. Such criticism had been freely given until 1959 when the British obscenity laws, which required literary merit in a work, turned criticism into legal testimony. The reviewer responded:

> ... one cause is obvious: the censorship of Mr. Burroughs has been made a challenge to the liberal-minded reader, to the publisher, and even to the scholar. If only we had a saner attitude towards obscenity, his works would fall as flat as its own boring and repetitious technique.[42]

The controversy continued into the week of Christmas 1963.
Harold Hobson confessed that he had met Burroughs and afterwards, upon reading Naked Lunch, found it uninteresting.
Nevertheless he balked at the criticism leveled at Calder,
whom he had known for many years and regarded as a man
of "absolute integrity."[43]

As the debate spilled over into the new year, John
Calder wrote once again. This time he debunked the charge
that Burroughs' work promoted perversity and drug addiction.
He asserted that the descriptions in the book were devoid of
the kind of glamour which invites imitation.

Anthony Burgess wrote that Burroughs was seriously
trying to extend the boundaries of the novel, and that his
books pointed toward new uses of language thought impossible
since Joyce had wrung it dry.[44]

Several humorous comments followed the next week.
Gollancz accused both Calder and Burroughs of literary
"coprophagy." Another correspondent observed that the discussion provided a good example of the confusion of literature
with lechery, and vision with voyeurism. And still another,
noting the weekly installment of "Ugh," called sarcastically
for a new Times supplement to be called the "Ugh Supplement" edited by Calder and Gollancz with Burroughs and Sitwell on the advisory board.[45] The next week another correspondent quipped that Naked Lunch would only extend the
novel form toward the lavatory.

Burroughs appeared in London at the Calder offices at
the time and read the "Ugh" letters. The author asked,
"Who is Mr. Gollancz?"[46] Then he too wrote to TLS in
defense of his own book. Contrary to the assertions of the
reviewer, Burroughs explained that he personally believed
that drugs were a destructive disease. He informed the reviewer that his views on drugs were well known, and bristled
at the reviewer's suggestion that he announce to the reader
whenever a character of dubious morality appeared in the
text. Burroughs reminded the reviewer tauntingly that his
job was to evaluate a book, not distort it. The reviewer
replied that the intentions and views of the author were not
well known outside his narrow circle of sympathizers, adding
that any serious writer would have enough imagination to
realize that.[47]

For another correspondent the "Ugh" controversy illustrated the vast ignorance of the true nature of the revolu-

tion taking place in the novel. [48] And another found the
book and the controversy boring. To end it he suggested that
the existence of the book in America was evidence enough that
Naked Lunch should be allowed in England, if for no other
reason than not to appear second to Americans in the toleration of the emetic in literature. [49]

A summary explanation of the debate over the Burroughs book ended, in print at least, the "Ugh" controversy. [50]
The anonymous writer explained that the reviewer had originally demonstrated that Naked Lunch and the other three books
inspired disgust and boredom. Only an overwhelming moral
message or an innovative extension of the forms of literature
and language could make that bearable, which in the opinion
of the reviewer Burroughs' books did not have. The critical
response which followed the original review was keen, none
keener in the history of the TLS according to the writer.
Yet the debate ultimately resolved nothing. No attitudes were
changed, but Burroughs did receive a great deal of publicity.
As far as the TLS writer was concerned, the controversy
cleared the air for future discussion of censorship and obscenity. He felt that now subjects and issues could be discussed intelligently without circumlocution.

The fight over Naked Lunch raised deeper questions,
however. What was at stake, as the TLS suggested, were
the criteria of literary judgment. The situation was explained
this way:

> reading some novel reviews nowadays one does
> indeed feel that a separate literary race has grown
> up whose standards are quite divorced from other
> people's; who seem to go less by their own judgment
> of the characters and events portrayed and the
> author's attitude toward them than by conventional
> literary opinion, and the pattern of other criticisms
> and other books. The only permanent cure for our
> troubles is to break this distinction down. [51]

The call for a reintegration of the standards of life and literature may have been too little, too late; if not downright reac-
tionary. The sentiment was a little like trying to retrieve a
roller coaster once it has crested the first hill.

The responses to Naked Lunch in both America and in
England were indicative of more intense assaults on estab-

lished values in music, art, politics; as well as in the novel.
Naked Lunch was part of a social, intellectual, and political
protest which affected the entire Western World in the late
1960's.

Chapter 12

BANNED IN BOSTON: THE TRIAL OF NAKED LUNCH

Part I: The Arrest

Boston's censorship record goes back to the Puritans. "When Governor William Bradford of Plymouth discovered in 1628 that the renegade Thomas Morton had, with his other misdeeds, 'composed sundry rhymes and verses, some tending to lasciviousness' the only solution was to send a military expedition to break up Morton's high-living settlement at Merrymount."[1] It was not until the 1920's, however, that Boston acquired its reputation as the censorship capital of America. The label "Banned in Boston" followed as a national joke. The Watch and Ward Society, its counterpart of the New York Society for the Prevention of Vice begun by the granddaddy of American censors Anthony Comstock, reflected the moral repugnance of Boston's citizens toward the recent trends in print. The center of publishing and the arts had shifted to Manhattan in the early part of the century, attracting a large community of artists and writers. "Having long since ceased to be a well-spring of literary creativity, Boston lacked the intellectual ferment generated by a resident community of authors, editors, publishers, and critics."[2] In the void created by the journalistic iconoclasm of the city, its people had to create a literary taste of their own, one opposed to the trends the novel had taken.

The Boston of President John F. Kennedy had not shaken its reputation for literary censorship, banning as obscene in the early 1960's Tropic of Cancer, God's Little Acre, Fanny Hill and Burroughs' Naked Lunch. The obscenity laws of the Commonwealth of Massachusetts were arbitrarily applied to the point of embarrassment. In the Boston University Law Review in 1962, a legal journalist noted:

> Massachusetts, which symbolized prudishness and propriety, has a long history of literary censorship.

> It has but recently emerged from a period of ex-
> treme severity in the application of its obscenity
> law.   With its newly liberalized interpretation of
> what is and is not obscene, and its recognition of
> First Amendment rights in the field of literature,
> "banned in Boston" may well disappear from dust
> jackets.   But Massachusetts still does not know
> what "obscenity" means, nor does it know whether
> or not its Supreme Judicial Court will continue to
> uphold its latest trend, in the light of the narrow
> majority presented [in the exoneration of Tropic of
> Cancer].

The call was not for new legislation, but for more definition
of the existing laws through judicial decisions.   A new Re-
publican Attorney General and his staff of young lawyers would
take on the task.   But the old law enforcement officers continued to arrest booksellers for peddling what they considered
illegal material.

At 545 Washington Street stood the bookshop of Theodore Mavrikos, only two or three blocks from what is now
called the "combat zone. "[4]   With predictable regularity fights
broke out in the working men's bars, often between the locals
and the students and sailors who frequented the zone.   Here
Mavrikos had a reputation of sorts in prudish Boston.   If
you wanted a certain kind of book, he was likely to have it.
The Boston Police had arrested him at least nine times for
selling "obscene" material prior to 1963. [5]

In January of that year Sergeant-Detective Edmund
Griffin was assigned to the Police Vice-Squad. [6]   A complaint
had been received by the Department from "concerned parents" that Mavrikos was selling a book called Naked Lunch. [7]
The bookseller was well-known to the Vice-Squad from his
arrest record.   Griffin drew the assignment, and with two
plain-clothes detectives went down to the store on Washington
Street.   He sent the two into the store while he remained
outside and out of sight.   One of the detectives asked Mavrikos
for a copy of Naked Lunch.   He reached under the counter.
As he handed them the book he said, "If that's what you want,
we got it. "   When the book was in sight, the detective asked
if Mavrikos knew the book was obscene, since the law required that the seller be aware of the quality of the contents
of an allegedly obscene book.   When he nodded affirmatively,
Griffin came into the store and arrested him. [8]

Mavrikos was loud and abrasive, according to his lawyer Frank Dardeno. He possessed the hubris of his Greek heritage and was a member of the Greek Orthodox Church. [9] But neither the people of Boston, nor the District Attorney's office, nor the Vice-Squad were sympathetic to obscenity cases. The only case harder to defend, from a lawyer's point of view, involves child molesting. At the time of the arrest, the Police were determined to clean up the "zone." Griffin and others in the Vice-Squad would routinely swear out general warrants against what they suspected might be inside a store, and then they would "go in and scoop up anything they could get their hands on. This was all illegal. The whole thing was illegal," Dardeno observed. The lawyer blamed the Boston political, religious, intellectual, and legal communities for the arrest of his client. Mavrikos' numerous arrests had reduced his $1,000 a day business to a mere $50. Dardeno noted, "You know his clientele was not just a bunch of perverts and kids. He had a lot of solid businessmen who bought his books. After all, at $10 a book you had to have some money."[10]

Mavrikos saw no evil in what he was doing. As far as he was concerned, people had a right to read what they wanted to read. However, he was a businessman, not a crusader. [11]

Barney Rosset learned of the arrest in Boston. It was not a totally unexpected development. He informed the major critic of his delay in the publication of Naked Lunch, Maurice Girodias, on February 7, 1963, "We have our first arrest on Naked Lunch ... a bookseller in Boston,"[12] as if to confirm his previous cautious actions. Because of the costs involved in his defense of Tropic of Cancer, he was in no financial position to attempt to defend every bookdealer arrested for selling Naked Lunch. And his contract on the book gave him the option to pay for such a defense if he chose. But unlike Mavrikos, Grove Press publisher Barney Rosset was a crusader, as well as a businessman. Exercising his option, he contacted Edward deGrazia to defend Naked Lunch in Boston.

Recognized as an excellent lawyer on First Amendment issues, deGrazia had published many articles in legal journals on the obscenity issue. His expertise made him a solid choice to defend Burroughs' book. "DeGrazia was a slim elegant Sicilian with a subtle diffidence in his manner, terribly hesitant, almost a stammer, but he was a Sicilian who somehow inspired the confidence that he knew where the next bit of information might reside.   Besides, he bore a pleasant resemblance to the way Frank Sinatra looked ten years ago. "[13]

On March 11, 1963, Louis Schrieber of the Massachusetts Library Association Intellectual Freedom Committee wrote a letter to Attorney General Edward Brooke, protesting the arrest of Mavrikos for selling a copy of Naked Lunch. The next day Albert Beisel, Chairman of the Massachusetts Civil Liberties Union, wrote a similar letter of protest to Brooke. [14]

Attorney General Brooke announced on May 6, 1963, a policy designed by his office to avoid the criminal aspects of the censorship of books and to assure booksellers due process of law.   The new policy called for the book to be placed on trial in an in rem (i. e. the thing itself) procedure in any censorship action.   A book had to be found obscene before a dealer could be arrested on criminal charges of selling it. The policy seemed humane, fair, and constitutional.

The arrest of Theodore Mavrikos on criminal charges for selling Naked Lunch, indicated the difference in the legal thinking between the office of District Attorney Garret Byrne and that of the Attorney General.   Frank Dardeno argued with the two offices, on behalf of his client, that the charges against Mavrikos be dropped in favor of the in rem action. In the anti-pornography atmosphere he perceived in Boston at the time, Dardeno felt that the actions of the Attorney General were politically motivated. [15]   No public official wanted to be perceived as favoring pornography, and according to Assistant Attorney General William I. Cowin, Brooke "may have been concerned in a political way that the public would view him as 'soft on pornography' were he simply to terminate the criminal case [against Mavrikos] without any substitute action; but that is, frankly, more in the nature of speculation ... rather than a conclusion based upon good evidence. "[16]

Little was resolved by the District Attorney or the Attorney General until late in the year.   By that time, Grove had decided that it would take up the Naked Lunch case, not by merely supporting the defense of the bookseller, but by actively arguing that the in rem action go forward.   On December 11, 1963, deGrazia wrote to Assistant District Attorney Joseph Nolan proposing that such action be initiated against the book and that the Mavrikos case be delayed until a decision was reached. [17]   He succeeded in obtaining a delay so that both the District Attorney and the Attorney General could hear motions on the matter. [18]

DeGrazia took advantage of the time to request more letters of protest urging the in rem procedure in place of the criminal action. At the end of January 1964, Schrieber of the Massachusetts Library Association wrote to District Attorney Byrne with a protest; Albert Beisel again wrote to Brooke; Marvin Geller of the American Jewish Congress wrote a letter of protest to both Byrne and Brooke. [19]

By March it appeared likely that the District Attorney's office would agree to delay criminal action against Mavrikos until a final ruling on the book was obtained. A meeting was set up between deGrazia and the two offices to discuss the problem. [20] He was scheduled to meet with Assistant Attorney General Leo Kozol and Assistant District Attorney Joseph Nolan on April 9, 1964, in Boston, and he was optimistic that the in rem action would be allowed to proceed. He also felt that Brooke's office considered Naked Lunch to be protected by the Constitution, and therefore was reluctant to begin the case against the book. However, it was deGrazia's opinion that Brooke would go ahead with the case in order to save Byrne's face for initiating it in the first place. [21] But as far as Brooke was concerned:

> It wasn't so much a question of saving any District Attorney's face--it was a question of coming up with an answer to a controversial legal problem which was fair to both sides and, I think, in the best civil libertarian tradition. [22]

The Boston meeting produced an agreement that the case against Naked Lunch should go forward. On May 1, 1964, deGrazia formally requested on behalf of Grove Press that the Attorney General bring action against Burroughs' book. [23]

On September 30, 1964, the Attorney General's office filed a petition with the Superior Court, stating that there was reason to believe that Naked Lunch was obscene. [24]

On October 5, 1964, Superior Court Judge Francis Good reviewed the petition and determined that there was indeed reasonable cause to believe the book was obscene. He then ordered that an Order of Notice be issued by the Attorney General against Naked Lunch, the author, and the publisher. [25] The Attorney General issued it the same day. [26] A show-cause hearing took place on October 13, and a date for a court trial in January 1965 was set.

DeGrazia began to prepare his case and assemble witnesses. He had proposed to Rosset that Burroughs testify at the trial, but was not certain that the author could, or would, show up. He considered that for the purpose of the trial Allen Ginsberg would perhaps be more effective. He assumed that Grove was going to pay the hotel and travel expenses of the witnesses, and offer nominal fees to psychiatrists who were scheduled to testify. [27]

Shortly before the trial date, deGrazia sent each witness a list of questions which he was going to ask them at the trial. He also asked that they prepare a written statement of their opinion concerning the social, psychological, literary, or medical value of the book. He added that they should not be concerned about saying the wrong thing on the witness stand. [28]

The night before the trial, deGrazia had a party in his hotel room for the witnesses who were to testify. [29]

Part II: The First Day of the Trial

Attorney General Brooke chose William I. Cowin from his staff to argue the case against Naked Lunch. Cowin was experienced in obscenity cases, having argued for Massachusetts against Memoirs of a Woman of Pleasure. The in rem procedure promised to be the humane alternative to the criminal prosecution of a bookseller. It also promised to ease some of the fear of a criminal prosecution for selling allegedly obscene material. In the past, if a dealer was arrested for selling a particular title in Boston, others in the neighboring communities became hesitant, even afraid, to stock that book for fear of similar charges and the possibility of imprisonment.

Not only was the in rem procedure the sensible way to act on the obscenity question, it was also politically ingenious. It afforded an official the opportunity to be simultaneously perceived as tough on smut, and liberal on the criminal prosecution of the bookdealer. In addition, placing the book itself on trial met with the approval of Ervin Gaines of the Massachusetts American Library Association. [30]

On January 12, 1965, at 10:00 a.m. in the Suffolk County Court House, Room 314, [31] deGrazia had waived the right of jury trial, choosing a judge's decision instead. Ex-

perience had taught lawyers that in cases which involved questions of sexual obscenity, juries were quite liberal and sympathetic until the magazine, book, or movie was shown to
them.   Emotion soon negated any abstract tolerance they may
have had toward free expression in sexual matters.   Judges,
on the other hand, were more objective, and swayed by the
law rather than emotion.

Massachusetts Superior Court Judge Eugene A. Hudson
presided over the trial.   He began by calling on Assistant
Attorney General Cowin to present his case against the book.
Just as the prosecutor had done in the obscenity hearing of
Big Table five years earlier in Chicago, Cowin offered a copy
of William S. Burroughs' Naked Lunch published in New York
by Grove Press into evidence.   He asked defense lawyer
Edward deGrazia if he would verify that what he had submitted was a correct copy.   DeGrazia assented, and Cowin
then informed Judge Hudson that his case was in (Trans., p.
4).

DeGrazia began the presentation of his case by introducing a list of articles and reviews of the book as documentary evidence of its social, literary, and artistic value.   The
documents on the list were also offered as evidence of the
contemporary community's standards of decency, since many
were published in some of the nation's foremost newspapers
and literary journals.

Cowin confirmed the authenticity of the documents and
the possibility of their use in defining community standards,
but he objected to their use of material evidence of the value
of the book because such judgments were strictly hearsay.
Hudson reserved a ruling on this objection until he had an
opportunity to read the reviews.

DeGrazia began to ask the judge a question concerning
the reviews and then stopped himself.   He had submitted the
articles as evidence of the recognition of the book, not their
content.   The list included the blasts which appeared in Time
and John Wain's caustic assessment in New Republic. 32   Hudson then taunted deGrazia:

> Hudson: Is it your intention to offer these reviews
> or do you expect me to find them somewhere?
>
> DeGrazia: Your Honor, we have and will offer a
> number of these reviews of the major, of the larger
> reviews.

> Hudson: Are you going to offer all the reviews
> which are listed on this sheet of paper that you
> have in your hand?
>
> DeGrazia: I can, if Your Honor wishes.   I had not
> intended to.
>
> Hudson: I have no pleasure in the matter one way
> or another.   So far as I am concerned, you don't
> have to offer anything (Trans. , pp. 6-7).

Hudson's unveiled sarcasm this early in the trial revealed
that he was not in the least sympathetic with the case before
him.   He may have been irritated at deGrazia's hesitation,
but his attitude was especially important considering that he
and not a jury would provide a decision.

After the judge's quip, deGrazia offered the list as
evidence and began to submit copies of the reviews as exhibits. [33]   Cowin objected to their use as evidence of the
social importance of the book.   Again the judge reserved a
ruling until he had a chance to read the documents in question.

A copy of Terry Southern's Candy was submitted as
evidence of the contemporary community standards for decency,
as was page eight of the January 10, 1965, New York Times
Book Review which indicated that the Southern book appeared
on the best seller list for thirty-three weeks.   Cowin objected
to both; Hudson reserved a ruling.

In an effort to establish Grove Press as a reputable
publisher, deGrazia offered as evidence a complete list of
their publications.   Cowin objected to this move altogether.
Judge Hudson agreed with the objection, and allowed the item
to be marked for identification only, excluding it from evidence.

A list of Burroughs' publications was also offered into
evidence.   Cowin objected to it too.   This time, however,
Hudson said that he failed to see how the list would prejudice
the prosecutor's case, and he allowed it as evidence.

DeGrazia made another attempt to convince the judge
to allow the list of Grove Press Publications into the record.
The list would demonstrate the seriousness of the publisher,
unlike fly-by-night pornographers.   The judge again refused,
reminding the lawyer that by noting his exception to the ruling,

his rights had been protected in the event the decision was
appealed.

     The Grove attorney had no other documentary evidence
to present.   Before he made his opening remarks and began
to present witnesses, he wanted the court to clarify for the
record the procedure which brought Naked Lunch to trial.
He questioned the propriety of Brooke's request of Superior
Court Judge Good to find reasonable cause of the book's obscenity and to issue an Order of Notice.   In his opinion there
was no interlocutory finding in this case, and in recent rulings
in June of 1964 in A Quantity of Books vs. Kansas and in
Jacobellis vs. Ohio called for such findings.   Judge Hudson
reminded deGrazia that Judge Good's ruling constituted the
required temporary finding in the case.

     In his opening remarks deGrazia asserted that it was
the duty of the Attorney General to introduce evidence which
would demonstrate three things before the judge could validly
say Naked Lunch was obscene before the law.   The prosecutor
had to demonstrate: one, the book appealed to the national
community; two, it went beyond the contemporary community
standards for decency and was "patently offensive or tanta-
mount to hard-core pornography"; and three, the book had
utterly no social importance (Trans. , p. 13).   The require-
ments underscored the lack of any such testimony offered
against Naked Lunch.

     DeGrazia informed the court that he would shortly
present witnesses for the sole purpose of demonstrating the
social importance of the book.   With such importance, he
argued, the book must be free of any ban.   He told the court,

> We'll call witnesses, having already offered re-
> views and other commentaries, to show how Naked
> Lunch, not only has literary, and artistic importance,
> but sociologic and psychiatric and moral importance
> (Trans. p. 23).

Ending his remarks, he observed that the book was socially
important because it portrayed "one of the country's newest
kinds of Hell. "   Startled, the judge asked abruptly, "Newest
kinds of what?" DeGrazia replied, "Hell.   Heroin addiction.
And that [the book] is manifestly a plea against this Hell and
related forms of it (Trans. p. 25). "

     John Ciardi was the first witness to be called to testify

for Naked Lunch. [34] Hudson asked that all witnesses present
step forward to either be sworn or affirm the testimony they
were to give.   Oddly Ciardi chose to affirm rather than be
sworn.   The other witnesses, except Paul Hollander, were
sworn in, including Norman Mailer and Allen Ginsberg.

Ciardi took the stand, gave his name and address to
the court, and stated that he was by profession a poet.   He
discussed his academic and professional background, listing
for the record his teaching positions at Harvard University,
Rutgers, and Tufts.   He mentioned his position as poetry
editor of Saturday Review and his membership in Phi Beta
Kappa, National Institute of Arts and Letters, and The Academy of Arts and Sciences.   He was past president of the College English Association, and he gave about fifty lectures
across the country during the year.

DeGrazia asked Ciardi if he had read the book and if
he would tell the court his opinion of its importance.

Ciardi said he had, and he mentioned the review he
had written earlier, "Book Burners and Sweet Sixteen" in
Saturday Review. [35]   He admitted that the review was written
on the appearance of excerpts from the book which appeared
in Big Table #1, because their quality tone excited him.
He hastened to add, however,

> My later opinion when I read the whole book, is
> that the structure is a little soggy and slow.   I am
> less enthusiastic about it as a piece of writing than
> I was (Trans. p. 28).

Like the disappointment on the face of a football coach whose
team has had the opening kick-off returned for a touchdown,
the effect of Ciardi's comment on the judge must have reflected in deGrazia's expression.   Sensing that his honest critical assessment had exaggerated legal ramification, Ciardi
quickly qualified himself,

> My only point in this was a literary one; to my
> reading Naked Lunch is a substantial work by an
> author of some talent and serious commitment.   I
> do not think Naked Lunch is a great work of art.
> It is, however, memorable, serious, and important
> (Trans p. 29).

He went on to point out that he found the book boring because

of the awkwardness of the writing.   But the record of the
personal battle with drug addiction, the soul's agony according
to Ciardi, made the lack of artifice appropriate.

Burroughs' account of his drug experience was com-
passionate and poetic, but it went beyond the problem of drug
addiction to a definition of the constant struggle between good
and evil.   Even though Ciardi considered the book terrifying,
it could not be immoral because of its attempt to stare into,
and record the depths of human agony.   Like a hell-fire sermon, the book made us uneasy as it awakened our awareness
of evil.   In that sense, he concluded, it could hardly be conceived as prurient.

Ciardi addressed his remarks to the use of four-letter
words in the book, comparing it to Dante's in the Divine
Comedy.

> I think the point is that when Dante dipped the sins
> in excrement, he did not call it excrement.   When
> you are dealing with depraved subject matter you
> must coarsen the language; you must take the rough
> rasp to the finish in order to indicate it's course.
> I don't see how a man can sin in following the
> Master in this.   When Burroughs wants to indicate
> a certain level of depravity he tries to roughen his
> language to achieve it (Trans. p. 32).

Ciardi finished his statement in defense of Naked Lunch.

William I. Cowin began his cross-examination of the
poet by asking if he thought Burroughs was conscious when he
compiled the notes for the book, and if he thought the author
knew what he was doing when he wrote those notes.

Puzzled by the question, Ciardi answered that Burroughs was certainly aware that he was writing.   DeGrazia
interrupted to clarify his own misunderstanding of the prosecutor's question and brought about the following exchange:

> DeGrazia: Excuse me.   Is this a question as to
> how the author constructed his material?
>
> Hudson: I think I could hear you better if you
> stood up.
>
> DeGrazia: Is this a question as to how the author
> constructed his material in Mr. Ciardi's opinion?

Cowin: Is this an objection to my question?

DeGrazia: I don't understand the question.

Hudson: The witness understood it and answered it.

DeGrazia: I hadn't heard the witness's answer.

Ciardi: I must confess I am a bit confused. Either he knew he was writing the book or indulging in all the writing to the extent, in some sort of trance. I don't believe he wrote it automatically in a trance (Trans. pp. 32-33).

Obviously Cowin was attempting to pin the witness on Bur-roughs' reference to the composition of the book on page v of the Introduction in which he declared, "I have no precise memory of writing the notes which have now been published under the title Naked Lunch. "[36] Cowin could use that state-ment to discredit the artistic integrity of the book. Ciardi explained that the reference was quite rational, adding that he personally would often begin a piece of writing, put it on the desk, forget it, but use it later without remembering the actual composition.

Cowin then asked the witness if some sections ap-peared "sexually morbid to him. " When Ciardi replied that the two terms were mutually exclusive in his opinion--nothing that was morbid was in the least sexy, Cowin asked if he thought some sections were sexually perverse.

Ciardi agreed some were, but sexual perversity was secondary to the theme of the book. DeGrazia objected to the questions because they were not relevant. The judge overruled the objection because Ciardi was given a great deal of lee-way in his statement, and it was only fair to give the same to the crossexaminer.

Cowin continued by asking if the book contained sub-stantial references to homosexuality and human excrement. Although Ciardi assented, he added that he was not aware that such references dominated the entire work.

A specific section of the book was referred for com-ment. Although it was not read, the passage was the first part of the "Benway" section in which Benway explains that

one of his method's is "to hypnotize a priest and tell him he
is about to consumate a hypostatic union with the lamb--then
steer a randy old sheep up his ass."[37]   Cowin asked Ciardi
if the lamb mentioned in the passage was the Lamb of God.
He agreed that it was, but when asked to interpret the passage,
he replied with an answer more appropriate of Robert Brown-
ing: "I doubt that Burroughs himself could interpret what this
paragraph was about (Trans. , p. 36). " He was not attempting
to be flip; the reference had been thrown at him unexpectedly.
However, the conclusion that Burroughs used the Benway character to satirize religion, belief in the Holy Ghost, and homosexuality in the priesthood would have been damaging indeed
in heavily Catholic Boston.   Ciardi took the opportunity to
comment that the primary response to Naked Lunch was literary.   Anyone not interested in it as a literary phenomenon
would get bored and stop reading.

Cowin asked Ciardi to look at this sentence: "A coprophage calls for a plate, shits on it and eats the shit, ex-
claiming, 'Mmmm, that's my rich substance (NL p. 38), "
and define the word "coprophage. "   Almost clinically, Ciardi
answered, "One who eats excrement. "   In an attempt to catch
the witness, he asked what that sentence had to do with the
discussion of good and evil which he had mentioned in his
statement.   By saying that the sentence had been taken out
of context, Ciardi neatly side-stepped another potentially
damaging answer, adding that within the context of an halluci-
nation the passage had something to say about good and evil.
Contrary to his remark, the coprophage appears as one of
the inmates of Dr. Benway's reconditioning center who was
released accidently with other inmates.   The scene is one of
utter madness and chaos, and could double for a scene from
Peter Weiss' Marat-Sade.   But it would be difficult indeed to
perceive this as predominantly prurient.

Cowin referred the witness to page 43 of the text, a
graphic description of a certain type of homosexual VD.   Ciardi agreed the reference was unmistakeably homosexual, but
this was an example of the very boring passages which he
paid little attention to.   Cowin followed up on this line of
questioning by asking if the book had many references to
baboons, especially to "certain parts of the baboon's anatomy
(Trans. p. 39). "

The purple rumps of baboons, Ciardi explained by
analogy, flashed through the author's imagination.   They were
like props in the mind's prop room.   He continued, like

Hieronymus Bosch, Burroughs' world was one of unreality
and madness.   The book was therefore powerful because it
tried to escape from that world.   Cowin interrupted, "Burroughs finds himself in a world of obscenity and unreality.
Are those your words?" Ciardi replied, "That is one part
of the thing. I think the power of the book is its effort to
come out of that world (Trans. p. 39). "

Cowin had slipped in the word obscenity, and then
closed his cross-examination.   DeGrazia tried to repair the
damage by asking on redirect if Ciardi had the legal concept
of obscenity in mind when he reacted to Cowin's last question.   Ciardi, aware of the response he had given, said "no"
flatly.   He added that he had no certain idea what the legal
concept of obscenity meant.

Cowin had no more questions.   The judge dismissed
him from the stand and took the opportunity to call a short
recess.   It was 11:30 a. m.

At 11:50 a. m. , the next witness was called to testify.
Paul Hollander, who also affirmed rather than swearing,
gave the court his name and address, and outlined his ac-
complishments and professional background.   He had earned
degrees in Sociology from University of London, University
of Illinois, and a doctorate from Princeton.   He had served
as a probation officer in London, and taught at a Massachusetts prison for the criminally insane.   He had taught at
Queens College and Princeton.   At the time of the trial he
was teaching a course in the sociology of literature at Harvard.

DeGrazia asked if he had read the book and if he had
formed any opinion concerning its worth.   Hollander asked if
he could refer to the notes he had prepared; the judge nodded.
It was his opinion that the book represented a statement of
social and moral importance.   It had value because it contained details of drug-related sickness and delirium.

On the question of the character of the depiction of
drug addiction, he felt that only an author with no artistic
merit, imagination, or moral indignation could depict addiction in a detached, neutral or aesthetically pleasing way.

> If an author or a writer wants to evoke the ethos
> of drug addiction he can hardly avoid producing a
> work that will be shocking and even revolting.   If
> in reality the results of addiction are revolting and

disgusting, one cannot expect its artistic or literary
reflection to be antiseptic, inoffensive or corresponding to one's conception of the normal and healthy
(Trans. p. 44).

As far as he was concerned the specific sociological
significance of the book lay in its concern with drug addic-
tion--a major social problem. The book confronted the reader
with the reality and consequences of addiction without attempting to trivialize or soften them.

Hollander explained that drug addiction was the type
of deviance which claimed the whole person, ultimately de-
stroying him. It was not just the subject which made the
book sociologically important, it was also Burroughs' success
in demonstrating the impoverished social relationships of the
addict as well as the interconnections between addiction and
other deviant behavior.

DeGrazia interrupted him to ask if he believed the
depraved, even cannibalistic sexual episodes were related to
the addict's destructiveness and loss of personality recalled
by the author in the book. He answered the question by noting
the sexual practices were directly related to the loss of moral
standards described in the text.

As a sociologist, he found the book useful because it
made concrete and believable some of the abstract scientific
notions of the field. The observations and information about
drug addiction corresponded to the scientific data available on
the subject. But the book was an articulate narrative from
one who actually had the experience. Because it did not
romanticize or glamorize drugs, but presented the inhuman
brutal world of the addict as horrible, hideous, frightening
and repulsive, the book would serve as a marvelous deterrent
toward addiction for any individual, in Hollander's opinion.

Seen from the perspective of the sociology of literature,
which seeks to understand society through novels, the book
presented invaluable information on a social type and sub-
culture.

He addressed himself to the significance of the four-
letter words in the book. The underworld depicted there
flaunts its opposition to social standards which is indicated
symbolically by the use of the taboo words. Because they are
commonplace in the drug-subculture, he concluded that "the

use of obscenities as a symbolic expression of rebellion
against society (Trans. p. 53)" is not peculiar.

He noted that the book required some intellectual background for appreciation, and anyone interested mainly in reading obscenities would soon get bored or puzzled reading Naked
Lunch. Both witnesses had made the same critical assessment. The book was boring for some readers, in spite of
its language and unique style.

Judge Hudson perceived another similarity between the
two witnesses; and in an effort to confirm his suspicion that
both Ciardi and Hollander were professional obscenity case
witnesses, he asked them both if either had testified at a
similar trial before. Neither had. In fact it was Ciardi's
first time in court. Hudson may have confused Paul Hollander
with John Hollander of Yale who testified for Fanny Hill in
New York in 1963. [38]

Cowin's cross-examination began with an effort to
discredit Hollander as an expert witness. Asked if he would
define the sociology of literature, Hollander explained that
the discipline was interested in the relationships between the
author and the work, the work and the reader's reaction, and
the information about society provided by the work. Cowin
wanted to know if one needed a technical, literary viewpoint
to accomplish the task. Correcting the prosecutor, Hollander
said that the sociologist was not concerned with the literary
aspects of a book, but the themes and information about society found there.

Still trying to shake his credibility, Cowin reminded
Hollander that he had observed that some intellectual sophis-
tication was needed to determine the theme of Naked Lunch.
Cowin taunted, "Do you have this level, Professor?" Hollander answered coolly, "I trust I do (Trans. p. 58)."

Cowin then began a new tack with the witness, realizing
that the insult was not well taken. He asked if the book would
deter anyone from addiction. Hollander agreed that it would,
although he conceded that it would be a difficult conclusion to
support empirically. Here the effect a book had on its reader
to act or not to act approaches the basis of the argument
against censorship, but from the back door. It has been interpreted that a book could not be considered a "clear and
present danger" because books do not act or actively provoke
an individual's behavior. The converse, that a book would

deter one's behavior, should also have been an irrelevant point. Hollander's answer was properly couched as an opinion.

As with his questioning of Ciardi, Cowin asked Hollander his opinion of a specific section of the novel, in this case "A. J. 's Annual Party" (NL, pp. 88-100). Cowin asked if the sexual gymnastics of Mary, John, and Mark which appeared as part of a blue movie shown at the party were a protest of anything in society. Hollander did not believe they were.

Then Cowin asked if the section contained a substantial amount of perversion and if the names--Johnny, Mary, Mark --had any Biblical significance. To Hollander the perversion was there, but not the Biblical allusion. Recalling Cowin's question of Ciardi on the Lamb as the Lamb of God in conjunction with this question, the prosecutor's attempt to read Naked Lunch as an anti-religious, anti-Catholic book becomes clear. The literary basis for it, as Hollander remarked, was quite shaky.

After some questions on the number of references to sex and perversion and the amount of profanity, Hollander said that such a quantitative assessment would be difficult, but what appeared in the book was "roughly adequate for the purposes he had (Trans. p. 64). " On that point, Hollander was excused.

The next witness identified herself as Gabriele Bernhard Jackson, Assistant Professor of English at Wellesley College. Her professional credits included a B. A. from Barnard, a Fulbright Grant for a year at Oxford, an M. A. and a Ph. D. at Yale, two forthcoming books on Ben Jonson, and courses in English and World literature.

She said she had read the book, and it had two values. One was the depiction of the addict's existence; and two, the assertion that the morals and motives of society are the objective correlative of the metaphor of addiction in the book. She explained that Burroughs used the techniques of realism and surrealism in the first two sections to create this microcosm of western society within the metaphor of addiction. According to Jackson, the realism used in the first section "provides real description of an addict's experience (Trans. p. 67). " Surrealism

provides metaphorical description of behavior in our

> society. As the book progresses the two merge
> and the apparently surrealistic descriptions may be
> realistic enough as depiction of an addict's fantasies
> and hallucinations, while simultaneously providing
> ... metaphors for general behavior (Trans. p. 67).

She suggested that Benway might represent the way an addict
would see a doctor or psychiatrist treating him, as well as
a satire of institutionalized medicine. Expanding on her point
she mentioned other instances in the book which appear realis-
tically--a cocktail lounge, and surrealistically--"The Meet
Cafe."

Jackson went on to observe that Burroughs directs the
reader's judgment by presenting evil as frightening, revolting,
ludicrous or at least unacceptable. Merely to assert one's
disdain for evil is not as effective as convincing your audience
that it is indeed evil. In his scenes of violence and perversion, Jackson felt Burroughs found "an image that revolts the
reader from the metaphorical action; and the evil involved in
the metaphorical action is always a version of victimization,
of the use of one human being by another (Trans. p. 70). "
The sex scene in which Mary devours Johnny's face suggests
the predatory nature of the American woman, and according to
the professor's interpretation, the homosexual hangings were
intended to depict an entire society corrupted by its need for
one human to exert power over another.

> In all these episodes, as well as in his treatment
> of the University, of religion in general and in
> particular of prejudice against Jews and Negroes,
> the conscious and often skilled use of parody is
> meant to reveal the fadishness and futility of the
> activity, the invalidity of the principles on which it
> is based, and the real, essential nature of the be-
> havior to which these lead (Trans. p. 72).

For Jackson and for many other critics, Burroughs is a moral
writer whose scenes of perversity were meant to revolt the
reader, not to titillate him to imitation.

Not only was the book derivative of experience, Jackson
explained that it also had roots in literary tradition. She noted
several references, allusions, and examples of diction in Naked Lunch which were drawn from classical mythology, Anglo-
Saxon battle poetry, Shakespeare, the 17th-century lyric, 18th-
century mock-heroic prose description, the Ancient Mariner,

and 20th-century poetry.   Most references and allusions are
distorted or altered in some way, or used unexpectedly or
intentionally inappropriately in the book by the author.   "The
total effect is of a literary tradition which has lost force and
vitality, which presents a series of unacceptable verbal actions, or verbal actions acceptable only as parody, just as
the contemporary society which relies on this tradition presents
a series of unacceptable real actions (Trans. p. 73). "   In
writing about the 20th century in Naked Lunch, Burroughs
draws on the techniques of T. S. Eliot, James Joyce, Aldous
Huxley, and Franz Kafka.   But according to Jackson, he tries
to affect a fusion in the styles and extend that synthesis beyond any one of its individual parts.   She concluded that "he
is clearly building an indictment of contemporary society in
its private and public behavior through the use of literary
technique (Trans. p. 74). "

　　DeGrazia had no questions of Jackson, so Cowin began
his cross-examination by asking if she felt the book had dis-
cernible characters.   After she said it did, Cowin asked her
to describe for him "autopsy Ahmed, " and "Salvador Hassan
O'Leary. "   She could not remember them, much less give a
description, but countering the attorney, "Did you ask me
whether the book had characters or memorable characters
(Trans. p. 75)?"

　　As he had done with the other witnesses, Cowin directed
Jackson to a specific passage of text.   She was asked to define
the word "Latah" which appears on page 37.   By Burroughs'
definition she replied that it referred to a person who imitates
another's behavior totally.   She added that it was an example
of the sort of unacceptable behavior she had just discussed.
With that answer she appeared to recover from what promised
to be an erosion of the credibility of her opening remarks, because she could not recall the details of the book.   Cowin
however continued to ask her questions about characters.

　　He wanted to know if in her opinion the character
Benway was intended to be an example of unpleasant human
behavior, or was his description included for its own sake.
She instructed the lawyer that any imaginative description is,
on one level, executed for its own sake, adding quickly that
it was a valid part of the theme.   If it were not, Burroughs
would not have included it.   Jackson's answer effectively undercut Cowin's point that some sections of the book had nothing
to do with the central theme and were inserted into the otherwise unoffensive novel to take advantage of the legal require-

ments that a book be judged as a whole. The passages then
were not mere dirt for dirt's sake, as the attorney contended.
He was undaunted, however, and asked if the scenes involving
heterosexuality were germaine to the theme. Jackson said
that they were.

He then asked if she considered the descriptions of
perversions, the use of profanity, and the continued references
to human excrement as contributions to the moral judgment
mentioned earlier in her statement. She said she did and
was about to refer to her notes in expressing her opinion
stated earlier when Judge Hudson asked her to express her
opinion without the notes if she could. Briefly she explained
that Burroughs described revolting activities in order to condemn the already unacceptable behavior by purposefully demonstrating and describing the perversions.

Cowin had no more questions, but Judge Hudson asked
Jackson about her professional training at Yale and Oxford
and about her teaching experience, which she detailed when
she took the stand. It may be that the Judge wanted to re-
assure himself of the degree of credibility he should ascribe
to the witness after some of the questions hurled at her by
Cowin had shaken her a bit. The court recessed for lunch.

Norman Holland, the next witness, had met William I.
Cowin in the men's room of the Suffolk County Court House.
Holland remembers the attorney confiding "that he was prose-
cuting this case because various old ladies would get on the
Attorney General's back and insist that he do something about
this or that book. He himself wished he were devoting this
time to something more important, and so did the A. G.
but they had to bow to public opinion. "[39]

The Judge resumed the proceedings with deGrazia's
next witness, Norman N. Holland, who told the court that he
was a Professor of English at M. I. T. and the author of two
books of criticism and over forty articles. He said he trained
as a psychological critic at the Boston Psycho-Analytic Institute for three years and had received his Ph. D. from Harvard.
Like the other witnesses, he told the court that he had read
Burroughs' book and had formed an opinion of it.

Holland explained that the novel was technically surreal,
that it was not written in best-seller style, and that it was
designed to give to the reader a vision of reality through
images and symbols.

He felt that the book was important both morally and
psychologically.   He explained the psychological use of addiction in the book by drawing an analogy with cigarette smok-
ing.   The appearance in the book, he continued, of "perversion and addiction psychologically are rather similar.   Both
are ways of trying to deal with some other reality which is
felt as intolerable ... (Trans. p. 83). "   Since both were regarded as distortions of a segment of reality, they were considered examples of deviant behavior.

At this point Cowin objected to Holland testifying on
psychological matters because he was an expert on literature.
Considering his years of training at the Boston Psycho-Analytic
Institute, Hudson overruled Cowin's point and allowed the witness to continue.   But before he could, Cowin asked that the
Judge note his exception to the ruling.   The exchange in the
men's room between Holland and Cowin had been quite friendly,
and Holland was surprised that the attorney had taken issue
with his credentials as a psychological critic. [40]   Cowin had
shaken the witness with an old lawyer's trick.   He had gained
the confidence of the witness, only to use the resulting com-
placence to the advantage of his own case.

Holland nevertheless maintained that Naked Lunch was
an articulation of the half-mad vision of the addict and the
pervert.   Burroughs showed that vision with artistic insight
and psychological truth.   The images of the body coming
apart, burning, turning into either protoplasm or an automaton
appeared to Holland as the artistic equivalent of the destruction of the self.

The moral importance of the vision lay in his feeling
that Burroughs used heroin as "a symbol for what he feels is
every man's position in the world (Trans. p. 85). "   He explained that the "Algebra of Need" as applied in the book to
clarify heroin addiction applies also to political control.   Holland felt that for Burroughs control is only a means to more
control, like junk is a means to more junk.

Then he extended his discussion of the moral value of
the book by trying to build on what Ciardi had earlier observed.

> Naked Lunch is a religious novel about original sin.
> I was struck [by] what Mr. Ciardi mentioned, St.
> Augustine.   If St. Augustine were writing today he
> might well write something like Naked Lunch (Trans.
> p. 86).

Obviously startled by the reference, Judge Hudson asked,
"What was that again, please? What did you say?" Holland
repeated himself, adding that Burroughs followed the idea of
original sin into almost every human activity. Some years
after the trial Holland recalled that Hudson, who "seemed to
me your average trial court judge, a man of modest cultural
means ... seemed to take umbrage at my suggestion that if
Saint Augustine were alive today, he might write something
like Naked Lunch ... When I tell the story I lapse into an
Irish brogue at that point: 'Do you mean to say, Professor,
that the blessed saint would write something like this book'
(holding it up like a dead mackerel between thumb and fore-
finger)? Alas, rereading the transcript I see I have been
exaggerating the man all these years."[41] But the story has
the seeds of interpretive truth when we remember Cowin's
questions which tried to expose the book as anti-Catholic in
religious Boston. Holland's anecdote may not be factually
correct, but captures the spirit of the trial which shaded his
memory of the event.

Shaken by the Judge's question, Holland took the opportunity to summarize his opinion of the moral and psychological
value of the book as a preface to his opinion of its literary
value. Its literary merit lay in the moral and psychological
vision, while its chief literary weakness "is Burroughs' failure
to shape and construct his material (Trans. p. 87)." Although in Holland's opinion the book had no beginning, middle,
or end, and by comparison was not the equal of Faulkner or
Proust, it was nevertheless certainly comparable to Saul Bellow, Mary McCarthy, or John Updike.

DeGrazia had no further questions and Cowin began his
cross-examination by attempting to establish Holland as a professional witness in censorship cases. Cowin asked him if
he had ever testified in an obscenity trial before. He knew
the answer before Holland could say yes. Cowin prosecuted
Memoirs of a Woman of Pleasure, a case he argued only a
few days before in Massachusetts Supreme Judicial court, and
Holland had also testified for that book. Cowin knew that
multiple appearances usually diluted the credibility of a witness.

Aware that he had gained the momentum with the witness, and quite possibly with the trial, Cowin launched a
series of questions pertaining to the numerous references to
homosexuality in the book. Cowin asked if the cause of homosexuality was drug addiction. Holland said that only a few

addicts turned to homosexual prostitution to secure money for
their habit. He described the other references to homosexuality as Burroughs' attempt to make the reader feel the peculiar mixture of love and disgust, just as addiction was
described to show a mixture of pleasure and pain.

As he had done with the others, Cowin directed the
witness to a passage from the text. This time he focused on
a paragraph which referred to the paternity suits incurred by
the character A. J. as a result of his use of a "water pistol
shooting jism [sperm] up career women at parties (NL p.
112)." The passage fades like a film into the next scene of
A. J.'s lawyer questioning one of the pregnant women: "Con-
clusive tests have established that my client has no uh personal
connection with the uh little accident of the charming plaintiff ... [elipsis in text] Perhaps she is preparing to emulate
the Virgin Mary and conceive immaculately naming my client
as a hurumph ghostly pander (NL p. 112)."

Cowin asked Holland if the reference to the Immaculate
Conception contributed to the general theme of the book. Holland stumbled to explain the reference, calling religious beliefs a type of addiction, possessing the same pain and shame
as drug addiction. The response was weak, so Cowin asked
if the reference in the text was an intentionally "sordid, perverse treatment (Trans. p. 90)" of the Immaculate Conception. Holland agreed that the reference was intended to be
perverse.

Judge Hudson took the opportunity to ask Holland to
explain his statement that Naked Lunch was the sort of book
St. Augustine would have written were he alive. The Professor tried to clarify his remark:

> Granted the difference in what a man, writing a
> book of confessions would write about today, in St.
> Augustine's time, it seems to me this is a confes-
> sion leading to a kind of repentance, although paro-
> doxically the confession appears in the introduction
> of the book rather than the conclusion (Trans. p.
> 91).

The surrealistic style might also have been used by the Saint
if he were writing today though Holland made little association
between the style of Naked Lunch and that of any Saint. Finally Hudson asked if Saint Augustine would refer to the Immaculate Conception the way Burroughs had done on the pages in
question. He replied, "I doubt it (Trans. p. 92)."

Cowin resumed his questioning by asking Holland to
look at the sexual encounter between Mary and Johnny, beginning "Johnny moves up her body (NL p. 100)." He asked the
significance of "this normal sexual scene after one hundred
pages of perversion (Trans. p. 93)." To Holland this scene
was not normal but was also associated with pain and disgust.
He pointed out that the bodies disintegrate in the paragraph
directly after the one in question.

Next Cowin asked for the significance of the title of
the section "A. J. 's Annual Party," and for a description of
its contents. Holland felt the title suggested either an office
function or a suburban affair. Generally the action involved
the showing of a stag movie at such a party. Cowin asked
what exactly led him to that conclusion, and Holland said,
"On page 89 where it says, 'On Screen.' And then there is
a complaint later on. Let me see if I can find it. As you
may have noted, Mr. Cowin, it is hard to find things in this
book. Cowin: It is indeed. Holland: Top of page 89, 'Many
an ill-starred actor had felt the icy blast of Slashtubitch's
displeasure (Trans. p. 94).' " The point of this line of questioning was whether or not the sex scenes had anything to do
with drug addiction. Holland was not sure that they did directly, but he repeated that the sexual descriptions dealt with
pleasure and disgust.

Judge Hudson in an attempt to determine the level of
the offensiveness in the book, asked Holland if it would be
offensive if it were published serially, without censorship, in
a daily newspaper. In his opinion the average newspaper
reader would not enjoy the book because it had no plot, was
difficult to follow, and would be boring. But the Judge wanted
to know if Holland thought that the obscene words in the book
would be offensive in the same context printed in a newspaper.
Holland told the Judge that newspapers were different because
their audience was captive. The reader "buys the newspaper
and finds the funnies, the news and sports and all of a sudden
he comes on Naked Lunch (Trans. p. 96)." He added in
response to Hudson's question that the book was not the type
that 14- to 16-year-olds should read, because it would be
disturbing to them.

Cowin asked if the perversion in the book was neces-
sary in order to illustrate the themes. Holland said yes.
Finally the attorney asked what Steely Dan III on page 91 was.
Holland replied, "It seems to be an artificial fallacy (sic)
(Trans. p. 97. This should read phallus.)."

The testimony had gone badly; and in an effort to lessen
the impact of Cowin's victories on cross-examination, and
counter the apparent prejudices of the judge, deGrazia commented that the legal test involved in the case did not hinge on
whether or not the material was intended for the general public in a newspaper. He asked several questions in order to
clarify the suggestion that homosexuality and addiction were
related themes in the book. Holland declared that the perversion described in the book was like an addiction, and he concluded that the two together became a metaphor for a series
of addictions.

Holland would describe his experience some years later
as "a rather trying cross-examination ... I spent an enter-
taining morning in court, and I felt thoroughly grilled. I
found it damned hard to do good literary criticism bound by
the question-and-answer format and the rules of evidence. In
the Fanny Hill case, they wouldn't let me refer to Dr. Johnson on the ground that would be hearsay!"[42]

Norman Mailer, the next witness, was sworn in and
took the stand. He gave his address, but before he could
tell the court his occupation, Judge Hudson asked if he were
"associated with Provincetown at one time (Trans. p. 101)."
The writer replied that he did indeed go there frequently.
More than just an idle question, the query exhibits the Judge's
interest in Mailer as a recognized American novelist. It is
only mildly strange that the Judge would ask questions of the
witness as he routinely identified himself for the record.
The Judge may have sought to establish in his own mind the
limits of Mailer's expertise in asking him about the nature
of his novels, but he was possibly curious about the writer
as anyone would be of a celebrity. As the other witnesses
had done, Mailer listed his publications.

Mailer's testimony in court under the direct examination of Edward deGrazia became part of the introductory
material in the paperback edition of the book. [43] The answers
he gave were forthright, and he was "cool and collected on
the stand."[44]

In his remarks, Mailer expressed his admiration for
Burroughs' work and confessed that he had been very impressed with the excerpts he had read in Big Table #1. When
the whole book was published, he read it all then. And in
preparing for the trial, he began to read it again for the third
time, slowly and carefully.

When Hudson interrupted Mailer to clarify the rela-
tionship between <u>Big Table</u> and <u>Naked Lunch,</u> both the novelist
and deGrazia referred him to the testimony Ciardi had given
earlier in the day and to his article in <u>Saturday Review.</u>   De-
Grazia hastened to add that the Federal case which involved
the Burroughs excerpts resulted in a decision declaring the
magazine as not obscene.   The previous decision, the lawyer
hoped, might influence the judge's.

Finally, after the preliminary questions cleared up
details for the judge, Mailer began to express his opinion of
the importance of the book, and the reactions he had during
his various readings of the text.   On his second reading of
<u>Naked Lunch</u> he was not as enthusiastic as he might have
been, and for that reason he approached the book for the
third time with "trepidation (Trans. p. 104)," because he knew
he was to testify in court on the literary importance of the
book.

The honest expression prompted Judge Hudson to ask
rhetorically:

> If you read a book once and took a fancy to it and
> read it a second time and didn't like it, you wouldn't
> want to stake your life under those circumstances,
> would you (Trans. p. 105)?

Mailer agreed generally with the notion, but promptly asserted
that his fear on the third reading proved unfounded.   He found
he respected the book more as literature and considered Burroughs an "extraordinary talent.   Possibly he is the most
talented writer in America.   As a professional writer I don't
like to go about bestowing credit on any other writers (Trans.
p. 105). "

Burroughs' ability to capture the beauty, viciousness,
meanness, and excitement of the ordinary talk of criminals,
soldiers, athletes, and junkies impressed Mailer; as did Burroughs' ability to capture disgusting, but nevertheless poetic
images.

On the composition of the book brought up earlier by
Cowin's questions of another witness, Mailer thought that
<u>Naked Lunch</u> was written while Burroughs became addicted,
as well as during and after addiction.   The result was a book
which had structure, though an imperfect one.   Burroughs'
experience with drugs was at fault in his opinion.   Drugs had

excited and damaged his talent. Mailer concluded: "This man might have been one of the greatest geniuses of the English language if he had never been an addict (Trans. pp. 108-109)." And the product of his efforts, Naked Lunch, drew Mailer "to read it further and further, the way Ulysses did when I read that in college, as if there are mysteries to be unanswered when I read it (Trans. pp. 109-110)."

Mailer ended his statement with a comment against the ban. He suggested that it should be sold in any bookstore in the U. S. If it were sold openly, Mailer predicted that the Great Society envisioned by Lyndon Johnson would be able to tolerate it. In his opinion it took a brave and morally honest society to look into the abyss described in Naked Lunch. "But a Great Society can look into the chasm of its own potential Hell and recognize that it is stronger as a nation for possessing an artist who can come back from Hell with a portrait of its dimensions (Trans. p. 114)."

Mailer's dramatic and powerful conclusion stemmed the course of the trial away from the prosecution, regaining some of the losses suffered in the preceding testimony. Content with Mailer's eloquent expression of the importance of the book, deGrazia turned the witness over to William Cowin for cross-examination.

Matched with the literary heavyweight, Cowin began slowly, as if to wait for an opening. He asked if Mailer would clarify for him the number of times he had read the book. [45] Mailer explained that he had read the book completely twice. In preparing for the trial he had begun it again, but had not finished more than 130 pages.

Cowin seized on this indecisiveness in Mailer's response to ask,

> Considering the difficulty of the work and your relatively indirect exposure to it, may I ask, Mr. Mailer, how you are so sure of the value that this book contains (Trans. pp. 114-115)?

Instead of challenging the insinuation that he was not even familiar with the book, let alone in a position to defend it as literature, Mailer answered with an analogy to his favorite sport--prizefighting. He could have scolded Cowin like a child, reminding him that he had followed Burroughs' career closely since the publication of the Naked Lunch excerpts in

Big Table, and that he had helped introduce the larger literary
community to Burroughs at the Edinburgh Conference in 1962.
But instead he explained that he could go into any gym, see
a young kid fighting, and tell in one minute if the kid were
going far or not. In other words, talent could be immediately
perceived, but the exact amount would require further study.
Concerning a novel, Mailer said he would have to read it five
or six times to evaluate its degree of worth. To his mind
Naked Lunch demonstrated: "extraordinary merit and may be
a great novel. There are a few novels that even make me
think of reading them twice, but I am compelled to go back
to this (Trans. p. 115). "

     Cowin wanted to know if Mailer felt the book had a
structure and if every item contributed to the overall meaning,
again setting up for questions on the relationship of sex scenes
to overall theme. Mailer of course saw the goal of the question and replied cautiously that the book appeared to have an
elaborate structure and that everything in it had meaning,
though it was not co-ordinated perfectly.

     Hudson broke in to ask if an elaborate autopsy were
required to understand the elaborate structure. Mailer agreed.
Hudson asked if the average person read a book other than
Dickens's Christmas Carol or the Bible more than once.
Cynically he replied that as far as he knew most readers
never finish a book at all.

     Cowin asked Mailer if Naked Lunch had artistic co-
ordinates. Mailer explained that the style of the book was
similar to the repetition of musical themes. It also contained parodies as diverse as of radio commercials and of
other writers. Often the parodies were more subtle than
those of Joyce in Ulysses. Then he asserted:

          At the very least, I feel that the man has an extra-
          ordinary talent. Perhaps he is the most talented
          writer in America today (Trans. p. 118).

     Failing to shake Mailer from his staunch support,
Cowin finally referred him to a specific passage, "You can
cut into Naked Lunch at any 'intersection point' (NL p. 224), "
and challenged: "Do you feel that may be intended to be an
admission by the author that the book has no structure, Mr.
Mailer (Trans. p. 118)?" Mailer had to agree; however,
he quickly explained that kind of structure was an Aristotelian
sense of having a beginning, a middle, and an end. He com-

pared the structure of Burroughs' book to Finnegans Wake,
which Joyce had intended to be opened anywhere and read
around--the last sentence of the book and the first running
together.   Though Burroughs used such a novelistic structure,
Mailer personally had no use for it in his own writing.

Before calling for a short recess, the judge apologized
to Mailer for having read none of his books, but asked if his
works "involve sex in the naked sense (Trans. p. 119)." Although all his books contained sexual passages, he admitted
that he wrote nothing comparable to Naked Lunch, adding innocently, "I write in a far chaster tradition (Ibid.)."

Cowin continued by noting that Mailer was a distinguished writer himself, and he asked him if his responses were
imposed by his own sense of order, rather than what appeared
in Naked Lunch.   The intellectual process of reading, according to Mailer, entailed an extraction of order from any
material.   He baited a trap for himself:

>   Mailer: In other words, any literary critic can
>   take the worst thing written--
>
>   Cowin: It can be done to pornography?
>
>   Mailer: I don't think I am going at it--I have ex-
>   perience reading books carefully, thinking about
>   them critically.   I would think by now my instinct
>   for determining what order is true and well-inte-
>   grated, or meritricious is more highly developed
>   than the average reader's (Trans. p. 121).

Having boxed Mailer into a corner of sorts, Cowin ended the
cross-examination.   It appears he was satisfied with the implication in Mailer's testimony that it was possible for a
literary critic to praise something as more important than it
actually was.   Mailer tried to explain the damaging admission,
but Cowin cut him off abruptly.

DeGrazia let him finish his answer on redirect examination.   Allowed now to expand on his answer, Mailer explained that any critic who called a work first rate when it
was not, had in his opinion, engaged in a "meritricious
activity....   Serious professionals and first-rate critics don't
go in for meretricious acts (Trans. p. 122)."   He returned to
his fight analogy, repeating his assertion that anyone with long
experience could identify a good fighter in a minute.   To this

analogy he added another, "just like a Judge may form an
opinion on the reliability of a witness on the basis of ten,
twenty, thirty years experience in law courts (Trans. p. 123)."
Hudson speculated that a judge would probably be fair and re-
serve judgment until the testimony was complete, and he asked
Mailer if he could determine in a minute if a fighter had
class or not. The novelist could determine that, but not if
the fellow would be a champion.

Neither lawyer had further questions, and Mailer
stepped from the stand. His answers had been dramatic, effective, and honest. At this point in the trial it seemed as
if the Judge had been won over in favor of the book by the
eloquent brashness of the writer.

The next witness called to testify by the defense was
Stanley Howard Eldred, Associate Psychiatrist at the McLean
Hospital in Belmont, Massachusetts and Assistant Professor
of Psychiatry at the Harvard Medical School. Dr. Eldred informed the court of his professional credentials which included training at the University of Michigan Medical School
and at the Washington Psycho-Analytic Institute. He was
certified to practice by the American Board of Psychiatry and
Neurology. In addition to his private practice, he served as
a consultant to the Walter Reed Army Hospital on the Psychological Evaluation Program of the U.S. Information Agency.
He told the court he was a member of the editorial board of
Psychiatry, and belonged to numerous professional societies
and associations.

Responding to deGrazia's opening questions, he told
the court that he read the book and formed an opinion of its
value. As a psychiatrist he found the book clinically interesting. "It portrays in a dramatic fashion aspects of the unconscious mind that are ordinarily not dealt with in other literature, technical and otherwise. Naked Lunch deals with
thoughts and feelings that most people learn to keep out of
their minds, out of their conscious minds in the process of
growing up (Trans. p. 126)."

Eldred said he considered the book a most effective
way of presenting to psychiatrists in training parts of the unconscious not found in other literature or encountered infre-
quently in normal clinical practice. It also portrayed "the
living death ... that ensues when human relationships are
based on greed, lust, desire without the intervening capacity
for love, affection, regard and respect (Trans. p. 127)."

Not only did the psychiatrist find it important for these reasons, it also went far beyond the implied subjects of drugs
and homosexuality to explore "the unconscious human condition (Trans. p. 128)."

Asked if he found the book useful as "hard-core pornography," the doctor replied with an emphatic, flat "no."
Startled by the abrupt answer, Judge Hudson asked: "You
mean to say, a book which contained hard-core pornography
would not ordinarily be of interest to a psychiatrist (Trans.
p. 128)?" Elred reiterated that such writing had no professional interest to a psychiatrist.

DeGrazia had no more questions.

Cowin wanted to know if he found the book difficult to
wade through, considering that his background was not literary.   Eldred admitted that at times reading the book was
hard work.   Cowin then began to set the witness up for a
damaging question by asking if he missed some things in the
book because his background was in medicine, not literature.
In all honesty the doctor had to agree.   Then the attorney
asked:

> By the same token do you think that there may be
> things in this book that you are creating rather than
> things that are actually there (Trans. p. 130)?"

The question revealed that the line of questioning was intended
to extract an admission from the witness that whatever value
he saw in the book was his own projection and not intrinsic
within the text.   Cowin had set the same trap for Mailer who
managed to wriggle painfully free.   If the proposition were
allowed to stand, then its corollary--that the book had no
intrinsic value--would devastate the case which conceded that
it went beyond the standards of the community and was patently
offensive, but contained redeeming social value.   All the witnesses and the documentary evidence were presented at the
trial to demonstrate the value of Naked Lunch.   In an effort
to avoid the trap and even the hint that a scientist would project his own ego on a book, Eldred answered, "No."

Undaunted Cowin referred the witness to a section of the
book in which Benway tells the story of a carnival character
who taught his anus to talk.   Eventually, according to Benway,
this anus takes over the body and the man becomes an all-
purpose blob. [46]   He asked what was being described in the

section. Eldred's reluctance to articulate the subject of the passage in open court is not only humorous, but also reveals the limits of candor in description.

> DeGrazia: Do you understand the question, Dr. Eldred?
>
> Eldred: He [Cowin] asked me what is being referred to on these pages.
>
> DeGrazia: [47] (Sic) Could you be more specific?
>
> Eldred: There are many things being referred to.
>
> Hudson: Give us some things that are referred to.
>
> Cowin: There is a general subject matter that is described, Doctor?
>
> Eldred: There seems to be some particular refer-ence to material that the analyst would call anal material, preoccupation with bowel functions (Trans. pp. 131).

The attorney asked if the psychiatrist considered the passage to be pornographic. He said no because he believed that hard-core pornography was designed to represent sexuality in a prurient manner, and the passage certainly did not.

Cowin wanted to know exactly how the doctor used the book, which sections he recommended and if he discussed it regularly with his colleagues. The psychiatrist did not dis-cuss the book except on rare occasions. It was the kind of book he referred to people. The suggestion that Naked Lunch was of tangetial rather than essential value to psychiatrists had been successfully established by Cowin through his ques-tions. As Eldred stepped from the stand, the momentum of the trial had shifted toward the prosecution once again.

The next witness, John Barry Sturrock was also a psychiatrist teaching at the Harvard Medical School. After the tough questioning Eldred had received, he could expect no less.

Dr. Sturrock summarized his professional credentials. He was trained in psychiatry at Woodsley Hospital in London where he was in charge of a large psychiatric observation

ward for acute psychotics from 1957 to 1959. He managed
and treated drug addicts there also.   At the time of the trial
he was associated with Boston Hospital and a consultant for
both the Alcoholism Clinic and the Long Island Hospital alco-
hol and drug rehabilitation program.

He had of course read the book and as a professional
psychiatrist found it "an extremely vivid and realistic por-
trayal (Trans. p. 134)" of the kind of unconscious material
displayed by psychotic patients.   Sturrock had recommended
the book to his psychiatric students and residents at Boston
Hospital.   Unlike a surgeon who could have a student observe
procedures and techniques, a psychiatrist had to depend on
secondary reports.   Because "it is quite rare to find a first-
hand account of material like this so clearly and dramatically
expressed (Trans. p. 134)," Sturrock found that Burroughs'
book provided a very valuable reference source for students of
psychiatry.

The book also helped him to treat drug addicts.   He
had not been able to understand their fantasies because most
of them were not verbal people.   Naked Lunch reproduced
material that might otherwise never have been available to
him.   The psychiatrist concluded:

> I feel that reading this has and will continue to help
> me understand and, therefore, to treat drug addicts
> better (Trans. p. 135).

Sturrock found that because the life of the addict was described
as so undesirable, the book could deter the general public
from drugs.

The book also dealt with solutions to the controversial
problem of drug addiction.   The psychiatrist considered narcotics addiction to be in the same place alcoholism had been
a generation before in terms of legal, social, and medical
attitudes.   The social problem, he admitted was far from
solved.

Cowin, on cross-examining the doctor, asked if he
too had trouble understanding the book.

> Sturrock: There are a few Americanisms in it
> which I wasn't quite certain of their meaning; but
> there are also some Britishisms on which I had the
> advantage.

Cowin: Some Anglo-Saxonisms?

Sturrock: No, I had heard, I think, all of them
before (Trans. p. 137).

Thwarted, the attorney asked if there were things in the book
the doctor did not see. The tactic which had failed with the
other witnesses, failed with Sturrock. He replied that he
would not be presumptuous enough to believe that he had gotten
everything from the book, though whatever was there, could
be perceived if one looked hard enough.

Cowin asked if he used the book for academic purposes, and if he thought the references in it "to perversion
and to homosexuality serve academic purposes (Trans. p.
138). " Sturrock did indeed recommend the book, and considered the references pointed out by Cowin to be valuable
preparation for medical students because patients often talked
of such fantasies during treatment.

Hudson interrupted to ask if the witness believed the
book to be of value to the general society beyond psychiatry.
Sturrock replied confidently, "To the extent, sir, that if it
helps me and if it helps psychiatry; and if it helps the medical profession, I suppose it must eventually help everyone
(Trans. p. 139). "

Cowin returned to his question on the description of
perversions and homosexuality by asking if the psychiatrist
felt it necessary to have the number of descriptions which
were found in the book. In short would he choose one example over the others for academic purposes. Miffed by the
insinuation, Sturrock asserted that he recommended medical
students and residents to read the entire book "for the total
impression, the wholeness of it (Trans. p. 139). " As a
psychiatrist he felt that the fantasies and drug related delirium
gave the reader a true picture of what an addict goes through.

Following his pattern of questioning, Cowin referred
the witness to the text. This time he chose "Hassan's Rumpus Room (NL, pp. 74-83). " The section features the hanging
and homosexual rape of a blond boy by the Mugwump, and
Cowin asked if this were relevant to the academic purposes
mentioned previously. Sturrock's reply was a positive "yes, "
adding that it was one of the more fascinating examples.

Still trying to corner the witness in a contradiction,

Cowin asked if he would define liquefactionist in Burroughs'
terms. He replied that it referred to one who absorbed everyone and everything into himself. Cowin asked what the academic interest of the term was. The psychiatrist, exasperated, blurted out: "Oh, I wouldn't justify every word, phrase,
name or sentence in the book (Trans. p. 141)." The admission was just a crack in the defense, but it was the opening
Cowin needed. He quickly took advantage of the opportunity
to ask,

> So, in effect, for academic purposes it is a ques-
> tion of picking bits and pieces that the doctor may
> be interested in and may get value from (Trans. p.
> 141)?

Clearly frustrated by the question, and its unveiled attempt
to draw him into a contradiction, Sturrock said again,

> No. For recommended purposes it is the very op-
> posite of not picking bits and pieces, but taking it
> as a whole (Trans. p. 141).

Cowin persisted in his effort to shake the witness,

> As a whole, Doctor? Isn't there an extraordinary
> amount of both natural and unnatural sex in this
> profanity, perversions, references to human excre-
> ment? Of what academic interest are these things?

> Sturrock: Could I ask what you mean by extra-
> ordinary?

> Cowin: A substantial number, and described in a
> a way that is unusual, that you would not be apt to
> see serialized in the Ladies Home Journal.

> Sturrock: I haven't read that.

> Cowin: Or in any family magazine (Trans. pp.
> 141-142). [48]

At this point deGrazia challenged Cowin on the purpose of his
line of questioning. Cowin wished to pin down the exact academic use Sturrock had made of Naked Lunch. Allowed to
explain unbadgered, Sturrock found that Naked Lunch made
available in print material on the conscious and unconscious
mind. The book was "a gold mine of material not otherwise
commonly available (Trans. p. 143)."

Judge Hudson asked the psychiatrist if the information could not also be found in hospital records on the treatment of such patients, records readily available to medical students. He instructed the judge that the Burroughs book contained a first-hand account which retained the immediacy of the feelings. Because of the immediacy, it gave students a more exact picture of what to expect from a mental patient, than could be obtained from the second-hand medical reports.

Finally Cowin asked if the descriptions of the perversions found in Naked Lunch would appear in a medical textbook. As direct quotations, the psychiatrist replied, they certainly would.

On redirect deGrazia allowed his witness to discuss the psychological interest of "Hassan's Rumpus Room." He commented on the hanging in a more cogent fashion,

> It's a common folklore, at least in Britain, and I understand here, that when a man is hanged he gets an erection and an ejaculation. The scientific evidence for this is fairly fuzzy, but it is a common belief. Perhaps you could call it the mandrake, the plant which was supposed to grow in a soil where a hanging man's semen fell, usually a highway man. That's why mandrake was considered to have all sorts of magical properties. There's some fantasies of disgorgement, somebody hanging down could produce what looks like an erection, the draining out of prostatic secretion could look like, I suppose, the results of an ejaculation. But it is to me very interesting that [Burroughs] should take this age-old myth and dwell on this (Trans. p. 145).

With that discussion of the psychological significance of the hangings in the book complete, the witness was excused.

DeGrazia called Thomas H. Jackson, the husband of Gabrielle Jackson who had testified earlier that day, to take the stand. He identified himself as an assistant Professor of English at Massachusetts Institute of Technology. He listed his academic credentials--a B. A. from Wayne University, an M. A. from the University of Michigan, and a Ph. D. from Yale.

Before he could begin his statement, Hudson adjourned until the next morning at 10:00.

The story reported the next morning in the Boston Globe revealed sympathy toward the case for the book. The reporter listed the names of the witnesses brought in to defend the book and quoted some of Mailer's praise. He observed that "Most of the spectators carried Naked Lunch under their arms and read along with the witness the passages referred to in testimony."[49]

Part III: The Second Day of the Trial[50]

The previous day, Professor Jackson had informed the court that he would not be able to arrive to continue his testimony until around 10:30.   DeGrazia suggested that the arguments on the admissability of the documentary evidence could be heard while they waited for him to arrive.   Hudson and Cowin agreed.

The Grove Press lawyer urged that the published reviews and commentaries be admitted as evidence of the opinions of national reviewers on the value of the book and on its social importance.   He argued that a precedent for such use of reviews existed in Massachusetts, and had been laid down in the case involving Miller's Tropic of Cancer.[51]   He reminded the judge that the U. S. Supreme Court explicitly refused to tolerate decisions in which the Federal principle of the "constitutional limits of free expression in the nation would vary with state lines (Trans. p. 154)."   A rejection of the reviews from journals published all over the country, deGrazia asserted, would also constitute a failure to consider the contemporary community standards in the case of Naked Lunch.

Anticipating the major objections to the reviews as hearsay and therefore not subject to proper cross-examination, deGrazia suggested that the documents "might properly be considered to be the full opinion of the reviewer in question (Trans. p. 155)."

Finally he argued that the list of books published by Grove Press should be admitted into evidence.   The list suggested that "a publisher who ... publishes some of the most important avant-garde writers, European and American, of the times, is not likely to be a publisher of a piece of pornography ... (Trans. p. 156)."

Cowin argued that because the reviews commented on the value of the book, "that they are hearsay and should be

excluded (Trans. p. 157)." He noted that he had no objection
to the limited use of the reviews to show current standards
of the community, but qualified, "The fact that a book is reviewed at all is relevant; what is in the review is not (Trans.
p. 159)." Such an assertion in the case of the reviews of
Naked Lunch cut both ways. If just the existence of the reviews were considered, the prominent journals and reviewers
spoke highly of the novel. If the content of the reviews were
also considered, some of the literary criticism would appear
legally damaging. It was the book reviewer's general opposition to censorship for any reason which prompted Cowin to
call for the rejection of the reviews as evidence of the social
value for two reasons: "No oath has been given when this
review was prepared ... [and] there is no opportunity to
cross-examine a magazine (Trans. p. 160)."

To counter this strong legal argument, deGrazia then
clarified the purpose for which the reviews had been submitted into evidence:

> The existence of these reviews throughout the coun-
> try ... displays quite clearly that the book in ques-
> tion, has, in the words of the Supreme Court, at
> least, some slight redeeming social importance
> (Trans. pp. 164-165).

With that statement deGrazia had modified his position that
the reviews be admitted for all purposes. He retreated to
the position that the articles constituted evidence of social
importance, as well as of contemporary community standards.

Immediately after the arguments of the two attorneys,
Judge Hudson ruled: "On these two limited grounds will they
be received (Trans. p. 166)."

By the time Hudson ruled, Professor Jackson had arrived in the courtroom, and was asked to continue his testimony. Because he had to rush to court, because he experienced the anxiety normal to testifying before a court of law,
because he sensed the disposition of the court against the
book, or a combination of all three reasons, Professor Thomas
Jackson was nervous. His anxiety showed in this rapid speech.

In his opinion the book was "a relatively successful
attempt to express the moral and psychic, and spiritual significance of narcotics addiction (Trans. p. 167)." Burroughs
accomplished this, he added, by using literary devices similar

to ones found in Dante's <u>Divine Comedy</u>. Jackson cited the
example of a parody of a military grafter who signals his
Commander, "as Dante says, 'By making a trumpet of his
anus, breaks wind in imitation of a military trumpet' (Trans.
p. 167). "

Judge Hudson interrupted the professor to ask if the
<u>Inferno</u> contained any "prurient language, " and would he point
out for the court. An exchange followed concerning a definition of the term "prurience. " DeGrazia instructed the judge
that the witness had not been called to testify to the prurience
of either the <u>Inferno</u> or of <u>Naked Lunch.</u> Hudson explained
that he was well aware of that, and he had only brought up
the question because Jackson himself had mentioned a comparison between the language of the two books.

Jackson tried to clarify his statements: "I would
maintain that there is [a comparison], though not perhaps on
the grounds of prurience (Trans. p. 170). "

Guided now by deGrazia's questions the professor explained that a book, or a part of a book, is often designed to
shock, disgust, or revolt the reader, and that <u>Naked Lunch</u>
was not a unique example. The <u>Inferno</u> and some of the
writings of Swift were intended to achieve a similar effect.
Hudson interrupted again to find out if Jackson included <u>Naked
Lunch</u> in the same class as the writings of Dante. Although
the professor agreed that the two were not in the same class,
he maintained that his comparison of the works was intended
to demonstrate that some of the characters and images used
by Burroughs were not different in content from those of
Dante.

Jackson said the passage from Dante in which two
sinners frozen in the ice to their necks are eating the head of
another employed a technique similar to the cannibalistic passage in <u>Naked Lunch</u> involving Mary, Mark, and John. Cowin
pointed out the same passage in which Mary sexually assaults
John, and, after orgasm, begins to devour his face and genitals. In making his point Jackson said, "We must be careful
again as I said before, I am not suggesting <u>Naked Lunch</u> is
the equal of the <u>Divine Comedy</u> (Trans. p. 173). "

The Judge interrupted to chide the witness, "Mr. Jackson, I don't think you intend to take over here, but you will
just have to listen to the question and answer the question.
Don't argue the case for them (Trans. p. 173). "

Surprised by the reprimand, Jackson repeated some of his earlier points before continuing his comparison. He then explained that Naked Lunch equated narcotics addiction and its misuse of the hypodermic needle with grotesque homosexuality and its misuse of the penis. According to Jackson addiction made the addict a victim, destroyed human personality, and assaulted dignity. The reader is also impressed by the parallel destructiveness of homosexuality.

Finally Jackson addressed himself to diction in the text. As he began to read to illustrate his point, deGrazia interrupted him to ask if he would face the judge. Hudson said that he would rather the remarks were addressed to the court stenographer who was struggling desperately to transcribe what Jackson was reading and saying.

Jackson seemed not to absorb the judge's comment. As he began to read the baboon description

So there I was completely out of K. Y. in the headwaters of the Baboonasshole when it came through by air drop my gratitude was indescribable. As a matter of fact, and I have never told this before to a living soul--elusive blighters (Trans. p. 176),

the judge interrupted, "Just a minute, please." Jackson assumed instantly that the content of the passage had in some way been very offensive to the judge, and he quickly apologized, "Perhaps I'll just refer to the passages (emphasis mine)." The judge explained,

I have no objection to your reading, but if you will simply be a little bit considerate of the stenographer. She is trying to take what you are saying (Trans. p. 176).

The witness began, slower this time. DeGrazia apologized for his behavior, reminding the judge that the language and syntax of the book were indeed unusual. Hudson said that he interrupted Jackson because,

There is no sense in his reading it if this girl is going to have a nervous breakdown in an effort to get it down. Now you know, yourself, that he (Jackson) is reading faster than it is humanly possible to take it down (Trans. pp. 176-177).

Jackson finished the passage, and interpreted it as a parody
of anthropologic jargon used to reveal the nonsense of ordinary conversation disguised as intellectual discourse.

The English professor then took on an explanation of
the appearance of the work "fuck" in "You're trying to fuck
me out of my commission (NL, p. 179)." He explained that
the word was used in the book as an image of what is physically involved in narcotics addiction. Such uses were an
indication of the author's disapproval of and moral indignation
toward the acts described in the book. He felt that Burroughs
tried to project a picture of the world of an addict which was
accurate in psychic terms, and negative in spiritual terms.

In an effort to discredit Jackson's comparison of Naked
Lunch and the Divine Comedy, Cowin began his cross-examination by asking if Jackson remembered the name of the
character who fed on the head of another, and if that scene
were preceded by a description of perverted sex. He identified the character as Uglino, and recalled that there was no
such scene preceding the one in question.

Cowin tried to drive a wedge in the comparison of the
two books, asking if the cannibalistic scene in Naked Lunch
involving Mary and Johnny was preceded by a sexual description. Jackson replied it was, establishing Cowin's point
that there was indeed a substantive difference in the treatment
of cannibalism in the books.

Cowin asked Jackson to return to a scene he mentioned before (NL, p. 59). Asked what sexual practice was
referred to, Jackson replied, "Sexual intercourse with a dead
woman (Trans. p. 185)." Cowin wanted to know what the
reference had to do with the fulfillment of the addict's need.
Jackson admitted it was not related. To avoid the implication
that the scene was detached from the rest of the book, and
therefore included for its perverse titillation, Jackson reminded the attorney that the particular passage was found in
a section labeled "Disintoxication Notes," which were the
delerious ramblings, the rotten outpouring of the addict's
mind.

Asked if the book had a plot and descriptions of characters, Jackson said it was organized, but contained no plot
because it was not a novel. Cowin wanted him to describe
"Hassan O'Leary." The character, Jackson instructed, was
not really described, but rather a name that drifts in and out

of the book. Challenged to give a purpose for the character's
appearance, Jackson mentioned the scene in Anthony and Cleo-
patra in which Anthony makes his men cry simply by shaking
hands and saying "Good-bye. " Considering it as part of the
whole play, Jackson confessed,

> To this day, as often as I have talked about Anthony
> and Cleopatra, I can't explain it to myself; and I
> wouldn't pretend to be able to explain every detail
> of Naked Lunch either (Trans. pp. 186-187).

The attorney asked the witness to explain the significance of the section-title "Lazarus Go Home (NL, p. 68). "
Jackson assumed that the title referred to the biblical figure
brought back from the dead by Christ. It suggested that the
narcotics addict is one who lives in the land of the dead "a
Lazarus who hasn't come back (Trans. p. 188). " Cowin
referred Jackson to "The Examination (NL, pp. 186-97)" and
asked if the frequent references to homosexuality were necessary when one considered that it was preceded by 186 pages
of such material. Irritated, Jackson stated that Naked Lunch
was not a list of references.

Cowin then turned to the main focus of his questions,
the continuity, or lack of it, in the book. If he could prove
that it had no structure or plot, then it could not be thought
of as a unit. The sexual sections could be singled out and
explained as prurient inserts in an otherwise formless mass.
Jackson admitted that the book did not pretend to have the
type of continuity found in conventional novels. Burroughs
had asserted as much at least twice in the text. Cowin wanted
to know why material was presented in the twelve pages of
the section in question which had been mentioned many times
before in the book. The professor explained that the material
was repeated as part of "a psychic state which has not been
presented in just this way any other place in the book (Trans.
p. 189). "

Still probing, Cowin asked if the imagery of homosexuality and addiction were sustained throughout the main
part of the book. Jackson agreed. Since the point had been
made elsewhere in the text, couldn't Burroughs have deleted
the twelve pages of "The Examination" and still made his
point. Jackson said no. Cowin attacked the issue from another angle, asking Jackson if in his opinion the impact of
the book would have been altered if twelve pages were ran-
domly left out. Reflecting the absurdity of the question, he
answered, "No, of course not (Trans. p. 190). "

Cowin had no further questions, having shaken the testimony of the witness to his satisfaction.

Judge Hudson took the opportunity to ask the professor a series of questions concerning the sexual descriptions, the addict's hallucinations, and the language of the book.   Jackson told the judge that he did not find the book to be hard-core pornography, that he considered the sexual cannibalism scene with Mary and Johnny repellent and repulsive, and that some of the language used by the characters was vulgar by every-day standards.

The Judge referred to the text and asked if there was anything in his opinion grossly offensive or vulgar in the first paragraph of "A. J. 's Annual Party. "   Jackson admitted that if he were at a party and someone behaved as the character in the book, he would certainly take offense.

Apparently unsatisfied with the explanation Jackson gave for the use of the vulgar language in the text, Hudson referred him to a sentence on page seventy-five, suggesting that no useful purpose would be served if he read it aloud in court.   The sentence he found so obviously offensive was spoken by a character called Mr. Naked America, "My ass-hole confounds the Louvre!   I fart ambrosia and shit pure gold turds! My cock spurts soft diamonds in the morning sun-light (NL p. 75). "   The character parodies the narcissism of beauty pageant contestants stripped of their clothes and changed into men.   Jackson, however, was caught off guard by the judge's reference to the passage from "Hassan's Rumpus Room, " and he explained that the description was a grotesque part of the phantasmagorical concept of what occurs psychically and spiritually in America's rumpus rooms.   The professor added that he would be grossly offended if something similar occurred in his own house.

Hudson wanted to know--disregarding Burroughs' talent --if he had heard obscene words or expressions filthier than those in the book.   Jackson admitted that he had heard one more distressing in college, but declined to say it in court. Asked if some of the words in the book would be defined in a dictionary, Jackson said the compounds would not because they were self-explanatory, but the others would be because they were "simply old commonplace words for actions or parts of the body (Trans. p. 195). "

Finally the judge asked if the writer who is granted

license in description should be limited in his use of obscenity.
Jackson hesitated, then said that from a literary point of
view a writer should not be limited in any way. In his opinion a writer should be free to write anything, and stand or
fall on the quality of the result. Legally "the artist should
not be restricted (Trans. p. 196)." Jackson's was not an
uncommonly held position among literary men. It was the
rule rather than the exception.

On redirect deGrazia allowed Jackson to clarify the
writing technique used in Naked Lunch. The professor thought
the repetition, disorganization, and dislocation found in the
text were a function of the new methods of experimental writing. The techniques used were a series of carefully laid out
images like that found in the Cantos of Ezra Pound and T. S.
Eliot's The Wasteland.

Cowin followed up the question of the writing technique
in re-cross-examination. Cowin asked if the pattern of Naked
Lunch and that of The Wasteland could be identified point for
point. Though both works, according to the witness, had a
rational pattern, it was impossible to determine the exact
meaning of each reference. He said that Burroughs, like
Eliot, gave instructions on how to read the book when he said:
"There is only one thing a writer can write about, what is in
front of his senses at the moment of writing. I am a recording instrument ... (NL p. 221 and Trans. p. 198)."

Cowin began to taunt the witness and precipitated this
exchange:

> Cowin: So the record that he [the author] makes of
> the psychic process depends upon how the psychic
> process develops and relates?
>
> Jackson: The record he makes depends upon the
> recorder, which is the sensibility of the artist--
>
> Cowin: He is recording his own psychic process in
> this?
>
> Jackson: No, he doesn't say that.
>
> Cowin: Whose psychic process is he recording?
>
> Jackson: I am not a psychologist of art, but I
> would assume he is either recording his own or his
> conception of psychics (sic) in general.

> Cowin: It is his conception of psychic process that it undergoes a series of experiences of perversion that take approximately two hundred and twenty-five pages to describe?
>
> Jackson: Yes, a process which takes two hundred and twenty-five pages of description to describe, yes. (Trans. pp. 198-199.)

Jackson's repetition of the question reflects his reaction to the absurdity of Cowin's questioning. He told the attorney that nothing could be left out, and no rephrasing could make him admit that the book would not suffer if even a single word, let alone a whole page, were dropped.

DeGrazia said that the book had 235 pages, 255 with the appendix, thinking Cowin had laid a technical trap for his witness.

A strange series of questions followed from the judge, deGrazia, and Cowin concerning the date and place of publication of Naked Lunch. It seems that Hudson was confused by the 1959 copyright date and the 1962 U.S. publication date. He was eventually informed of the Paris and New York publications.

More pertinent, however, was his question on the method of distribution of the book. Books of obvious pornographic content are handled differently than other publications. DeGrazia informed Hudson that Naked Lunch had been distributed and sold "coast to coast for two years in the U.S. (Trans. p. 201)."

Neither lawyer nor the judge had anything further of Professor Jackson, and he was allowed to step down. Cowin and Judge Hudson had extracted some damaging answers from him. His cross-examination had been more intense than that of the earlier witness. The advantage the case for the book had gained had eroded dangerously. Cowin's and Hudson's questions revealed that their interest was in the use of particular words and isolated scenes. Their frustrated effort to find a definable plot on which to judge the whole book resulted in their focus on individual passages in which "shit," "fuck," and "cunt" were used.

Having read the reviews submitted as evidence, the judge may have formed an opinion of the value of Naked Lunch based on the negative opinions of the literary critics. The use of vulgar words within sexual contexts only contributed to the alledged obscenity of Naked Lunch.

The next and final witness would have to be convincing in order to turn the tide in favor of the book. He was Burroughs' close friend for twenty years, Allen Ginsberg. According to Norman Holland, Ginsberg "cut a picturesque figure in the courtroom all dressed up in a business suit (three piece, I think) with a briefcase, but his bare feet sticking out of sandals."[52]

Ginsberg took the stand, swore to tell the truth, stated his New York address, and informed the court that he was a poet by profession. He listed his publications: "Howl," "Kaddish," "Empty Mirror," "Reality Sandwiches." Judge Hudson asked incredulously, "Reality Sandwiches? (Trans. p. 204)." Ginsberg said that was correct, and continued with the list of his book reviews, essays, and teaching experiences.

After a short recess the proceeding resumed with de-Grazia's direct examination. Judge Hudson continued to interrupt with questions. For example, he asked Ginsberg about Provincetown Review, which he assumed was associated with a literary club. Ginsberg explained that there was a weekly by that description, but not of the same name. The one he had written for was a literary magazine published four years before. Hudson may have been trying to determine if a connection existed between Ginsberg and the censorship of Hubert Selby's "Tra La La" in Provincetown Review which became a chapter in Last Exit to Brooklyn.

DeGrazia asked Ginsberg to identify himself in a picture with Burroughs and Kerouac which appeared in Time magazine November 30, 1962. That issue was submitted as evidence and carried a scathing review of Naked Lunch, so scathing Burroughs went to court over it.[53] It seems odd that the defense would take the trouble to point out a piece of evidence so obviously detrimental to the case. Its purpose may have been simply to show Allen Ginsberg as the "beardless boy (Trans. p. 207)," of the picture in order to cast him more conservatively for the judge. They did not dwell on the picture, but began immediately to discuss Ginsberg's opinion of the social importance of Naked Lunch.

Ginsberg informed the court that an important discussion of the theory of drug addiction as a metaphor for other addictions was articulated clearly in the section "The Algebra of Need. "[54] Judge Hudson interrupted Ginsberg[55] as he discussed the metaphor of drug addiction to ask the meaning of the phrase "Son Cosas de la vida" which Ginsberg suggested meant, " 'That is the way life is, ' or 'That is the way the cookie crumbles. ' Literally, 'These are the things of life. ' (Trans. p. 210). " The Judge continued to interrupt, asking at one point if Ginsberg considered the book obscene. He asked for explanations of phrases such as "as always the lunch is Naked, " and "newspaper spoon. " Finally he asked him to interpret the title of the book. Ginsberg explained that Naked "relates to nakedness of seeing, to be able to see clearly without any confusing disguises, to see through the disguise ... and 'Lunch' would be a complete banquet of all this naked awareness (Trans. p. 213)."

DeGrazia resumed his questions, extracting Ginsberg's opinion on the merit of drug addiction as a subject for fiction, and the plausibility of the cure expressed in the book.

However, Hudson did not understand Ginsberg's interpretation of the title. He stopped the poet again to find out if he saw any connection between the words "Bill's Naked Lunch Room (NL, p. XIV), " and the title of the book. Ginsberg explained that Burroughs had assumed the voice of a carnival pitch-man in that instance, exhorting the crowd to step right up. Revealing the intent of his previous question Hudson asked:

> Hudson: You wouldn't even remotely associate the title with any incident in this book which portrays unnatural acts?
>
> Ginsberg: Yes, that part of it, too. The unnatural acts portrayed are part of exhibitions of control.
>
> Hudson: Would you go so far as to say it is associated with a description of a person eating excrement, served on a plate here in the front part of the book?
>
> Ginsberg: That particular association had not literally ever occurred to me.
>
> Hudson: Well, what do you say now?
>
> Ginsberg: I am sure that could be included, too. Certainly that would be included also. All levels

in the title would be acceptable, I think.   (Trans.
pp. 216-217).

Hudson associated the title with the eating of excrement. His
association indicates that in reading the book the judge must
have favored the risque, if not the pornographic interpretation, in any instance which was even slightly ambiguous or
suggestive.

In another attempt by Hudson to pin down the date and
place of publication, Ginsberg surprisingly could not remember
the date of publication. He said, "I think, 1959 or '60. I
am not sure (Trans. p. 218)." Finally he recalled the English-language publication in France in 1959, and the U.S. publication in 1962. To avoid some sensational implication which
might be drawn from its apparently clandestine publication in
France, deGrazia hastened to have his witness mention other
books published in just that fashion such as Tropic of Cancer
and Lady Chatterley's Lover. Hudson challenged, "Was that
of any significance? Am I to draw an inference from that?
(Trans. p. 219)."

DeGrazia explained, "I was trying to answer the inference you were raising in your question, which, perhaps,
I didn't completely understand. (Trans. p. 219)." The
judge denied that he had any question of censorship in mind.
On the contrary, he felt that his questions were material to
the case since there was obvious confusion over the basic facts
of the time and place of publication. His questions did establish, in open court, that Naked Lunch had a publication history
similar to countless books barred from publication for many
years in this country because they dealt frankly with sex. 56

The examination continued on another point as Ginsberg
discussed the political significance of the parodies of political
parties (NL p. 144-165). Again Hudson interrupted Ginsberg,
probing for an interpretation of the fictional depictions of the
political groups. Finally the judge asked in which group the
author would place himself. When Ginsberg said "Burroughs
considers himself a Factualist (Trans. p. 221)," Hudson observed, "The Birch Society deals with factuality doesn't it?"
Ginsberg snapped, "Actually I haven't read their prose (Trans.
p. 221)."

DeGrazia eased Ginsberg away from political references
by asking his opinion of the character the County Clerk (NL
pp. 169-177). The section containing the character involves

a court room scene in which a city dweller finds himself before the Sheriff, whose questions and statements are filled
with anecdotal asides revealing his sexual, social, and racial
preoccupations.   Ginsberg called the rendering of the character in Naked Lunch a factual portrait of the kind of person
they had read about in the newspaper stories on segregation
in the South.

Before the trial Ginsberg had made rather extensive
notes on the book.   He described the character this way:

> The County Clerk: complete portrait of the style
> of an antinegro, antinorthern, antiliberal, and anti-
> semitic antipluralistic southern red-neck bureau-
> crat. ...   This is one of the funniest and most bril-
> liant sections of the book, written prophetically in
> the mid-fifties, drawing on the author's extensive
> living experience in Missouri, Florida, Texas, and
> Louisiana; exposing basic sexual and social obses-
> sion and provincialism of such types as form the
> backbone of Ku Klux Klan dominated communities. [57]

While quoting part of the dialogue of the character to demonstrate how Burroughs parodied the character's anti-Semitism,
the judge asked if he found the reference grossly offensive to
him as a Jew.   Ginsberg exploded, "No, Burroughs is defending the Jews here.   Don't you realize he is making a
parody of the monstrous speech and thought processes of a
red-necked Southern, hate-filled type, who hates everybody,
Jews, Negros, Northerners.   Burroughs is taking a very
moral position, like defending the good here, I think (Trans.
pp.   228-229). "

Ginsberg won the point, and deGrazia moved on quickly,
wishing not to dilute the impact of the poet's emotional reaction.

The next question concerned the section titled "The
Hospital" (NL pp.   55-68), and the effect on the books as a
whole if it were left out. [58]   Ginsberg said that the section
could not be removed because it "consists of very specific
factual notes on disintoxication and withdrawal symptoms in the
hospital (Trans. p.   229). "   Revealing once again the type of
inference Hudson made from the text, he interrupted to ask,
"You are talking about the ejaculation in the jar now?"   Totally
startled by the question, Ginsberg asked, "Where is that now?"
Exasperated, Hudson replied, "Some place in the book (Trans.
pp.   229-230). "

However, the next interruption by the judge proved a
sticky one for Ginsberg. He was asked whether the line
"Makes me feel sorta like a dirty old man? (NL p. 59)"
displayed really good talent. [59]   Ginsberg said the line displayed great talent.   Hudson explained that he had intended
to refer to the entire paragraph, not just the isolated phrase
in his question.   The line occurs directly before the Spanish
phrase, "Son cosas de la vida. " The Spanish sentence was
attributed to a Mexican criminal "Soberla de la Flor ... when
the fuzz upbraids him for blasting this cunt and taking the
dead body to the Bar O Motel and fucking it ... (NL p. 59). "
Hudson asked if the entire paragraph were grossly offensive in
his opinion.   Ginsberg replied that on the contrary, the inclusion of the references by Burroughs were "quite honorable
(Trans. p. 231). "

DeGrazia, in an effort to counteract the implication
of the Judge's questions, asked Ginsberg if the section just
mentioned was related in any way to "Hassan's Rumpus Room"
and "A. J. 's Annual Party" (NL pp. 74-83; 88-103).   He explained that the "Hospital" came before the two, and that it
was natural for them to follow the sections dealing with the
crisis of drug withdrawal.   The return of the libidinous urge,
he argued is a normal occurrence following heroin withdrawal.
The connection between the return to sexual desire and withdrawal was established by the psychiatrists.

Although deGrazia made a good effort to salvage the
weak response Ginsberg gave to Hudson's question, it is
doubtful that the judge viewed the explanation of the sexual
passages as convincing.

DeGrazia completed his examination of the poet by
asking if Burroughs and Naked Lunch had any importance for
his own creative work.   He replied that he considered the
book personally important for its confessional honesty, "absolutely nothing hidden or left out (Trans. p. 233), " its duplication of common speech, and its poetic language.   Ginsberg
concluded by quoting from his Reality Sandwiches on Naked
Lunch.

> The method must be purest meat
>   and no symbolic dressing,
> actual visions & actual prisons
>   as seen then and now.
>
> Prisons and visions presented
>   with rare descriptions

corresponding exactly to those
of Alcatraz and Rose.

A naked lunch is natural to us,
  we eat reality sandwiches.
But allegories are so much lettuce.
  Don't hide the madness. [60]

DeGrazia had no more questions.

Ginsberg considered the so-called pornographic sec-
tions--"Hassan's Rumpus Room" and "A. J.'s Annual Party"
--as Burroughs' deeply personal expression. Of the first,
Ginsberg wrote in pretrial notes, "Perhaps a projection of
the author's horrible image of himself which reinforced his
escape to junk and reappears after junk cure."[61] His notes
on "A. J.'s Annual Party" comment on Burroughs' use of
repetition, and begin to define some of Burroughs' sexual
images. Ginsberg felt that the section was

> an examination of the authors' sexual fantasies many
> of which are repellent to himself, and an exorcism
> of them by repetition, scrambling of them, & paro-
> dy ... An exploration here of all the pavlovian,
> that is, conditioned & habitual, images associated
> with the author's sense of eroticism. By becoming
> conscious of his own fetishistic stimuli he becomes
> free of his obsessional imagery.

> At the end of this mental blue movie we have the
> return of the hangman, orgasm as a form of death
> to the author, seen in the light of a carnival show. [62]

The poet's observations, though made with an eye toward his
court appearance, reveal the feeling that underneath a great
deal of Burroughs' work was a self-loathing manifested in
sexual fantasy. Such a reading did not surface in the direct
examination, but promised to be revealed when Cowin questioned Ginsberg on the two sections believed to be obscene.

Cowin's first question dealt with the homosexuality
described in "Hassan's Rumpus Room" and its possible relationship to drug withdrawal. He wanted to know why the section continued with the homosexual references even after the
withdrawal from drugs. Ginsberg explained that it is at that
time, after withdrawal, that sexuality reasserts itself, and
that the addict in the book was a homosexual to begin with.

Cowin asked, "And so, therefore, this is a book about homosexuality that does not necessarily relate to narcotics addiction? (Trans. p. 237)." Sensing the implication in the attorney's question, Ginsberg replied,

> Well there is a relationship between the homo-
> sexuality which the author finds very horrifying
> to himself, which he sees in himself, and the
> motivation for going on narcotics and also the
> fear of coming off narcotics. When he comes
> off narcotics he has to face the whole homo-
> sexual syndrome in himself. (Trans. p. 237).

Cowin drew Ginsberg's attention to "The Hospital"
section. He referred specifically to the following sentence
which occurs in the middle of a parody of Dr. Benway's explanation of the medical performances of a Dr. Tetrazzini.
Cowin read Benway's line, "Tumors put him [Tetrazzini] in
a frenzy of rage." The lawyer stopped short, skipping a
word before continuing, "undisciplined cells." Then he asked
Ginsberg to explain the reference to tumors and undisciplined
cells, and their relevance to drug withdrawal. The poet felt
that the Benway section was a satire of the paranoid suspicions experienced by an addict during withdrawal, and that
this reference amounted to "a fantasy of an insane doctor
making insane operations (Trans. p. 239)."

Getting to the point of his question, Cowin asked for
an explanation of Benway's specific characterization of the
cells. Ginsberg read from the text the word the attorney had
so scrupulously avoided, " 'Fucking undisciplined cells!' he
would snarl, advancing on the tumor like a knife-fighter
(Trans. p. 239, and NL. p. 61)." He then explained to Cowin,
again, that the instance was a fantasy that an addict had during withdrawal, since, after all, the section carried the heading, "Disintoxication Notes." Ginsberg had neatly sidestepped
an apology for the use of the word "fucking," which was obviously the intention of the question.

Cowin then referred to a parody of a radio station
(NL. p. 64), in which a diplomat delivers a speech, and the
"Star Spangled Banner" is sung by a lisping tenor. There is
a technician in a control room which is blowing up. Cowin
referred to the lines, "The technician, naked, his body burned
black, staggers about like a figure in Gotterdammerung,
screaming: 'Thubber. thonic! Oth. thu thair!!!' A Final
blast reduces the technician to a cinder (Trans. p. 242, and

NL p. 64). " Evidently the 'th' spellings suggested an effemi-
nate lisp to the attorney, and he asked if the technician were
meant to be portrayed as a homosexual.

Ginsberg corrected the misreading of the passage by
referring to the earlier description of the character as tooth-
less and suggesting, "his plate of teeth fall out and that is
why he is speaking with a lisp (Trans. p. 242). " Cowin had
confused the lisping tenor with the technician.

Cowin continued to question Ginsberg on the homosexuality found in the book, and on Burroughs' attitude toward
the subject. It was Ginsberg's opinion that Burroughs was
disturbed and frightened by it, and that the book acted as an
attack and defeat of his own fear. According to Ginsberg,
the book "would have a certain cathartic effect (Trans. p.
243)" for the reader who was able to follow it.

Cowin turned from homosexuality to ask Ginsberg to
explain the reasons for the apparent differences in style between the main body of the text and the style of both the introduction and the appendix. Specifically he wanted to know
if the styles were chosen consciously. Ginsberg replied that
no writer's creation was "that consciously chosen (Trans. p.
245). "

He asked Ginsberg to comment on the depiction of drug
addiction treatment, and to explain the differences between that
depiction in the main and in the introduction and appendix.
Ginsberg observed that in the main part of the book drug treatment was criticized in dramatic form. Cowin implied:

> So actual treatment by the author of suggested
> changes of the approach toward narcotics addic-
> tion really are found, either in the introduction
> or the appendix, is that true?
>
> Ginsberg: No. Negative criticism of present
> treatment is throughout the whole book.
>
> Cowin: I am not referring to the criticism, I
> am referring to suggestions for change. (Trans.
> p. 246).

Aware of the corner Cowin had placed him in, Ginsberg said he
could not answer until he had a chance to look through the
main text to see if references to apomorphine occurred there

or not. Cowin was satisfied with Ginsberg's implication that even if the main text indeed contained those references, they were so obscure as to be easily forgotten. He thanked the witness, completing his cross-examination.

Judge Hudson took the opportunity to ask Ginsberg some added questions of his own. The line, "Motel, Motel, Motel, broken neon arabesque, loneliness moans across the continent like fog horns over still oil water of tidal rivers, (NL. p. 225)" had been quoted earlier by Ginsberg as a particularly poetic example of Burroughs' diction. Hudson wanted to know what was so poetic about it, and if the same line could not be placed anywhere in the book and make just as much sense as it did where it was.

Ginsberg explained that the line occurred in the "Wouldn't You" section, which was made up of fragments from the book placed together like a mosaic in a long prose poem. It made sense in that place, and not in the preface or anywhere else, because it appeared within the context of a series of images of America seen from a moving auto, in this case passing by motels near a polluted river.

The Judge was also concerned with the paragraph just above that line. He began to explain to the court, "Johnny is on all fours with Mary, and I don't want to read it..." Ginsberg did, however, "Johnny on all fours and Mary sucking him and running her fingers down the thigh backs and light over the outfields of the ballpark (Trans. p. 250)," pointing out that the attention of the writer is drawn from the thighs out to the ballpark.

Hudson wondered if the paragraph after "Motel ..." was also concerned with America seen from an automobile. Ginsberg said it was not, and the judge taunted, "What happened there? Did the car break down (?) (Trans. p. 251)." Exasperated, Hudson revealed the point of his questions.

> Frankly, what I am concerned about is whether or not the insertion of hard-core pornography at any place in a description of an addict's hallucinations becomes seriously and grossly offensive (Trans. p. 251).

Then he repeated his earlier observation that the book lacked continuity, which suggests that he felt that pornography had indeed been inserted in the descriptions.

DeGrazia and Ginsberg tried to correct Hudson's misconception by saying that like a newspaper, or life for that
matter, Naked Lunch had no plot. Its continuity, rather, lay
in its ability to duplicate the often illogical process of thought
within the structure of a fiction.

Hudson stopped them to explain himself quite explicitly.
One of the concerns he had, which he considered a prerequi-
site to rule on the whole book, was "whether or not under the
guise of portraying the hallucinations of a drug addict, the
author has ingeniously satisfied his own whim or fancy, and
inserted in this book hard-core pornography (Trans. p. 254)."
Hudson admitted his understanding of the opinion of the literary
experts that the book necessarily lacked continuity in the descriptions of the thoughts of the homosexuals and drug addicts.
However, he explained, "in several places here I just fail to
see the association between what appears to me to be a grossly vulgar and obscene phrase with the thought expressed in
the preceding paragraph or the paragraph which follows (Trans.
p. 255)."

The Judge, after more argument asked rhetorically:

> But what are we headed for? My mind is entirely
> open so far as this book is concerned ... But is it
> conceivable that in our lifetime, probably in the
> lifetime of the next generation, that there will be
> no censorship whatsoever, so far as freedom of
> writing and publication is concerned? Is that the
> thought that is expressed by him [Burroughs] in this
> book? (Trans. p. 257).

The complaint, when considered in the context of the events
which followed on the censorship of obscenity, is ironic.

The Judge then asked Ginsberg if he were in London
in 1959 and,

> Did you write on the report of the homosexual com-
> mission which was appointed in London? Are you
> familiar with that? ...
>
> Ginsberg: I read about it in a newspaper, but I
> didn't write anything about it ... I think I was in
> Paris [at the time] (Trans. pp. 257-258).

The judge appeared to search for some connection that would

weaken Ginsberg's credibility as a witness on the basis of a previously established prejudice.

Hudson had no more questions and deGrazia took the opportunity to clarify several damaging points established under cross-examination. He asked Ginsberg to explain again the difference between the style of the main text and that of the appendix and introduction. To his previous statement Ginsberg added that the introduction, beginning with "Post Script ... Wouldn't You," was an improvised fantasy which was related stylistically to the last chapter, and bore a similar title. Under the lawyer's questions he concluded, "This introduction just presents the main idea dramatically presented during the book (Trans. p. 264)." He reaffirmed the definite relationship between the introduction and the main text. Had Cowin been resourceful, he would have compared the Grove Press edition with the Olympia edition, and found strong evidence in the absence of end pieces that were of course added with the U.S. censor in mind. [63]

Finally deGrazia asked if the poet would explain the appearance of both homosexual and heterosexual prostitution in the book. He explained that an addict, to satisfy his drug habit, was often forced to sell his body "as a practical thing, to get money for the drugs (Trans. p. 265)." Prostitution was often a result of addiction, and was therefore one of the themes of the book.

Neither lawyer, nor the judge, had anything further of Ginsberg, and he stepped from the stand.

DeGrazia asked Hudson to clarify his decision to allow the book reviews and articles as evidence of the book's recognition. He was concerned over the content of the reviews. He intimated that Hudson did not have to read the reviews, since it was not their substance which demonstrated public recognition, but their mere existence. Hudson stated flatly, "I am not going to ad lib upon the ruling ... (Trans. p. 268)." It is no surprise that deGrazia did not wish the reviews to stand as evidence of the book's value. The unfavorable ones implied that Naked Lunch assaulted the Freudian belief which suggests that sex must be repressed for art to emerge; unrepressed sexual energy accelerates a decline in the concern for art and civilization. Also on trial with Burroughs' book was repression for art's sake vs. liberation for art's sake. Such a non-legal question could not be decided by the judge, but the reviews which broached the subject could easily be misinterpreted by him.

DeGrazia began his final argument by quoting Mary
McCarthy's review of Naked Lunch in the New York Review
of Books, and continued with a discussion of recent obscenity
decisions. He explained that the Roth test required that no
book could be banned if it had the slightest social importance.
Hudson would have to conclude from the testimony of witnesses,
the documentary evidence, and the book itself that it was
totally worthless and devoid of social value before he could
properly rule Naked Lunch obscene. He asserted:

> It does not matter, Your Honor, that the book may
> be shocking, revolting, disgusting, indecent or of-
> fensive. As our Supreme Court said in Roth:
> 'Books expressing ideas having even the slightest
> redeeming importance, ' unorthodox ideas, contro-
> versial ideas, even ideas hateful to the prevailing
> climate of opinion, have the full protection of the
> guarantee. For once a book is seen to have any
> importance at all, it is entitled, its entitlement to
> freedom is not to be weighed against its otherwise
> objectionable features. (Trans. p. 280).

To impress on Hudson the new national limits of free expression, deGrazia mentioned that the Supreme Court in Illinois
extended to night club entertainer and satirist Lenny Bruce
the right of free expression. He also reminded the judge
that Burroughs' book dealt with the hell of drug addiction,
and he asked rhetorically, "Whoever, suggested that Hell
could be anything other than shocking, revolting, disgusting,
indecent and offensive? (Trans. p. 282). "

Finally deGrazia quoted from a letter written to him
by Burroughs on sex. [64] He then read from Sigmund Freud
and John Dewey on the absolute necessity of artistic freedom
for the public health. In his closing remarks to the court,
deGrazia indicated his resolve to fight for the freedom of the
book.

> Your Honor, I agree, I think the witnesses we
> heard here today, who have read Naked Lunch,
> and have testified for the court and for us and
> for you also agree: I am sure the U. S. Supreme
> Court will if necessary agree: I hope you agree.
> (Trans. p. 287).

With that hope, deGrazia thanked the court for its careful
consideration.

Immediately Hudson asked deGrazia if <u>Naked Lunch</u> had
been tried before.   He was looking for a legal benchmark.
DeGrazia told him that the entire book had never been tried,
but excerpts were tried in Federal District Court in Chicago.

Cowin informed the judge he would cite the cases he
used in the brief he would file later.   He began his final remarks by instructing the court in the legal history of obscenity,
and quoted Justice of the U. S. Supreme Court Brennan:

> "Implicit in the history of the First Amendment is
> the fact that obscenity is completely without re-
> deeming parlance and is not entitled to protection
> of the guarantees of the First Amendment (Quoted
> Trans. p. 288). "

Cowin reviewed the three pronged test for obscenity outlined
in <u>Roth</u> and <u>Manual Enterprises vs. Day</u>--social value, prurient interest, patent offensiveness.

He directed his attention to the last part of the test
and concluded that the book on trial met the criteria because

> the total effect of the book, the profanity, the
> references to homosexuality, the perversion that
> characterizes page after page of this writing, will
> so overwhelm any other material that he may find
> any other point he may get from the book, that, in
> effect, he will be affronted, if not by the language,
> then by some of the descriptions (Trans. pp. 290-
> 291).

The reasons Cowin gave may not have been within the spirit
or the letter of the test, since he had obtrusively weighed
social value against offensiveness, something the court had
warned against.   He explained that the prurient interest test
required that the dominant appeal of the book be toward a
morbid or shameful interest in sex, nudity, or excretion.
<u>Naked Lunch</u> contained many descriptions of sexual acts and
substantial references to excrement.   The attorney conceded
that if such things were mentioned once or twice or even
fifteen times in a work it would possibly be considered within
normal limits.   But he observed that it becomes abnormal

> when out of approximately two-hundred and thirty to
> forty pages of the book they appear on virtually
> every single page, described, characterized in a

fashion that the average reader ... is not used to,
but I submit would be shocked by, then I submit
this appeals to the prurient interests (Trans. p.
292).

The questions Cowin fired at the witnesses on cross-examination concerning the frequency of the references to homosexuality, sexual intercourse, and excretion were designed to establish and support his claim that the whole of Naked Lunch appealed to the prurient interest.

Then in evaluating the opinions of the witnesses for the
book, Cowin demonstrated a commonly held misconception of
critical literary opinion. He asserted what he had suggested,
while cross-examining Mailer, that is, the testimony the court
heard was not Burroughs', but the point of view of each wit-
ness--Ginsberg, Ciardi, Mailer. Not only did he suggest
biased, self-aggrandizement in their judgments, he went on
to accuse the witnesses of professional incompetence by observing that these witnesses had the ability to find value in
any piece of writing. Cowin claimed that each of the witnesses could not discriminate, for whatever reason, a piece
of good writing from a bad one, though he said he was not
attempting to discredit the witnesses. His argument led
finally to this conclusion:

What value has been brought out in testimony relative
to this book is value created by the witnesses; it is
not value inherent in the book (Trans. p. 294).

When one considers this statement in isolation, its logic falls
flat. Value defined simply deals not with the "inherent" worth
of the thing itself, but that which is assigned or agreed upon.

In spite of the number of witnesses who testified, he
urged the ban of the book because it had no social value.
The witnesses, Cowin contended, were experts who would have
no book banned. The value the book may have had, was lost,
overwhelmed by the frequent references to homosexuality and
perversion, and by the use of profanity. In short "this book
is hard-core pornography" (Trans. p. 295) according to the
law and precedent in Massachusetts defining the term.

Finally Cowin pleaded to the sensibility of the judge,
and reminded him that the case strained the social value test
to breaking. If he did not find Naked Lunch obscene, Cowin
warned, he was abdicating his legal responsibility, and "leaving

[it] to a series of witnesses all of whom are strongly opposed
to the idea of the right of the state to censor material at all
(Trans. p. 297)." He ended with a call for the declaration
of Naked Lunch as obscene, the denial of its constitutional
protection, and a ban on its publication and distribution.

DeGrazia reminded Hudson that the Attorney General
had brought no witnesses to refute the social importance of
the book. Calling it hard-core pornography, deGrazia interpreted, "shows how hardpressed [Cowin] is in this case
(Trans. p. 298)." The law required that all three tests be
met before a work could be obscene, deGrazia noted. His interpretation of the three-pronged test for obscenity was not
totally accepted at that time. It was this clarification of Roth
which had to be decided before Naked Lunch could be judged
properly under the Constitution.

However, Hudson had only to judge the book in the
context of the laws of Massachusetts. He took the case under
advisement, and awaited the submission of legal briefs before
he would hand down a ruling.

All arguments concluded, the court was adjourned.

Chapter 13

CENSORSHIP IN LOS ANGELES

The Boston newspapers reported the highlights of the final day of testimony, failing to mention either Cowin's cross-examination or final statement. Judge Hudson's constant questions on the second day were also unmentioned by the press, though one report included a picture of Ginsberg and quoted his praise of Burroughs' book. [1]

The first of the trial witnesses to write about the event was John Ciardi, who took advantage of his Saturday Review column to comment on the Boston trial of Naked Lunch in a fashion similar to his previous articles on the Big Table controversy in Chicago. [2] The trial was the first he had witnessed personally, and the court action impressed him as a "torrent of reason" released down "an unerodable molehill." The whole book banning process was absurd and ineffective, and as far as he was concerned, the unbanning of a book amounted to pocket-book justice, making the censorship situation disgraceful.

> Precedents now firmly established make it as nearly inevitable as the law can be that any book defended long enough to a high enough court, which is to say expensively enough, will finally be cleared. It follows, with negligible exceptions, that a book can be banned only by exhaustion of the defendant's resources. [3]

Ciardi observed that censorship actions wastefully encumbered the courts, constituted harassment, and perverted justice. Even before Hudson had time to issue his verdict, Ciardi felt sure Naked Lunch would be found obscene, making an appeal to a higher court necessary in order to reverse the ban.

Defense attorney Edward deGrazia, on the other hand, was not nearly as pessimistic. He expressed his optimism in a letter to California attorney Frank D. Laven:

We expect a rapid decision within one or two months,
and there is an excellent chance that we will get a
favorable decision. [4]

Laven had been selected as the legal representative of Isaac
Galanti and Sidney Earle Frank.

On the 11th of September of the previous fall, 1964,
two complaints were filed in Los Angeles Municipal Court.
Complaint number W33846 charged Frank, and complaint number W33845 charged Galanti with a misdemeanor violation of
Section 311. 2 of the Penal Code of the State of California--
the state's obscenity statute. [5] The complaint alleged that
on August 4, 1964, Frank sold and distributed obscene matter,
a book titled The Sex Scholar by Monte Steele and one titled
Naked Lunch by William S. Burroughs. Galanti was similarly
charged for selling and distributing the two books on August
7, 1964. The court action which followed was different from
the Boston trial. The Los Angeles case involved criminal
proceedings against the bookseller and distributor, in contrast
to the in rem action against the book itself. If the books were
found to be obscene, and the men to have in fact sold them,
then they would go to jail.

On January 28, 1965, only a few weeks after the Boston trial, the case which involved Naked Lunch was heard in
Division 2A of the Municipal Court of Los Angeles Judicial
District by Judge Alan G. Cambell. Roland Fairfield argued
the case for Los Angeles City Attorney Roger Arnebergh.
For Judge Cambell, the principle question in the case was
whether or not either of the books in question should be received into evidence. He had read all of The Sex Scholar and
most of Naked Lunch. Although he found Burroughs' text "revolting, nauseating, repugnant, ... it perhaps cannot be said
that its predominant appeal taken as a whole, is to the prurient
interest and so on. "[6] There was no doubt in his mind that
the content of the book went substantially beyond the customary
limits of candor in description. But if the whole text were
considered, he felt it did not meet the prurient interest test.

Not surprisingly however, Cambell referred to "A. J. 's
Annual Party (NL, pp. 88-103), " as a sticking point. Both
Cowin and Hudson found the section objectionable. The Los
Angeles judge felt the section was independent within itself
and had relatively little to do with the rest of the book. He
was concerned over the possibility that an author or an editor
could put together a book beyond the reach of an obscenity

statute, and then "put in it a section which is clearly and totally obscene (L. A. Partial Trans., p. 5)" as a way of circumventing the law.

The judge was quick to qualify his general observations, reminding those in court:

> However the complaints here do not charge the distribution, possession, and so on, of this chapter entitled "A. J.'s Annual Party" or of any other specified portion of the book and separate it from the rest; it undertakes to say that the whole book is obscene (L. A. Partial Trans., p. 6).

Whatever else the book was, Cambell concluded, it did not appeal predominantly to the prurient interest. He offered several alternative appeals the book might have:

> One person might say its predominant interest is to complete boredom; that it is tiresome and difficult to read. And another one would say that no one in his right mind would have any interest in reading it. Another one might say it says nothing (L. A. Partial Trans., p. 6).

But he repeated his belief that Naked Lunch did not appeal to the prurient interest.

Judge Cambell then advised the prosecutor that if he chose to stand on count II of the complaint against Frank and Galanti, the Naked Lunch count, he would "not be authorized to receive the book in evidence and consequently that I may not be authorized to elect that a charge under either of the count II's to go to the jury (L. A. Partial Trans., p. 6)." The suggestion that the Burroughs book be dropped from the case was unmistakeable and strong.

In an effort to persuade the judge to reconsider his recommendation on Naked Lunch, prosecutor Fairfield directed the judge's attention to selected pages of the text. Cambell, however, stood firm on his suggestion. But the attorney tried another approach to convince the judge to reconsider.

> Fairfield: Your honor, I would just like to point out to the court that the following words are used in the book a total of 234 times on 235 pages; and I will spell them rather than say them in the court--

Cambell: Go ahead and say them. We hear them
here probably at least once a week.

Fairfield: Fuck, shit, ass, cunt, prick, asshole,
cock-sucker. Two hundred and thirty-four times
on two-hundred and thirty-five pages.

Cambell: You mean each of those happen to be
used exactly the same number of times?

Fairfield: No your Honor (L. A. Partial Trans.,
pp. 9-10).

At this point the judge reminded the attorney for the city that
the courts had refused to go along with the notion that the
obscene character of a work could be determined by counting
words, or counting the pages on which they appeared.

Judge Cambell subsequently ruled that Naked Lunch
could not be allowed into evidence, but the case against The
Sex Scholar continued. [7]

Although the case against Naked Lunch appeared to be
coincidental, Grove helped defray the legal costs. Both Frank
and Galanti were associated with California Magazines, Inc.,
and received $1,500 in credit against their account with Grove
to cover Laven's $1,840.50 fee for the defense of the Bur-
roughs book. [8]

Laven was not unknown to Grove Press, having defended Miller's Tropic of Cancer previously. The case against
Naked Lunch could have signaled a repeat of the numerous
state and local actions similar to those which plagued Miller's
Tropic. But a barrage of legal actions did not take place. [9]

Neither did the censorship in Los Angeles have the
importance of the case being decided in Boston by Judge Hudson.

Chapter 14

DECISION IN BOSTON

Both William I. Cowin and Edward deGrazia filed briefs
with the court shortly after the trial of Naked Lunch ended on
January 13, 1965. On March 23, 1965, Judge Hudson issued
his decision titled "Findings of Material Facts and Order for
Decree."

To the surprise of no one, the judge ruled that the
book was "obscene, indecent, and impure ... [and] taken as a
whole is predominantly prurient, hard-core pornography, and
utterly without redeeming social importance."[1] He rejected
the main contention of the defense that the book was of social
and scientific value because it contained detailed descriptions
of the drug addict's delirium. He refused the claim because,
it seemed to him, that if he agreed, then the door of the First
Amendment protection would, in his opinion, be open to the
publication of "trash" by a "mentally sick" author.

Hudson also felt the book contained graphic descriptions
of the visions of an addict, but had nothing that even remotely
resembled plot. From this the judge concluded "that the
author first collected the foulest and vilest phrases describing
unnatural sexual experiences, and tossed them indescriminate-
ly...."[2] Hudson also found the book saturated with profanity
and filthy language.

In applying the law to the text, Hudson complained that
the legal principles since the 1957 Roth decision were not
clear. To resolve his quandary, he relied on Justice Stewart's
much quoted, and often ridiculed, definition of hard-core
pornography set forth in Jacobellis vs. Ohio, "I know it when
I see it."[3]

Reaction to the ban of Naked Lunch was quick, and
ranged from dismay to outrage over the application of the
law to Burroughs' book.[4] Defense attorney Edward deGrazia
reacted to the decision by appealing it on March 25, 1965.

Shortly after the ban was placed formally on Naked
Lunch, the "action against a defendant named Theodore Mavrikos for sale of the book, Naked Lunch, was dismissed by
the District Attorney's Office on an oral motion on April 12,
1965. "[5] It appears odd that the District Attorney would drop
the charges, especially since the recent ban made the sale of
the book a violation of the obscenity law.   But the explanation in this instance is more political than legal.   The State
Attorney General's Office under Edward Brooke, shortly after
the Naked Lunch trial, "announced formally a policy of termi-
nating any unauthorized prosecution of a bookseller by a district attorney. "[6] So Mavrikos, arrested in January of 1963
for selling a copy of the book to undercover vice-squad detectives, was released from the charges. [7] The spirit of the
in rem procedure developed by Brooke's office prevailed, but
Naked Lunch remained banned in Boston.

On October 8, 1965, the case to reverse the decision
against the Burroughs book was argued before the Massachusetts Supreme Judicial Court. [8] The Naked Lunch appeal came
as three other cases involving obscenity laws were before the
United States Supreme Court.   The three cases reflected the
jumble of misinterpretation which had followed in the wake of
the Roth case, and promised to clear the air on the issue.
As an example of the muddled state of the application of the
obscenity statute, Hudson used Jacobellis vs. Ohio as the precedent in the banning of Naked Lunch.   That case was considered in 1965 as a clarification of the test for obscenity
by stipulating that:

> The constitutional status of the questioned material
> cannot be made to turn on a "weighing" of its said
> importance against its "prurient appeal, " for a work
> cannot be prosecuted unless it is "utterly" without
> social importance. [9]

Cowin's closing remarks at the trial concluded that Burroughs'
book was obscene based on the "weighing" of value and prurience.   Apparently that was the guide Hudson used in making
his decision.

The three obscenity cases were argued before the
U. S. Supreme Court on December 7 and 8, 1965.   They were
Ginzburg vs. U. S. 383 U. S. 463, Mishkin vs. New York 383
U. S. 502, and Memoirs of a Woman of Pleasure vs. Attorney
General 383 U. S. 413.   The third, commonly referred to as
Fanny Hill, began with a ban in Massachusetts in 1821; re-

tried on January 8, 1965, and banned once again on April 4,
1965. The case was contemporary with the one involving
Naked Lunch, and tried by the same prosecutor, William I.
Cowin. All three of the cases before the U. S. Supreme Court
sought clarifying definition. In the nine years since the Roth
decision, the high court had avoided the obscenity issue, choosing not to turn obscenity tests into dogma. However, it had
decided to clear up the confusion.

The Mishkin case involved the 1960 arrest of Edward
Mishkin in New York for selling pornographic books. Richard
Kuh, the attorney who prosecuted Lenny Bruce on obscenity
charges for the use of prohibited language and gestures in his
nightclub act, described Mishkin as "probably America's
leading pornographer of the offbeat."[10] He published books
on aberrations such as sado-masochism, lesbianism, and
fetishism. Under a no royalty contract, he paid writers between $100 and $200 to write pamphlets which carried such
titles as "Cult of the Spankers," "Dance with the Dominant
Whip," "Screaming Flesh," "Mistress of Leather," and "The
Tainted Pleasure." It cost 40¢ to print the material which
he sold for $5 to $15. In the New York court, Mishkin was
found guilty on the obscenity charges, fined $12,000, and
sentenced to three years in jail.[11] This was not Mishkin's
first appearance in court on obscenity charges. He was involved in Kingsley Books, Inc. vs. Brown (354 U. S. 436) in
1957. In that case a lower court injunction against the sale
of a series of Mishkin's books titled Nights of Horror was
upheld by the Supreme Court.

Because the latest Mishkin case did not involve literature or material which could reasonably fit into the gray
area of redeeming social value, it was singled out by a group
of literary intellectuals to formally put the Roth obscenity
tests to rest. The lawyer who defended Naked Lunch Edward
deGrazia was asked to file an amici curiae (friends of the
court) brief on behalf of Mishkin by Robert Silvers of The
New York Review of Books, Jason Epstein of Random House,
Barney Rosset of Grove Press, Richard Poirier of Partisan
Review, Norman Podhoretz of Commentary, Walter Hincle of
Ramparts, Walter Minton of G. P. Putnams', Eric Larrabee,
Paul Goodman, and Marshall Cohen. Generally, deGrazia
took the position in his brief that the constitutional guarantees
of free-expression were absolute. He recommended that the
Roth tests be put aside, and Mishkin be saved.[12]

On December 7, 1965, defense lawyer Emanuel Red-

field argued before the Supreme Court for Mishkin. He asserted that the sado-masochistic books in question did not appeal to the prurient interest of the average person. Though
they did appear disgusting and repelling, he conceded that only
the special audience for whom they were intended would be
sexually aroused by the material. The court would decide
this case on the question of the definition of the audience,
and the interpretation of the community standards. [13]

The second case before the court concerned another
controversial New York publisher, Ralph Ginzburg. He was
arrested for violating the Federal obscenity statutes by using
the mail to sell and distribute copies of the magazine Eros,
the newsletter Liaison, and a book titled The Housewife's
Handbook on Selective Promiscuity. The Federal District
Court sentenced him to five years in jail, and fined him
$42,000. An Appeals Court affirmed the conviction, con-
cluding that all three of the Roth tests had been met by each
publication.

Contrary to the findings of the lower court, Ginzburg's
lawyer argued before the Supreme Court justices that the publications had social importance. The prosecutor, on the other
hand, urged the continued proscription of the material, because
stories and pictures conceded to have value had been incor-
porated with highly objectionable material in what appeared to
be a blatant effort to short-circuit the redeeming social value
test. The question of the manner in which Ginzburg advertised his publication was mentioned only tangentially. However, the decision in the Ginzburg case would turn on just
this point, and would directly affect the decision on Naked
Lunch in Massachusetts. [14] The court was irritated with the
obscenity issue, and the fear of the possible consequences of
their decisions was jokingly expressed by Chief Justice Warren during the Ginzburg oral arguments:

> I'm sure the Court doesn't want to be a final censor
> in reading all the prurient literature in the country
> to determine whether it has any social value [laugh-
> ter]. [15]

The third case before the Supreme Court had many
links to the Naked Lunch case. A Book Named John Cleland's
Memoirs of a Woman of Pleasure vs. Attorney General of
Massachusetts (383 U.S. 413) involved a book which was often
called a classic of 18th-century pornography. The attorney
arguing the case for Massachusetts was Edward Brooke's

Assistant Attorney General William I. Cowin, the same man who argued against Naked Lunch less than a year before. John Cleland's book was written while he was in English debtor's prison, and published in that country in 1749. In 1821 Peter Holmes was arrested in Massachusetts for publishing the book. When in 1963 Putnams' announced the republication of the book, it would not escape the attention of the authorities. The Massachusetts Supreme Judicial Court heard an appeal of the lower court's ban on January 8, 1965, only a few days before the Naked Lunch trial on the 12th and 13th. On April 4, 1965, a verdict was returned deeming the book obscene. 16 In spite of a decision absolving the text in New York, Massachusetts banned the book. The case went to the Supreme Court of the United States.

Charles Rembar presented the case for the book before the high court. In his oral argument, he reminded the justices that overwhelming evidence had been presented at the lower court trials, affirming the social value of Fanny Hill. Norman Holland, who appeared on behalf of Naked Lunch, also was among the witnesses for Fanny Hill. Rembar insisted that the court view each test for obscenity independently, not weighed against one another.

Cowin, on the other hand, argued that the book was obscene except for ten pages in the beginning which conveyed Fanny from the outskirts of England to the center of London, and thirty-two intermittent transitional pages. The rest of the book, he told the Court, was full of sexual scenes, descriptions, and references. He rejected the testimony of expert witnesses as biased, reflecting their vested interest in obscenity cases. Although they were honest men, it was his opinion that such witnesses came to court determined to protect any piece of writing. 17

The cases were in, and the justices began their deliberations while the legal and literary communities awaited the decisions. The Supreme Judicial Court of Massachusetts also delayed its decision on the Naked Lunch appeal, pending the outcome of Memoirs, Mishkin, and Ginzburg.

On March 21, 1966, the U.S. Supreme Court handed down its decision in each of the three obscenity cases. The majority opinion of the Court upheld the conviction of Ralph Ginzburg, because "each of the accused publications was originated or sold as stock in trade of the sordid business of pandering--'the business of purveying textual or graphic matter

openly advertised to appeal to the erotic interest of their
customers. ' "18 The court cited the efforts, revealed in
the lower court testimony, of the editors of Eros to secure
mailing privileges from the postmasters in Intercourse and
Blue Ball, Pennsylvania for the salacious appeal of their
names. The two towns turned down the requests because
they could not handle the expected volume of mail. But Middle-
sex, New Jersey granted the publisher the privileges. The
court pointed out the "leer of the sensualist in the advertising
which boasted of sexual candor in the publication as erotically
arousing therefore stimulated the reader to accept them as
prurient. "19 Unlike other obscenity cases, Ginzburg did not
offer clarified definitions, but added new complications to the
concept of obscenity. In proper legalese, the court explained
its interpretation:

> Where an exploitation of interests in titillation by
> pornography is shown with respect to material lend-
> ing itself to such exploitation through pervasive
> treatment of description of sexual matters, such
> evidence may support the determination that the
> material is obscene even though in other contexts
> the material would escape such condemnation. 20

In other words, even if a work were not obscene, it could be
judged as such if it were so advertised.

Justice Douglas dissented, because he considered the
use of sex "an advertiser's technique as old as history. "21
He observed that the sexuality of ads did not detract nor add
to the quality of the merchandise offered for sale, mentioning
the use of thighs, calves, bosoms, and eyes to sell lotions,
tires, cars, clothes, liquor, and food.

Justice Black also dissented, reiterating this belief
that the First Amendment prohibited censorship of any kind.
Even conservative Justice Harlan objected to the question of
advertising, because it appeared to him as an eleventh hour
rationalization. Justice Stewart thought the material was vulgar and unedifying, but dissented because the First Amendment
protected all forms of expression. Stewart considered censorship as a reflection of society's lack of confidence in itself.

The conviction of Edward Mishkin was also upheld by
a six to three vote of the Justices. Writing the majority
opinion, Justice Brennan noted that the material was designed
and directed toward a sexually deviant group. The defense

had made no effort to refute the charge that the books appealed to the prurient interest of such groups. They contended, however, that the average person would not be titillated by the material, merely repulsed. In his opinion, Brennan explained that the "average person" text, as defined in Roth, amounted to a rejection of the previous precedent, modeled after the 1868 English case, Queen vs. Hicklin, which required that the "most susceptible" member of the society be protected. Brennan considered that the reference to "average" in Roth did not exclude material directed toward a clearly defined deviant group. Because no attempt was made to counter the evidence establishing the prurient appeal of the material, the conviction was allowed to stand.

Justices Black, Stewart, and Douglas dissented. Black called censorship un-American, and prescribed that the Supreme Court "decline to act as a national board of censors over speech and press."[22]

Both the Mishkin and Ginzburg decisions indicated that the high court was in no mood to interpret the First Amendment as absolute dogma. For liberal observers, the two rulings to uphold the convictions of the publishers was a repressive gesture, strongly and dramatically affirming the concept in Roth that "obscenity" was not constitutionally protected expression.

The majority opinion in the Memoirs case was also written by Justice Brennan. He noted that the term "obscene" had the same range of meaning in Massachusetts as it did in constitutional interpretation. He then reviewed the Roth definition, and for the first time articulated the three tests for obscenity:

> Under this definition, as elaborated in subsequent cases, three elements must coalesce: it must be established that (a) the dominant theme of the material taken as a whole appeals to a prurient interest in sex; (b) the material is patently offensive because if affronts contemporary community standards relating to the description or representation of sexual matters; and (c) the material is utterly without redeeming social value.[23]

Brennan cautioned that each element be applied independently; no single criterion must be weighed against or cancelled by another. The justice concluded that because the Massachu-

setts court determined that the literary value, which was not
disputed, was outweighed by its prurient appeal and patent
offensiveness, the ruling must be reversed under the new interpretation of the test. He qualified the new interpretation
by noting that a classification of obscenity might not be improper under all circumstances in which redeeming social
value was evident. He was referring to the new criterion
of pandering spelled out in the Ginzburg decision. In other
words, if a book such as Fanny Hill were commercially ex-
ploited for the sake of prurient appeal, excluding all other
values, a conclusion that it was utterly without social value
might very well be justified. As long as it had value, however minimal, and it was published and distributed on the
basis of that value, it was due the full protection of the First
Amendment.

The Memoirs decision, especially the social value test,
signaled a great victory in the opinion of attorney Charles
Rembar for the free exploration of sexual questions in literature. His book, The End of Obscenity, [24] was based on
that reading. To others, the pandering qualification marked
a return to Victorian prudery, placing a plain cover on sexually candid books once again. [25]

The three March 21, 1966 Supreme Court decisions
had for the moment cleared the air and resolved some of the
legal questions on the obscenity issue. The Supreme Judicial
Court could now rule on the question of the obscenity of Naked
Lunch, which had been before it since the previous Fall, in
an atmosphere of greater constitutional assurance and definition.

The decision of the Massachusetts high court was
rendered on July 7, 1966, in Attorney General vs. A Book
Named 'Naked Lunch' 351 Mass., 298. [26] The ruling marked
the first application of the new obscenity tests to a work of
contemporary literature. [27] In the more relaxed interpretation of the obscenity laws, the social and literary value of the
book established at the trial would count favorably toward
reversing the ban.

The Massachusetts court felt that Naked Lunch "may
appeal to the prurient interest of deviants and those curious
about deviants," [28] and to the members of that group "it is
grossly offensive and is what the author himself says, 'brutal,
obscene, and disgusting.' "[29] Although the first two tests
for obscenity had been met, the justices conceded that the
value of the book had been demonstrated in the reviews and

articles submitted as evidence, and through the testimony of expert witnesses.   The court realized that it was not bound by such opinion, but it was difficult for them to ignore the serious treatment of the book by the literary community.   Applying the new tests outlined in the Memoirs decision, they concluded that Naked Lunch could not be considered "utterly without redeeming social value."   It was therefore not obscene.

Still mindful of the other two Supreme Court rulings, the Massachusetts justices considered the question of pandering.   They recognized that the Ginzburg decision took into account the manner of publication and distribution of the book, and that commercial exploitation of a book's sexual appeal could result in the loss of its First Amendment privileges. In reversing the ban on the Burroughs book decreed by Judge Hudson, they qualified their ruling with this warning:

> This final decree shall be without prejudice to the bringing of new proceedings with respect to this book under the appropriate sections of the G. L. c. 272 [General Laws], if it shall appear that, after March 21, 1966, the date of the three recent Supreme Court cases, already cited, any persons have been or are advertising this book in this Commonwealth in a manner to exploit it for the sake of its possible prurient appeal. [30]

The majority ruling carried a note that Chief Justice of the Commonwealth Raymond S. Wilkins did not take part in the consideration of this case.   There was nothing sinister in his refusal.   Quite simply, he was ill when the case was argued in October 1965, and for that reason excluded himself from the judgment.

The qualified victory secured in Massachusetts was a limp one, but a victory nevertheless.   The book could be freely purchased, as long as the advertising remained pristine.

The decision to remove the ban on Naked Lunch was not unanimous, as the duplication of only the majority opinion in the paperback edition of the book might suggest.   Two justices, Paul C. Reardon and Paul G. Kirk dissented. [31]   Although Kirk found the book disgusting, his dissenting opinion was based largely on the undeserved weight he felt his colleagues had given to the testimony of the expert witnesses. As far as he was concerned, the acceptance by the court that the opinion of a witness in any proceeding was valid, binding,

or decisive of the case amounted to "a surrender of the judicial function to absolutism."[32]   Kirk had of course misinterpreted the use the majority had made of the testimony.   It
had not been considered decisive or binding as he thought;
rather it had been used as evidence of social value.   Since no
evidence to the contrary had been introduced by the prosecutor,
the testimony of the expert witnesses stood as evidence of the
book's importance.

Justice Reardon, on the other hand, objected to the
majority opinion in much stronger terms.   He prefaced his
remarks by recalling that Massachusetts led the call for a
national Bill of Rights in 1788, and asserted the disinclination
of the Commonwealth's high court to act as a final censor for
published material.   But he added that he did not agree with
Justice Black that the First Amendment was absolute.

Since the obscenity statute still had power, Reardon
concluded that he must rule on the book:

> Consonant with the duty laid upon us by the statute,
> I have read the book and found it to be a revolting
> miasma of unrelieved perversion and disease, graph-
> ically described in the finding of the trial judge.   It
> is, in truth, literary sewage....[33]

Reardon did not overlook the recent decisions of the U. S.
Supreme Court, but he did take issue with the other justices
who considered the testimony of the expert witnesses and the
book reviews as evidence of literary value.   Citing no less
than six cases, he observed:

> Our experience with allegedly pornographic works
> over the years in Massachusetts has revealed that
> there is no dearth of experts ready to leap to the
> defense of such of them as have come under scrutiny
> from time to time.[34]

To emphasize his point, he asserted that the testimony of
Ciardi, Mailer, Jackson, and Ginsberg "became weak under
examination."[35]   He also pointed out that the reviews submitted as evidence were less than praiseworthy, and of course
he emphasized that the court did not enjoy the privilege of a
cross-examination of their authors.[36]   The qualification which
left future prosecution open in the case of pandering disturbed
Reardon.   In his opinion the case should have been decided
differently on this point.

> To remand the matter for a hearing on advertising
> would eliminate the likelihood of a complete retrial
> on all points in the event that the Attorney General
> desires to take new action in the light of the Mem-
> oirs decision. [37]

Reardon brought up the point because he had seen in the exhibits an ad for Naked Lunch which claimed, "Not for minors--
for adults only. Exactly as Printed in Paris by Olympia
Press. A literary masterpiece by some, and a piece of pornography by others. Shocking! Startling! Definitely not for
the squeamish. A searing experience."[38]

Reardon concluded his remarks with a final opinion on
the obscenity of the book:

> In sum it is my view that this book should not be
> allowed to slide by the statutory prohibitions on the
> grounds set forth in the majority opinion. We should
> not cease in our endeavor to uphold our own statute
> when it still possesses some vitality. In the light
> of the findings of the trial judge and the foregoing
> discussions I would remand this matter to the Su-
> perior Court for the limited purpose of taking evi-
> dence on the matter in which this book was pro-
> duced, publicized, and sold. [39]

But the opinions of Reardon and Kirk formed the minority.

For the first time since its original publication as excerpts in Big Table #1, Naked Lunch was free of obscenity
litigation.

Shortly after the decision was reached, Grove Press
expressed some anxiety over the possibility of future litigation related to pandering as outlined by Reardon. According
to the Boston Globe, the publisher felt the decision had resolved nothing. They had no control over individual bookdealers, and were not certain how to prevent commercial exploitation once the book was released for sale in Massachusetts. [40]

A Boston editorialist, commenting on the recent decision, called Naked Lunch "a dirty book and we think its literary importance has been greatly overrated."[41] Yet it was
not merely the contents which were of concern, it was the
new pandering interpretation which appeared most ominous.

There was no way for bookdealers to avoid prosecution under
the ruling "if they accurately described the book's contents
in their advertising."[42]

No subsequent action against the book was taken by the
Attorney General. Nevertheless Grove Press did not wish to
precipitate another court action in Boston. Instead it used the
court fight itself as a selling point by incorporating into the
introduction of the paperback edition, excerpts from the testimony given at the Superior Court trial, as well as the entire
majority decision of the Massachusetts Supreme Judicial Court.
In this way the book could be advertised effectively without
pandering to any notion of prurience.

The author and publisher were certainly satisfied with
the outcome in Boston. Even Attorney General Edward Brooke
was pleased that the in rem strategy his office had devised to
cope with the obscenity question had proved to be humane and
legally sound. The procedure had worked well.

Brooke, while Senator from Massachusetts, had this
comment on the case:

> I am still convinced that our answer was the cor-
> rect one even though it has the elements of cumber-
> someness and takes a good deal more time to pur-
> sue.[43]

Brooke's Assistant Attorney General William I. Cowin
was also satisfied with the decision. After the U.S. Supreme
Court ruling on Memoirs, Cowin felt that the majority decision to reverse the ban on Naked Lunch was inevitable. Only
the dissent by the two justices surprised him.

Looking back at the case, Mr. Cowin, who is now in
private law practice in Boston, observed:

> As far as the merits were concerned, I think the
> decision was correct then and is correct now. I
> do not believe that very much is left of the First
> Amendment if its strength is so reduced that it does
> not protect a book of the quality of Naked Lunch
> from proscription.[44]

Chapter 15

NAKED LUNCH AFTER 1966:
THE LAST OF THE OBSCENE

In her chapter "From the Warren Court to the Burger Court" in Literature Obscenity and Law, [1] Felice Flanery Lewis demonstrates that the legal question of obscenity after 1966 no longer concerned works of literature. She wrote that after that date:

> A multitude of obscenity cases continued to come before the courts, but one must search deligently to find any involving a specific work on fiction. In California, litigation arose in 1968 over Michael McClure's one-act play The Beard, but the charge was that McClure and two performers were responsible for 'lewd and dissolute conduct in a public place' rather than the play itself was obscene. In New York, an unpublished play by Lennox Raphael, Che, was held obscene in 1970. In Utah, a book dealer was arrested in 1973 for selling a number of books, among them Anthony Burgess's A Clockwork Orange, but authorities later dropped the charges. Although litigation over paper back pulps occurred occasionally, censorship actions seem to have been directed primarily against other types of material: magazines, tabloids, paintings and photography, miscellaneous articles such as an artificial penis, and particularly motion pictures. [2]

This shift in focus of obscenity related litigation supports Charles Rembar's contention in his book, The End of Obscenity, that the Memoirs decision would mark the end of the censorship of literature in the United States. One need only consider how distant the cases of actor Harry Reems, for his role in the film Deep Throat, and publisher Larry Flynt, for his Hustler magazine, are from the cases which involved recognized works of literature such as Tropic of Cancer, Lady Chatterley's Lover, Ulysses, and Naked Lunch.

The controversy over the right of Americans to choose what they could view and read did not disappear after 1966, by any means. But works of literature proved a ridiculous target for enforcement of existing obscenity statutes. The situation reached a point in 1970 at which the repeal of all obscenity laws was urged in the conclusion of the Report of the Commission on Obscenity and Pornography. However, that absolute interpretation of the First Amendment would not prevail. Then President Richard Nixon, of course, disassociated himself from the findings of the commission which was appointed by Lyndon Johnson.

Obscenity law interpretation took a decidedly conservative turn in 1973 when the U.S. Supreme Court redefined the criteria for a legal determination of the obscene in Miller vs. California, 413 U.S. 15 (1973). This particular case dealt not with literary works, but unsolicited pictoral advertisements for a film and four books--Intercourse, Man-Woman, Sex Orgies, Illustrated, An Illustrated History of Pornography. Although the defense argued that the case was essentially involved with the question of the invasion of privacy and with the possibility of a minor receiving the material, the high court saw this case as a chance to clear up what it considered the judicial over statement in Memoirs which required that material be proved to be "utterly without redeeming social value." Its ruling in the Miller case softened the absolute interpretation of the value test, and modified the definition of "community standard" to be applied to the local rather than the national community by saying:

> It is neither realistic nor constitutionally sound to read the First Amendment as requiring that the people of Maine or Mississippi accept public depiction of conduct found tolerable in Las Vegas, or New York City. [3]

The redefinition of the community standard created a great deal of concern and fear that the censorship issue and its relationship to literature would again heat up. However, an empirical study of the effect of the Miller decision on the actions of prosecutors indicates that just the opposite has occurred after the 1973 ruling. The study undertaken by the New York University Law Review concludes that prosecutors are less willing to begin an obscenity action against all but the most obvious, hard-core pornography, and that even then they are unwilling to take court action. [4]

The Post Office, of course, changed its method of
dealing with questionable material shortly after the Big Table
case when the question of obscenity became a judicial, rather
than a departmental matter. And the U.S. Customs is now
reluctant to act against adult pornographic magazines in plain
wrappings requested by an American subscriber. A recent
case heard by Federal Judge Pierre N. Leval sitting in the
U.S. District Court for the Southern District of New York
handed down an opinion in U.S. vs. Various Articles of Obscene Merchandise 78-2475, on July 28, 1978, voiding a Customs seizure. Neither attorney sought to establish a community standard, leaving that process up to the judge. His
remarks reflect reluctance to serve as an ultimate censor:

> Heavy-handed censorship I think is a far more
> dangerous abuse than the discreet private consump-
> tion of adult materials intended for sexual stimula-
> tion. [5]

Such an attitude is not uncommon among judges, assuring the
relative safety of a work of literature from proscription in an
intellectual and legal climate which tolerates extremes in
sexual discussion.

The experience of Naked Lunch, then signals an end
to the censorship of literature in the United States; not an
end to obscenity censorship, but an end to literary censorship.
The battle between the First Amendment tradition of free expression and our Puritan heritage, which was first given con-
creteness by the granddaddy of American censors Anthony
Comstock, was brought to an uneasy rest with the decision to
reverse the ban on Naked Lunch. Critics of American literature have since been free to deal with Burroughs as a serious
artist, without the pressure of defending his work before a
hostile court. His book is no longer a literary oddity, or a
cause célèbre, but an accepted part of many university
courses.

Censorship of some sort will almost always exist, but
unless drastic changes occur in the way the courts deal with
explicit discussion of sex, Burroughs' book will retain its
spot in the literary history of the United States. Naked Lunch
has earned its unique distinction as the last work of literature
to be censored by the academy, the U.S. Post Office, the
U.S. Customs Service, and state and local government.

CHAPTER NOTES

CHAPTER 1

1. Maurice Girodias, "Confessions of a Booklegger's Son," Censorship No. 3, 1965, p. 10. This first person account is an excellent condensation of Girodias' publishing career. It is a witty as well as factual narrative. Among the topics handled in the article is a humorous, yet sensitive bombast of the bourgeois censorship policies of the deGaulle government.

2. Ibid.

3. Victor Bockris, "Information about the Operation: A Portrait of William Burroughs," The New Review, Vol. 13, No. 25 (April 1976), pp. 42-43. Essentially the same material appears as: Victor Bockris, "First Meetings: One Dozen Memories from the Files of William Burroughs as told to Victor Bockris," National Screw, Vol. 1, No. 5 (April 1977), pp. 9-14.

4. Girodias, p. 10.

5. Ibid. , p. 4.

6. Ibid. , p. 7.

7. Ibid. , p. 8.

8. An interesting though thoroughly misinformed discussion in George Dardess, "The Invisible William Burroughs," Dissertation: Rutgers University, 1970, makes the case that Burroughs wrote books for Olympia Press under the pen name Akbar del Piombo. Even though the undocumented argument is convincing, it rests on the unsupported assertion that Burroughs was indeed behind the pen. Instead of discussing the similarities between the two, while assuming they were the same individual, Dardess could have compared del Piombo's Fuzz Against Junk with Naked Lunch in demonstrating the thematic and stylistic affinities of the two books. But even such a comparison would have been equally fallacious if offered as proof that Burroughs was indeed del Piombo. On September 17, 1975, where Burroughs read to a crowd of almost 1,000 gathered at SUNY at Stony Brook, I asked him if he had written anything for Olympia Press under the name Akbar del Piombo. Almost irritated that the rumor still cir-

culated, he said flatly that the only pen name he ever used
was "Willy Lee" for his first book Junkie. After that one
instance he only used his own name. Burroughs went on to
identify del Piombo as the artist Rubington, who is credited
with the illustrations of some of the del Piombo books. In
the article cited above Girodias identified del Piombo as "an
American painter long established in Paris. "
    9.   Girodias, p. 8.
    10. "Maurice Girodias: In Trouble for His 'd. b. 's, "
Publishers' Weekly 188 (October 11, 1965), p. 34. See also
"Shy Pornographer, " Time 78 (November 3, 1961), pp. 88-89.
    11. Girodias, p. 9.
    12. Ibid. , p. 10.
    13. Allen Ginsberg, Howl and Other Poems, San
Francisco: City Lights, 1956, dedication page.
    14. William S. Burroughs, "from 'Naked Lunch', "
Chicago Review, Vol. 12, No. 1 (Spring 1958), pp. 23-30.
See also pages 1-8 of Naked Lunch, New York: Grove Press,
1959.
    15. Burroughs, "Chapter 2 of Naked Lunch, " Chicago
Review, Vol. 12, No. 3 (Autumn 1958), pp. 3-12. See also
pages 9-20 of Naked Lunch.

CHAPTER 2

    1.   Jack Mabley, "Filthy Writing on the Midway, "
Chicago Daily News, Saturday, October 25, 1958, p. 1.
    2.   Ibid.
    3.   Ibid.
    4.   Norman Mailer, "The Faith of Graffiti, " Esquire,
May, 1974, p. 77ff.
    5.   Mabley, "Filthy Writing on the Midway. "
    6.   Ibid.
    7.   Ibid.
    8.   The reconstruction which follows documents the
nature of the extra-legal supression of the Winter 1959 issue
of the Chicago Review which was scheduled to publish extensive excerpts from Burroughs' Naked Lunch. To demonstrate
the kind of censorship which greeted the author's work, this
chapter employs several sources, primarily Albert N. Podell's
"Censorship on the Campus" in San Francisco Review No. 2
and Report of the Special Committee of the Student Government Organization in re: The Chicago Review, 1959. Each
contributes valuable facts, evaluations, and comments on the
suppression of the Winter issue, however through only their
proximity to the time of the events do both incorporate the

opposing perspectives with the available facts.   In addition, the Report of the Special Committee (hereafter Report) is now only available through the archives of the University of Chicago. It is nevertheless invaluable because it was compiled by students unassociated with the magazine only a short time after the publication of the issue was stopped.   Because it includes information from meetings and interviews, it forms a solid primary source.

9.   Albert N. Podell, "Censorship on the Campus: The Case of the Chicago Review," San Francisco Review, Vol. 1, No. 2, 1959, pp. 73-74.   Podell was on the staff of the magazine at the time.   His article and the short account by Irving Rosenthal on pages 3-6 of Big Table #1 together form the best first person account from the magazine editor's point of view.   Considering the temptation to fall into excited rhetoric over the emotionally charged issue of "obscenity" and "censorship," both accounts show objectivity.

10.   Both Maroon charges and Mabley's response are quoted in Podell, "Censorship on Campus," p. 74.

11.   William S. Burroughs, "Chapter 2 of Naked Lunch," Chicago Review, Vol. 12, No. 3 (Autumn 1958), p. 4.   An interesting error appears on the first page of the Burroughs contribution, page 3.   His middle initial in the credit line is erroneously printed as "C." not "S." indicating his relative obscurity to the proofreader at least.

12.   Burroughs, "Chapter 2 of Naked Lunch," p. 7.

13.   Burroughs, p. 7.

14.   Burroughs, p. 8.

15.   Ibid. , p. 9.

16.   Ibid. , p. 10.

17.   Ibid. , p. 12.   Here "shit" refers not to excrement, but rather to the half-baked ideas and theories of the pimp.

18.   Chicago Review, Vol. 12, No. 3, p. 17.

19.   Ibid. , p. 44.

20.   Ibid. , p. 46.

21.   Ibid. , p. 48.

22.   Ibid. , p. 49.

23.   Podell, "Censorship on Campus," p. 74.

24.   Roth vs. United States, 354 U. S. 476 (1957).

25.   Podell, p. 76.

26.   Report of the Special Committee of the Student Government Organization in re: The Chicago Review, University of Chicago, 1959, p. 21.   Hereafter as Report.

27.   Podell, p. 77.

28.   Report, p. 21.

29.   Podell, p. 77.

30. Ibid., p. 78.
31. Report, p. 7.
32. Ibid., p. 6.
33. Ibid., p. 7. Based on interviews with two of the members present, the student committee investigating the Chicago Review prepared a summary of this meeting. It was then submitted to three of the others present for additions and corrections. All five substantiated the summary as correct. Chancellor Kimpton would not and submitted his own account of that meeting. It is included in the Report as "Appendix A" on pages 14ff.
34. In June of 1959 the question of the obscenity of the material was heard before a postal hearing officer in Chicago. The particulars leading up to that hearing and the subsequent Federal Court appeal are discussed below in Chapters 4, 5, and 6 which deal with Big Table #1. The suppression of the Chicago Review occasioned the birth of Big Table.
35. Report, p. 7.
36. Ibid.
37. Ibid., p. 8. This was the conclusion of the student committee which investigated the affair. Kimpton of course denied that pressure motivated his actions in his own account of the meeting.
38. Ibid.
39. Ibid.
40. Ibid.
41. Ibid.
42. Podell, p. 78.
43. Report, p. 9.
44. Podell, p. 78.
45. Report, p. 21.
46. Ibid.
47. Report, p. 15.
48. Report, p. 17.
49. Ibid.
50. Ibid.
51. Report, p. 18.
52. Ibid.
53. Report, p. 21.
54. Podell, p. 79. On Friday, December 5, 1978 the student investigators asked Kline about the manuscript (spelled K L E I N erroneously in the Report). He refused to comment, but referred them to his superior Mr. Trout. Trout asserted that the manuscripts had never left the press offices. On Tuesday, December 9, confronted with Trout's statement, Kline substantiated the story and added that he had lied to Rosenthal. The manuscripts, he admitted, had indeed been

in his safe all along. He also indicated that he "had been
under orders from the Comptroller's Office not to let Rosenthal see or have his manuscripts until they had given clear-
ance to do so (Report, p. 22)."

The investigators went to the Comptroller's office
to check on Kline's story on Friday December 12. The comptroller assured them that he "knew nothing about anything in
the foregoing account (Report, p. 22.)" All the members of
the Faculty Advisory Board of the Chicago Review were asked
about the incidents at the press. They replied that they had
not seen the manuscripts, nor been in contact with either the
press or the comptroller. Chancellor Kimpton also had neither seen the manuscripts nor talked with the press or comptroller. The investigators concluded: "The committee finds
this somewhat mysterious account of the events quite incon-
clusive. If either of Klein's [sic] statements is true the
administration is clearly implicated in some sort of nebulous
dealing; if neither of Klein's accounts is true we know even
less (Report, p. 22). "

55. Report, p. 5.
56. Ibid.
57. Report, p. 4. The administration officials referred to here by Dean Wilt in his two meetings with the
students investigating the matter are identified only as "financial authorities of the University. " Asked by the committee
if he could be more specific about the identity of the officials,
Wilt replied that he was not at liberty to do so. One could
speculate that the reference could have been anyone from
Chancellor Kimpton or a member of the Board of Trustees to
the Comptroller.

58. Pak was unable to issue a totally new Winter
issue. He admitted later that he could not assemble a staff
and new manuscripts then select and edit them in time for
the Winter deadline. The issue was scuttled. This explains
the conspicuous absence of Number 4 of Volume 12.

59. Joel Rosenthal to Lem Coley, 12-16-1977, in
Mr. Coley's possession. Joel Rosenthal is no relation to
Irving Rosenthal. He was charged with the setting up of the
student committee which reported to him as the student body
president.

60. Report, p. 20.
61. Ibid.
62. Ibid.
63. Report, p. 19.
64. Report, p. 20.
65. Report, p. 2.
66. Irving Rosenthal, "Editorial, " Big Table # 1,
Spring 1959, p. 6.

67.   Nelson Algren, "Chicago is a Wose," Nation 188,
February 28, 1959, p. 191.   Algren poked fun at the lisp of
one of the readers in his title by using "wose" for "rose."

                         CHAPTER 3

        1.   Irving Rosenthal, "Editorial," Big Table #1,
Spring 1959, pp. 3-6.
        2.   Report of the Special Committee of the Student
Government in re: The Chicago Review, Chicago: Student
Government of the University of Chicago, 1959.   The copy
held in the University archives was used in this and the pre-
ceding sections.   The Report is a valuable primary source.
Difficulty in its use, however, may be attributable to its fol-
lowing a chronology of the investigation of the incident, rather
than of the incident itself.
        3.   "August Derleth, Prolific Author," New York
Times, July 6, 1971, p. 36.
        4.   Ibid.
        5.   "Derleth, August (William)," in Contemporary
Authors, Vols. 1-4, ed. Kinsman and Tennenhouse, Detroit:
Gale Research, 1967, p. 244.
        6.   "The Hallucinatory Operators Are Real (An Inter-
view)," S F Horizons, No. 2 (1965), p. 3.
        7.   "Derleth, August (William)," p. 244.
        8.   William S. Burroughs, Naked Lunch, New York:
Grove Press, 1959, 1962, p. 221.
        9.   Big Table Magazine, Issue Number 1, Spring
1959, Post Office Department Docket # 1/150, Transcript of
Hearing, p. 31.   Hereafter referred to as "P. O. D. Docket
1/150, Transcript" by page number.
        10.   18 U.S. Code, Section 1461.
        11.   39 U.S. Code, Sections 259a, 259b, 259c.
        12.   James C. N. Paul and Murry L. Schwartz,
Federal Censorship: Obscenity in the Mail, New York: The
Free Press, 1961, p. 291.
        13.   P. O. D. Docket # 1/150, Transcript, p. 39.
        14.   P. O. D. Docket # 1/150, Transcript, p. 30.
        15.   Ibid.
        16.   "Initial Decision of the Hearing Examiner,"
P. O. D. Docket # 1/150, July 9, 1959, p. 1, in American
Civil Liberties Union, Illinois Division Papers, University of
Chicago, Box 38, Folder # 3.
        17.   Ibid.
        18.   Ibid., pp. 1-2.

19. Quoted in "Complaint Big Table vs. Carl A.
Schroeder, " no date, A. C. L. U. , Illinois Division Papers,
Box 38, Folder # 2.
20. Quoted in Richard Farr to Albert Podell, April
30, 1959, P. O. D. Docket # 1/150.
21. Quoted in "Complaint Big Table vs. Carl Schroeder, " A. C. L. U. , Illinois Division Papers, Box 38, Folder # 3.
22. Richard Farr to Albert Podell, April 30, 1959,
P. O. D. Docket # 1/150.
23. Richard Farr to Chicago Postmaster [Carl Schroe-
der], April 30, 1959, P. O. D. Docket # 1/150.
24. Albert Podell to Herbert B. Warburton, May 7,
1959, P. O. D. Docket # 1/150.
25. Ibid.
26. Al [Podell] to Irv [Rosenthal], Friday Morn [May
8, 1959], A. C. L. U. Archives Vol. 18-21a, "Big Table (mag),
P. O. Mail Ban, Chicago, Illinois, " Mudd Manuscript Library,
Princeton University Library.
27. Ibid. , p. 2.
28. Joel J. Sprayregen to Rowland Watts, May 8,
1959, A. C. L. U. Archives, Vol. 18-21a, "Big Table Mail
Ban" Mudd Manuscript Library, Princeton University Library.
29. Irving Rosenthal to Mr. Watts, May 11, 1959,
"Big Table Ban" Mudd Manuscript Library, Princeton University.
30. Receipt signed by Albert Podell, May 14, 1959,
P. O. D. Docket # 1/150.
31. Carl A. Schroeder to Docket Clerk, May 18,
1959, P. O. D. Docket # 1/150.
32. Mel Wulf to Joel Sprayregen, May 22, 1959.
"Big Table Ban, " Princeton University Library.
33. "Post Office Rules Off New Quarterly as Obscene, "
New York Post, May 24, 1959, clipping in "Big Table Ban, "
Princeton.
34. Farr to Podell, May 22, 1959, P. O. D. Docket
1/150.
35. Roth vs. U. S. 354 U. S. 476, quoted in Farr to
Podell, May 22, 1959, P. O. D. Docket # 1/150.
36. Dorothy C. Lang, Docket Clerk to Postmaster
[Schroeder], May 25, 1959, P. O. D. Docket # 1/150.
37. "Notice of Hearing, " May 25, 1959, P. O. D.
Docket # 1/150.
38. "Complaint, " no date, P. O. D. Docket # 1/150.
39. "Order, " May 25, 1959, P. O. D. Docket # 1/150.
40. Memo, May 28, 1959, P. O. D. Docket # 1/150.
41. Paul Carroll to Hearing Examiner, May 26, 1959,
P. O. D. Docket # 1/150.

42. Receipt, May 28, 1959, P. O. D. Docket # 1/150.
43. Carl A. Schroeder to Docket Clerk, June 1, 1959, P. O. D. Docket # 1/150.
44. Joel A. Sprayregen to Hearing Examiner, May 28, 1959, P. O. D. Docket # 1/150.
45. Joel Sprayregen to Melvin Wulf, May 29, 1959, typed on a copy of Sprayregen to Hearing Examiner, May 28, 1959, A. C. L. U. Archives, "Big Table Ban," Princeton University.
46. Melvin Wulf to Irving Rosenthal, May 29, 1959, "Big Table Ban," Princeton University.
47. Irving Rosenthal to Joel [Sprayregen], June 1, 1959, "Big Table Ban," Princeton University.
48. Ibid.
49. Ibid.
50. "Order," June 1, 1959, P. O. D. Docket # 1/150.
51. "Complainant's Reply to Mailer's Request for Transfer of Hearing," June 1, 1959, P. O. D. Docket # 1/150.
52. "Complainant's Reply to Mailer's Request for Continuance of Hearing and Supplemental Request for Transfer," June 2, 1959, P. O. D. #1/150.
53. William A. Duvall to Joel Sprayregen, June 3, 1959, and "Order," June 3, 1959, P. O. D. Docket # 1/150.
54. "Order," June 10, 1959, P. O. D. Docket # 1/150.
55. Herbert Levy to Rowland Watts, June 8, 1959, "Big Table Ban," Princeton University.
56. Joel [Sprayregen] to Mel [Wulf], June 11, 1959, "Big Table Ban," Princeton University.
57. "Post Office Morals," The Nation 188, May 30, 1959, pp. 486-487.
58. Ibid.
59. Ibid.
60. Ibid.
61. James Paul, Federal Censorship, p. 176. See Paul's discussion of the revision of the postal regulations governing such impounding actions described in this chapter on pages 176-178 in his book. The legislative debate led eventually to a change in the law and required direct court action for any detention of mail. The original Granahan Bill which revised the postal regulations in 1959, had sought at first to give the Post Office the power to impound for a 45-day period without a hearing. Fearing, and rightly so, an abuse of such untrammeled power to impound, Senators Monroney and Clark virtually rewrote the legislation, stipulating that the Post Office be required to apply to the appropriate Federal District Court for any temporary order of restraint.
62. Ibid., p. 177.

63. "Report of the Committee on Obscene Matter
Sent through the Mail, " U. S. Government Printing Office,
August 1959, p. 20.
64. Sprayregen, "Answer, " June 18, 1959, A. C. L. U.
Illinois Div. Papers. University of Chicago, Box 38, Folder
3.
65. Ibid.
66. Ibid.
67. Ibid.
68. The date given in Sprayregen's "Answer, " April
16, is an obvious error. All other references set the deposit
of the magazines at the Post Office on March 18.
69. See Chapter 8 below for a detailed discussion of
the French publication of Naked Lunch. Unfortunately the
Olympia Press records have not been carefully preserved in
a university library like similar documents of Grove Press.
Not only have the Olympia records not been preserved, but
according to Girodias they do not exist at all. The firm went
bankrupt in Paris in 1964 after the French government banned
virtually all books on his list and prosecuted him for at least
two titles he never published. A 1968 effort to revive the
company ended in bankruptcy as well. Following the financial
failures, Girodias informed me in a letter of June 21, 1976,
"various landlords threw away all of that unfortunate company's
properties, which have been presumably lying at the bottom
of the river ever since (Girodias to Goodman, June 21, 1976.
In my possession).
Burroughs had "no agent at the time" and "accepted
the contract as it was (Telephone conversation between Burroughs and Goodman, April 21, 1976, notes in my possession).
The contract gave Olympia the world rights on the English-
language edition. According to Girodias, "hopes of ever
seeing that particular book issued in a regular American edition were practically nil (Girodias to Goodman, June 21,
1976), " considering the censorship climate there. For the
book Burroughs received a rather modest advance 600, 000 to
800, 000 francs, i. e. $300 to $400 against a 10 percent
royalty. Naked Lunch had a standard print run of 5, 000
copies selling for roughly $2. 50 each. During that time
Girodias applied the same terms to everything he published--
straight dirty books and literary books. The literature, however, sold very slowly. In fact none of the three Burroughs
books published by Olympia--Soft Machine and Ticket That
Exploded were also printed under similar contracts--went
into a second printing. According to Burroughs, Girodias
got a basic 33 percent on all foreign rights which was high
considering that most publishers did not get any. Referring

to the contract Burroughs said it was "not advantageous to me (Telephone conversation, April 21, 1976). " He accepted un-favorable terms, but he needed the money at the time.   According to Girodias, Burroughs "was happy with that miserable contract (Girodias to Goodman, June 21, 1976). "

CHAPTER 4

1.   Post Office Department Docket #1/150, Tran-script of Hearing, p. 25. Further references will be made parenthetically by page number. This discussion of the Post Office hearing is based on the official transcript, the postal file, and the American Civil Liberties Union documents per-taining to the case.

2.   Al [Podell] to Irv [Rosenthal], Friday Morn [May 8, 1959], "Big Table (mag), P. O. Mail Ban, Chicago, Illi-nois, " A. C. L. U. Archives Vol. 18-21a, Mudd Manuscript Library, Princeton University Library. See Chapter 3 above for a discussion of this letter and its contents.

3.   Post Office Department Docket #1/150, "Initial Decision of the Hearing Examiner, " Appendix A.

4.   Ibid.

5.   Big Table #1, Spring 1959, p. 2.

6.   Jack Kerouac, "Old Angel Midnight, " Big Table #1, Spring 1959, pp. 7-42.

7.   Kerouac, "Old Angel Midnight, " p. 9.

8.   The following is a list of the offensive words found in the Kerouac story: "Goddam, " p. 7; "Shit, " p. 8; "ass-hole"; "cucksucker" (sic); "Fuckin"; "Damn lick lip twillerin fishmonger! Kiss my royal ass baboon! poota! Whore! You and yr retinue of chariots & fucks"; "ass-warlerin ratpole"; "scriptural apocraphylizers fucking their own dead mothers, " p. 9; "horseshit, " p. 10; "cunt" (three times), p. 11; "fuck it, " p. 12; "Krap" (sic), p. 16; "crap" (two times), p. 18; "shit, " p. 19; "fuck, " p. 21; "shittly" (sic), p. 22; "half-ass, " "farting, " "shit, " p. 28; "shit, " p. 29; "shit, " "ass-hole, " "slut" (three times), "twat, " "fuckface, " "Faust fuck, " p. 31; "twat & tit, " "the ass of God, " p. 34; "shit" (twice), "fuck, " p. 35; "shit, " p. 36; "fuck, " p. 39; "kiss my ass, " p. 40; "fuck off, " p. 42.

9.   Edward Dahlberg, "Further Sorrows of Priapus, " Big Table #1, Spring 1959, pp. 43-62.

10.   Dahlberg, "The Garment of Ra, " pp. 63-78.

11.   William S. Burroughs, "Ten Episodes from Naked Lunch, " Big Table #1, pp. 79-136.

12. The following is a list of the questionable words found in the Burroughs story in Big Table # 1: "we see God through our ass holes in the flashbulb of orgasm, " p. 79; "ass, " "turd, " p. 80; "shit, " "fuck, " p. 81; (Pages 81-86 comprise section 2 and was printed previously in Chicago Review for Spring 1958); "real ass-hole, " p. 81; "bull shit, " p. 84; "shit" (here the reference is to heroin, now in use referring to almost any thing), p. 86; "piss, " "asshole, " p. 90; "cunt, " "fucking, " p. 93; "fucking, " p. 94; (Pages 95-104, comprising Section 5, was printed in Chicago Review, Autumn 1958, and is discussed in Chapter 2); "nigger-killing, " p. 99; "shit, " "fuck um all, " p. 100; "shit, " p. 104; "allah fucked me, " p. 106; "son of a bitch, " p. 107; "nigger, " "crap, " p. 110; "got fucked up the ass, " "Bastards, " p. 111; "fucking, " p. 115; "shit, " p. 117; "fucking, " p. 118; "shit, " "fuck up, " p. 119; "fucking, " "How in the fuck should I know?" p. 121; "nameless assholes, " p. 123; "shitting and pissing on passers-by, " p. 124; "cunts, " p. 125; "asshole, " "cunt, " p. 128; "shit, " p. 129; "nameless asshole, " p. 130; "shit, " p. 133; "asshole, " p. 134; "shit, " p. 136.

13. James C. N. Paul and Murry L. Schwartz, Federal Censorship: Obscenity in the Mail (New York: The Free Press, 1961), p. 187.

14. For a recent discussion of this notion see: "An Empirical Inquiry into the Effects of Miller v. California on the Control of Obscenity, " New York University Law Review, Vol. 52, No. 4, October 1977; as well as W. H. Eich, "From Ulysses to Portnoy: A Pornography Primer, " Marquette Law Review, Vol. 53, No. 2 (Summer 1970), pp. 155ff.

15. "Brief in Support of Plaintiff's Motion for Summary Judgment and in Opposition to Defendant's Cross Motion for Summary Judgment, " A. C. L. U. Collection Manuscripts, Box # 38, Folder # 5, February 1, 1960, p. 5, Regenstein Library, University of Chicago. Referred to here as "Brief" followed by a page number.

16. Ibid.

17. "Initial Decision of the Hearing Examiner, " p. 17.

18. "Transcript of Hearing, " pp. 63-64. See William B. Lockhart and Robert C. McClure, "Literature, The Law of Obscenity, and the Constitution, " Minnesota Law Review 38 (March 1954), pp. 295-395, which is regarded as the seminal article in the contemporary censorship debate.

19. Evergreen Review, the literary periodical of Grove Press, published works-in-progress by new authors whose books often appeared in their totality under the Grove imprint. The publisher was not merely interested in the fee

for the ad in Big Table, but had a genuine interest in the works of the writers represented in that journal, particularly that of Burroughs. The role of Grove Press in the American publication of Naked Lunch is the subject of Chapter 9 below.

20. Lewis in Literature, Obscenity, and Law makes this argument in discussing the case of Joyce's Ulysses on pp. 125-130 of her book.

21. Allen Ginsberg, "Two Letters from Allen Ginsberg," Chicago Review (Autumn 1958), p. 47. This is quoted with spelling and punctuation variants on page 92 of the Transcript.

22. Brief, p. 6.

23. In his summary of the hearing, Duvall chose only to mention that Norris had reviewed the magazine unfavorably and that that represented the majority critical opinion. The misrepresentation reveals the hearing examiner's prejudice, and indicates that he was convinced of the obscenity of Big Table early in the proceedings. In this instance, what appeared in a literary review as a defense of accepted standards, became legally detrimental in the hearing room.

24. Brief, p. 8.

25. Brief, p. 9.

26. See Transcript, p. 188 and New York Herald Tribune, June 21, 1959, p. 1

27. Fletcher Martin, "Smut or Art? Barred Magazine, P. O. Tangle at Hearing," New York Post, Wednesday, June 24, 2959, p. 6.

28. John Ciardi, "Bookburners and Sweet Sixteen," Saturday Review 42, July 27, 1959, p. 22.

29. Ibid.

30. Ibid.

31. Ciardi, p. 30.

32. Ibid.

33. Ibid.

34. Ibid.

35. Ibid.

36. Ibid.

37. Marc D. Schleifer, "Big Table #1," Village Voice Vol. 14, No. 24 (April 8, 1959), p. 5.

38. "First Big Table," Wagner Literary Magazine, No. 1 (Spring 1959), pp. 72-73.

39. "Initial Decision of the Hearing Examiner," p. 1.

40. Saturday Review, July 14, 1959, contents page.

41. "Letters to the Editor," Saturday Review 42 (July 11, 1959), p. 23.

42. Ibid.

43. Ibid.

44. Ibid.
45. See Chapter 2 above.
46. "Letters to the Editor, " Saturday Review 42 (July 18, 1959), p. 21.
47. Ibid.
48. Ibid.
49. Ibid.
50. In a phone conversation in November 1977, Burroughs' secretary James Grauerholz informed me that Irving Rosenthal and Allen Ginsberg were not related. In a memo to Lem Coley, December 16, 1977, Joel Rosenthal asserts that he is no relation to Irving Rosenthal.
51. Saturday Review, July 18, 1959, p. 21.
52. Ibid.
53. Three responses which agree with Ciardi's position are also found in the July 18, 1959 Saturday Review. They were written by Jack Lindeman, Albert Ball, and Joan Mebius.
54. Jack Mabley, "Filthy Writing on the Midway, " Chicago Daily News, October 25, 1958, p. 1. Emphasis mine.
55. "Letters to the Editor, " Saturday Review 42 (August 1, 1959), p. 25.
56. Ibid.
57. Ibid.
58. Ibid.
59. In his Saturday Review column six months later on February 6, 1960, Ciardi published an article, "Epitaph for Dead Beats, " in which he said that the movement was "not only juvenile but related to juvenile delinquency. " However, venemous towards the movement as a whole, his blast retained its critical judgment of the writers he had previously defended. Ciardi refused to classify Burroughs as a Beat writer, observing instead that "he is, in simple fact, his own kind of madman ... who would have written exactly as he does write had there never been a Beat Generation. " This was not faint praise considering the caustic tone of the rest of the article.

CHAPTER 5

1. "Initial Decision of the Hearing Examiner, " P. O. Department Docket # 1/150 July 9, 1959. Also in A. C. L. U. Manuscripts Collection Box 38, folder 5 at the Regenstein Library of the University of Chicago. Afterwards cited as "Initial Decision. "
2. "Brief in Support of Plaintiff's Motion for Summary Judgment and in Opposition to Defendant's Cross Motion

for Summary Judgment, " A. C. L. U. Collection Manuscripts,
Box # 38, folder # 5, Regenstein Library at the University of
Chicago, February 1, 1960, p. 8. Afterwards cited as "Brief"
followed by page number.
    3.   "Initial Decision, " p. 16.
    4.   "Initial Decision, " pp. 14-15. The nine articles
as listed by Duvall are:
3. 1. book, "The Beat Generation and the Angry Young Men, "
    edited by Gene Feldman and Max Gartenberg, published
    by the Citadel Press (1958), see:
    (a)   Introduction, pp. 9-18.
    (b)   "Disengagement: the art of the beat generation"
         by Kenneth Rexroth, pp. 323-38.
    (c)   "The White Negro, " by Norman Mailer, pp.
         342-63.
3. 2. Chicago Review, Spring 1958, see:
    (a)   "The Origins of Joy in Poetry, " by Jack Kerouac,
         p. 3.
    (b)   "Note on Poetry in San Francisco, " by Lawrence
         Ferlinghetti, p. 4.
3. 3.   Evergreen Review, Vol. 1, No. 2 see "San Francisco
    Letter, " by Kenneth Rexroth, pp. 5-14.
3. 4.   article, "The Philosophy of the Beat Generation, " by
    John Clellon Holmes, Esquire, February, 1958, pp.
    35-38.
3. 5.   article, "Kerouac's Beat Generation, " by Ralph Gleason,
    Saturday Review, Jan. 11, 1958, p. 75.
3. 6.   article, "The Origins of the Beat Generation, " by Jack
    Kerouac, based on 1958 address to Brandeis University
    seminar, Playboy, June, 1959, pp. 31-32, 42, 79.
3. 7.   excerpts, book review of "On the Road, " by Jack Kerouac;
    reviewed by Gilbert Milstein, N. Y. Times, Sept. 5,
    1957, p. 27, col. 2.
3. 8.   article, "King of the Beats, " by Seymour Krim, the
    Commonweal, Jan. 2, 1959, pp. 359-60.
3. 9.   article, "California's Young Beat Writers, Angry and
    Otherwise, " by Basil Ross, Library Journal, June 15,
    1958, pp. 1850-54.
    5.   "Initial Decision, " p. 15.
    6.   The writers as listed and identified by Duvall in
Appendix B of the "Initial Decision" included: Harold Taylor
--President of Sarah Lawrence College. John Ciardi--Rutgers
University, President, College English Association. Norman
Mailer--Author of The Naked and the Dead. Allen Ginsberg.
Anthony West--Author and New Yorker book critic. Hugh Ken-
ner--Prof. of English and Chairman of the Department Uni-
versity of California at Santa Barbara. Robert Greeley--Editor

of the Black Mountain Review.   Robert W. Spike--Congrega-
tional Minister--Secretary, Board of Home Missions of the
Congregational and Christian Churches.   Alfred G. Aronowitz
--Author, New York Post reporter.   Randolph H.
Hudson-- Acting Director, Department of English, Stanford University.
James Laughlin--Publisher, New Directions Press.   Roy H.
Miller--Editor and Publisher, San Francisco Review.   Francis
Golffing--Department of English, Bennington College.   Rev.
Pierre Delattre--Congregational Minister, Bread and Wine
Congregation, San Francisco.   William Butler--Director, Lit-
erature and Drama; Production Director, Radio Station KPFA,
Berkeley, California.   James Boyer May--Director, Villiers
Publications, London; Editor, Trace.   Lawrence Ferlinghetti
--Publisher, City Lights Press, San Francisco; bookseller
and poet.   Marc D. Schleifer--Author and critic, contributor
to the Greenwich Village Voice.   Jacques Barzun--Critic,
Dean of Colleges, Columbia University.   Kenneth Burke--Crit-
ic, member of the Institute for Advanced Studies, Princeton
University.   Thomas Parkinson--Associate Professor of Eng-
lish, University of California.   Le Roi Jones--Editor of Yugen
and publisher of Totem Press, New York City.   Gerhart
Piers, M. D. --Director, Institute of Psychoanalysis of Chicago.
Lionel Trilling--Critic and Professor of English, Columbia
University.
    7.   The sections of the statements allowed into evi-
dence are in Appendix B, pp. 1-14 of the "Initial Decision."
    8.   "Initial Decision," pp. 11-12.
    9.   "Initial Decision," p. 12.
    10.   Norman Mailer, White Negro, San Francisco: City
Lights, 1957, 1970 from Dissent.
    11.   "Initial Decision of the Hearing Examiner," copy
in the A. C. L. U. Archive at the University of Chicago, Box
38, Folder # 5, p. 12.   This marginal note, which I presume
is in Sprayregen's hand, is found at the bottom of page 12 in
this copy.   In fairness to Duvall, Mailer's book was included
as an example in the collection of Beat writings submitted as
evidence.   See Exhibit B, 3-1 cited above.
    12.   "Initial Decision," Appendix B, p. 2.
    13.   "Initial Decision," Appendix B, p. 6.
    14.   "Initial Decision," Appendix B, p. 2.
    15.   "Initial Decision," Appendix B, p. 13.
    16.   "Initial Decision," Appendix B, p. 1.   This state-
ment submitted to the court by Ciardi should not be equated
with his article "Book Burners and Sweet Sixteen" (see Chapter
4 above for a discussion) which appeared in Saturday Review.
    17.   "Initial Decision," p. 13.
    18.   Quoted in "Brief," p. 22.

19.   Quoted in "Initial Decision, " p. 16.
20.   Quoted in "Initial Decision, " p. 17.
21.   Quoted in "Initial Decision, " p. 18.
22.   "Initial Decision, " p. 20.
23.   Ibid.
24.   "Initial Decision, " p. 19.
25.   "Initial Decision, " p. 20.
26.   Quoted in "Initial Decision, " p. 21, from United
States v. Limehouse, 285 U.S. 424, 426.
27.   "Initial Decision, " p. 21.
28.   "Initial Decision, " p. 22.
29.   "Initial Decision, " p. 23.
30.   Joel Sprayregen to Roland Watts and Melvin Wulf,
July 10, 1959, "Big Table (mag.)--Post Office Mail Ban,
Chicago, Illinois, " A. C. L. U. Archives 1960 Vol. 18-21a,
Seely Mudd Manuscript Library, Princeton University.
31.   Sprayregen, "Appeal Memorandum, Exceptions, "
"Post Office Department Docket # 1/150.
32.   Ibid.
33.   "Initial Decision, " p. 19.
34.   "Appeal, Memorandum, Exceptions, " P. O. Dept.
Docket # 1/150.
35.   Ibid.
36.   "Big Table, " Press Release, n. d. , 2 pages--"Big
Table (mag.) P. O. Mail Ban, Chicago, Illinois, " A. C. L. U.
Archives 1960, Vol. 18-21a, Princeton University, Mudd
Manuscript Library.
37.   Saul Mindel, "Application for Extension of Filing
Date for Complainant's Reply Brief, " P. O. Dept. Docket
1/150.   I have been unable to find any mention of why
Schueler was replaced by Mindel on the case.   Both had handled the Lady Chatterley's Lover litigation, Mindel taking the
larger role.   The assignment of Mindel to the case may indicate its escalating importance to the Post Office.
38.   "Order--July 31, 1959, " Memo.   P. O. Dept.
Docket # 1/150.
39.   Charles Rembar, The End of Obscenity (New
York: Random House, 1968), p. 62.
40.   Saul Mindel, "Complainant's Reply Brief on Appeal, " August 3, 1959, Post Office Department Docket # 1/150.
41.   Quoted in "Complainant's Reply Brief on Appeal, "
p. 2.
42.   Ibid.
43.   Ibid. , p. 3.
44.   Sprayregen to Post Office Department, August 3,
1959, P. O. Dept. Docket # 1/150.
45.   Ibid.

46.   Charles D. Ablard, "Departmental Decision,"
August 12, 1959, A. C. L. U. Collection, Illinois Division Papers, Manuscript Box 38, Folder #3, Regenstein Library,
University of Chicago.   Hereafter "Departmental Decision"
followed by a page reference.
47.   "Departmental Decision," p. 3.
48.   Quoted in "Departmental Decision," p. 4.
49.   "Departmental Decision," pp. 4-5.
50.   "Departmental Decision," p. 6.   Again, this is
Ablard using a definition from the American Law Institute.
51.   Ibid.
52.   Ibid., p. 7.
53.   Ibid., p. 10.

CHAPTER 6

1.   Congressional Record Appendix for August 19,
1959, p. A 7152.   Senator Andrew F. Schoepel of Kansas
ordered the Summerfield address into the Record.   The
A. C. L. U. maintained several files on the anti-smut campaigns
of the Post Office.   In Volume 23 1959 of the ACLU Archive
at Mudd Manuscript Library at Princeton University, see
"P. O. Censorship," "P. O. Attitude Toward Censorship," and
"Summerfield, Postmaster General (Speeches on Mail Obscenity)."
2.   Richard McGowan and David Rusk, "Billion $
Cesspool," New York News, Tuesday, March 17, 1959, p.
24.   The other three articles in the series carried only Mc-
Gowan's by-line.   They were: "Pornographers' Poison is
Easily Available to Kids," N. Y. News, March 18, 1959, p.
40; "Your Name Could Be on Mail Lists of Smut Dealers,"
N. Y. News, Thursday, March 19, 1959, p. 44; "Smut Dealers:
How Far Can They Go?" N. Y. News, Friday, March 20, 1959,
p. 36.
3.   Alfred C. Roller, "How Smut Seduces Youths to
Violence," Chicago Sun Times, August 13, 1959, p. 22.   The
other articles in this series are: "A Blueprint Is Offered
For War Against Smut," Chicago Sun Times, August 10, 1959,
p. 1 & 6; "How 2 Cities Battle Much," Chicago Sun Times,
August 11, 1959, p. 3 & 20; "You Can Strike a Blow Against
Smut," Chicago Sun Times, August 13, 1959, p. 8.
4.   Report on Obscene Matter Sent Through the Mail
to the House Committee on the Post Office, Washington, D. C.:
U. S. Government Printing Office, August 1959, p. 19.   Afterwards cited as: Report on Obscene Matter.
5.   Ibid.

6. Ibid.
7. See Paul, Federal Censorship, pp. 176-178. Mrs.
Granahan introduced a bill calling for the 45-day period which
easily passed in the House. Senators Clark and Monrony,
however, had reservations because of past abuses of "temporary" mail blocks by the Post Office. The Senators held
the bill in committee for almost a year, then rewrote it to
require the Post Office to operate through the court system.
This is what civil libertarians had argued for all along as a
way to erase the inequities in the Post Office's administrative
actions in obscenity cases.
8. Report on Obscene Matter, p. 21.
9. See the A. C. L. U. file at Princeton 1959, Vol.
23, "P. O. Censorship," especially the clipping file for 1959
which contains a Parade magazine article of that summer with
the picture of a blond, blue-eyed boy with a crew-cut peering
innocently into a rural mailbox. The picture is accompanied
by a caption warning of the smut problem.
10. Paul, Federal Censorship, p. 291.
11. The copy of the complaint in my possession (see
note 12 below) is undated. I have deduced the date from a
reference on page 12 of Sprayregen's Brief in Support ...
Summary Judgment. "
12. "Complaint: Big Table vs. Carl Schroeder, "
n. d. , n. p. , A. C. L. U. Collection Manuscripts, Illinois Division Papers, Box # 38, Folder # 1, University of Chicago
Regenstein Library.
13. Ibid. , point 17.
14. Ibid. , point 19.
15. "Brief, " p. 12.
16. "Brief in Support of Plaintiff's Motion for Summary Judgment and in Opposition to Defendant's Cross Motion
for Summary Judgment, " A. C. L. U. Collection Manuscripts,
Box # 38, folder # 5, February 1, 1960, Regenstein Library
of the University of Chicago. Cited above and hereafter as
"Brief" followed by page number.
17. See Chapter 5, page 9 above quoting "Initial Decision, " p. 19; and Chapter 5, page 18 quoting "Departmental
Decision, " pp. 4-5.
18. "Brief, " p. 18.
19. Ablard, "Departmental Decision, " p. 14.
20. "Brief, " p. 27.
21. "Brief, " p. 21.
22. Ibid.
23. Ibid.
24. Grove Press vs. Christenberry 175 F. Supp. 502.
This case involved Grove Press as the publisher of Lady

Chatterley's Lover and New York City Postmaster Christenberry who barred the mailing of the book under Section 1461.
   25.   Ibid.
   26.   "Brief, " p. 30.
   27.   Time, December 4, 1959, p. 4.
   28.   Paul O'Neill, "The Only Rebellion Around, " Life,
November 30, 1959, pp. 115-130. See Chapter 8 below for
Burroughs' comments to Allen Ginsberg on the Life reporters
and photographers who interviewed him in Paris for this article.
   29.   Ibid. , pp. 115-126, quoted by Sprayregen in
"Brief, " pp. 32-3.
   30.   "Brief, " Appendix B, p. 2.
   31.   Ibid.
   32.   The other members of the panel were Louise
Bagan, Charles Boni, Thomas Hess, Henri Payre.
   33.   Grove Press vs. Christenberry.
   34.   William B. Lockhart and Robert C. McClure,
"Literature, The Law of Obscenity, and the Constitution, "
Minnesota Law Review 38, March 1954, pp. 295 ff. Professor Lockhart would later chair the President's Commission
on Obscenity and Pornography. The Report of that commission in 1970 created more controversy on the obscenity and
pornography question.
   35.   "Brief, " p. 34. Emphasis in text.
   36.   "Brief, " pp. 43-44.
   37.   See Chapter 3 above for a description of the cover
of Big Table #1.
   38.   "Brief, " p. 46. It was the opinion of some legal
interpreters that the Post Office operated as the civil censorship body for the entire country, actions far in excess of its
statutory mandates. See Edward de Grazia, "Obscenity and
the Mail, " Law and Contemporary Problems 20, 1955, p. 608.
   39.   On this point these cases were cited: Hannegan
vs. Esquire 327 U.S. 146 (1946); Roth vs. U.S. 354 U.S. 476
(1957); Sunshine vs. Summerfield 355 U.S. 372 (1958); Grove
Press vs. Christenberry 175 F. Supp. 488 (SDNY 1959).
   40.   Sprayregen cited Walker vs. Popence 149 F. 2nd
511, 513-14 (D.C. Cir. 1945) as the precedent on the impounding of mail. In that case the court determined that mail
could not be seized and impounded under Section 1461 without
a prior hearing. DeGrazia noted in his article "Obscenity and
the Mail" that in spite of Walker vs. Popence the Post Office
continued to refuse magazines for mailing, holding hearings
at a much later time. The action taken against Big Table was
similar to that ruled illegal in Walker vs. Popence.
   41.   "Brief, " p. 41.

42. "Brief," p. 53. <u>Kingsley Books vs. Brown</u> 354
U. S. 436 (1954) was cited as providing the legal mechanism
which safeguarded the right to a hearing when material was
impounded on the suspicion of an obscenity violation.
43. "Brief," pp. 59-60.
44. "Brief," p. 61.
45. The contents of the brief submitted by the Post
Office in support of its motion for summary judgment is taken
from Sprayregen's "Plaintiff's Reply Memorandum in Support
of Its Motion for Summary Judgment and in Opposition to De-
fendants's Cross Motion for Summary Judgment" filed on May
2, 1960 in Illinois Federal District Court. I have used the
copy found in "Big Table (mag.) P. O. Mail Ban, Chicago,
Illinois," 1960--A. C. L. U. Archive Vol. 18-21a at Mudd Manuscript Library at Princeton University.
46. "Plaintiff's Reply Memorandum in Support of Its
Motion for Summary Judgment ...," May 2, 1960.
47. <u>Smith vs. California</u> 80 S. Ct. 215 (1959). Referred to in above "Plaintiff's Reply Memorandum ... " on
pp. 3-5.
48. "Plaintiff's Reply Memorandum ...," p. 9.
49. <u>Big Table vs. Carl A. Schroeder</u> 186 F. Supp.
254 (1960). The following discussion of Judge Julius J. Hoffman's decision is taken from the official report recorded in
the <u>Federal Supplement</u> Vol. 186, pp. 254-262.
50. Ibid., p. 257.
51. <u>Niemalko vs. Maryland</u> (340 U. S. 268) and <u>Joseph</u>
<u>Burstyn vs. Wilson</u> (343 U. S. 495) were the cases which set
the precedents.
52. <u>Big Table vs. Schroeder</u> (186 F. Supp 254) at
259.
53. <u>Big Table vs. Schroeder</u> at 260.
54. Ibid.
55. <u>Big Table vs. Schroeder</u> at 261.
56. Ibid.
57. Ibid.
58. Ibid.
59. <u>Big Table vs. Schroeder</u> at 262.
60. In London ten years later, Burroughs would play
the role of Judge Hoffman in a dramatization of the Chicago
Seven trial. See Irving Wardle, "Conspiracy Trial Is Given
as Drama: William Burroughs Seen as Judge Hoffman," <u>The</u>
<u>New York Times</u>, August 26, 1970, p. 35. Wardle wrote
that Burroughs "occupied the bench with a most chilling authority: immovable and expressionless as though a smile
might tear his parchment features."
61. Memo, August 11, 1960, "Big Table (mag.)--P. O.

Mail Ban, " A. C. L. U. Collection, Mudd Manuscript Library,
Princeton.
   62. Ibid.

CHAPTER 7

     1. In the fall of 1959 U. S. Customs Service inspec-
tors at the port of New York seized copies of the Olympia
Press edition of Burroughs' Naked Lunch as obscene material.
The books were barred from entry under provisions of Title
19, Section 1305 of the U. S. Code. No hearing or inquiry on
the book's obscenity was held, nor was notice of seizure
served on Grove Press publisher Barney Rosset until August
29, 1960.
     The Customs Service retains a file on Naked Lunch in both
New York and in Washington, D. C. After I made a request
under the Freedom of Information Act, both files were released to me. The two files are identical in content except
that the New York file contains two memos, dated March 14,
1963 and October 2, 1962, which do not appear in the Washington file. What the Customs sent, however, was suspiciously
incomplete. In fact the file provided began in 1962, almost
two years after the book was seized. It is so incomplete that
it does not even contain a copy of the August 29, 1960 notice
of seizure which I obtained from the Grove Press Collection:
Burroughs, Box # 1, "Burroughs, William. Naked Lunch.
Editorial Correspondence # 1. 1959-1962, " in the George
Arents Research Library for Special Collections at Syracuse
University. An additional request from Customs yielded nothing (see notes 14 and 16 below), not even confirmation that
the rest of the file had been lost or destroyed. The publication records of Grove Press at Syracuse University and the
A. C. L. U. Archive at Princeton University were used to supplement the deficiencies of the Customs file.
     Since the Customs files are so sketchy, some of their
specific actions and motives suggested in this chapter are
based on similar seizures, circumstantial evidence, and conjecture. Also the actions taken by the University of Chicago
and by the U. S. Post Office against the book must be considered indirectly related to the Customs' seizures. Without
consideration of the previous efforts to suppress Burroughs'
book, the steps taken by Customs might appear random and
incidental.
     2. Fran Muller to Judith Schmidt, September 21,
1959. Grove Press Collection: Burroughs, Box # 1, "Burroughs, William. Naked Lunch. Editorial Correspondence # 2.

1962-1967, " in the George Arents Research Library for Special
Collections at Syracuse University. This letter should pro-
perly be included in "Editorial Correspondence # 1, 1959-1962. "
       3.   Judith Schmidt to Miriam Worms, October 14,
1959, Grove Press Collection: Burroughs, Box # 1, "Bur-
roughs, William. Naked Lunch. Editorial Correspondence
1, 1959-1962, " in the George Arents Research Library for
Special Collections at Syracuse University.
       4.   See "Initial Decision" of Duvall and "Departmental
Decision" of Ablard in either the Post Office Department's file
"Big Table, Docket # 1/150, " or in the A. C. L. U. Collection
at the University of Chicago Library, Box # 38, folder # 3.
       5.   Schmidt to Worms, October 14, 1959.   Grove
Press Collection.
       6.   Paul Boyer, Purity in Print (New York: Scrib-
ner's, 1968), p. 209.   Boyer quotes The New York Times,
January 23, 1924, p. 9 on this point and concludes: "In 1923,
French erotica was excluded with special diligence, not from
a sudden access of prudery among Customs inspectors, but
because the Franco-American Board of Commerce and Industry, suspecting that such books were giving Americans a distorted idea of France, had secured the cooperation of the
Customs Bureau in a campaign to bar them at the ports. "
       7.   Joel J. Sprayregen to Charles Rembar, October
14, 1959.   Grove Press Collection: Burroughs, Box # 1
"Naked Lunch.   Editorial Correspondence # 1, " in the George
Arents Research Library at Syracuse University.
       8.   E. R. Hutchinson, Tropic of Cancer on Trial:
A Case History of Censorship (New York: Grove Press,
1968), pp. 1-2.
       9.   Some of the recipients of the form letter were:
Dr. Milton Schwebel, William Barrett, Nat Waldman, and
Ephriam London.   Schmidt to the above, April 1, 1960.
Grove Press Collection.   "Editorial Correspondence # 1. "
Syracuse University.
       10.   Irving Fishman to Barney Rosset, August 29,
1960, Grove Press Collection.   The numbers on the three
letters of seizure are: 8451/2/3-6; 8499-60; and 8464-60.
       11.   Richard McGowen, "Smut Dealers: How Far Can
They Go?" New York Daily News, March 20, 1959, p. 36.
This article was the last in a series dealing with the pornography industry.   He reported that the 600 Customs inspectors in the Restricted Merchandise Division worked effectively
against smut.   He wrote, "Without concerning themselves with
the dissenting of judges, when they spot something they regard
as obscene they set it aside for burning. "   That attitude came
from Fishman who expressed the feeling to Senator Kefauver's

subcommittee on juvenile delinquency that the courts were too
soft in their rulings on what did or did not constitute obscenity.

12. In James C. N. Paul and Murray L. Schwartz,
Federal Censorship: Obscenity in the Mail (New York: The
Free Press of Glencoe, 1961), pp. 347-48. The statute allows classics of literary or scientific merit only if the works
are "imported for non-commercial purposes." The law ex-
cludes works that are "treason or insurrection against the
United States," drugs and articles used for abortion or con-
traception, and lottery tickets.

13. The Report of the Commission on Obscenity and
Pornography, U.S. Government Printing Office, 1970, p. 392.
We can assume for our purposes that the procedures described
in the Report are similar to the ones in force in 1959. Since
its controversial advocacy of the repeal of censorship laws,
we can also assume that the procedures were described accurately.

14. Personal notes on a telephone conversation between myself and John Atwood of the Restricted Materials
Department of the U.S. Customs, May 18, 1976, 2:20-2:40
p.m., e.d.t. I found Mr. Atwood to be a cautious, helpful,
skeptical, polite, and realistic civil servant. Aside from being
evasive on the specifics of Customs methods, he was most
helpful with all other questions and clarified the procedure for
obtaining records through the Freedom of Information Act.

15. Paul, Federal Censorship, pp. 68-69.

16. In a letter on August 23, 1976 I in fact asked the
Customs Service to verify the completeness of the file sent
to me. I provided several alternative subject headings for
the additional search. Acting Director of Entry Procedures
and Penalties, E. J. Doyle replied, "The files disclosed no
further records. Because of changing concepts and positions
in the obscenity field over the years, much of the material
accumulated in this field by the Customs Service was destroyed
as having no application to casework of a legal nature upon
the retirement of Mr. Irving Fishman and Mr. Reuben Klaben,
both of whom handled these cases exclusively for many years."
The letter implies that the Burroughs file was one of many
to be discarded. I am still not fully sure why only part of
the file was destroyed and not all of it.

17. Dan [Bell] to Alan [Reitman], November 17, 1958,
in A.C.L.U. Archives at Princeton University, 1959--Volume
23, "Customs Bureau Seizures of Olympia Press Books."
Bell subsequently wrote an article on the incident titled " 'What
You Can't Read to Your Daughter'," in The New Leader, Vol.
42, No. 21 (May 25, 1959), pp. 23-24.

18. Ibid.

19. Al Reitman to Dan Bell, November 13, 1958.
A. C. L. U. Archives at Princeton, 1959--Vol. 23.
20. Ibid.
21. Malin to Anderson, December 30, 1958. A. C. L. U.
Archives at Princeton, 1959--Vol. 23.
22. A. Gilmore Flues to Patrick Malin, March 16,
1959. A. C. L. U. Archives at Princeton, 1959--Vol. 23. Section 305 of the Tariff Act is the same as Title 19, Section
1305 of the U. S. Code.
23. D. Upton to Patrick Malin, May 20, 1959.
A. C. L. U. Archives at Princeton, 1959--Vol. 23.
24. J. A. Sigler, "Customs Censorship," Cleveland--
Marshall Law Review Vol. 15 (January 1966), p. 63. Sigler
has quoted from a letter he received from Irving Fishman
dated February 10, 1965. One can assume that Fishman was
Sigler's source of information on the existence of an informal
list of books.
25. In the U. S. Customs file on Naked Lunch. This
memo is only in the New York file.
26. Farr to Podell, April 30, 1959, in the Post Office Department file on Big Table, Docket # 1/150.
27. Maurice Girodias to William Burroughs, June 6,
1959, in the Spencer Library at the University of Kansas.
28. Even though the supporting materials no longer
exist, it is safe to conclude from the seizure of the book
that its obscenity had been determined by the Customs Service.
29. Quoted in the October 2, 1962 memo in the Customs file. As far as I have been able to determine, the February 21, 1961 letter has been destroyed along with all material before October 1962.
30. Klaben to Fishman, October 1, 1962, U. S. Customs file.
31. Fishman to Klaben, October 4, 1962, U. S. Customs file.
32. Fishman to Klaben, December 4, 1962, U. S. Customs file.
33. Telephone conversation between myself and Detective (retired) Edmund Griffin of the Boston Police, May 24,
1976, 4:35-5:00 p. m. , e. d. t. See Chapter 12 below for details of the Boston arrest.
34. Shapiro to Customs, February 15, 1963, U. S.
Customs file.

CHAPTER 8

1. William S. Burroughs, Jr. , "Life with Father,"
Esquire (September 1971), p. 141.

2. Paul Bowles, "Burroughs in Tangier," Big Table
#2 (Summer 1959), pp. 42-43. Also reprinted in Thomas
Parkinson's A Casebook on the Beat, pp. 114-115.

3. William Burroughs to Jack Kerouac [1954], p. 3.
Rare Books and Manuscripts, Butler Library at Columbia
University in the City of New York.

4. William Burroughs to Jack Kerouac, December 7,
1954. Columbia University.

5. In an interview some years later he expressed his
desire to write a best seller. The facetiousness of his dry
wit humorously masks his need for funds. See Gerard Malanga, "An Interview with William Burroughs," The Beat Book
4 (1974), p. 90ff.

6. William Burroughs, Naked Lunch (New York:
Grove Press), 1959, 1962, pp. 177-78.

7. William Burroughs to Jack Kerouac, December 7,
1954. Columbia.

8. The letter discussed here is found in another letter
which Allen Ginsberg wrote to Bob Lavigne from Tangier on
June 8, 1957. The letter along with the Burroughs material
enclosed is found in the Humanities Research Center of the
University of Texas at Austin. The letter from Burroughs
to Ginsberg is not in Burroughs' hand nor signed by him, but
appears to be a typed copy. The type face is different than
the one which appears in letters Burroughs typed during the
same period. References in the letter by Burroughs to his
lack of a typewriter are further evidence that the contents
were typed by someone other than himself in an effort to obtain a readable copy. In other words the Burroughs letter to
Ginsberg which begins, "Feb. 7, 1954, Tangier, Dear A----:"
was copied from a hand written page. This calls the date into
question. Considering the letter to Kerouac dated December
7, 1954 and the one to Ginsberg dated February 12, 1955,
the substance of the two letters suggests the Feb. 7 letter to
Ginsberg followed the letter to Kerouac and should properly
be dated 1955 not 1954. Both letters discuss the Hauser and
O'Brien section of Naked Lunch which Burroughs was writing
at the time. I will refer to this letter as "William Burroughs
to Allen Ginsberg, Feb. 7, 1954--probably 1955--in Ginsberg
to Bob Lavigne, June 8, 1957, Humanities Research Center,
Austin."

9. Naked Lunch, pp. 131-135.

10. Naked Lunch, p. 134.

11. William Burroughs to Allen Ginsberg February 7,
1954--probably 1955--in Ginsberg to Lavigne, June 8, 1957,
Humanities Research Center, Austin.

12. William Burroughs to Jack Kerouac, February 12,
1955, Columbia.

13.   William Burroughs, "Literary Autobiography, " in Catalogue of the William S. Burroughs Archive, London: Miles Associates, 1973, p. 77.

14.   William Burroughs to Allen Ginsberg, February 7, 1954--probably 1955--in Ginsberg to Lavigne, June 8, 1957, Humanities Research Center.

15.   Burroughs to Kerouac, February 12, 1955.   Columbia.

16.   Naked Lunch, p. 221.

17.   Burroughs to Kerouac, February 12, 1955.   Columbia.

18.   Ibid.

19.   Ibid.   Burroughs' elipsis.

20.   Naked Lunch, p. 212.

21.   Ibid. , p. 209.

22.   William S. Burroughs, "Tangier, " Esquire, 62 (September 1964), p. 114.

23.   Burroughs, Dead Fingers Talk (London: Calder, 1963), pp. 1 ff.

24.   Burroughs to Kerouac, May 24, 1955.   Columbia.

25.   Naked Lunch, pp. 135-136.   This reproduces the version in the letter with only minor additions.

26.   Burroughs, "The Coming of the Purple Better One, " Esquire 70 (November 1968), pp. 89-91.

27.   Burroughs to Ginsberg, n. d. (circa April 1952), Ginsberg Deposit, Rare Books and Manuscripts, Butler Library of Columbia University in the City of New York.   This letter and the others from Burroughs are owned by Ginsberg and held by Columbia.   Access to them is by permission only. In the folder for 1952 in the Ginsberg Deposit, several versions of this letter exist as if parts were typed and edited for possible publication.   The quotation here is taken from the only version in the file signed in Burroughs' hand.   Other letters to Ginsberg from this collection will be referred to as "Ginsberg Deposit. "

28.   Queer was not published, nor is it expected to be since Burroughs considers the writing similar to an artist's school sketches and therefore not very interesting.

29.   At this time Burroughs indicated his perception of himself as a professional writer.   He wrote Ginsberg, "Better save my letters maybe we can get out a book of them later on when I get a rep (Burroughs to Ginsberg, c. April 1952, p. 2). "   The suggestions which Burroughs made in 1952 may have convinced them that their letters were an art form or at least of general public interest.   In fact City Lights published The Yage Letters in 1963, a record of the correspondence between the two in the early 1950's when Burroughs

was in South America. Most of the letters in this edition follow faithfully the originals held at Columbia.

30. "Stunt Shooting of Wife Denied, " New York Times,
Saturday, September 8, 1951, p. 3.

31. "Trial Ordered in Killing, " New York Times,
September 11, 1951, p. 6.

32. Burroughs to Ginsberg, April 14, 1952. Ginsberg
Deposit.

33. Burroughs to Ginsberg, July 1, 1952. Ginsberg
Deposit.

34. Burroughs to Ginsberg, July 13, 1952, Ginsberg
Deposit.

35. Burroughs, Junkie, p. 6.

36. William Burroughs, Jr. , "Life with Father, " p.
113.

37. Conrad Knickerbocker, "William Burroughs:
Paris Review Interview, " Paris Review (Fall 1965), p. 40.

38. See especially Burroughs to Kerouac, December
26, 1950, Columbia.

39. Naked Lunch, p. 19.

40. Ibid. , p. 20.

41. His travels there are recorded in his correspondence with Ginsberg and collected in The Yage Letters.

42. Burroughs to Kerouac, April 22, 1954, Columbia.

43. Burroughs to Kerouac, [1954], Columbia.

44. Burroughs to Kerouac, April 22, 1954, Columbia.

45. Burroughs, "Literary Autobiography, " in Catalogue
of the William S. Burroughs Archive, p. 77.

46. Burroughs to Ginsberg, September 20, 1957.
Ginsberg Deposit.

47. Ibid.

48. Ibid. Burroughs was involved in a murder case
as a material witness in the 1940's in New York City. In late
August 1944 Lucien Carr fatally stabbed Dave Kammerer and
tossed his body into the Hudson River. Burroughs knew them
both. Carr came to Burroughs after the stabbing for advice,
and he told him to go to the police. See Frank S. Adams,
"Columbia Student Kills Friend and Sinks Body in Hudson
River, " N. Y. Times, August 17, 1944, pp. 1 and 13; "Student
Silent on Slaying Friend, " N. Y. Times, August 18, 1944, p.
14; "Student in 2D Murder, " N. Y. Times, August 25, 1944,
p. 15. A recent article on the case appears in Aaron Latham,
"The Columbia Murder that Gave Birth to the Beats, " New York
Magazine (April 19, 1976), pp. 41ff.

49. Burroughs to Ginsberg, September 20, 1957, Ginsberg Deposit.

50. Burroughs to Ginsberg, n. d. (Probably sometime
between September 20 and October 14, 1957), Ginsberg Deposit.

51.   See Knickerbocker, Paris Review, 1965.
52.   See Burroughs to Ginsberg, October 28, 1957,
Ginsberg Deposit.
53.   Burroughs to Ginsberg, October 28, 1957.
54.   Ibid.
55.   Burroughs to Ginsberg, October 31, 1957, Ginsberg Deposit.
56.   Burroughs to Ginsberg, November 10, 1957.
Ginsberg Deposit.
57.   Burroughs to Ginsberg, November 26, 1957, Ginsberg Deposit.   See Chapter 1 for the Olympia Press publication.
58.   Ibid.
59.   Burroughs to Kerouac, December 4, 1957, Columbia.
60.   Burroughs to Ginsberg, December 4, 1957, Ginsberg Deposit.
61.   Ibid.
62.   Burroughs to Ginsberg, February 10, 1958, Ginsberg Deposit.
63.   Burroughs to Ginsberg, n. d. [1958].
64.   The infrequency of their correspondence after 1958
suggests a cooling in their relationship.   See Burroughs to
Kerouac letters at Columbia.
65.   Burroughs to Paul Bowles, July 20, 1958, Humanities Research Center, Austin.   See Chapter 2 above for a
detailed discussion of the Chicago Review and Burroughs' excerpts from Naked Lunch.
66.   Burroughs to Ginsberg, August 25, 1958, Ginsberg
Deposit.
67.   Burroughs to Paul Bowles, October 19, 1958,
Humanities Research Center.
68.   Burroughs to Ginsberg, October 10, 1958, Ginsberg Deposit.
69.   Burroughs to Paul Bowles, October 19, 1958,
Humanities Research Center.
70.   Burroughs to Paul Bowles, n. d. [1958], Humanities Research Center.
71.   Burroughs to Ginsberg, n. d. [1958], Ginsberg
Deposit.
72.   See also Burroughs to Ginsberg, January 2, 1959,
Ginsberg Deposit.   Burroughs expands upon the paranormal
experience he mentioned in his Christmas card.   He also included some calligraphy in the letter.
73.   Burroughs to Paul Bowles, January 12, 1959,
Humanities Research Center.
74.   Ibid.

75. Burroughs to Paul Bowles, February 20, 1959,
Humanities Research Center.
76. See accounts of the incident in Burroughs to Ginsberg, April 2, 1959, Burroughs to Ginsberg, May 5, 1959 in
the Ginsberg Deposit; and in Burroughs to Paul Bowles May
5, 1959 in the Humanities Research Center.
77. Naked Lunch, p. 1.
78. Burroughs to Ginsberg, April 21, 1959, Ginsberg
Deposit.
79. See above mentioned in Burroughs to Kerouac,
February 12, 1955.
80. Burroughs to Ginsberg, May 5, 1959, Ginsberg
Deposit.
81. Many published accounts of the composition of
Naked Lunch exist. See versions in: Gerard Malanga, "An
Interview with William Burroughs," The Beat Book, vol. 4
(1974), p. 109; Robert Palmer, "Rolling Stone Interview:
William Burroughs," Rolling Stone No. 108 (May 11, 1972),
p. 52; Conrad Knickerbocker, "The Art of Fiction: William
Burroughs," Paris Review 35 (1965), pp. 31-32; Jack Kerouac,
Desolation Angels (N. Y.: Coward-McCann, 1965), pp. 310-
311; John Tytell, Naked Angels (N. Y.: McGraw-Hill, 1976),
p. 49; William S. Burroughs, "Literary Autobiography," in
Catalogue of the William S. Burroughs Archive (London: Cov-
ent Garden Press, 1973), pp. 77-78.
82. Burroughs to Paul Bowles, July 30, 1959, Humanities Research Center.
83. Burroughs to Ginsberg, n. d. [c. July 30, 1959]
Ginsberg Deposit. Compare the contents of this letter with
the above letter to Paul Bowles, July 30, 1959.
84. Burroughs to Ginsberg, September 5, 1959, Ginsberg Deposit.
85. Burroughs to Ginsberg, August 24, [1959], Ginsberg Deposit.
86. See Maurice Girodias to Michael Goodman, June
21, 1976 in my possession, and Burroughs to Ginsberg, August 24, 1959, Ginsberg Deposit.
87. Burroughs to Ginsberg, n. d. [c. July 30, 1959],
Ginsberg Deposit, and Burroughs to Paul Bowles, July 30,
1959, Humanities Research Center.
88. Burroughs to Ginsberg, September 11, 1959, Ginsberg Deposit.
89. Such disbelief in the validity of Burroughs' assertion that the hanging scenes satirized capital punishment was
voiced by Thomas Parkinson when he observed, "It boggles
my mind to imagine any reader of the text, without Burroughs'
intervention, stumbling unaided on the notion that those obscene,

barbaric and disgusting passages are anything more than an
exhibit of the kind of depravity that the human mind can sink
to, and of the guilt and sorrow of humanity, we are all capa-
ble. But the text itself gives no clue to Burroughs' intended
effect. " He concluded that the whole notion of the text as a
tract against capital punishment was "Hogwash. " Prof. Parkinson's remarks are quoted from page six of a typescript of
an unpublished paper read at the Burroughs Special Session
at the MLA Convention in Chicago on December 30, 1977.
      90.   Burroughs to Ginsberg, September 25, 1959,
Ginsberg Deposit. Although the text is not contained in the
Ginsberg Deposit, this letter has a finished copy of the "Deposition" article enclosed. Also in this letter he emphasized
that he was off drugs and that drugs were a dead end. Burroughs again asserted that there was nothing dishonest in the
"Deposition, " though he had written it as an insurance policy
to cover himself in the event of misunderstanding.
      91.   Burroughs to Ginsberg, October 7, 1959, Ginsberg
Deposit. See George Malko's Scientology (New York: Delta,
1970) for a fully documented expose of Hubbard and his religion of Scientology.
      92.   William S. Burroughs, "Uncle Bill Burroughs
(Alias Technical Tilly) On Scientology, " Rat 2, No. 24 (1969),
pp. 12-13.
      93.   Harry G. Polkinhorn, "William Burroughs: In the
Radical Tradition, " DAI Vol. 36 (1976), pp. 7424-A-7425-A.
He says, "Since the publication of his experimental works, he
has influenced a group of European writers who call themselves the International Cut-Up Conspiracy. Claude Pelieu,
Carl Weissner, and Jeff Nuttall are indebted to Burroughs for
themes, imagery, and techniques. " Even the most casual look
at the experiments of these writers confirms the limitations
of the cut-up method.
      94.   Burroughs to Ginsberg, October 7, 1959, Ginsberg
Deposit.
      95.   Burroughs to Ginsberg, November 17, 1959, Gins-
berg Deposit.
      96.   Paul O'Neill, "The Only Rebellion Around, " Life
47 (November 30, 1959), pp. 124-125.
      97.   Ibid.
      98.   Burroughs to Ginsberg, October 7, 1959, Ginsberg
Deposit.
      99.   Burroughs to Ginsberg, October 29, 1959, Gins-
berg Deposit.
      100.   Burroughs et al. Minutes to Go (Paris: Two
Cities Press, 1960).

101. Burroughs to Ginsberg, October 29, 1959, Ginsberg Deposit.
102. Burroughs to Ginsberg, November 17, 1958, Ginsberg Deposit.
103. Ibid.
104. See Lemuel Coley's unpublished doctoral dissertation on Burroughs, SUNY at Stony Brook, 1979, for an excellent discussion of Burroughs' cut-up method.

CHAPTER 9

1. Fred Warshofsky, "Grove Press: Little Giant
of Publishing," Paperback Trade News, Vol. 1, No. 1 (March
1962), pp. 10-17 passim.
2. Joel J. Sprayregen to Charles Rembar, October
14, 1959. In "Burroughs, William. Naked Lunch. Editorial Correspondence #1, 1959-1962," Grove Press Collection:
William S. Burroughs in the George Arents Research Library
for Special Collections of Syracuse University. Further references to material in the Grove Press Collection will be cited
by the title found on the file folder, and followed by "Grove
Press Collection: Burroughs, Syracuse."
3. Barney Rosset to Maurice Girodias, November 11,
1959. "Burroughs, Naked Lunch, Editorial Correspondence
#1," Grove Press Collection: Burroughs, Syracuse.
4. Maurice Girodias to Barney Rosset, November 25,
1959. "Naked Lunch, Editorial Correspondence #1." Grove
Press Collection: Burroughs, Syracuse.
5. Odette Hummel is not mentioned by name in this
letter to Rosset of November 25, 1959, but subsequent contract negotiations were made through her. Also in this letter
Girodias mentions the possible publication of Miller's Tropics.
He tells Rosset, too, an anecdote concerning a meeting between himself and Nabokov at a Paris cocktail party. It seems
a minor scandal arose over the publication of Lolita by both
Olympia and Gallimard. The meeting promised a scene and
photographers were there to capture the moment. But no
exchange of insults or blows occurred. According to Girodias,
when Nabokov was asked later about the meeting he replied
like Humbert Humbert that he had not met the publisher at
the party at all.
6. Rosset to Girodias, November 30, 1959. "Naked
Lunch, Ed. Correspondence #1," Grove Press Collection:
Burroughs, Syracuse. Rosset also continues the discussion of
the publication of Miller's books in this letter. This seemed
hopeless because he was yet to secure the author's permission
to do so.

7. Maurice Girodias to Michael Goodman, June 21, 1976 in my possession. Girodias detailed the contract he had with Burroughs for Naked Lunch since the original and other records of Olympia Press had been lost or destroyed by various landlords during the financial troubles of the company.

8. Rosset to Girodias, November 30, 1959 "Naked Lunch, Ed. Correspondence # 1, " Grove Press Collection, Syracuse.

9. Girodias to Rosset, December 19, 1959 "Naked Lunch, Ed. Correspondence # 1, " Syracuse. Some detailed discussion of a restaurant Girodias had purchased is included here. That venture would prove the publisher's financial albatross, draining his resources.

10. Rosset to Girodias, December 28, 1959 "Naked Lunch, Ed. Correspondence # 1, " Syracuse.

11. Odette Hummel to Rosset, January 13, 1960. "Naked Lunch, Ed. Correspondence # 1, " Syracuse.

12. Rosset to Hummel, January 20, 1960, "Naked Lunch, Ed. Correspondence # 1, " Syracuse.

13. Hummel to Rosset, February 3, 1960, "Naked Lunch, Ed. Correspondence # 1, " Syracuse.

14. Rosset to Hummel, February 8, 1960, "Naked Lunch, Ed. Correspondence # 1, " Syracuse.

15. Hummel to Rosset, February 20, 1960. "Naked Lunch, Ed. Correspondence # 1, " Syracuse.

16. Rosset to Hummel, February 24, 1960. "Naked Lunch, Ed. Correspondence # 1, " Syracuse.

17. Charles Rembar to Rosset, April 6, 1960 and Rosset to Hummel, April 14, 1960. "Naked Lunch, Ed. Correspondence # 1, " Syracuse.

The Swiss connection was to prove more than just a bothersome complication, and Rosset was not the only one who had doubts about it. In a letter to New York artist Charles Henri Ford, Burroughs explained that he was "not altogether happy about Miss Hummel (September 20, 1960, Humanities Research Center, Austin). " He continued to be dissatisfied until he finally wrote to Rosset on May 13, 1963 asking, "Is it at all possible to send me my [royalty payments] direct[ly]. All this clearing through Switzerland and Licktenstein (sic) drags out interminably ("Naked Lunch, Ed. Correspondence # 2, 1962-1967, " Syracuse.). " Rosset replied that he could not do anything about the payment arrangements unless Girodias approved a contract change.

The matter remained unresolved until Grove received a letter from Paul Bowles in December 1963. Bowles expressed his sympathy over Burroughs' financial trouble, and told Richard Seaver that it was his understanding that Girodias had

lost money for Burroughs on Naked Lunch (Bowles to Seaver,
December 11, 1963. "Ed. Correspondence # 2. ") According
to Seaver the remark exploded like a bomb at the office of
Grove, and he informed him of the Swiss arrangement, adding
that they assumed Hummel was a wholly reputable agent (Seaver to Bowles, February 19, 1964. "Ed. Correspondence
2. ").

It appears that Girodias, not Hummel was at fault. He
wrote to Rosset on March 5, 1964 requesting information
about royalties on Naked Lunch. He explained bluntly, "The
idea concerning Naked Lunch royalties is that I owe Burroughs
a good deal of money and should like to pay him with what is
due to me (March 5, 1964, "Ed. Correspondence # 2. ") On
March 10, 1964 Burroughs wrote to Seaver with an explanation of what had happened to the money. Girodias was having
censorship trouble with the French government, in addition to
the financial drain of the restaurant. According to Burroughs
he had gotten the money due both of them from Hummel. He
concluded, "The plain fact is he spent the money to cover what
he evidently considered more pressing debts and I was barely
able to squeeze out of him enough to get myself back to Tangier. Of course I told him that the Swiss arrangement must
be canceled so that my share of royalties comes directly to
me in the future. He agreed to this and I have just received
a letter from him to the effect he has written you giving notice
of the new arrangement (March 10, 1964, Ed. Correspondence
2.). " He went on to explain his attitude toward what had oc-
curred, "Despite my understandable annoyance with Maurice
I still sympathize with his position which could hardly be
worse. More and more trouble with the French authorities,
suspended sentences piling up, a twenty-year publishing ban,
inevitable debacle of that unfortunate restaurant venture, owing
money to his staff, social security to the government, fines,
lawsuits, the lot (Ibid.). " The next royalty payment was sent
directly to Burroughs. Seaver added that considering what had
happened, his attitude toward Girodias was indeed admirable
(Seaver to Burroughs, April 1, 1964, "Ed. Correspondence
2. ").

18.   Burroughs to Paul Bowles, March 1, 1960. Humanities Research Center.

19.   Rosset to John Ciardi, April 13, 1960. "Ed.
Correspondence # 1, " Syracuse.

20.   Ciardi to Rosset, April 17, 1960. "Ed. Correspondence # 1, " Syracuse.

21.   Burroughs to Seaver, August 5, 1960. "Ed. Correspondence # 1, " Syracuse. The forward included with this
letter is a single page of typescript, all in capital letters, and
bears the title "NAKED LUNCH?". Its contents reassert the

general ideas expressed in the "Atrophied Preface" section
that the text is a how-to book.

22.   Two check requests dated July 7, 1960 and July
18, 1960 to Irving Rosenthal are in "Ed. Correspondence #1. "
Four letters concerning corrections to be made in the text
are included in this file: Seaver to Girodias, May 26, 1960;
Miriam Worms to Seaver, May 31, 1960; Judith Schmidt to
Miriam Worms, June 6, 1960; Worms to Schmidt, June 15,
1960. Another file, "Burroughs' Naked Lunch," contains
twenty-three carbon copy pages of textual insertions.

23.   Burroughs to Rosenthal, July 20, 1960. "Ed.
Correspondence #1. "

24.   Ibid. , p. 2. A brown envelope with twenty-five
calligraphs is contained in the file "Burroughs' Naked Lunch. "
Burroughs sent them from Paris to Allen Ginsberg on March
26, 1959. Ginsberg supplied the illustrations to Grove Press
after Burroughs requested they be inserted in the book. The
idea was not carried out.

25.   Ginsberg to Burroughs, April 29, 1960. "Ed.
Correspondence #1. " Syracuse.

26.   Ibid. , p. 2. The book is of course Thomas
Parkinson's Casebook on the Beat.

27.   Burroughs to Ginsberg, July 3, 1960 (sic). "Ed.
Correspondence #1, " Syracuse. Since it was written in response to Ginsberg's letter of July 29, the date should properly
read August 3, 1960, not July 3.

28.   The twelve-page manuscript of the essay and the
one-page cut-up of it mentioned in the letter cited above are
found in the Grove Press Collection file on Evergreen Review #4 at Syracuse.

29.   Burroughs to Seaver, August 5, 1960. "Ed. Correspondence #1. "

30.   See Chapter 7 above and the Notice of Seizure
sent to Rosset on August 29, 1960 in "Ed. Correspondence
#1. "

31.   E. R. Hutchinson, Tropic of Cancer on Trial,
N. Y. : Grove 1968, p. 50. See also chapters four and five
for Hutchinson's account of Grove's publication of Tropic of
Cancer.

32.   Burroughs to Seaver, November 25, 1960. "Ed.
Correspondence #1. "

33.   See Seaver to Girodias, December 21, 1960 and
Miriam Worms to Judith Schmidt, February 1, 1961. "Ed.
Correspondence #1. "

34.   Henry Miller to Maurice Girodias, December 8,
1960. "Ed. Correspondence #1. "

35.   Rosset to Miriam Worms, February 28, 1961.
"Ed. Correspondence #1. "

36. Girodias to Rosset, May 17, March 31, July 19, August 2, 1961. All four letters are in "Ed. Correspondence #1."

37. In "Burroughs' Naked Lunch," Grove Press Collection: Burroughs, Syracuse.

38. Hutchison, Tropic of Cancer on Trial, p. 63.

39. Ibid.

40. Ibid., p. 65.

41. Floating Bear #14 (1961), p. 23 reprinted in The Floating Bear: A Newsletter Nos. 1-37, 1961-1969, ed. Diane diPrima and LeRoi Jones (LaJolla, California: McGilvery, 1976), p. 156a. Pages xiii-xv of diPrima's "Introduction" to the collection contains a discussion of the incident with the authorities. Floating Bear #9 was sold by subscription only. One of its subscribers was a black poet named Harold Carrington who was an inmate in a New Jersey prison. DiPrima concluded that the Post Office and the FBI found out about the contents of the issue from a prison censor.

42. Hutchinson, pp. 74-75.

43. "Censorship Issues and Legal Cases." Publishers' Weekly (January 15, 1962), p. 68.

44. Edward deGrazia, "Defend the Freedom to Read in the Courts," ALA: Bulletin 49 (June 1965), p. 508. The lawyer who would later defend Naked Lunch in Boston observed in this article, "As you know, some years ago Grove Press essayed to defend at their own expense, coast to coast, anyone prepared to handle Tropic of Cancer, with results which I am told almost bankrupted the company."

45. Girodias to Rosset, December 4, 1961. "Ed. Correspondence #1."

46. Rosset to Girodias, December 7, 1961. "Ed. Correspondence #1." For recent status of the obligation of a writer in case of a law suit related to his work see Herbert Mitgang, "Authors Guild Challenges Indemnity Clause as Threat to Freedom," New York Times, April 23, 1978, p. 55.

47. Burroughs to Rosset, December 12, 1961. Box 2: "Nova Express," Grove Press Collection: Burroughs, Syracuse.

48. Rosset to Girodias, January 31, 1962, "Ed. Correspondence #1."

49. Burroughs to Rosset, June 23, 1962. Box 2: "Nova Express," Grove Press Collection: Burroughs, Syracuse.

50. Rosset to Burroughs, June 25, 1962. Box 2: "Nova Express," Grove Press Collection: Burroughs, Syracuse.

51.   Burroughs to Rosset, August 7, 1962.   "Ed. Correspondence #1."
52.   Burroughs to Paul Bowles, August 17, 1962.
Humanities Research Center, U. T. Austin.

CHAPTER 10

1.   The discussion of the conference and its relation
to Burroughs is reconstructed from a transcript of the proceedings which has been published in mimeographed form.
Each of the five discussions is paged separately and appears
under the common title: International Writers' Conference.
Edinburgh International Festival [Proceedings ... Monday-
Friday, August 20-24, 1962], Edinburgh: The Conference,
1962. The discussions were also broadcast over the radio,
greatly expanding the 2,000 who attended at McEwan Hall.
Although the transcript contains many gaps, misinterpreted
names, and questionable statements, it is useful as a record
of the sessions.   References to the transcript will be made
as "Edinburgh Conference Proceedings" followed by the date
and page number.
Also used in this chapter were reports in The Times of
London.   See: "Diary of the Week's Events," The Times,
August 18, 1962, p. 10; "Writers' Conference Draws an
Audience of 2,000," The Times, August 21, 1962, p. 4; "Authors' Meeting Breaks Up with Song," The Times, August
22, 1962, p. 6; "Modern Writers 'Failing in Task of Commitment,' " The Times, August 23, 1962, p. 5; "Authors Disappointed with Edinburgh Conference," The Times, August 24,
1962, p. 6; "Future of the Novel Discussed at Writers' Conference," The Times, August 25, 1962, p. 8.
2.   After the conference Mary McCarthy expanded her
opinions of Naked Lunch in articles published in Encounter and
in the New York Review of Books.   A discussion of her written comments follows in Chapter 11 below.
3.   Edinburgh Conference Proceedings, Monday,
August 20, 1962, p. 15.   Emphasis mine.
4.   Ibid. , p. 17.
5.   Edinburgh Conference Proceedings, Tuesday,
August 21, 1962, pp. 10, 11, 12, 27.
6.   Raymond Walters, "In and Out of Books," The
New York Times Book Review, September 16, 1962, p. 8.
7.   Burroughs' remarks on this topic were later
printed as "Censorship," Transatlantic Review, No. 11 (Winter
1962) p. 5ff, and reprinted under the same title in New American Story, eds. Allen and Creeley (New York: Grove Press,
1965), p. 254 ff.

8. Edinburgh Conference Proceedings, Thursday, August 23, 1962, p. 5.

9. Ibid.

10. Ibid. , p. 9.

11. Edinburgh Conference Proceedings, Friday, August 24, 1962, p. 2.

12. Ibid., p. 9.

13. Ibid. , p. 17.

14. Ibid.

15. Ibid. , p. 18. Burroughs' comments on the novel found in the transcript have been reprinted as a section titled "The Future of the Novel" in "Censorship," cited above at note 7.

16. Ibid.

17. Ibid.

18. Ibid.

19. Ibid. , p. 19.

20. Ibid. , p. 29.

21. Ibid. , p. 32.

22. Ibid. , p. 33.

23. Walters, "In and Out of Books," The New York Times Book Review, September 16, 1962, p. 8.

24. Cable from Milton Perlman to Barney Rosset, November 15, 1962, Grove Press Collection: Burroughs, "Naked Lunch, Editorial Correspondence # 1, 1959-1962," Syracuse University Library.

25. A single page bearing the date August 7, 1961 appears to be a printer's estimate of the production costs of Burroughs' book. The page is found in the "Naked Lunch Editorial Correspondence # 1" file at Syracuse. On the page is a notation that the work would be done by the "Hallmark Lithograph Co. " This may be a reference to Halliday Lithograph Corporation, but I have not been able to substantiate that speculation. Recalling Grove's plans to publish the book on 1961, the date which appears seems accurate.

26. Russel Halliday to Richard Seaver, October 11, 1962, "Editorial Correspondence # 1, " Grove Press Collection: Burroughs, Syracuse.

27. Copy of this agreement with the Book Press signed only by Rosset in Box # 1, "Burroughs' Naked Lunch, " Grove Press Collection: Burroughs, Syracuse.

28. Lionel Trilling to Barney Rosset, October 28, 1962, Box # 1, "Burroughs' Naked Lunch, " Grove Press Collection: Burroughs, Syracuse.

29. Advertising flyer: "Dear Bookseller, October 30, 1962, " p. 2, Box # 2, "Naked Lunch, Los Angeles, Editorial and Legal, " Grove Press Collection: Burroughs, Syracuse.

30. Barney Rosset to William Burroughs, March 14, 1963, Box #2 "Nova Express," Grove Press Collection: Burroughs, Syracuse.

CHAPTER 11

1. Allen Ginsberg, Howl and Other Poems (San Francisco: City Lights, 1956), Dedication page.
2. Arthur Flynn, "William Burroughs: Walden Revisited," Wagner Literary Magazine, No. 2 (1960-1961), p. 47.
3. Norman Mailer, Advertisements for Myself (New York: Putnam's Sons, 1959), p. 472.
4. "William Burroughs Naked Lunch," Grove Press publicity pamphlet, 1962, p. 4. Grove Press Collection: Burroughs, Syracuse.
5. Ibid., p. 3.
6. Ibid., p. 6.
7. Ibid., p. 7.
8. Ibid., p. 16.
9. Charles Poore, The New York Times, November 20, 1962, p. 33.
10. Ibid.
11. Herbert Gold, "Instead of Love, The Fix," New York Times Book Review, November 25, 1962, p. 4.
12. Richard Kluger, "The Absurdities of Existence Savagely Seen," New York Herald Tribune, November 25, 1962, p. 8.
13. Curt Gentry, "A Scream from the Junkie's Hell," San Francisco Chronicle. This World Magazine, January 6, 1963, p. 23. Some years later as co-author of Helter Skelter, Gentry would encounter description far more horrible and disgusting in the tale of Charles Manson.
14. Ibid.
15. Ibid.
16. "Strange Taste," Newsweek, November 26, 1962, p. 94.
17. "King of the YADS," Time, Vol. 80, No. 22 (November 30, 1962), pp. 96 and 98.
18. Diana Franklin, Time Archives to Michael B. Goodman, November 29, 1977. In my possession.
19. John Wain, "The Great Burroughs Affair," New Republic 147 (December 1, 1962), p. 21.
20. Ibid.
21. Richard Kostelanetz, "Senility of the Young Rebel," New Republic, December 15, 1962, p. 30.

22. George Siegel, "Naked Lunch," New Republic, December 29, 1962, p. 29.
23. Ibid.
24. Kay Boyle, "Naked Lunch," New Republic, December 29, 1962, p. 30.
25. Florence Howe, "Naked Lunch," New Republic, January 12, 1963, p. 31.
26. Alfred Chester, "Burroughs in Wonderland," Commentary Vol. 15, No. 1 (January 1963), p. 90.
27. Ibid.
28. John Gross, "Disorganization Men," New Statesman, February 8, 1963, p. 203.
29. Ibid., p. 204.
30. David Malcolm, "The Heroin of Our Times," The New Yorker, February 2, 1963, p. 114.
31. Ibid., p. 120.
32. Mary McCarthy, "Dejeuner sur l'Herbe: The Naked Lunch," New York Review of Books Vol. 1, No. 1 (n. d.), p. 4. A similar review by McCarthy appeared at the same time in England as "Burroughs' Naked Lunch," Encounter 20 (April 1963), pp. 92-98. Both reviews were revised and expanded for a chapter in her book The Writing on the Wall, New York: Harcourt, 1970, pp. 42-53. Though she could easily have reversed her previous positive views on Burroughs' book, the chapter revised from her reviews does not alter the high praise for Naked Lunch.
33. Lionel Abel, "Beyond the Fringe," Partisan Review 30 (Spring 1963), p. 110.
34. "Ugh ...," TLS, No. 3220, November 14, 1963, p. 919.
35. TLS, No. 3221, November 21, 1963, p. 947.
36. Ibid.
37. Mottram was later to write a full-length treatment of Burroughs titled William Burroughs: The Algebra of Need, New York: Intrepid Press, 1971. It was, however, an oddly chaotic and often muddled work which received this recent evaluation from Thomas Parkinson at the 1977 MLA Convention in Chicago: "I have the uneasy feeling reading Eric Mottram's William Burroughs that a handful of very uneven novels and a rather goofy theory of composition are being treated as if they were the major works and theories of a Conrad, Hardy, or James. I am mildly relieved when I note that Mottram has absolutely no clue about how to handle routine matters like bibliographies and notes and is no scholar, but when the question of Burroughs' world view is given so Germanic a presentation, I become irreverent ... " The remarks are taken from page 4 of a typescript copy of

the paper Parkinson read at the Burroughs Special Session on December 30, 1977.

38. TLS, No. 3222, November 28, 1963, p. 993.
39. TLS, No. 3223, December 5, 1963, p. 1011.
40. TLS, No. 3224, December 12, 1963, p. 1031.
41. TLS, No. 3225, December 19, 1963, p. 1049.
42. Ibid.
43. TLS, No. 3226, December 26, 1963, p. 1065.
44. TLS, No. 3227, January 2, 1964, p. 9.
45. TLS, No. 3228, January 9, 1964, p. 27.
46. TLS, No. 3229, January 16, 1964, p. 53.
47. TLS, No. 3230, January 23, 1964, p. 73.
48. Ibid.
49. Ibid.
50. "Whither Ugh?" TLS, No. 3231, January 30, 1964, p. 87.
51. Ibid.

CHAPTER 12

1. Paul S. Boyer, Purity in Print, New York: Scribner's, 1968, p. 167.
2. Ibid., p. 169. For a detailed discussion of censorship in Boston in the 1920s, see the entire chapter, pp. 167-206.
3. Chris F. Gillatti, "Book Censorship in Massachusetts: The Search for a Test for Obscenity," Boston University Law Review Vol. 42 (Fall 1962), p. 491.
4. Ed Zuckerman, "Boston Gets an Erogenous Zone," Vol 5, No. 9 Oui (September 1976), pp. 76-78; 128-131. The area is zoned by the city of Boston as "E," which euphemistically stands for "entertainment subdistrict." The area is similar to Baltimore's Baltimore Street and New York City's West 42nd Street with adult movies, clubs, bars, and book stores. The "E" district is represented by a beautiful public relations woman who escorts visiting city officials, who are interested in establishing similar "zones" in their home towns, through that section of Boston.
5. Boston Police Commissioner Robert diGrazia to Michael Goodman, May 6, 1976. In my possession. He is no relation to lawyer Edward deGrazia.
6. The account which follows was reconstructed from responses to questions put to Sergeant-Detective Griffin by phone on May 24, 1976 between 4:30 and 5:00 p.m., e.d.t. Griffin is now retired.
7. Commissioner diGrazia to Michael Goodman, May 6, 1976. There is, however, some confusion over who filed

the initial complaint. District Attorney Garret Byrne's office told me that the complaint was originally sworn out by the Vice-Squad (Asst. D. A. Joseph A. Laurano to M. Goodman, April 21, 1976), and Frank Dardeno in a phone conversation with me on July 19, 1976 said essentially the same thing, Mavrikos was arrested for the sale of Naked Lunch under a general warrant sworn out by the Police. Byrne is still the District Attorney in the Boston area. His office was co-operative, but not helpful. I asked access to their records of the case and any follow-up records through an official application under the freedom of information statutes which govern the Commonwealth. I was denied access to the information on Mavrikos and Naked Lunch. The reason given by the Judge was that the law forbade the publication of any names from the criminal offender records. They considered my dissertation as publication, and denied my request. There is a possibility, which Byrne's office would not confirm or deny, that the records had been routinely destroyed. What may still exist on microfilm is a record of the case in a Police journal, which are kept by the Boston Police back to 1930. Let me hasten to add here that Commissioner diGrazia and his office were very helpful. And Mr. Griffin was exceptionally precise and helpful in his recollections of the events surrounding the arrest of Mavrikos for selling Naked Lunch. Some of the details which might be found in the Police and District Attorney's records must remain a mystery for the moment.

      8.   Phone conversation between Griffin and M. Goodman, May 24, 1976. The awareness of a book's contents is the proof of "scienter" in an obscenity case.

      9.   This characterization of Mavrikos and other details of his arrest were provided by his lawyer Frank Dardeno in a phone conversation with me, July 19, 1976. Notes of this conversation are in my possession.

      10.   Phone conversation between Frank Dardeno and M. Goodman, July 19, 1976. The following statement found on page 25 of The Report of the Commission on Obscenity and Pornography, 1970, corroborates Dardeno's claim: "Patrons of adult bookstores and adult movie theatres may be characterized as predominantly white, middle class, middle aged, married males dressed in a business suit or neat casual attire, shopping or attending the movie alone."

      11.   Ibid.

      12.   Barney Rosset to Maurice Girodias, February 7, 1963. Grove Press Collection: Burroughs "Naked Lunch, Editorial Correspondence #2, 1962-1967." Syracuse University.

13. Norman Mailer, The Armies of the Night, New York: The New American Library, 1968, pp. 21-22.

14. Copies of the two letters are enclosed with a letter from deGrazia to Barney Rosset, March 21, 1963. Box #2, "Naked Lunch, L. A., Editorial and Legal," Grove Press Collection: Burroughs, Syracuse.

15. Phone conversation with Dardeno, July 19, 1976.

16. William I. Cowin to Michael B. Goodman, April 26, 1976. In my possession. Mr. Cowin is now in private practice in Boston.

17. Edward deGrazia to Joseph Nolan, December 11, 1963. Box #2, "Naked Lunch, L. A. Editorial and Legal," Grove Press Collection: Burroughs, Syracuse.

18. Edward deGrazia to Ervin Gaines, January 7, 1964. Box #2, "Naked Lunch, L. A. Editorial and Legal," Grove Press Collection: Burroughs, Syracuse.

19. Edward deGrazia to Barney Rosset, February 5, 1964. Box #1, "Naked Lunch, Editorial Correspondence #2, 1962-1967," Grove Press Collection: Burroughs, Syracuse. Attached to this letter are copies of Schrieber to Byrne, January 22, 1964; Geller to Byrne, January 27, 1964; Geller to Brooke, January 27, 1964; and Beisel to Byrne, January 27, 1964.

20. Edward deGrazia to Barney Rosset, March 4, 1964. Box #1, "Naked Lunch, Editorial Correspondence #2, 1962-1967," Grove Press Collection: Burroughs, Syracuse. Rosset was concerned with the payment of Mavrikos' overdue bill to Grove Press, and did not want deGrazia to go ahead with the case until it was paid. DeGrazia received an assurance from Dardeno that the bill would be paid.

21. Edward DeGrazia to Barney Rosset, March 26, 1964. Box #2, "Naked Lunch, L. A. Editorial and Legal," Grove Press Collection: Burroughs, Syracuse.

22. Senator Edward Brooke to Michael Goodman, June 29, 1976, in my possession. On this point, William I. Cowin suggested that Brooke "would not--in my opinion--have cared, one way or the other, what the fellow [Byrne] thought" (Cowin to Goodman, April 26, 1976, in my possession). Since the book was widely distributed, while containing material shocking and offensive to some people and also since it posed many interesting, unresolved legal questions, Cowin believed it offered a worthwhile test of the new in rem procedure.

23. Edward deGrazia to Edward Brooke, May 1, 1964. Box #2, "Naked Lunch, L. A. Editorial and Legal," Grove Press Collection: Burroughs, Syracuse. The letter was sent only after deGrazia received confirmation that Mavrikos had settled his debt with Grove Press.

24.   Transcript of "Attorney General vs. A Book Named Naked Lunch" Massachusetts Superior Court #83001, p. 18.

25.   "Opinion of Justice of the Superior Court that There IS Reasonable Cause to Believe that a Book Named 'Naked Lunch' Is Obscene, Indecent, and Impure and Order of Issuance of Order of Notice" attached to deGrazia to Milton Perlman, October 12, 1964, Box #2 "Naked Lunch, L. A. Editorial and Legal, " Grove Press Collection: Burroughs, Syracuse.

26.   "Order of Notice Directed Against a Book Named 'Naked Lunch', " in Box #1, "Naked Lunch, Editorial Correspondence #2, 1962-1967, " Grove Press Collection: Burroughs, Syracuse.

27.   Edward deGrazia to Barney Rosset, December 31, 1964.   Box #2, "Naked Lunch, L. A. Editorial and Legal, " Grove Press Collection: Burroughs, Syracuse.

28.   Edward deGrazia to Witnesses, January 1964 (it should read January 1965).   Box #2 "Naked Lunch, L. A. Editorial and Legal, " Grove Press Collection: Burroughs, Syracuse.

29.   Norman Holland to Michael Goodman, March 6, 1978, in my possession.

30.   Ervin Gaines, "Model Obscenity Statute, " ALA Newsletter on Intellectual Freedom, March 1964, p. 16.

31.   The following account of the trial is reconstructed from the transcript of "Attorney General Edward W. Brooke vs. A Book Named Naked Lunch, " Massachusetts Superior Court #83001.   Further references will be made parenthetically as (Trans.) followed by a page number.   Obvious errors have been corrected in quoting from the record.

32.   See Chapter 11 above for a detailed discussion of the two reviews.

33.   The exhibits are listed on pages 2, 3, and 148 of the Transcript.

34.   Asked why he took up the Burroughs cause, Ciardi wrote to me on April 17, 1978, "Burroughs is not exactly my favorite author, but he is honest (which is legally sufficient), talented (which is esthetically sufficient), and he carried me to a madness I could experience as real (which is emphatically sufficient). " He characterized Judge Hudson as "an able man trying to go through the formal motions of a job that made no sense. "

35.   The review was submitted as Exhibit #11.

36.   William S. Burroughs, Naked Lunch, New York: Grove Press, 1959, 1966, p. v.   This is the paperback edition which appeared after the trial.

37. Burroughs, Naked Lunch, New York: Grove Press, 1959, 1962, p. 27. Further references to this edition, which was the one on trial, will be made parenthetically as ("NL") followed by page number.

38. Richard Kuh, Foolish Figleaves?, New York: MacMillan, 1967, p. 131.

39. Norman Holland to Michael Goodman, March 6, 1978, p. 1. In my possession.

40. Ibid.

41. Ibid.

42. Ibid.

43. Part of Mailer's testimony is found in the 1966 paperback edition of Naked Lunch on pages x-xviii. It coincides with pages 102 to 114 of the trial transcript.

44. Holland to Goodman, March 6, 1978.

45. Cross-examination questions and responses are not reproduced in the paperback edition of the text. They are found on pages 114 to 123 of the transcript and include deGrazia's redirect examination.

46. This section is on pages 131-133 of Naked Lunch. See Chapter 8 above for a discussion of this section of the book.

47. It is quite possible that this is one of Cowin's questions incorrectly attributed to deGrazia, or addressed to Cowin by deGrazia.

48. Burroughs' letter to Jack Kerouac on December 7, 1954 contains an expression of his frustration over his inability to write popular magazine fiction. See Chapter 8 above for a discussion of this letter.

49. Joseph M. Harvey, "Defenders of Naked Lunch compare Burroughs to Authors of Classics," Boston Globe, January 13, 1965, p. 14.

50. The second day's testimony is recorded in Volume II of the Transcript on pages 148-300. Because of the sequential pagination, no mention of the volume number seems necessary for identification. References to the Transcript will continue as (Trans.). References to the book will continue as (NL).

51. Attorney General vs. A Book Named Tropic of Cancer. 345 Mass. 11.

52. Norman Holland to Michael B. Goodman, March 6, 1978, in my possession.

53. See the text accompanying note 18 in Chapter 11 above.

54. Naked Lunch, Black Cat (paperback) Edition, pp. xviii-xxxiv. Ginsberg's testimony is found on pages 203-269 of the Transcript. When prepared for inclusion in the paper-

back edition of Naked Lunch, only parts of the direct examination were kept. The cross-examination was eliminated,
though some questions by Cowin and Hudson remained. As
they appear in the edition of the book, both Ginsberg's and
Mailer's testimony were edited to show the best case for the
Burroughs book, and misrepresent the events slightly for
maximum dramatic effect.

55.   Their exchange was deleted from the reproduction
of the testimony, and should appear just after "have you found
..." on page x of the Black Cat Edition. The exchange may
have been deleted because it was considered tangential, and
the failure to note an elipsis a simple oversight. Coupled
with other deletions, however, a more positive impression of
Ginsberg's performance on the final day of the trial emerges.

56.   The deletion of this exchange makes that part of
the trial appear tamer than it was. It also eliminates an
important circumstance which may have influenced the judge's
application of the censorship laws to Naked Lunch.

57.   Allen Ginsberg, Unpublished notes for the Boston
trial of Naked Lunch, p. 6.   Box #1, Editorial Correspondence
#2, 1962-1967, Grove Press Collection: Burroughs, Syracuse
University.

58.   This exchange was also deleted from the paperback edition. It may have been blue-penciled because these
few pages, 229-233 of the Transcript, deal with one of the
so-called pornographic sections of Naked Lunch.

59.   The same line is part of the passage mentioned
during the questioning of Jackson in which there is a reference
to sexual intercourse with a dead woman.

60.   Naked Lunch (paperback edition), p. xxxiv.   At
the request of Allen Ginsberg, the arrangement of the lines
he read at the trial follows the text as it appears in Reality
Sandwiches (City Lights), p. 40.   The poem appeared on page
236 of the trial transcript as follows: "The method must be
purest meat and no symbolic dressing, actual visions and
actual prisons, as seen then and now. Prisons and visions
presented with rare descriptions corresponding exactly to those
of Alcatraz and rose. A Naked Lunch is natural to us. We
eat reality sandwiches, but allegories are so much lettuce.
Don't hide the madness." The court stenographer Ursula E.
Nurse recorded the Ginsberg poem as if it were prose. When
Grove Press published portions of the transcript of the trial
in Naked Lunch, the poetic arrangement of Ginsberg's lines
was restored.

61.   Ginsberg, Unpublished notes for the trial of Naked
Lunch.

62.   Ibid., p. 4.

63. At note 88 in Chapter 8 above, see the discussion of the September 11, 1959, letter from Burroughs to Ginsberg. He explains his reasons for the additional material for the American edition.

64. DeGrazia's summation appears on pages 285-287 of the Transcript; pages xxxiv-xxxvi of the book.

CHAPTER 13

1. See Joseph M. Harvey, "Poet Ginsberg Defends Naked Lunch," AM Globe, January 14, 1965, p. 35; and "Two Give Praise to Naked Lunch," The Boston Herald, January 14, 1965, p. 3.

2. John Ciardi, "Banned in Boston," Saturday Review 48 (March 1965), p. 14.

3. Ibid.

4. Edward deGrazia to Frank D. Laven, January 25, 1965. Box #2 "L. A. Editorial and Legal," Grove Press Collection: Burroughs, Syracuse.

5. Copies of the complaints are located in Box #2, "L. A. Editorial and Legal," Grove Press Collection: Burroughs, Syracuse.

6. Partial Transcript of "California vs. Galanti/ Frank," p. 1, in Frank D. Laven to Edward deGrazia, February 4, 1965, Box #2, "L. A. Editorial and Legal." Hereafter referred to parenthetically as "L. A. Partial Trans."

7. See clippings in "L. A. Editorial and Legal," Grove Press Collection: "Lewd Literature Trial Still Awaiting Jury," Evening Outlook, Wednesday, January 27, 1965, p. 8; "Jury Weighs Obscenity," Citizen News, February 1, 1965, n. p.; "Judge Dismisses Case Against Naked Lunch," Evening Outlook, n. d., p. 1 & 6; "Court Rules Book Not Obscene," Citizen News, n. d., n. p.

8. Laven to Grove Press, April 1, 1965; Richard Gallen, Grove General Council to Frank Laven, April 6, 1965. Both letters in Box #1, "Naked Lunch, Editorial Correspondence #2, 1962-1967," Grove Press Collection: Burroughs, Syracuse.

9. Burroughs' work has also been banned in at least two other instances, not by judicial authorities, but by local librarians. Naked Lunch was banned along with Lawrence Durrell's Justine in Norwich, England. The town's Library Committee chairman is reported to have complained, "I don't see why we should be a party to the lowering of moral or library standards (The Guardian, Manchester, England, Friday, February 19, 1965, p. 4.)." The librarian was not as au-

thoritative and apologized, "If the reviews had been better, we might have bought him. But we were warned off a bit (Ibid.)."

In Tar Heel, North Carolina, a tobacco-growing and pig-farming area, Burroughs' The Wild Boys was ordered removed from the High School library along with twenty other books including three Hemingway novels ("School Ban Includes Hemingway Novels," The Dallas Morning News, May 17, 1976, p. 8B.).

CHAPTER 14

1. Judge Eugene Hudson, "Findings of Material Facts and Order for Decree," Massachusetts Superior Court, March 23, 1965.
2. Ibid.
3. Jacobellis vs. Ohio, 378 U.S. 184 (1964). Although this case involved a movie, books were considered to come under its definitions of the obscene and the pornographic.
4. See "Naked Lunch Obscene, Bay State Judge Rules," The Boston Globe, March 23, 1965, p. 16; "Banned Here," The Boston Globe, March 24, 1965, p. 24; John Ciardi, "The Book Banners Again (and Again and Again)," Saturday Review 48 (August 28, 1965), p. 21.
5. Joseph A. Laurano, Executive Assistant to Suffolk Country District Attorney to Michael Goodman, April 12, 1976. In my possession.
6. William I. Cowin to Michael Goodman, April 26, 1976, p. 2.
7. After the formal charges were dropped, Dardeno said that he "advised him to clean out his store because they were after him. I told him, 'Griffin's after you (Phone conversation with Dardeno on July 19, 1976)'." And shortly afterward, Mavrikos, whose family had a history of mental illness, was committed to the West Borough Institution where he subsequently died in 1968, according to Dardeno.
8. Attorney General vs. "Naked Lunch." 351 Mass. 298; 298.
9. Jacobellis vs. Ohio. 378 U.S. 184 (1964).
10. Richard Kuh, Foolish Figleaves?, New York: Macmillan, 1968, p. 99.
11. See Kuh, Foolish Figleaves?, pp. 77-83; 123-143 for a complete discussion of these cases and the arguments before the U.S. Supreme Court. For the text of the oral arguments see Obscenity, ed. Leon Friedman, New York: Chelsea House, 1970, pp. 203-277.

12.   Edward deGrazia, "Introduction, " Censorship Landmarks, New York: Bowker, 1969, pp. xxx-xxxi.

13.   Obscenity, ed. Leon Friedman, New York: Chelsea House, 1970, pp. 226-243.

14.   Ibid. , pp. 203-225.

15.   Ibid. , p. 217.

16.   Paul I. Hennessey, "Constitutional Law: Attorney General vs. Memoirs, " Portia Law Journal, Spring 1966, pp. 250-259.

17.   Obscenity, ed. Friedman, pp. 244-267 for the oral argument in the Memoirs case.

18.   Ginzburg vs. U. S. 383 U. S. 463.

19.   Ibid.

20.   Ibid.

21.   Ibid.

22.   Mishkin vs. New York. 383 U. S. 502.

23.   Memoirs vs. Massachusetts. 383 U. S. 413.

24.   Charles Rembar, The End of Obscenity, New York: Random House, 1968.

25.   David Wilson, "Pre-Publication Fanfare: New Obscenity Test?" and James Doyle, "Fanny Hill Obscured, " both articles in Boston Sunday Globe, April 10, 1966, p. 73.

26.   Attorney General vs. 'Naked Lunch. ' 351 Mass. 298.   Only the majority opinion of the decision is reproduced on pages viii-ix of the 1966 paperback edition of Naked Lunch issued after the resolution of the case.

27.   Edward deGrazia, "Introduction, " Censorship Landmarks, pp. xxvi-xxvii.

28.   Attorney General vs. 'Naked Lunch. ' 351 Mass. 298; 299.

29.   Ibid.

30.   Ibid. , p. 306. Also on p. ix of the paperback Naked Lunch.

31.   Ibid. , pp. 300-301.

32.   Ibid. , p. 311.

33.   Ibid. , p. 302.

34.   Ibid. , p. 303.

35.   Ibid. , pp. 304-305.

36.   On page 195 of Foolish Figleaves?, Richard Kuh comments on the use of witnesses in obscenity cases. "Happily, the rules of evidence permit a so-called expert to be cross-examined, after he has given his opinion, as to the reasoning, the logic--if any exists--to support this viewpoint. If the expert's reasoning inadequately justifies the expert's conclusions, the trier-of-fact (jury or judge) is free to discard completely the expert's opinions. "

37.   Attorney General vs. 'Naked Lunch. ' 351 Mass. 298; 308.

38. Ibid. The Massachusetts decision says that the quotation was found in exhibit 20, the New York Times Book Review for January 10, 1965. No page reference was given. A search through that issue failed to turn up the words quoted, as did a similar search of preceding and following issues.

39. Ibid. , p. 311.

40. "Naked Lunch Ban Off, " Boston Globe, July 7, 1966, p. 27; and "Naked Lunch Declared Not Obscene by Massachusetts Supreme Court, " Library Journal 91 (August 1966), pp. 3667-8.

41. "Naked Lunch, " Boston Herald, July 9, 1966, p. 4.

42. Ibid.

43. Senator Edward Brooke to Michael Goodman, June 29, 1976. In my possession.

44. William I. Cowin to Michael Goodman, April 26, 1976. In my possession.

CHAPTER 15

1. Felice Flanery Lewis, Literature, Obscenity, and Law, Carbondale: Southern Illinois University Press, 1976.

2. Ibid. , p. 255.

3. Miller vs. California, 413 U. S. 15 (1973).

4. "Project: An Empirical Inquiry into the Effects of Miller vs. California on the Control of Obscenity, " New York University Law Review Vol. 52, No. 4 (October 1977), pp. 819-939. See especially pages 858-859, 900, 903-904, and 917-918.

5. "U. S. Judge Voids Customs' Seizure of Sex Magazine, " New York Law Journal, August 1, 1978, p. 2.

REFERENCES

The following list of works cited in the text is divided into two parts: I) published material arranged alphabetically; II) unpublished material arranged chronologically. For a fuller bibliography see my William S. Burroughs: An Annotated Bibliography of His Works and Criticism (New York: Garland Publishing Co., 1975). For a descriptive rather than critical bibliography of only Burroughs' works to 1973 see Joe Maynard and Barry Miles, Williams S. Burroughs, 1953-1973: A Bibliography (University of Virginia Press, 1977).

I. PUBLISHED WORKS

Abel, Lionel. "Beyond the Fringe." Partisan Review, 30 (Spring 1963), pp. 109-112.

Adams, Frank S. "Columbia Student Kills Friend and Sinks Body in Hudson River." New York Times, (August 17, 1944), pp. 1 and 13.

Algren, Nelson. "Chicago Is a Wose." Nation 188, (February 28, 1959, p. 191.

Attorney General vs A Book Named "Naked Lunch." 351 Mass. 298.

Attorney General vs A Book Named "Tropic of Cancer." 345 Mass. 11.

"August Derleth, Prolific Author." New York Times, (July 6, 1971), p. 36.

"Authors Disappointed with Edinburgh Conference." The Times, (August 24, 1962), p. 6.

"Authors' Meeting Breaks Up with Song." The Times, (August 22, 1962), p. 6.

"Banned Here." Boston Globe, (March 24, 1965), p. 24.

Bell, Dan. "What You Can't Read to Your Daughter." The
    New Leader, Vol. 42, No. 21 (May 25, 1959), pp.
    23-24.

"Big Table" vs Carl A. Schroeder 186 F. Supp. 254 (1960).

Bockris, Victor. "First Meetings: One Dozen Memories
    from the Files of William Burroughs." National Screw,
    Vol. 1, No. 5 (April 1977), pp. 9-14.

_____. "Information About the Operation: A Portrait of
    William Burroughs." The New Review, Vol. 13, No.
    25 (April 1976), pp. 42-43.

Bowles, Paul. "Burroughs in Tangier." Big Table #2 (Sum-
    mer 1959), pp. 42-44.

Boyer, Paul. Purity in Print. New York: Scribner's,
    1968.

Boyle, Kay. "Naked Lunch." New Republic, (December 29,
    1962), p. 30.

Burroughs, William S. "Censorship." Transatlantic Review,
    No. 11 (Winter 1962), pp. 5-1-.

_____. "Chapter 2 of Naked Lunch." Chicago Review
    Vol. 12, No. 3 (Autumn 1958), pp. 3-12.

_____. "The Coming of the Purple Better One." Esquire,
    70 (November 1968), pp. 89-91.

_____. Dead Fingers Talk. London: Calder, 1963.

_____. "from 'Naked Lunch.'" Chicago Review, Vol.
    12, No. 1 (Spring 1958), pp. 23-30.

_____. Junkie. New York: Ace, 1953.

_____. "Literary Autobiography," in Catalogue of the
    William S. Burroughs Archive. London: Miles As-
    sociates, 1973.

_____. Minutes to Go. Paris: Two Cities Press, 1960.

_____. The Naked Lunch. Paris: Olympia Press, 1959.

_____. Naked Lunch. New York: Grove Press, 1962.

_____. Naked Lunch. New York: Grove Press, 1966.

_____. "Tangier. " Esquire, 62 (September 1964), pp.
       114-119.

_____. "Uncle Bill Burroughs (Alias Technical Tilly) on
       Scientology. " Rat, Vol. 2, No. 24 (1969), pp. 12-13.

_____, and Allen Ginsberg. The Yage Letters. San
       Francisco: City Lights, 1963.

Burroughs, William S. , Jr. "Life with Father. " Esquire,
       (September 1971), pp. 113-115, 140-141, 144-145.

"Censorship Issues and Legal Cases. " Publishers' Weekly,
       (January 15, 1962), p. 68.

Chester, Alfred. "Burroughs in Wonderland. " Commentary,
       Vol. 15, No. 1 (January 1963), p. 90.

Ciardi, John. "Banned in Boston. " Saturday Review, 48
       March 1965), p. 14.

_____. "The Book Banners Again (and Again and Again). "
       Saturday Review, 48 (August 28, 1965), p. 21.

_____. "Bookburners and Sweet Sixteen. " Saturday Re-
       view, 42 (July 27, 1959), p. 22.

_____. "Epitaph for Dead Beats. " Saturday Review,
       (February 6, 1960), p. 11.

Coley, Lemuel. Unpublished Doctoral Dissertation on William
       S. Burroughs. SUNY at Stony Brook, 1979.

Congressional Record. Appendix for August 19, 1959, p.
       A7152.

Dahlberg, Edward. "Further Sorrows of Priapus. " Big
       Table #1, (Spring 1959), pp. 43-62.

Dardess, George. "The Invisible William Burroughs. " Diss:
       Rutgers University, 1970.

deGrazia, Edward. Censorship Landmarks. New York:
Bowker, 1969.

_____. "Defend the Freedom to Read in the Courts. "
ALA Bulletin, 49 (June 1965), p. 508.

_____. "Obscenity and the Mail. " Law and Contemporary
Problems, 20 (1955), p. 608.

"Derleth, August (William). " In Contemporary Authors Vols.
1-4, eds. Kinsman and Tannenhouse. Detroit: Gale,
1967, p. 244.

"Diary of the Week's Events. " The Times, (August 18, 1962),
p. 10.

Doyle, James. "Fanny Hill Obscured. " Boston Globe,
(April 10, 1966), p. 73.

Eich, W. H. "From Ulysses to Portnoy: A Pornography
Primer. " Marquette Law Review, Vol. 53, No. 2
(Summer 1970), p. 155-171.

"An Empirical Inquiry into the Effects of Miller vs. California on the Control of Obscenity. " New York University
Law Review, Vol. 52, No. 4 (October 1977), pp. 810-
939.

Epstein, Jason. "The Obscenity Business. " Atlantic Monthly,
Vol. 218, No. 2 (August 1966), pp. 56-60.

"First Big Table. " Wagner Literary Magazine, No. 1 (Spring
1959), pp. 72-73.

Floating Bear: A Newsletter Nos. 1-37, 1961-1969. eds.
Diane di Prima and Le Roi Jones. La Jolla, California: McGilvery, 1976.

Flynn, Arthur. "William Burroughs: Walden Revisited. "
Wagner Literary Magazine, No. 2 (1960-1961), p. 47.

"Future of the Novel Discussed at Writers' Conference. "
The Times, (August 25, 1962), p. 8.

Gains, Ervin. "Model Obscenity Statute. " ALA Newsletter
on Intellectual Freedom, (March 1964), p. 16.

Gentry, Curt. "A Scream from the Junkie's Hell." San
    Francisco Chronicle: This World Magazine. (January
    6, 1963), p. 23.

Gillotti, Chris F. "Book Censorship in Massachusetts: The
    Search for a Test for Obscenity." Boston University
    Law Review, Vol. 42 (Fall 1962), pp. 476-491.

Girodias, Maurice. "Confessions of a Booklegger's Son."
    Censorship, No. 3 (Summer 1965), pp. 2-16.

Ginsberg, Allen. Howl and Other Poems. San Francisco:
    City Lights, 1956.

_____. "Two Letters from Allen Ginsberg." Chicago
    Review, Vol. 12, No. 3 (Autumn 1958), p. 47.

Ginzburg vs U. S.   383 U. S. 463.

Gold, Herbert. "Instead of Love, The Fix." New York
    Times Book Review, (November 25, 1962), p. 4.

Gross, John. "Disorganization Men." New Statesman (Feb-
    ruary 8, 1963), p. 203.

Grove Press vs Christenberry.   175 F. Supp. 502.

The Guardian (Manchester, England). (Friday, February 19,
    1965), p. 4.

"The Hallucinatory Operators Are Real (An Interview)." SF
    Horizons, No. 2 (1965), p. 3.

Harvey, Joseph M. "Defenders of Naked Lunch Compare
    Burroughs to Authors of Classics." Boston Globe,
    (January 13, 1965), p. 14.

_____. "Poet Ginsberg Defends Naked Lunch." Boston
    Globe. (January 14, 1965), p. 35.

Hennessey, Paul I. "Constitutional Law: Attorney General
    vs Memoirs." Portia Law Journal (Spring 1966), p.
    250-259.

Howe, Florence. "Naked Lunch." New Republic, (January
    12, 1963), p. 31.

Hudson, Eugene. "Findings of Material Facts and Order for
    Decree. " Massachusetts Superior Court, March 23,
    1965.

Hutchinson, E. R. Tropic of Cancer on Trial: A Case His-
    tory of Censorship. New York: Grove Press, 1968.

International Writers' Conference. Edinburgh International
    Festival [Proceedings ... Monday-Friday, August 20-
    24, 1962], Edinburgh: The Conference, 1962.

Jacobellis vs Ohio.   378 U. S. 184 (1964).

Kerouac, Jack. Desolation Angels. New York: Coward-
    McCann, 1965.

_____. "Old Angel Midnight. " Big Table # 1, (Spring
    1959), pp. 7-42.

"King of the YADS. " Time, Vol. 80, No. 22 (November 30,
    1962), pp. 96 and 98.

Kluger, Richard. "The Absurdities of Existence Savagely
    Seen. " New York Herald Tribune, (November 25,
    1962), p. 8.

Knickerbocker, Conrad. "William Burroughs: Paris Review
    Interview. " Paris Review, (Fall 1965), p. 40.

Kostelanetz, Richard. "Senility of the Young Rebel. " New
    Republic, (December 15, 1962), p. 30.

Kuh, Richard. Foolish Figleaves? New York: Macmillan,
    1967.

Latham, Aaron. "The Columbia Murder That Gave Birth to
    the Beats. " New York Magazine, (April 19, 1976),
    pp. 41ff.

"Letters to the Editor. " Saturday Review, 42 (July 11, 1959),
    p. 23.

_____. Saturday Review, 42 (July 18, 1959), p. 21.

_____. Saturday Review, 42 (August 1, 1959), p. 25.

Lewis, Felice Flanery. Literature, Obscenity, and Law.
    Carbondale: Southern Illinois University Press, 1976.

Lockhart, William B. and Robert C. McClure. "Literature, the Law of Obscenity, and the Constitution." Minnesota Law Review, 38 (March 1954), pp. 295-395.

Mabley, Jack. "Filthy Writing on the Midway." Chicago Daily News, (October 25, 1958), p. 1.

Mailer, Norman. Advertisements for Myself. New York: Putnam's, 1959.

_____. The Armies of the Night. New York: New American Library, 1968.

_____. "The Faith of Graffiti." Esquire, (May 1974), pp. 77ff.

_____. White Negro. San Francisco: City Lights, 1970.

Malanga, Gerard. "An Interview with William Burroughs." The Beat Book, No. 4 (1974), pp. 90-112.

Malcolm, David. "The Heroin of Our Times." The New Yorker, (February 2, 1963), p. 114.

Malko, George. Scientology. New York: Delta, 1970.

Martin, Fletcher. "Smut or Art? Barred Magazine, P. O. Tangle at Hearing." New York Post, (June 24, 1959), p. 6.

"Maurice Girodias: In Trouble for His 'd. b. 's'." Publishers' Weekly, 188 (October 11, 1965), p. 34.

McCarthy, Mary. "Burroughs' Naked Lunch." Encounter, 20 (April 1963), pp. 92-98.

_____. "Dejeuner sur l'Herbe: The Naked Lunch." New York Review of Books, Vol. 1, No. 1 (n. d.), pp. 4-5.

_____. The Writing on the Wall. New York: Harcourt, 1970.

McGowan, Richard. "Billion $ Cesspool." New York News, (March 17, 1959), p. 24.

_____. "Pornographers' Poison Is Easily Available for Kids." New York News, (March 18, 1959), p. 40.

_____. "Your Name Could Be on Mail Lists of Smut Dealers." New York News, (March 19, 1959), p. 44.

Memoirs vs. Massachusetts. 383 U.S. 413.

Miller vs. California. 413 U.S. 15.

Mishkin vs. New York. 383 U.S. 502.

Mitgang, Herbert. "Authors' Guild Challenges Indemnity Clause as Threat to Freedom." New York Times, (April 23, 1978), p. 55.

"Modern Writers' Failing in Task of Commitment." The Times, (April 23, 1962), p. 5.

Mottram, Eric. William Burroughs: The Algebra of Need. New York: Intrepid Press, 1971.

"Naked Lunch." Boston Herald, (July 9, 1966), p. 4.

"Naked Lunch Ban Off." Boston Globe, (July 7, 1966), p. 27.

"Naked Lunch Declared Not Obscene by Massachusetts Supreme Court." Library Journal, 91 (August 1966), pp. 3667-8.

"Naked Lunch Obscene, Bay State Judge Rules." Boston Globe, (March 23, 1965), p. 16.

Obscenity, Leon Friedman, ed. New York: Chelsea House, 1970.

O'Neil, Paul. "The Only Rebellion Around." Life, 47 (November 30, 1959), pp. 115-130.

Palmer, Robert. "Rolling Stone Interview: William Burroughs." Rolling Stone, No. 108 (May 11, 1972), pp. 48ff.

Parkinson, Thomas. A Casebook on the Beat. New York: Crowell, 1961.

_____. "William S. Burroughs: Critical Approaches." Unpublished paper read at Burroughs' Special Session, MLA Convention, Chicago, Illinois, December 30, 1977.

Paul, James C. N. and Murry L. Schwartz. Federal Cen-
     sorship: Obscenity in the Mail. New York: The Free
     Press, 1961.

Podell, Albert N. "Censorship on the Campus: The Case of
     the Chicago Review. " San Francisco Review, Vol. 1,
     No. 2 (1959), pp. 71-87.

Polkinhorn, Harry. "William Burroughs: In the Radical
     Tradition. " DAI, 36 (1976), 7424A-7425A (New York
     University).

Poore, Charles. The New York Times. November 20, 1962,
     p. 33.

"Post Office Morals. " The Nation, 188 (March 30, 1959),
     pp. 486-487.

"Post Office Rules Off New Quarterly as Obscene. " New
     York Post. May 24, 1959.

Rembar, Charles. The End of Obscenity. New York: Ran-
     dom House, 1968.

The Report of the Commission on Obscenity and Pornography.
     U. S. Government Printing Office, 1970.

"Report of the Committee on Obscene Matter Sent Through the
     Mail. "   U. S. Government Printing Office, August
     1959.

Roller, Alfred C. "A Blueprint Is Offered for War Against
     Smut. " Chicago Sun Times, August 10, 1959, pp.
     1 & 6.

_____. "How Smut Seduces Youths to Violence. " Chicago
     Sun Times, August 12, 1959, pp. 22.

_____. "How 2 Cities Battle Muck. " Chicago Sun Times,
     August 11, 1959, pp. 3 & 20.

_____. "You Can Strike a Blow Against Smut. " Chicago
     Sun Times, August 13, 1959, p. 8.

Rosenthal, Irving. "Editorial. " Big Table #1 (Spring 1959),
     pp. 3-6.

Roth vs. U.S.   354 U.S. 476.

Schleifer, Marc D.   "Big Table #1."   Village Voice, Vol. 4,
     No. 24 (April 8, 1959), p. 51.

"School Ban Includes Hemingway Novels."   The Dallas Morning
     News, May 17, 1976, p. 8B.

"Shy Pornographer."   Time, 78 (November 30, 1961), pp.
     88-89.

Siegel, George.   "Naked Lunch."   New Republic, (December
     29, 1962), p. 29.

Sigler, J. A.   "Customs Censorship."   Cleveland-Marshall
     Law Review, Vol. 15 (January 1966), p. 63.

"Strange Taste."   Newsweek, (November 26, 1962), p. 94.

"Student Is Indicted in 2d Degree Murder."   New York Times,
     August 25, 1944, p. 15.

"Student Silent on Slaying Friend."   New York Times, August
     18, 1944, p. 14.

"Stunt Shooting of Wife Denied."   New York Times, Septem-
     ber 8, 1951, p. 31.

Time, December 4, 1959, p. 4.

TLS, No. 3221, November 21, 1963, p. 947.

TLS, No. 3222, November 28, 1963, p. 993.

TLS, No. 3223, December 5, 1963, p. 1011.

TLS, No. 3224, December 12, 1963, p. 1031.

TLS, No. 3225, December 19, 1963, p. 1049.

TLS, No. 3226, December 26, 1963, p. 1065.

TLS, No. 3227, January 2, 1964, p. 9.

TLS, No. 3228, January 9, 1964, p. 27.

TLS, No. 3229, January 16, 1964, p. 53.

TLS, No. 3230, January 23, 1964, p. 73.

"Trial Ordered in Killing." New York Times, September 11, 1951, p. 61.

"Two Give Praise to Naked Lunch." Boston Herald, January 14, 1965, p. 3.

Tytell, John. Naked Angels. New York: McGraw-Hill, 1976.

"Ugh ... " TLS. No. 3220, November 14, 1963, p. 919.

"U. S. Judge Voids Customs' Seizure of Sex Magazine." New York Law Journal, (August 1, 1978), p. 1-2.

Wain, John. "The Great Burroughs Affair." New Republic, 147 (December 1, 1962), p. 21.

Walters, Raymond Jr. "In and Out of Books." The New York Times Book Review, September 16, 1962, p. 8.

Wardle, Irving. "Conspiracy Trial Is Given as Drama: William Burroughs Seen as Judge Hoffman." New York Times, August 26, 1970, p. 35.

Warshofsky, Fred. "Grove Press: Little Giant of Publishing," Paperback Trade News, Vol. 1, No. 1 (March 1962), pp. 10-17.

"Whither Ugh?" TLS. No. 3231, January 30, 1964, p. 87.

Wilson, David. "Pre-Publication Fanfare: New Obscenity Test?" Boston Globe, April 10, 1966, p. 73.

"Writers' Conference Draws an Audience of 2,000." The Times, August 21, 1962, p. 4.

Zuckerman, Ed. "Boston Gets an Erogenous Zone." Oui, Vol. 5, No. 9 (September 1976), pp. 76-78 ff.

II. UNPUBLISHED MATERIAL

A. 1. William S. Burroughs Letters to Allen Ginsberg, Ginsberg Deposit, Rare Books and Manuscripts, Butler Library of Columbia University in the City of New York.

Burroughs to Ginsberg n. d. (c. April 1952).
Burroughs to Ginsberg, April 14, 1952.
Burroughs to Ginsberg, July 1, 1952.
Burroughs to Ginsberg, July 13, 1952.
Burroughs to Ginsberg, September 20, 1957.
Burroughs to Ginsberg, N. D. (probably between September 20 and October 14, 1957).
Burroughs to Ginsberg, October 28, 1957.
Burroughs to Ginsberg, October 31, 1957.
Burroughs to Ginsberg, November 10, 1957.
Burroughs to Ginsberg, November 26, 1957.
Burroughs to Ginsberg, December 4, 1957.
Burroughs to Ginsberg, February 10, 1958.
Burroughs to Ginsberg, n. d. (1958).
Burroughs to Ginsberg, August 25, 1958.
Burroughs to Ginsberg, October 10, 1958.
Burroughs to Ginsberg, January 2, 1959.
Burroughs to Ginsberg, April 2, 1959.
Burroughs to Ginsberg, April 21, 1959.
Burroughs to Ginsberg, May 5, 1959.
Burroughs to Ginsberg, n. d. (c. July 30, 1959).
Burroughs to Ginsberg, August 24, 1959.
Burroughs to Ginsberg, September 5, 1959.
Burroughs to Ginsberg, September 11, 1959.
Burroughs to Ginsberg, September 25, 1959.
Burroughs to Ginsberg, October 7, 1959.
Burroughs to Ginsberg, October 29, 1959.
Burroughs to Ginsberg, November 17, 1959.

A. 2.   William S. Burroughs letters to Jack Kerouac, Rare Books and Manuscripts, Butler Library, Columbia University in the City of New York.

Burroughs to Kerouac, December 26, 1950.
Burroughs to Kerouac, n. d. (1954).
Burroughs to Kerouac, April 22, 1954.
Burroughs to Kerouac, December 7, 1954.
Burroughs to Kerouac, February 12, 1955.
Burroughs to Kerouac, May 24, 1955.
Burroughs to Kerouac, December 4, 1957.

B.   American Civil Liberties Union Archives, Mudd Manuscript Library, Princeton University.

"Customs Seizures of Olympia Press Books." 1959-- Vol. 23: Al Reitman to Dan Bell, November 13, 1958.

Dan [Bell] to Alan [Reitman], November 17, 1958.
Exec. Dir. Patrick Murphy Malin to Secretary of
   the Treasury Robert B. Anderson, December
   30, 1958.
A. Gilmore Flues to Patrick Malin, March 16,
   1959.
D. Upton to Patrick Malin, May 20, 1959.
"Post Office Censorship." 1959--Vol. 23.
"Big Table (mag.)--Post Office Mail Ban, Chicago,
Illinois." 1960--Vol. 18-20a.
   "Big Table." Press Release, n.d.
Al [Podell] to Irv [Rosenthal], Friday Morn [May
   8, 1959].
Joel J. Sprayregen to Rowland Watts, May 8, 1959.
Joel Sprayregen to Melvin Wulf, May 29, 1959.
Melvin Wulf to Irving Rosenthal, May 29, 1959.
Irving Rosenthal to Joel [Sprayregen], June 1, 1959.
Herbert Levy to Rowland Watts, June 8, 1959.
Joel Sprayregen to Melvin Wulf, June 11, 1959.
Joel Sprayregen to Melvin Wulf, July 10, 1959.
Joel Sprayregen, "Plaintiff's Reply Memorandum in
   Support of Its Motion for Summary Judgment and
   in Opposition to Defendant's Cross Motion for
   Summary Judgment," May 2, 1960.
Melvin Wulf to Joel Sprayregen, May 22, 1959.
Memo, August 11, 1960.

C. Grove Press Collection: Burroughs, George Arents Research Library for Special Collections, Syracuse University.

C. 1. Box #1, "Burroughs' Naked Lunch."

Copy of Printing Agreement with the Book Press for
   Naked Lunch.
"William Burroughs/Naked Lunch," Grove Press Pub-
   licity Pamphlet.
"Questionnaire" from Burroughs on editorial changes.
Judith Schmidt to Dr. Milton Schwebel, William Bar-
   ret, Nat Waldman, Ephriam London, April 1, 1960.
   (A form letter).
Lionel Trilling to Barney Rosset, October 28, 1962.
25 Calligraphs sent to Allen Ginsberg by Burroughs,
   March 26, 1959.
23 pages of textual insertions.

C. 2. Box #1, "Burroughs, William. Naked Lunch. Editorial Correspondence #1, 1959-1962."

Judith Schmidt to Miriam Worms, October 14, 1959.
Joel Sprayregen to Charles Rembar, October 14, 1959.
Barney Rosset to Maurice Girodias, November 11, 1959.
Maurice Girodias to Barney Rosset, November 25, 1959.
Barney Rosset to Maurice Girodias, November 30, 1959.
Maurice Girodias to Barney Rosset, December 19, 1959.
Barney Rosset to Maurice Girodias, December 28, 1959.
Odette Hummel to Barney Rosset, January 13, 1960.
Barney Rosset to Odette Hummel, January 20, 1960.
Odette Hummel to Barney Rosset, February 3, 1960.
Barney Rosset to Odette Hummel, February 8, 1960.
Odette Hummel to Barney Rosset, February 20, 1960.
Barney Rosset to Odette Hummel, February 24, 1960.
Charles Rembar to Barney Rosset, April, 6, 1960.
Barney Rosset to John Ciardi, April 13, 1960.
Barney Rosset to Odette Hummel, April 14, 1960.
John Ciardi to Barney Rosset, April 17, 1960.
Allen Ginsberg to Irving Rosenthal, April 29, 1960.
Richard Seaver to Maurice Girodias, May 26, 1960.
Miriam Worms to Richard Seaver, May 31, 1960.
Judith Schmidt to Miriam Worms, June 6, 1960.
Miriam Worms to Judith Schmidt, June 15, 1960.
Check request, July 7, 1960.
Check request, July 18, 1960.
William Burroughs to Irving Rosenthal, July 20, 1960.
William Burroughs to Allen Ginsberg, July 3, 1960
    (sic, probably August 3, 1960).
William Burroughs to Richard Seaver, August 5, 1960.
Irving Fishman to Barney Rosset, August 29, 1960.
William Burroughs to Richard Seaver, November 25, 1960.
Richard Seaver to Maurice Girodias, December 21, 1960.
Henry Miller to Maurice Girodias, December 8, 1960.
Miriam Worms to Judith Schmidt, February 1, 1961.
Barney Rosset to Miriam Worms, February 28, 1961.
Maurice Girodias to Barney Rosset, March 31, 1961.
Maurice Girodias to Barney Rosset, May 17, 1961.
Maurice Girodias to Barney Rosset, July 19, 1961.
Maurice Girodias to Barney Rosset, August 2, 1961.
Copy of printer's estimate, August 7, 1961.

Maurice Girodias to Barney Rosset, December 4, 1961.

Barney Rosset to Maurice Girodias, December 7, 1961.

Barney Rosset to Maurice Girodias, January 31, 1962.

William Burroughs to Barney Rosset, August 7, 1962.

Russel Halliday to Richard Seaver, October 11, 1962.

Milton Perlman to Barney Rosset, November 15, 1962.

C. 3. Box #1, "Burroughs, William. Naked Lunch. Editorial Correspondence #2, 1962-1967."

Fran Muller to Judith Schmidt, September 21, 1961.

Barney Rosset to Maurice Girodias, February 7, 1963.

William Burroughs to Barney Rosset, May 13, 1963.

Paul Bowles to Richard Seaver, December 11, 1963.

Edward deGrazia to Barney Rosset, February 5, 1964.

Richard Seaver to Paul Bowles, February 19, 1964.

Edward deGrazia to Barney Rosset, March 4, 1964.

Maurice Girodias to Barney Rosset, March 5, 1964.

William Burroughs to Maurice Girodias, March 10, 1964.

Richard Seaver to William Burroughs, April 1, 1964.

Frank Laven to Grove Press, April 1, 1965.

Richard Gallen to Frank Laven, April 6, 1965.

Allen Ginsberg, Notes for the Boston trial of Naked Lunch.

"Order of Notice Directed Against a Book Named Naked Lunch."

C. 4. Box #2, "Naked Lunch. Los Angeles, Editorial and Legal."

Advertising flyer "Dear Bookseller," October 30, 1962.

Edward deGrazia to Barney Rosset, March 21, 1963.

Edward deGrazia to Joseph Nolan, December 11, 1963.

Edward deGrazia to Ervin Gaines, January 7, 1964.

Edward deGrazia to Barney Rosset, March 26, 1964.

Edward deGrazia to Edward Brooke, May 1, 1964.

Edward deGrazia to Milton Perlman, October 12, 1964.

Edward deGrazia to Barney Rosset, December 31, 1964.

Edward deGrazia to Witnesses, January 1964 (sic, probably January 1965).

Edward deGrazia to Frank D. Laven, January 25, 1965.

Frank Laven to Edward deGrazia, February 4, 1965.
Copies of Los Angeles County complaints W33845 and
W33846 against the sellers of Naked Lunch.
Newspaper clippings on the L. A. trial.
Partial Transcript, "California vs. Galanti/Frank. "

C. 5. Box #2, "Nova Express. "

William Burroughs to Barney Rosset, December 12,
1961.
William Burroughs to Barney Rosset, June 23, 1962.
Barney Rosset to William Burroughs, June 25, 1962.
Barney Rosset to William Burroughs, March 14, 1963.

C. 6. Copy of trial transcript, "Attorney General vs. A
Book Named Naked Lunch, " Massachusetts Superior Court
83001.

C. 7. Twelve page manuscript of Burroughs' essay "Deposition: Testimony Concerning a Sickness" in the file for
Evergreen Review # 4.

D. American Civil Liberties Union, Illinois Division Papers,
Regenstein Library, University of Chicago, Box # 38.

Charles D. Ablard, "Departmental Decision, " August
12, 1959.
"Complaint: Big Table vs. Carl Schroeder, " n. d.
"Brief in Support of Plaintiff's Motion for Summary
Judgment and in Opposition to Defendant's Cross
Motion for Summary Judgment, " February 1, 1960.
"Initial Decision of the Haring Examiner, " July 9,
1959.
Joel Sprayregen, "Answer, " June 18, 1959.

E. Archives of the University of Chicago, Regenstein Library,
University of Chicago.

"Report of the Special Committee of the Student Government Organization in re: The Chicago Review, "
Chicago: The Student Government, 1959.

F. Letters in The Humanities Research Center, University
of Texas at Austin.

Burroughs to Paul Bowles, July 20, 1958.
Burroughs to Paul Bowles, October 19, 1958.

Burroughs to Paul Bowles, n. d. (c. 1958).
Burroughs to Paul Bowles, January 12, 1959.
Burroughs to Paul Bowles, February 20, 1959.
Burroughs to Paul Bowles, May 5, 1959.
Burroughs to Paul Bowles, July 30, 1959.
Burroughs to Paul Bowles, March 1, 1960.
Burroughs to Paul Bowles, May 17, 1962.
Burroughs to Charles Henri Ford, September 20, 1960.
Burroughs to Allen Ginsberg, February 7, 1954 (probably 1955) in Allen Ginsberg to Bob Lavigne, June 8, 1957.

G. "Big Table, Inc. Big Table, Issue No. 1, Spring 1959, Post Office Department Docket # 1/150, U. S. Postal Service, Office of Administrative Law Judges.

Richard Farr to Albert Podell, April 30, 1959.
Richard Farr to Chicago Postmaster Carl Schroeder, April 30, 1959.
Albert Podell to Herbert Warburton, May 7, 1959.
Receipt signed by Podell, May 14, 1959.
Carl A. Schroeder to Docket Clerk, May 18, 1959.
Richard Farr to Albert Podell, May 22, 1959.
Dorothy Lang to Schroeder, May 25, 1959.
"Notice of Hearing," May 25, 1959.
"Complaint," n. d.
"Order," May 25, 1959.
Paul Carroll to Hearing Examiner, May 26, 1959.
"Memo," May 28, 1959.
Receipt, May 28, 1959.
Joel Sprayregen to Hearing Examiner, May 28, 1959.
Carl Schroeder to Docket Clerk, June 1, 1959.
"Order," June 1, 1959.
"Complainant's Reply to Mailer's Request for Continuance of Hearing and Supplemental Request for Transfer." June 2, 1959.
"Order," June 10, 1959.
Transcript of Hearing, "Big Table Magazine, Issue Number 1, Spring 1959," Post Office Department Docket # 1/150.
"Initial Decision of the Hearing Examiner," July 9, 1959.
Joel Sprayregen, "Appeal, Memorandum, Exceptions."
Saul Mindel, "Application for Extension of Filing Date for Complainant's Reply Brief."
"Order--July 31, 1959."

Saul Mindel, "Complainant's Reply Brief on Appeal,"
August 3, 1959.
Joel Sprayregen to Post Office Department, August 3,
1959.
Charles D. Ablard, "Departmental Decision," August
12, 1959.

H.   Naked Lunch File, U.S. Customs Service, Washington,
D. C. and New York City.

Reuben Klaben to Irving Fishman, October 1, 1962.
Eleanor Suske to Irving Fishman, October 2, 1962.
Irving Fishman to Reuben Klaben, October 4, 1962.
Irving Fishman to Reuben Klaben, December 4, 1962.
Harold F. Shapiro to Commissioner of Customs, Feb-
ruary 15, 1963.

I.   Other References.

Senator Edward Brooke to M. Goodman, June 29,
1976.
John Ciardi to M. Goodman, April 17, 1978.
William I. Cowin to M. Goodman, April 26, 1976.
Boston Police Commissioner Robert deGrazia to M.
Goodman, May 6, 1976.
E. J. Doyle, Acting Director of Entry Procedures
and Penalties to M. Goodman, September 21, 1976.
Diana Franklin, Time Archives to M. Goodman, Nov-
ember 29, 1977.
Maurice Girodias to M. Goodman, June 21, 1976.
M. Goodman to John Atwood, Restricted Materials
Department of U.S. Customs, May 18, 1976.   Tele-
phone conversation.
M. Goodman to William Burroughs, April 21, 1976.
Telephone conversation.
M. Goodman to Frank Dardeno, July 19, 1976.   Tele-
phone conversation.
M. Goodman to James Grauerholz, November 3, 1977.
Telephone conversation.
M. Goodman to Boston Police Detective Edmund Grif-
fin, May 24, 1976.   Telephone conversation.
M. Goodman to U.S. Customs, August 23, 1976.
Norman Holland to M. Goodman, March 6, 1978.
Asst. D.A. Joseph Laurano to M. Goodman, April 12,
1976.
Asst. D. A. Joseph Laurano to M. Goodman, April 21,
1976.
Joel Rosenthal to Lemuel Coley, December 16, 1977.